D1105272

The World and Africa
and
Color and Democracy

THE OXFORD W. E. B. DU BOIS

Henry Louis Gates, Jr., Editor

The Suppression of the African Slave-Trade to the United States of America: 1638–1870
Introduction: Saidiya Hartman

The Philadelphia Negro: A Social Study
Introduction: Lawrence Bobo

The Souls of Black Folk
Introduction: Arnold Rampersad

John Brown
Introduction: Paul Finkelman

Africa, Its Geography, People and Products
Africa—Its Place in Modern History
Introductions: Emmanuel Akyeampong

Black Reconstruction in America
Introduction: David Levering Lewis

Black Folk: Then and Now
Introduction: Wilson J. Moses

Dusk of Dawn
Introduction: Kwame Anthony Appiah

The World and Africa
Color and Democracy: Colonies and Peace
Introductions: Mahmood Mamdani and Gerald Horne

In Battle for Peace: The Story of My Eighty-third Birthday
Introduction: Manning Marable

The Black Flame Trilogy: Book One
The Ordeal of Mansart
Introduction: Brent Edwards
Afterword: Mark Sanders

The Black Flame Trilogy: Book Two
Mansart Builds a School
> *Introduction: Brent Edwards*
> *Afterword: Mark Sanders*

The Black Flame Trilogy: Book Three
Worlds of Color
> *Introduction: Brent Edwards*
> *Afterword: Mark Sanders*

Autobiography of W. E. B. Du Bois
> *Introduction: Werner Sollors*

The Quest of the Silver Fleece
> *Introduction: William L. Andrews*

The Negro
> *Introduction: John K. Thornton*

Darkwater: Voices from Within the Veil
> *Introduction: Evelyn Brooks Higginbotham*

Gift of Black Folk: The Negroes in the Making of America
> *Introduction: Glenda Carpio*

Dark Princess: A Romance
> *Introduction: Homi K. Bhabha*

THE WORLD AND AFRICA

W. E. B. Du Bois

Series Edition, Henry Louis Gates, Jr.

Introduction by Mahmood Mamdani

OXFORD
UNIVERSITY PRESS

For Cornel West

OXFORD
UNIVERSITY PRESS

Oxford University Press, Inc., publishes works that further
Oxford University's objective of excellence in research,
scholarship, and education.

Oxford New York
Auckland Cape Town Dar es Salaam Hong Kong Karachi
Kuala Lumpur Madrid Melbourne Mexico City Nairobi
New Delhi Shanghai Taipei Toronto

With offices in
Argentina Austria Brazil Chile Czech Republic France Greece
Guatemala Hungary Italy Japan Poland Portugal Singapore
South Korea Switzerland Thailand Turkey Ukraine Vietnam

Published by Oxford University Press, Inc.
198 Madison Avenue, New York, NY 10016
www.oup.com

Library of Congress Cataloging-in-Publication Data is available.

ISBN: 9780195311808 (Series)
ISBN: 9780195325843 (Volume)

1 3 5 7 9 8 6 4 2

Printed in the United States of America
on acid-free paper

TO

NINA

FOR

OUR GOLDEN WEDDING

Contents

ILLUSTRATIONS

The Black Letters on the Sign:
W. E. B. Du Bois and the Canon

"... the slave master had a direct interest in discrediting the personality of those he held as property. Every man who had a thousand dollars so invested had a thousand reasons for painting the black man as fit only for slavery. Having made him the companion of horses and mules, he naturally sought to justify himself by assuming that the negro was not much better than a mule. The holders of twenty hundred million dollars' worth of property in human chattels procured the means of influencing press, pulpit, and politician, and through these instrumentalities they belittled our virtues and magnified our vices, and have made us odious in the eyes of the world. Slavery had the power at one time to make and unmake Presidents, to construe the law, and dictate the policy, set the fashion in national manners and customs, interpret the Bible, and control the church; and, naturally enough, the old masters set themselves up as much too high as they set the manhood of the negro too low. Out of the depths of slavery has come this prejudice and this color line. It is broad enough and black enough to explain all the malign influences which assail the newly emancipated millions to-day. . . . The office of color in the color line is a very plain and subordinate one. It simply advertises the objects of oppression, insult, and persecution. It is not the maddening liquor, but the black letters on the sign telling the world where it may be had . . . Slavery, stupidity, servility, poverty, dependence, are undesirable conditions. When these shall cease to be coupled with color, there will be no color line drawn."

—FREDERICK DOUGLASS, "The Color Line," 1881.

William Edward Burghardt Du Bois (1868–1963) was the most prolific and, arguably, the most influential African American writer of his generation. The novelist and poet James Weldon Johnson (1871–1938) once noted the no single work had informed the shape of the African American literary tradition, except perhaps *Uncle Tom's Cabin*, than had Du Bois's seminal collection of essays *The Souls of Black Folk* (1903). While trained as a sociologist at Berlin and as a historian at Harvard, Du Bois was fearless in the face of genre—even when some of the genres that he sought to embrace did not fully embrace him in return. Du Bois published twenty-two single-author works, twenty-one in his lifetime (his *Autobiography*, edited by his friend and literary executor, Herbert Aptheker, would not be published until

1968). A selection of his greatest works, *An ABC of Color: Selections from over a Half Century of the Writings of W. E. B. Du Bois*, appeared in 1963, the year he died. And while these books reflect a wide variety of genres—including three widely heralded and magisterial books of essays published in 1903, 1920, and 1940 (*The Souls of Black Folk*, *Darkwater: Voices from within the Veil*, and *Dusk of Dawn: An Essay toward an Autobiography of a Race Concept*), one biography, five novels, a pioneering sociological study of a black community, five books devoted to the history of Africa, three historical studies of African American people, among others—Du Bois was, in the end, an essayist, an essayist of the first order, one of the masters of that protean form that so attracted Du Bois's only true antecedent, Frederick Douglass (1818–1895) as well as Du Bois's heir in the history of the form, James Baldwin (1924–1987). (Baldwin, like Du Bois, would turn repeatedly to fiction, only to render the form as an essay.)

Du Bois, clearly, saw himself as a man of action, but a man of action who luxuriated within a verdant and fecund tropical rainforest of words. It is not Du Bois's intoxication with words that marks his place in the history of great black public intellectuals—persons of letters for whom words are a vehicle for political action and their own participation in political movements. After all, one need only recall Du Bois's predecessor, Frederick Douglass, or another of his disciples, Martin Luther King Jr. for models in the African American tradition of leaders for whom acting and speaking were so inextricably intertwined as to be virtually coterminous; no, the novelty of Du Bois's place in the black tradition is that he wrote himself to a power, rather than spoke himself to power. Both Douglass and King, for all their considerable literary talents, will be remembered always for the power of their oratory, a breathtaking power exhibited by both. Du Bois, on the other hand, was not a great orator; he wrote like he talked, and he talked like an extraordinarily well-educated late Anglo-American Victorian, just as James Weldon Johnson did; no deep "black" stentorian resonances are to be found in the public speaking voices of either of these two marvelous writers. Booker T. Washington (1856–1915) spoke in a similar public voice.

First and last, W. E. B. Du Bois was a writer, a writer deeply concerned and involved with politics, just as James Baldwin was; as much as they loved to write, Douglass and King were orators, figures fundamentally endowed with a genius for the spoken word. Even Du Bois's colleague, William Ferris, commented upon this anomaly in Du Bois's place in the tradition, at a time (1913) when he had published only five books: "Du Bois," Ferris wrote, "is one of the few men in history who was hurled on the throne of leadership by the dynamic force of the written word. He is one of the few writers who leaped to the front as a leader and became the head of a popular movement through impressing his personality upon men by means of a book" ("The African Abroad," 1913). Despite the fact that Du Bois by this time had published his Harvard doctoral dissertation in history, *The Suppression of the African Slave-Trade* (1896), his sociological study, *The Philadelphia Negro* (1899), *The Souls of Black Folk* (1903), the sole biography that he would publish, *John Brown* (1909), and his first of five novels, *The Quest of the Silver Fleece* (1911), Ferris attributed Du Bois's catapult to leadership to one book and one book alone, *The Souls of Black Folk*. Indeed, it is probably true that had Du Bois published this book alone, his place in the canon of African American literature would have been secure, if perhaps not as fascinating!

The Souls of Black Folk, in other words, is the one book that Du Bois wrote which most of us have read in its entirety. It is through *The Souls of Black Folk* that we center Du Bois's place in the literary canon; it is through *Souls* that we structure the arc of his seven decade career as a man of letters. There are many good reasons for the centrality of this magical book to Du Bois's literary career, but it is also the case that the other works that comprise Du Bois's canon deserve fresh attention as a whole. And it is for this reason that my colleagues and I have embarked upon this project with Oxford University Press to reprint Du Bois's single-authored texts, and make them available to a new generation of readers in a uniform edition. The only other attempt to do so—Herbert Aptheker's pioneering edition of Du Bois's complete works, published in 1973—is, unfortunately, long out of print.

The Souls of Black Folk is such a brilliant work that it merits all of the attention that it has been given in the century since it was published. In April 1903, a thirty-five-year-old scholar and budding political activist published a 265 page book subtitled "Essays and Sketches," consisting of thirteen essays and one short story, addressing a wide range of topics, including the story of the freed slaves during Reconstruction, the political ascendancy of Booker T. Washington, the sublimity of the spirituals, the death of Du Bois's only son Burghardt, and lynching. Hailed as a classic even by his contemporaries, the book has been republished in no fewer than 120 editions since 1903. In fact, it is something of a rite of passage for younger scholars and writers to publish their take on Du Bois's book in new editions aimed at the book's considerable classroom market.

Despite its fragmentary structure, the book's disparate parts contribute to the sense of a whole, like movements in a symphony. Each chapter is pointedly "bicultural," prefaced by both an excerpt from a white poet and a bar of what Du Bois names "The Sorrow Songs" ("some echo of haunting melody from the only American music which welled up from black souls in the dark past.") Du Bois's subject was, in no small part, the largely unarticulated beliefs and practices of American Negroes, who were impatient to burst out of the cotton fields and take their rightful place as Americans. As he saw it, African American culture in 1903 was at once vibrant and disjointed, rooted in an almost medieval agrarian past and yet fiercely restive. Born in the chaos of slavery, the culture had begun to generate a richly variegated body of plots, stories, melodies, and rhythms. In *The Souls of Black Folk*, Du Bois peered closely at the culture of his kind, and saw the face of black America. Actually, he saw two faces. "One ever feels his two-ness—an American, a Negro," Du Bois wrote. "Two souls, two thoughts, two unreconciled strivings; two warring ideals in one dark body, whose dogged strength alone keeps it from being torn asunder." He described this condition as "double consciousness," and his emphasis on a fractured psyche made *Souls* a harbinger of the modernist movement that would begin to flower a decade or so later in Europe and in America.

Scholars, including Arnold Rampersad, Werner Sollors, Dickson Bruce, and David Levering Lewis, have debated the origins of Du Bois's use of the concept of "double consciousness," but what's clear is that its roots are multiple, which is appropriate enough, just as it is clear that the source of one of Du Bois's other signal metaphors—"the problem of the twentieth-century is the problem of the color line"—came to him directly from Frederick Douglass's essay of that title. Du Bois had studied in Berlin during a Hegel revival, and Hegel, famously, had written on the relationship between master and bondsman, whereby each defines himself through the recognition of the other. But the concept comes up, too, in Emerson, who wrote in 1842 of the split between our reflective self, which wanders through the realm of ideas, and the active self, which dwells in the here and how, a tension that recurs throughout the Du Bois oeuvre: "The worst feature of this double consciousness is that the two lives, of the understanding and of the soul, which we lead, really show very little relation to each other."

Even closer to hand was the term's appearance in late-nineteenth-century psychology. The French psychologist, Alfred Binet, writing in his 1896 book, *On Double Consciousness*, discusses what he calls "bipartititon," or "the duplication of consciousness": "Each of the consciousnesses occupies a more narrow and more limited field than if there existed one single consciousness containing all the ideas of the subject." William James, who taught Du Bois at Harvard, talked about a "second personality" that characterized "the hypnotic trance." When Du Bois transposed this concept from the realm of the psyche to the social predicament of the American Negro, he did not leave it unchanged. But he shared with the psychologists the notion that double consciousness was essentially an affliction. "This American world," he complained, yields the Negro "no true self-consciousness, but only lets him see himself through the revelation of the other world. It is a peculiar sensation, this double-consciousness, this sense of always looking at one's self through the eyes of others, of measuring one's soul by the tape of a world that looks on in amused contempt and pity." Sadly, "the double life every American Negro must live, as a Negro and as an American," leads inevitably to "a painful self-consciousness, an almost morbid sense of personality and a moral hesitancy which is fatal to self-confidence." The result is "a double life, with double thoughts, double duties and double social classes," and worse, "double words and double ideas," which "tempt the mind to pretense or revolt, hypocrisy or to radicalism." Accordingly, Du Bois wanted to make the American Negro whole; and he believed that only desegregation and full equality could make this psychic integration possible.

And yet for subsequent generations of writers, what Du Bois cast as a problem was taken to be the defining condition of modernity itself. The diagnosis, one might say, outlasted the disease. Although Du Bois would publish twenty-two books, and thousands of essays and reviews, no work of his has done more to shape an African American literary history than *The Souls of Black Folk*, and no metaphor in this intricately layered book has proved more enduring than that of double consciousness, including Du Bois's other powerfully resonating metaphors, that of "the veil" that separates black America from white America, and his poignant revision of Frederick Douglass's metaphor of "the color line," which Du Bois employed in that oft-repeated sentence, "The problem of the twentieth-century is the problem of the color line"—certainly his most prophetic utterance of many.

Like all powerful metaphors, Du Bois's metaphor of double consciousness came to have a life of its own. For Carl Jung, who visited the United States in the heyday of the "separate but equal" doctrine, the shocking thing wasn't that black culture was not equal, the shocking thing was that is was not separate! "The naïve European," Jung wrote, "thinks of America as a white nation. It is not wholly white, if you please; it is partly colored," and this explained, Jung continued, "the slightly Negroid mannerisms of the American." "Since the Negro lives within your cities and even within your houses," Jung continued, "he also lives within your skin, subconsciously." It wasn't just that the Negro was an American, as Du Bois would note, again and again, but that the American was, inevitably and inescapably, a Negro. The bondsman and the slave find their identity in each other's gaze: "two-ness" wasn't just a black thing any longer. As James Baldwin would put it, "Each of us, helplessly and forever, contains the other—male in female, female in male, white in black, black in white."

Today, talk about the fragmentation of culture and consciousness is a commonplace. We know all about the vigorous intermixing of black culture and white, high culture and low—from the Jazz Age freneticism of what the scholar Ann Douglass calls "mongrel Manhattan" to Hip Hop's hegemony over American youth in the late-twentieth and early-twenty-first centuries. Du Bois yearned to make the American Negro one, and lamented that he was two. Today, the ideal of wholeness has largely been retired. And cultural multiplicity is no longer seen as the problem, but as a solution—a solution to the confines of identity itself. Double consciousness, once a disorder, is now the cure. Indeed, the only complaint we moderns have is that Du Bois was too cautious in his accounting. He'd conjured "two souls, two thoughts two unreconciled strivings." Just two, Dr. Du Bois, we are forced to ask today? Keep counting.

And, in a manner of speaking, Du Bois did keep counting, throughout the twenty two books that comprise the formal canon of his most cogent thinking. The hallmark of Du Bois's literary career is that he coined the metaphors of double-consciousness and the veil—reappropriating Frederick Douglass's seminal definition of the semi-permeable barrier that separates and defines black-white racial relations in America as "the color line"—to define the place of the African American within modernity. The paradox of his career, however, is that the older Du Bois became, the more deeply he immersed himself in the struggle for Pan-Africanism and decolonization against the European colonial powers, and an emergent postcolonial "African" or "Pan-Negro" social and political identity—culminating in his own life in his assumption of Ghanaian citizenship in 1963. And the "blacker" that his stand against colonialism became, the less "black," in a very real sense, his analysis of what he famously called "The Negro Problem" simultaneously became. The more "African" Du Bois became, in other words, the more cosmopolitan his analysis of the root causes of anti-black and -brown and -yellow racism and colonialism became, seeing the status of the American Negro as part and parcel of a larger problem of international economic domination, precisely in the same way that Frederick Douglass rightly saw the construction of the American color line as a function of, and a metaphor for, deeper, structural, economic relations—"not the maddening liquor, but the black letters on the sign telling the world where it may be had," as Douglass so thoughtfully put it. The Negro's being-in-the-world, we might say, became ever more complex for Du Bois the older he grew, especially as the Cold War heated up and the anti-colonial movement took root throughout Africa and the Third World.

Ironically, Du Bois himself foretold this trajectory in a letter he wrote in 1896, reflecting on the import of his years as a graduate student at Friedrich Wilhelm University in Berlin: "Of the greatest importance was the opportunity which my *Wanderjahre* [wander years] in Europe gave of looking at the world as a man and not simply from a narrow racial and provincial outlook." How does the greatest black intellectual in the twentieth century—"America's most conspicuously educated Negro," as Werner Sollors puts it in his introduction to Du Bois's *Autobiography* in this series—make the rhetorical turn from defining the Negro American as a metaphor for modernity, at the turn of the century, to defining the Negro—at mid-century—as a metonym of a much larger historical pattern of social deviance and social dominance that had long been central to the fabric of world order, to the fabric of European and American domination of such a vast portion of the world of color? If, in other words, the Negro is America's metaphor for Du Bois in 1903, how does America's history of black-white relations become the metaphor of a nefarious pattern of economic exploitation and dominance by the end of Du Bois's life, in 1963? Make no mistake about it: either through hubris or an uncanny degree of empathy, or a mixture of both, throughout his life, W. E. B. Du Bois saw his most naked and public ambitions as well as his most private and intimate anxieties as representative of those of his countrymen, the American Negro people. Nevertheless, as he grew older, the closer he approached the end of his life, Du Bois saw the American Negro as a metaphor for class relations within the wider world order.

In order to help a new generation of readers to understand the arc of this trajectory in Du Bois's thinking, and because such a large part of this major thinker's oeuvre remains unread, Oxford University Press and I decided to publish in a uniform edition the twenty-one books that make up Du Bois's canon and invited a group of scholars to reconsider their importance as works of literature, history, sociology, and political philosophy. With the publication of this series, Du Bois's books are once again in print, with new introductions that analyze the shape of his career as a writer, scholar, and activist.

Reading the canon of Du Bois's work in chronological order, a certain allegorical pattern emerges, as Saidiya Hartman suggests in her introduction to *The Suppression of the African Slave-Trade*. Du Bois certainly responded immediately and directly to large historical events through fierce and biting essays that spoke adamantly and passionately to the occasion. But he also used the themes of his books to speak to the larger import of those events in sometimes highly mediated ways. His first book, for example, proffers as its thesis, as Hartman puts it, a certain paradox: "the slave trade flourished under the guise of its suppression," functioning legally for twenty years following the Compromise of the Federal Convention of 1787 and "illegally for another half century." Moreover, Du Bois tackles this topic at precisely the point in American history when Jim Crow segregation is becoming formalized through American law in the 1890s, culminating in 1896 (the year of the publication of his first book) with the infamous *Plessy v. Ferguson* "separate but equal" decision of the Supreme Court—exactly twenty years following the end of Reconstruction. Three years later, as Lawrence Bobo shows, Du Bois publishes *The Philadelphia Negro* in part to detail the effects of the "separate but equal" doctrine on the black community.

Similarly, Du Bois's biography of John Brown appeared in the same year as a pioneering band of blacks and whites joined together to form the National Association for the Advancement of Colored People (NAACP), the organization that would plot the demise of legal segregation through what would come to be called the Civil Rights Movement, culminating in its victory over de jure segregation in the Supreme Court's *Brown v. Board of Education* decision, which effectively reversed the *Plessy* decision, and in the Civil Rights Act of 1964 and the Voting Rights Act of 1965. John Brown, for Du Bois, would remain the emblem of this movement.

Likewise, Du Bois's first novel, *The Quest of the Silver Fleece*, published just two years following his biography of John Brown, served as a subtle critique both of an unreflective assimilationist ideology of the early NAACP through its advocacy of "a black-owned farming cooperative in the heart of the deep South," as William Andrews puts it, just as it surely serves as a critique of Booker T. Washington's apparently radical notion that economic development for the newly freed slaves could very well insure political equality in a manner both irresistible and inevitable, an argument, mind you, frequently made today under vastly different circumstances about the role of capitalism in Du Bois's beloved Communist China.

Du Bois registers his critique of the primitivism of the Harlem Renaissance in *The Gift of Black Folk*, as Glenda Carpio cogently argues, by walking "a tightrope between a patriotic embrace of an America in which African American culture has become an inextricable part and an exhortation of the rebellion and struggle out of which that culture arose." In response to the voyeurism and faddishness of Renaissance Harlem, Du Bois harshly reminds us that culture is a form of labor, too, a commodity infinitely exploitable, and that the size of America's unprecedented middle class can be traced directly to its slave past: "It was black labor that established the modern world commerce which began first as a commerce in the bodies of the slaves themselves and was the primary cause of the prosperity of the first great commercial cities of our day"—cities such as New York, the heart of the cultural movement that some black intellectuals passionately argued could very well augur the end of racial segregation throughout American society, or at least segregation between equal classes across the color line.

Paul Finkelman, in his introduction to *John Brown*, quotes the book's first line: "The mystic spell of Africa is and ever was over all America." If that is true, it was also most certainly the case for Du Bois himself, as John Thornton, Emmanuel Akyeampong, Wilson J. Moses, and Mahmood Mamdani show us in their introductions to five books that Du Bois published about Africa, in 1915, 1930, 1939, and 1947. Africa, too, was a recurring metaphor in the Duboisian canon, serving variously as an allegory of the intellectual potential of persons of African descent; as John K. Thornton puts it, "What counted was that African history had movement and Africans were seen as historical actors and not simply as stolid recipients of foreign techniques and knowledge," carefully "integrating ancient Egypt into *The Negro* as part of that race's history, without having to go to the extreme measure of asserting that somehow the Egyptians were biologically identical to Africans from further south or west." The history of African civilization, in other words, was Du Bois's ultimate argument for the equality of Americans white and black.

Similarly, establishing his scholarly mastery of the literature of African history also served Du Bois well against ideological rivals such as Marcus Garvey, who attacked Du Bois for being "too assimilated," and "not black enough." Du Bois's various studies of African history also served as a collective text for the revolutions being formulated in the forties and fifties by Pan-African nationalists such as Kwame Nkrumah and Jomo Kenyatta, who would lead their nations to independence against the European colonial powers. Du Bois was writing for them, first as an exemplar of the American Negro, the supposed vanguard of the African peoples, and later, and more humbly, as a follower of the African's lead. As Wilson J. Moses notes, Du Bois once wrote that "American Negroes of former generations had always calculated that when Africa was ready for freedom, American Negroes would be ready to lead them. But the event was quite opposite." In fact, writing in 1925 in an essay entitled "Worlds of Color," an important essay reprinted as "The Negro Mind Reaches Out" in Alain Locke's germinal anthology *The New Negro* (as Brent Staples points out in his introduction to Du Bois's fifth novel, *Worlds of Color*, published just two years before he died), Du Bois had declared that "led by American Negroes, the Negroes of the world are reaching out hands toward each other to know, to sympathize, to inquire." And, indeed, Du Bois himself confessed at his ninety-first birthday celebration in Beijing, as Moses notes, that "once I thought of you Africans as children, whom we educated Afro-Americans would lead to liberty. I was wrong." Nevertheless, Du Bois's various books on Africa, as well as his role as an early theorist and organizer of the several Pan-African Congresses between 1900 and 1945, increasingly underscored his role throughout the first half of the century as the father of Pan-Africanism, precisely as his presence and authority within such civil rights organizations as the NAACP began to wane.

Du Bois's ultimate allegory, however, is to be found in *The Black Flame Trilogy*, the three novels that Du Bois published just before repatriating to Ghana, in 1957, 1959, and 1961. The trilogy is the ultimate allegory in Du Bois's canon because, as Brent Edwards shows us in his introductions to the novels, it is a fictional representation of the trajectory of Du Bois's career, complete with several characters who stand for aspects of Du Bois's personality and professional life, including Sebastian Doyle, who "not only studied the Negro problem, he embodied the Negro problem. It was bone of his bone and flesh of his flesh. It made his world and filled his thought," as well as Professor James Burghardt, trained as a historian at Yale and who taught, as Du Bois had, at Atlanta University, and who believed that "the Negro problem must no longer be regarded emotionally. It must be faced scientifically and solved by long, accurate and intense investigation. Moreover, it was not one problem, but a series of problems interrelated with the social problems of the world. He laid down a program of study covering a hundred years."

But even more important than these allegorical representations of himself, or early, emerging versions of himself, Du Bois used *The Black Flame* novels to underscore the economic foundation of anti-black racism. As Edwards notes, "The real villain," for Du Bois, "is not an individual Southern aristocrat or racist white laborer, but instead capitalism itself, especially in the corporate form that has dominated the economic and social landscape of the world for more than a century," which underscores Du Bois's ideological transformations from an integrationist of sorts to an emergent mode of African American, first, and then Pan-Africanist cultural nationalism, through socialism, landing squarely in the embrace of the Communist Party just two years before his death.

Despite this evolution in ideology, Mansart, Du Bois's protagonist in the triology, ends his series of intellectual transformations precisely where Du Bois himself began as he embarked upon his career as a professor just a year after receiving his Harvard PhD in 1895. In language strikingly familiar to his statement that the time he spent in Berlin enabled him to look "at the world as a man and not simply from a narrow racial and provincial outlook," Du Bois tells us in the final volume of the trilogy that Mansart "began to have a conception of the world as one unified dwelling place. He was escaping from his racial provincialism. He began to think of himself as part of humanity and not simply as an American Negro over against a white world." For all of his ideological permutations and combinations, in other words, W. E. B. Du Bois—formidable and intimidating ideologue and ferocious foe of racism and colonialism—quite probably never veered very far from the path that he charted for himself as a student, when he fell so deeply in love with the written word that he found himself, inevitably and inescapably, drawn into a life-long love affair with language, an affair of the heart to which he remained faithful throughout an eighty-year career as a student and scholar, from the time he entered Fisk University in 1885 to his death as the Editor of "The Encyclopedia Africana" in 1963. And now, with the publication of the Oxford W. E. B. Du Bois, a new generation of readers can experience his passion for words, Du Bois's love of language purely for its own sake, as well as a conduit for advocacy and debate about the topic that consumed him his entire professional life, the freedom and the dignity of the Negro.

✦ ✦ ✦

The first volume in the series is Du Bois's revised dissertation, and his first publication, entitled *The Suppression of the African Slave-Trade to the United States of America*. A model of contemporary historiography that favored empiricism over universal proclamation, *Suppression* reveals the government's slow movement toward abolition as what the literary scholar Saidiya Hartman calls in her introduction "a litany of failures, missed opportunities, and belated acts," in which a market sensibility took precedence over moral outrage, the combination of which led to the continuation of the Atlantic slave trade to the United States until it was no longer economically beneficial.

Lawrence D. Bobo, one of the foremost urban sociologists working today, argues in his introduction to *The Philadelphia Negro: A Social Study* (1899), that Du Bois was not only an innovative historian, as Hartman properly identifies him, but also a groundbreaking social scientist whose study of Philadelphia displays "the most rigorous and sophisticated social science of its era by employing a systematic community social survey method." Although it was well reviewed at its publication—which coincided with the advent of the field of urban sociology—*The Philadelphia Negro* did not become the subject of significant scholarly attention until the 1940s, and has become, since then, a model for the study of black communities.

The distinguished scholar of black literature and culture, Arnold Rampersad, calls *The Souls of Black Folk* "possibly the most important book ever penned by a black American"—an assertion with which I heartily agree. A composite of various essays, subjects, and tones, *Souls* is both very much of its time, and timeless. It contributed to the American lexicon two terms that have been crucial for more than a century in understanding the African American experience: the "color line" and "double consciousness." For Rampersad, that we have learned so much about both issues since Du Bois first wrote, but have not made either irrelevant to our twenty-first century experience is, in a real way, our scholarly blessing and burden.

Abandoning the scholarly and empirical prowess so vividly on display in *Suppression* and *Philadelphia Negro*, Du Bois meant his biography of John Brown to be not a work of scholarship but rather one "about activism, social consciousness, and the politics of race," argues the legal historian Paul Finkelman in his introduction to *John Brown* (1909). The only biography in Du Bois's vast oeuvre, the book grew out of his participation in the Niagara Movement's meeting at Harpers Ferry in 1906 (an event the centenary of which I had the good fortune to celebrate), and—with the myth of John Brown taking precedence at times over the facts of his life—marks Du Bois's transition from professional academic to full-time activist.

There was not a genre that Du Bois did not attempt in his long career as a writer. After the John Brown biography, Du Bois turned to the novel. In his introduction to *The Quest of the Silver Fleece* (1911), Du Bois's first novel, the literary historian William Andrews looks beyond the Victorian diction and sometimes purple prose to see a work that is the "most noteworthy Great *African American Novel* of its time." *Quest* is a "Southern problem" novel writ large on a national and even mythic canvas, and one that is ultimately radical in its endorsement of strong black womanhood, equality and comradeship between the sexes, and, in Du Bois's words, "a bold regeneration of the land," which for Andrews means a hitherto-unheard-of proposed economic alliance between poor blacks and poor whites in the rural South.

Moving from a national to an international canvas, Du Bois published *The Negro* (1915), more than half of which is devoted to African history. In this way, John K. Thornton argues in his introduction, Du Bois firmly grounded for an educated lay readership the history of African Americans in the history of Africa. Drawing on the emergent disciplines of anthropology and linguistics and including, even sketchily, accounts of what would now be called Diaspora communities in the Caribbean and Latin America, *The Negro* is important in that it presents, in Thornton's words, "African history [as having] movement and Africans . . . as historical actors and not simply as stolid recipients of foreign techniques and knowledge."

Dismissed by some critics and lauded by others as the "militant sequel" to *The Souls of Black Folk*, *Darkwater: Voices from Within the Veil* (1920) appeared in a world radically transformed by the ravages of World War I. In addition to these international upheavals, and to the "crossing and re-crossing" of the color line engendered by the war, the historian Evelyn Brooks Higginbotham tells us in her magisterial introduction to this volume that blacks at home in the U.S. faced major changes and relocations. The Great Migration was in full swing when Du Bois wrote *Darkwater*, and the change in the center of black life is reflected in the change of scene to the North, a far, urban cry from the rural setting of most of *Souls*. If *Souls* saw the American landscape in black and white, Higginbotham finds that *Darkwater* is like chiaroscuro, the painting technique developed by artists of the Italian Renaissance: "Du Bois, like these Renaissance painters, moves beyond the contouring line of the two-dimensional and introduces depth and volume through his representation of color—through his contrast and shading of white and various darker peoples." Higginbotham goes on to say that "Du Bois continually undermines the fixedness of racial boundaries and subverts the visual coherence of racial identities to an extent that cannot be accidental." The Du Bois who emerges in *Darkwater* is increasingly a citizen of the world, whose gaze may be fixed on his native land but whose understanding of that land is inextricably bound to the larger world around him.

The Gift of Black Folk (1924) had an odd genesis as part of the Knights of Columbus's series on "Racial Contributions to the United States." In her introduction, Glenda Carpio notes that Du Bois's celebration of black accomplishments did not turn away from the bitter history of slavery that spawned them: these were not gifts always rendered freely, Carpio points out. Though less substantial than many of his other works, and primarily a catalog of black accomplishments across different fields, *Gift* is notable for the complex ways Du Bois links African American contributions in the arenas of labor, war, church and social life, fraternal organizations, and especially the arts, by both women and men, to the bitter history of slavery.

Homi Bhabha sees *The Dark Princess* (1928) as another odd work, a "Bollywood-style Bildungsroman," in which the race-man Mathew Towns teams with Kautilya, the "dark Princess of the Tibetan Kingdom of Bwodpur," to combat international colonialism in the struggle for global emancipation. But in this somewhat messy novel, which renders the international scenes with a Zolaesque precision, Bhabha detects a serious philosophical purpose: to elaborate on the "rule of juxtaposition" (first defined in *Darkwater*), which "creat[es] an enforced intimacy, an antagonistic proximity, that defines the color-line as it runs across the uncivil society of the nation."

Du Bois moved from the esoteric exercise of *The Dark Princess* to a more accessible form for his next publications, *Africa, Its Geography, People and Products*, and

Africa—Its Place in Modern History (1930). Published as Blue Books for the educated lay reader by E. Haldeman-Julius of Girard, Kansas, the two volumes are, for the African historian and African Emmanuel Akyeampong, remarkably useful and trenchant. The first volume is a relatively straightforward analysis of Africa's geography, climate, and environment, and the impact these physical factors have had on the development of African civilization. The second volume, which seeks "to place the continent at the very center of ancient and modern history," is more polemical, with economics cited as the central motivating factor behind modern colonialism and the slave trade.

The anger that was evident in the second of the two Blue Books came to full flower in *Black Reconstruction* (1935), a sweeping corrective to contemporary histories of the Reconstruction era, which (white) historians had shaped with the view of blacks as inadequate to the task of capitalizing on the freedom that emancipation had given them, and black history as "separate, unequal, and irrelevant," in the words of Du Bois's Pulitzer Prize-winning biographer, David Levering Lewis. Inspired by *The Gift of Black Folk* and from Du Bois's own withdrawal of his article on the Negro in the *Encyclopedia Britannica*, which demanded an excision of "a paragraph on the positive Reconstruction role of black people," *Black Reconstruction* provided original interpretations of black labor's relation to industrial wealth and, most radically, of the *agency* of black people in determining their lives after the Civil War. In his introduction, Lewis contends, rightly, that the books marks a progression in Du Bois's thought, from his early faith in academic knowledge and empiricism as a cure-all for the nation's problems, to the "more effective strategy of militant journalism informed by uncompromising principles and vital social science."

Wilson J. Moses presents *Black Folk Then and Now* (1939) as a midway point between *The Negro* (1915) and *The World and Africa* (1946). While all three volumes sought to address the entire span of black history, the special mandate of *Black Folk* was to "correct the omissions, misinterpretations, and deliberate lies that [Du Bois] detected in previous depictions of the Negro's past." In this volume, he went back to the original Herodotus and provided his own translation, which led him to affirm, with other black writers, that the Egyptians were, indeed, black (a conclusion he had resisted earlier in his career). But even in this work, with such evidence of his intellectual background on display, Du Bois is less interested in intellectual history than in social history. Even as he tracks developments in the United States, the Caribbean, Latin America, Du Bois neglects the Pan-African movement and his own involvement in it.

Du Bois's autobiography, on the other hand, shows a man far more interested in writing about his intellectual journey than his personal or social life. The philosopher Anthony Appiah, in his subtle introduction to *Dusk of Dawn*, tells us that Du Bois was famous for nothing so much as his accomplishments as an intellectual and a writer; his institutional affiliations (with the NAACP, with the Pan-African Congress) were fleeting, and his internal contradictions were vexing (he was both a committed Socialist and a committed elitist). The aim of this account, like so much of Du Bois's other work, was to address the problem of the color line, and he presents his distinguished, singular life as emblematic of that problem, and himself as hopeful for its solution.

At the time he rejoined the NAACP to oversee its global programming in 1944, Du Bois was prepared to dedicate himself completely to the abolition of colonialism, which he saw as the driving force behind all global conflicts. What was remarkable about his anti-colonialism was, as Gerald Horne rightly points out in his introduction to *Color and Democracy* (1946), Du Bois's inclusion of Asia, and particularly Japan, in the discussion. As fertile ground for colonial enterprises, Asia yielded still more evidence of the "inviolate link between color and democracy."

Color continued to preoccupy Du Bois, and in The World and Africa, he attempted to correct the ways in which color (black) had affected history. Mahmood Mamdani tells us in his introduction that Du Bois's motivation in writing this somewhat hasty volume was to tell the story of "those left out of recorded history" and to challenge, in effect, "an entire tradition of history-writing . . . modern European historiography." Du Bois was aware that this was just a beginning to a much larger project, to connect the history of Europe that dominated the academic discipline of history to events and progress in the world at large, including Africa.

In Battle for Peace: The Story of My 83rd Birthday features an embattled Du Bois enduring prosecution by (and eventually winning acquittal from) the federal government whose indictment of him as an unregistered agent for the Soviet Union was, according to Manning Marable, a trumped-up means by which to discredit the great black leader and frighten his fellow supporters of international peace into silence. It worked, at least in part: while Du Bois drew support from many international associations, the NAACP essentially abandoned him. Ten years later, in 1961, Du Bois would permanently leave the United States for Ghana.

Brent Hayes Edwards in his introduction calls the *Black Flame* trilogy of novels Du Bois's most neglected work. Written in the last few years of life, *The Ordeal of Mansart* (1957), *Mansart Builds a School* (1959), and *Worlds of Color* (1961) follow the life of Manuel Mansart from his birth in 1876 (the last year of Reconstruction) to his death in 1956, a period which spans his rise from a noted but provincial Southern educator to a self-educating citizen of the world of color. With its alternating apocalyptic and utopian tone, its depiction of real historical figures and events, and its thoughtful "animation of economic history and especially labor history," the Black Flame trilogy offers, according to Edwards, "the clearest articulation of Du Bois's perspective at the end of his life, and his reflections on an unparalleled career that had stretched from Reconstruction through the Cold War."

Du Bois was a largely marginalized figure in the last decade of his life, and his work published at that time, most notably the *Black Flame* trilogy, went into the critical and cultural abyss. Mark Sanders suggests that the "invisibility" of the trilogy, then and now, can be explained by an evolution in literary "taste" in the 1950s, wrought by new trends in literary criticism and magazine culture, the emergence of the Civil Rights Movement, and Du Bois's own development. Even if we have rejected in many real ways the ethos of the 1950s, for Sanders, our prescriptions for taste still owe a great deal to that decade.

Werner Sollors finds "four major narrative strains" in the posthumously published *Autobiography of W. E. B. Du Bois* (1968): the personal (including "startling" sexual revelations from the famously staid Du Bois); the academic, editorial, and organizational, in which his work is fully explored, and the political is always personal even while science and reason are held to be the solution to the race problem; the Communist, first as interested onlooker and then as Party member; and the elderly, in which an old man takes stock of contemporary youth culture with something of a jaundiced eye. Sollors suggests that far from being disjointed, the various strands of the *Autobiography* are united by Du Bois's ongoing quest for recognition. I would argue that there is nothing pathetic in this quest; it is simply the desire for respect from the society (black and white) that Du Bois spent his long life trying to understand.

Henry Louis Gates, Jr.
Cambridge, Massachusetts
December 7, 2006

Introduction

Mahmood Mamdani, Columbia University

"How do we know what man did in West Africa," asks W. E. B. Du Bois in *The World and Africa: An Inquiry into the Part Which Africa Has Played in World History* (1947), "since black Africa has no written history? This brings the curious assumption that lack of written record means lack of matter and deed worth recording."

How do you tell the story of those left out of recorded history? How do you tell the stories of the poor and the oppressed, of minorities, of women—really, the stories of subaltern majorities? For those left out of documented records, where do you find the documentation? And if the documentation is not conclusive, what do you do?

Du Bois's answer was threefold. First, look at the written record yet again, to move "from direct narrative to indirect allusion and confirmation," because "the deeds of men that have been clearly and accurately written down are as pinpoints to the oceans of human experience"; second, lean on memory, "the memory of contemporary onlookers, of those who heard their word, of those who over a lapse of years interpreted it and handed it on"; and third, rely on "the mute but powerful testimony of habits, customs, and ideals, which echo and reflect vast stretches of past time." At the end of it all, he suggests that "we agree upon as true history and actual fact any interpretation of past action which we today believe and want to believe is true." Du Bois had no illusion that this would necessarily solve the problem: "The relation of this last historical truth to real truth may vary from fact to falsehood."

But this lack of certainty did not turn into a moment of doubt, freezing Du Bois into an intellectual posture. He wrote in the 1946 foreword to *The World and Africa*, "I feel now as though I were approaching a crowd of friends and enemies, who ask a bit breathlessly, whose and whence is the testimony on which I rely for something that even resembles Authority?" Du Bois's opening and main response was unequivocal: "I am challenging Authority ... the herd of writers of modern history who never heard of Africa or declare with Guernier *'Seule de tous les continents l'Afrique n'a pas d'histoire!'*" (alone of all the continents Africa has no history).

Du Bois's work was aimed at a tradition of scholarship that had racialized Africa and then draped "black" Africa in a curtain of ignorance. This racialized prejudice was summed up most systematically, even if not most originally, in the writings of the great philosopher George Wilhelm Friedrich Hegel (1770–1831). Hegel divided Africa into three geographies. He considered two of these—North Africa, which he called "European Africa," and Northeast Africa, the "land of the Nile"—to be appendages of Europe and Asia, respectively. Of "Africa Proper," the land to the south and the west, this human reserve from which were drawn captives for the transatlantic slave trade, Hegel wrote: "Africa proper, as far as history goes back, has remained—for all purposes of connection with the rest of the world—shut up; it is the gold land compressed within itself—the land of childhood, which lying beyond the day of conscious history is enveloped in the dark mantle of Night."[1]

These views were echoed down the generations by others, also perched at the rooftops in the Western academy, and they reverberated a million times over as common sense. As late as 1965, Hugh Trevor-Roper, the Regius Professor of Modern History at Oxford, wrote in *The Rise of Christian Europe*: "Undergraduates, seduced, as always, by the changing breath of journalistic fashion, demand that they should be taught the history of black Africa. Perhaps, in the future, there will be some African history to teach. But at present there is none, or very little: there is only the history of the Europeans in Africa. The rest is largely darkness, like the history of pre-European, pre-Columbian America, and darkness is not a subject for history."[2]

The questions that W. E. B. Du Bois raised made it clear that his concern was not with writing just another history of Africa but with questioning an entire tradition of history writing. Unlike nationalist historians whose concern was to write a history of the new nation-states or of Africa, Du Bois wanted to outline a world history that would provincialize Europe. The object of his critique was no less than modern European historiography. This is why the big question that he raised about Africa—What has been Africa's contribution to world history? —directly led to another big question: How has the obscuring of this history been a necessary consequence of a modern traffic in humans that has debased humanity in the black?

If modern historiography had draped Hegel's "Africa Proper" in "the dark mantle of the night," nothing less than a scholarship that would highlight Africa's relations with humanity—through history—would be necessary to remove that mantle. Fully aware that no one individual could completely remove the mantle, Du Bois strove to gather the intellectual courage and clarity to begin it.

In fine, I have done in this book the sort of thing at which every scholar shudders. With meager preparation and all too general background of learning, I have essayed a task, which, to be adequate and complete, should be based upon the research of a lifetime! But I am faced with the dilemma, that either I do this now or leave it for others who have not had the tragedy of life which I have, forcing me to face a task for which they may have small stomach and little encouragement from the world round about. If, out of my almost inevitable mistakes and inaccuracies and false conclusions, I shall have at least clearly stated my main issue—that black Africans are men in the same sense as white Europeans and yellow Asiatics, and that history can easily prove this—then I shall rest satisfied even under the stigma of an incomplete and, to many, inconclusive work.

The questions that Du Bois asked sketched the outlines of an intellectual project that would reverberate into the next century. With the upsurge of anti-colonial nationalism in Africa and the civil rights movement in the United States, a new generation of intellectuals came to share Du Bois's political and intellectual concerns. *The World and Africa* was published in 1947. About a decade later, in 1955, Cheikh Anta Diop wrote and published *Nations nègres et culture*. Around that same time the Ibadan School of Historians in Nigeria pioneered the development of methods in the documentation of oral history. Standing on these shoulders Martin Bernal could begin his multivolume ambition, *Black Athena: The Afroasiatic Roots of Classical Civilization*, in 1987.

W. E. B. Du Bois had the intellectual vision to realize that any effort to restore Africa's place in history would have to go beyond Africa's geography and question key assumptions that have informed the writing of the history of Europe in modern times. The book identifies the main points around which this rethinking will need to be: ancient Greece, the European Renaissance, and the industrial revolution, each pivotal in the story of Europe as told by its historians. To reevaluate this story, Du Bois proposed to relocate each of these turning points in context, so as to highlight in each instance the connections with the world at large, including Africa. Such an approach raised a new set of questions about the very assumptions underlining the dominant historiography.

Is it possible to make sense of ancient Greece as a stand-alone civilization, without taking into consideration its connections with the rest of the Mediterranean world, especially Egypt and Asia—as did, indeed, the traditional school associated with Herodotus? "When persons wished to study science, art, government, or religion, they went to Egypt. The Greeks, inspired by Asia, turned toward Africa for learning, and the Romans in turn learned of Greece and Egypt."

Similarly, was the Renaissance a secular miracle, a civilizational pool with no tributaries, or does it, too, have a history? For Du Bois, the Renaissance is the "new light with which Asia and Africa illumined the Dark Ages of Europe" and brought "new hope for mankind." So Du Bois alerts us to the unintended bridge-building consequences of some of the most brutal invasions during the European Middle Ages. "It was Asia and Africa which in the thirteenth century prepared Europe for the Renaissance through Genghis Khan and the Crusades." In that same vein, Cu Bois could have discussed the role of Andalusia (Spain) in the onset of the Renaissance.

And finally, even the forces that propelled the industrial revolution in its totality cannot be understood without an account of the story of Africans in America. "From being a mere stopping place between Europe and Asia or a chance treasure house of gold, America became through African labor the centre of the sugar empire and the cotton kingdom and an integral part of that world history and trade which caused the Industrial Revolution and the reign of capitalism."

At the heart of the industrial revolution was the story of African slaves, and of the triangular trade among the Americas, Europe, and Africa. What accounts for the explosive demand for slaves in the modern era, an era that eulogized freedom as a distinctly human endeavor and yet chained humanity in the millions? Orlando Patterson has shown that whereas the growing demand for slaves in the premodern period came mainly from the centralizing monarchy—whether in the emperor's household such as *familia Caesaris* in early imperial Rome, the imperial civil service in Byzantium, or the military in the Indian Deccan—seeking autonomy from an aristocratic elite, the major demand for slaves in the modern period came from the insertion of slaves in the productive economy, the capitalist plantation system.[3] Du Bois insisted that the two slave systems, the premodern and the modern, were radically different: "The mild domestic slavery of the African tribes and of the Arabs and Persians, which did not preclude the son of a slave becoming a king, a statesman, or a poet was changed into chattel slavery with hard tasks and cruel tasks."

In like manner, Du Bois insists that the modern capitalist market is the real thread that tied the eighteenth- and nineteenth-century Arab slave trade with the European slave trade in a subordinate relationship: the Arab slave trade was a subsidiary of the European slave trade because the Arab trade supplied a rapidly growing European and American demand (whether for ivory or for slaves to work in plantations). "In this whole story of the so-called 'Arab slave trade' the truth has been strangely twisted. Arab slave trading was at the beginning, and largely to the end, a secondary result of the British and American slavery and slave trade and specifically was based on American demand for ivory."

How could the slave come to be debased so totally in an era that exalted freedom as key to being human? But it makes sense that in a society where large numbers enjoy civic freedom and where it is believed that to be human is to be free would turn around and conclude that only the free are truly human. Where freedom is supposed to be the birthright of humans, the temptation to explain away continuing unfreedom by systematically debasing the unfree as subhuman—in deed as well as in thought—is not all that surprising.

There is a tension that runs through the story of world history as Du Bois tells it, because that story is told in two different ways. On the one hand, Du Bois is determined to take on the libel of racial deficiency with which black Africa and its descendents have been stigmatized in the modern era. To remove the stigma of racial inferiority he is compelled to gauge the historical landscape through racially coded lenses. So, fully aware that they "had no name for race," he looks for the "race" of the ancient Egyptians, if only to show that their origins were Negroid. "We conclude, therefore, that the Egyptians were Negroids, and not only that, but by tradition they believed themselves descended not from the whites or yellows, but from the black peoples of the south." But the preoccupation with origins does not blind Du Bois to the nature of subsequent developments. "Gradually, of course, the Egyptians became a separate inbred people with characteristics quite different from their neighbors . . . brown in color." And yet the text that follows is full of explorations into different times and places, each preoccupied with bringing to light the presence of "black" or "Negroid" people in the flow that we call civilization.

On the other hand, Du Bois tells a story in which civilization is not an inbred product but is incubated in precisely those places and times that made possible a confluence of different cultures. One of the most poignant observations in this regard comes in the course of a discussion on Arabs and Arabia: "There was but scant indigenous culture in Arabia. The rise of civilization among Arabs, as among all peoples, took place where they were fired by contact with Mongoloids at Bagdad, Negroids in the valley of the Nile; and in Spain after the Arabs had passed slowly and in comparatively small numbers through Africa and augmented their numbers with black and brown Negroids and mixed Berbers."

This tension gives the text a contradictory character. On the one hand, its preoccupation with origins gives it a familiar nineteenth- and twentieth-century "nationalist" feel. On the other hand, even as he succumbs to this nationalism, Du Bois is fully aware of its dangers. Not surprisingly, the text opens itself to an alternate possibility. Exasperated with modern attempts to paint Egyptians as anything but black, he has this to say: "We may give up entirely, if we wish, the whole attempt to delimit races, but we cannot, if we are sane, divide the world into whites, yellows, and blacks, and then call blacks whites." Thus opens a radically different possibility: not only to doggedly defend the record of the race— "black" or "Negroid"—but also to think through the relationship between emancipation and deracialization.

Geography has a history, and we will do well to historicize the geographies of Africa. Africa was a name that Romans gave to their southernmost province, what we now know as North Africa. With the Atlantic slave trade, "Africa Proper" became the name of the land south of the Sahara. From being a civilizational bridge, the Sahara became a barrier. The flow of goods and ideas shifted westward, from the Sahara to the Atlantic. Tarnished with the modern European tendency to racialize peoples and places, the place Africa became synonymous with a race and a color—as in black Africa, or Bantu Africa. For Du Bois the challenge was twofold: to deracialize the meaning of the African experience in the world and to join it to the struggle for Pan-Africanism.

Writing in the *National Guardian*, Du Bois recalled the antecedents of Pan-Africanism among Negro Americans: "In the eighteenth century they had regarded Africa as their home to which they would eventually return when free. They named their institutions 'African' and started migration to Africa as early as 1815." The mass movement for a return to Africa was led by Marcus Garvey. Du Bois thought it "poorly conceived," but he acknowledged its strength: "this was a peoples' movement rather than a movement of intellectuals." As a popular movement, however, "back to Africa" had a short life. "[T]he American Negroes were soon sadly disillusioned: first their immigrants to Liberia found that Africans did not regard them as Africans; and then it became clear by 1830 that colonization schemes were a device to rid America of free Africans so as to fasten slavery more firmly to support the cotton kingdom." As

American Negroes "turned to a new ideal"—"to strive for equality as American citizens"—Pan-Africanism in the United States became more of an intellectual preoccupation.

Why would natives who had never left home (continental Africans) be ambivalent to the return of natives who had been forcibly kidnapped from home (African Americans)? To what extent was this ambivalence rooted in the recognition that returning natives were not just freed persons coming home but the front paw of a new colonizing movement? Du Bois wrestled with these questions for the rest of his life. On the one hand, Pan-Africanism was born of the experience of bondage in the New World: "The idea of one Africa to unite the thought and ideals of all native peoples of the dark continent belongs to the twentieth century and stems naturally from the West Indies and the United States. Here various groups of Africans, quite separate in origin, became so united in experience and so exposed to the impact of new cultures that they began to think of Africa as one idea and one land."

On the other hand, the more committed that African Americans became to fighting for equal citizenship in the United States, the more Du Bois thought "American Negroes learned from their environment to think less and less of their fatherland and its folk" and began "to acquiesce in color prejudice." Du Bois wrote in the *National Guardian* of the effects of this specifically American complex: "American Negroes of former generations had always calculated that when Africa was ready for freedom, American Negroes would be ready to lead them. But the event was quite opposite." Neither did he exempt himself fully from this tendency. He recalled the time that his wife, Shirley Graham, returned from reading his message to the All-African Conference in Accra, Ghana, in 1958. When she told him "of Lumumba there demanding independence for Congo, I [Du Bois] thought he was an unthinking fanatic." In that same mood, he told Africans in the Peking University audience gathered to celebrate his ninety-first birthday: "Once I thought of you Africans as children, whom we educated Afro-Americans would lead to liberty. I was wrong."

Right up to the end of his life this giant of an intellectual kept his feet solidly on the ground and his gaze into the horizon, refusing to capitulate either to romance or to cynicism. More than six decades after W. E. B. Du Bois wrote *The World and Africa*, his twin preoccupation—to deracialize the meaning of the African experience and to use that knowledge to illuminate the quest for an African unity—remains a worthy guide for thought and action in the twenty-first century.[4]

NOTES

1. G. W. F. Hegel, *The Philosophy of History* (New York: Dover, 1956), p. 91. See also Hegel, "Introduction: Reason in History," in *Lectures on the Philosophy of World History* (Cambridge, U.K.: Cambridge University Press, 1975), pp. 173–174.
2. Hugh Trevor-Roper, *The Rise of Christian Europe* (New York: Harcourt, Brace and World, 1965), p. 9.
3. Orlando Patterson, *Slavery and Social Death: A Comparative Study* (Cambridge, Mass: Harvard University Press, 1982).
4. I would like to thank Mamadou Diouf for a critical reading of this text.

Foreword

Since the rise of the sugar empire and the resultant cotton kingdom, there has been consistent effort to rationalize Negro slavery by omitting Africa from world history, so that today it is almost universally assumed that history can be truly written without reference to Negroid peoples. I believe this to be scientifically unsound and also dangerous for logical social conclusions. Therefore I am seeking in this book to remind readers in this crisis of civilization, of how critical a part Africa has played in human history, past and present, and how impossible it is to forget this and rightly explain the present plight of mankind.

Twice before I have essayed to write on the history of Africa: once in 1915 when the editors of the Home University Library asked me to attempt such a work. The result was the little volume called *The Negro*, which gave evidence of a certain naïve astonishment on my own part at the wealth of fact and material concerning the Negro peoples, the very existence of which I had myself known little despite a varied university career. The result was a condensed and not altogether logical narrative. Nevertheless, it has been widely read and is still in print.

Naturally I wished to enlarge upon this earlier work after World War I and at the beginning of what I thought was a new era. So I wrote *Black Folk: Then and Now*, with some new material and a more logical arrangement. But it happened that I was writing at the end of an age which marked the final catastrophe of the old era of European world dominance rather than at the threshold of a change of which I had not dreamed in 1935. I deemed it, therefore, not only fitting but necessary in 1946 to essay again not so much a history of the Negroid peoples as a statement of their integral role in human history from prehistoric to modern times.

I still labor under the difficulty of the persistent lack of interest in Africa so long characteristic of modern history and sociology. The careful, detailed researches into the history of Negroid peoples have only begun, and the need for them is not yet clear to the thinking world. I feel compelled nevertheless to go ahead with my interpretation, even though that interpretation has here and there but slender historical proof. I believe that in the main my story is true, despite the fact that so often between the American Civil War and World War I the weight of history and science supports me only in part and in some cases appears violently to contradict me. At any rate, here is a history of the world written from the African point of view; or better, a history of the Negro as part of the world which now lies about us in ruins.

I am indebted to my assistant, Dr. Irene Diggs, for efficient help in arranging the material and reading the manuscript.

I feel now as though I were approaching a crowd of friends and enemies, who ask a bit breathlessly, whose and whence is the testimony on which I rely for something that even resembles Authority? To which I return two answers: I am challenging Authority—even Maspero, Sayce, Reisner, Breasted, and hundreds of other men of highest respectability, who did not attack but studiously ignored the Negro on the Nile and in the world and talked as though black folk were nonexistent and unimportant. They are part of the herd of writers of modern history who never heard of Africa or declare with Guernier *"Seule de tous les continents l'Afrique n'a pas d'histoire!"*

For chapters one and two I have relied upon my own travel and observation over a fairly long life. For confirmation I have resurrected William Howitt's *Colonization and Christianity*, a popular history of how Europeans treated the natives in their colonies. The book was published in London in 1838, and since then imperial Europe had tried to forget it. I have also made bold to repeat the testimony of Karl Marx, whom I regard as the greatest of modern philosophers, and I have not been deterred by the witch-hunting which always follows mention of his name. I like Robert Briffault's *The Decline and Fall of the British Empire* (1938) and George Padmore's *How Britain Rules Africa* (1936). I have mentioned the work of Anna Graves, who is usually ignored because she does not follow the conventions of historical writing and because no publisher has thought that he could make money out of her work.

In chapter three, on the slave trade, I have especially relied on Eric Williams' new and excellent work, *Capitalism and Slavery;* also on Wilson Williams' work published in the first number of the Howard University *Studies in the Social Sciences.* My own *Suppression of the Slave Trade* has continued to be of service. Rayford Logan's work on the United States and Haiti and Chapman Cohen's *Christianity, Slavery, and Labor* (1931) have also been used. Reginald Coupland's *East Africa and Its Invaders* (1938) has been valuable. But my greatest help in this chapter after Eric Williams, has been E. D. Moore's *Ivory: The Scourge of Africa* (1931); it is an invaluable book and I am deeply indebted to its author for facts.

In chapter four I have relied on Edwin W. Smith, now Editor of *Africa* and Julian Huxley; also on C. G. Seligmann, whose *Races of Africa* (1930), is priceless and marred only by his obsession with the "Hamites."

In chapter five on Egypt there is naturally the greatest diversity of opinion. My attention to the subject was first aroused by the little pamphlet published by Alexander F. Chamberlain in 1911, "The Contribution of the Negro to Human Civilization." Naturally one must read Maspero, Breasted, Rawlinson, and the other earlier and indefatigable students; but I have mainly depended upon W. M. Flinders Petrie's *History of Egypt* and on the sixth volume of the work on Egypt in the Middle Ages by E. Stanley Lane-Poole edited by Petrie. The travels of Ibn Batuta and Duarte Barbosa form a firm background to the modern research of Arthur Thomson, David Randall-MacIver, and Grace Caton-Thompson. Especially *Egyptian Civilization* by Alexandre Moret, published in French in 1927 and shortly thereafter in English has been illuminating. I have looked through the splendid reproductions of Karl R. Lepsius' *Denkmäler*. I have read Eduard Meyer's *Geschichte des Altertums* (1910–13); but of greatest help to me has been

Leo Hansberry. Mr. Hansberry, a professor at Howard University, is the one modern scholar who has tried to study the Negro in Egypt and Ethiopia. I regret that he has not published more of his work. The overwhelming weight of conventional scientific opinion on Africa has overawed him, but his work in manuscript is outstanding. Arthur E. P. B. Weigall's *Short History of Egypt* has also been of use.

In chapter six I have depended upon Hansberry. One always turns back to Winwood Reade's *Martyrdom of Man* for renewal of faith. The works of Sir Ernest Budge, George A. Reisner, A. H. Sayce, and F. L. Griffith have naturally been of use when they were not indulging their opinions about Negroes.

I should like to have used the researches on the Negro in classic Europe of Dr. Frank Snowden of Howard University. But classical journals in America have hitherto declined to publish his paper because it favored the Negro too much, leaving the public still to rely on Beardsley's stupid combination of scholarship and race prejudice which Johns Hopkins University published. I tried to get Dr. Snowden to let me see his manuscript, but he refused.

In chapter seven I have relied upon Leo Frobenius. Frobenius is not popular among conventional historians or anthropologists. He indulged his imagination. He had strong beliefs; but he was a great man and a great thinker. He looked upon Africa with unprejudiced eyes and has been more valuable for his interpretation of the Negro than any other man I know. The many works of Robert S. Rattray and Meek, Westermann and Schapera, cannot be ignored. African students like Soga and Caseley-Hayford have helped me, and younger men like Orizu. Mbadiwe, and Ojiki. Basic is the fine unprejudiced work of Maurice Delafosse. I have used Flora Lugard, although she is not a scientist; and also a new young Negro writer, Armattoe.

In the eighth chapter I have naturally depended upon Sir Harry H. Johnston and his study of the Bantu languages; the splendid work of Miss Caton-Thompson. I have learned much from James A. Rogers. Rogers is an untrained American Negro writer who has done his work under great difficulty without funds and at much personal sacrifice. But no man living has revealed so many important facts about the Negro race as has Rogers. His mistakes are many and his background narrow, but he is a true historical student.

In chapter nine there is reliance on Lane-Poole and Cooper, whom I have mentioned before, and on the new points of view brought by Jawaharlal Nehru in his *Autobiography* (1940) and his *Glimpses of World History* (1942). The study of Egypt and the East by Alfred T. Butler and Palon have shed much needed light; and general anthropology is gradually revealing the trend of the Negro in Africa as we emerge from the blight of the writers of current history.

Chapter ten is built on the work of Maurice Delafosse and of William D. Cooley (1841), with help from H. R. Palmer, Flora Lugard, and many others.

Chapter eleven depends on current thought and documents; and books like Leonard Barnes' *Soviet Light on the Colonies* (1944) and Harold Laski's *Rise of Liberalism* (1936).

In fine, I have done in this book the sort of thing at which every scholar shudders. With meager preparation and all too general background of learning, I have essayed a task, which, to be adequate and complete, should be based upon the research of a lifetime! But I am faced with the dilemma, that either I do this now or leave it for others who have not had the tragedy of life which I have, forcing me to face a task for which they may have small stomach and little encouragement from the world round about. If, out of my almost inevitable mistakes and inaccuracies and false conclusions, I shall have at least clearly stated my main issue—that black Africans are men in the same sense as white European and yellow Asiatics, and that history can easily prove this—then I shall rest satisfied even under the stigma of an incomplete and, to many, inconclusive work.

W. E. Burghardt Du Bois

New York
May 1946.

The World and Africa

CHAPTER I

---◆---

The Collapse of Europe

This is a consideration of the nature of the calamity which has overtaken human civilization.

We are face to face with the greatest tragedy that has ever overtaken the world. The collapse of Europe is to us the more astounding because of the boundless faith which we have had in European civilization. We have long believed without argument or reflection that the cultural status of the people of Europe and of North America represented not only the best civilization which the world had ever known, but also a goal of human effort destined to go on from triumph to triumph until the perfect accomplishment was reached. Our present nervous breakdown, nameless fear, and often despair, comes from the sudden facing of this faith with calamity.

In such a case, what we need above all is calm appraisal of the situation, the application of cold common sense. What in reality is the nature of the catastrophe? To what pattern of human culture does it apply? And, finally, why did it happen? In this search for reasons we must seek not simply current facts or facts within the memory of living men, but we must also, and especially in this case, seek lessons from history. It is perhaps the greatest indictment that can be brought against history as a science and against its teachers that we are usually indisposed to refer to history for the settlement of pressing problems. We realize that history is too often what we want it to be and what we are determined men shall believe rather than a grim record of what has taken place in the past.

Manifestly the present plight of the world is a direct outgrowth of the past, and I have made bold to add to the many books on the subject of our present problems because I believe that certain suppressions in the historical record current in our day will lead to a tragic failure in assessing causes. More particularly, I believe that the habit, long fostered, for forgetting and detracting from the thought and acts of the people of Africa, is not only a direct cause of our present plight, but will continue to cause trouble until we face the facts. I shall try not to exaggerate this thread of African history in the world development, but I shall insist equally that it be not ignored.

At the beginning of the twentieth century, when I was but ten years out of college, I visited the Paris Exposition of 1900. It was one of the finest, perhaps the very finest, of world expositions, and it typified what the European world wanted to think of itself and its future. Wealth and Science were the outstanding matters of emphasis: there was the new and splendid Pont Alexandre crossing the Seine, named for the Czar of Russia; there was an amazing exhibit of Russian industry at Jaroslav; and I had brought with me, as excuse for coming, a little display showing the development of Negroes in the United States, which gained a gold medal. All about me was an extraordinary display of wealth, luxury, and industrial technique, striking evidence of a Europe triumphant over the world and the center of science and art, power and human freedom.

It was easy to see what the great countries of Europe thought of themselves: France stood pre-eminently for art, for taste in building, technique, and pure expression; Germany stood for science and government; England for wealth and power with a high level of comfort; and America for freedom of human initiative.

There was even in this French exposition a certain dominance of the British Empire idea. The British paper promise-to-pay was actually worth more to the traveler than gold. British industry was unrivaled in efficient technique. British investments were the safest; and Great Britain was the widest and most successful administrator of colonies. Every kind of tribute was paid to her; she was the acknowledged leader in such various things as men's cloth and clothing, public manners, the rate of public expenditure—and all this showed in the deference a British subject could demand everywhere throughout the world.

Then came five crashing events in quick succession. First, in 1905, at Saint Petersburg, the shooting down in cold blood of Russian workingmen in the first organized attempt of the twentieth century to achieve relief; and by that murderous volley the Czar killed the faith of working Russia in the Little White Father. He revealed that Russian industry was paying 50 per cent and more in profits to Germans and other investors, while the workers starved. The Czar himself thus sowed the seeds of revolution.

Second, in 1911 a German warship sailed into Agadir, North Africa, and demanded in the name of the Emperor that the German Reich be consulted concerning the future of Morocco. I remember how the incident startled London. I was there at the time, attending the First Races Congress. It is a meeting now forgotten, but it might have been of world significance. Its advice might have changed the course of history had not World War I followed so fast. Meeting at the University of London was probably the largest representation of the groups of the world known as races and subraces; they were consulting together under the leadership of science and ethics for a future world which would be peaceful, without race prejudice; and which would be cooperative, especially in the social sciences. Among the speakers were world leaders—Giuseppe Sergi, Franz Boas, John A. Hobson, Felix Adler, Sir Sidney Olivier, and Wu Ting-fang. A hymn to the peoples was read:

So sit we all as one
So, gloomed in tall and stone-swathed groves,

The Buddha walks with Christ!
And Al-Koran and Bible both be holy!

Almighty Word!
In this Thine awful sanctuary,
First and flame-haunted City of the Widened World,
Assoil us, Lord of Lands and Seas!

We are but weak and wayward men,
Distraught alike with hatred and vainglory;
Prone to despise the Soul that breathes within—
High-visioned hordes that lie and steal and kill,
Sinning the sin each separate heart disclaims,
Clambering upon our riven, writhing selves,
Besieging Heaven by trampling men to Hell!

We be blood-guilty! Lo, our hands be red!
Let no man blame the other in this sin!
But here—here in the white Silence of the Dawn,
Before the Womb of Time,
With bowed hearts all flame and shame,
We face the birth-pangs of a world:
We hear the stifled cry of Nations all but born—
The wail of women ravished of their stunted brood!
We see the nakedness of Toil, the poverty of Wealth,
We know the Anarchy of Empire, and doleful Death of Life!
And hearing, seeing, knowing all, we cry:

Save us, World-Spirit, from our lesser selves!
Grant us that war and hatred cease,
Reveal our souls in every race and hue!
Help us, O Human God, in this Thy Truce,
To make Humanity divine![1]

There were a few startling incidents. I remember with what puzzled attention we heard Felix von Luschan, the great anthropologist of the University of Berlin, annihilate the thesis of race inferiority and then in the same breath end his paper with these words: "Nations will come and go, but racial and national antagonism will remain; and this is well, for mankind would become like a herd of sheep if we were to lose our national ambition and cease to look with pride and delight, not only on our industries and science, but also on our splendid soldiers and our glorious ironclads. Let small-minded people whine about the horrid cost of dreadnoughts; as long as every nation in Europe spends, year after year, much more money on wine, beer, and brandy than on her army and navy, there is no reason to dread our impoverishment by militarism. *Si vis pacem, para bellum;* and in reality there is no doubt that we shall be the better able to avoid war, the better we care for our armor. A nation is free only in so far as her own internal affairs are concerned. She has to respect the right of other nations as well as to defend her own, and her vital interests she will, if necessary, defend with blood and iron."[2]

We were aghast. Did German science defend war? We were hardly reassured when in printing this speech the editor appended the following note: "To prevent the last few paragraphs from being misinterpreted, Professor von Luschan authorizes us to state that he regards the desire for a war between Germany and England as 'insane or dastardly.' "[3]

But it was in vain. In 1914 came World War I; in 1929 came the depression; in 1939 came World War II. The cost of these wars and crises in property and human life is almost beyond belief; the cost in the destruction of youth and of faith in the world and mankind is incalculable. Why did these things happen?

We may begin with the fact that in 1888 there came to the throne of Germany a young, vigorous German emperor of British descent. Wilhelm II had utter faith in the future of Germany. As a student I used to see him often on the Unter den Linden. Time and again we students swung to the curb, and through the central arch of the Brandenburg Gate came the tossing of plumes and the prancing of horses, and splendid with shining armor and blare of trumpet there rode Wilhelm, by the Grace of God, King of Prussia and German Emperor.

Back of Wilhelm's faith in Germany lay deep envy of the power of Britain. In his soul strove unceasingly the ambition of Bismarck of Prussia and the aristocratic imperialism of his mother, a daughter of Queen Victoria. The French-British *Entente Cordiale* of the new century was faced by a German demand for "a place in the sun," a right to extract from colonial and semicolonial areas a share of the wealth which was going to Britain. When Germany invaded Belgium, and with that invasion brought war with England, it must be remembered that by that same token Germany was invading the Belgian Congo and laying claim to the ownership of Central Africa.

World War I then was a war over spheres of influence in Asia and colonies in Africa, and in that war, curiously enough, both Asia and Africa were called upon to support Europe. Senegalese troops, for example, saved France and Europe from the first armed German onslaught. They were the shock troops brought to be slaughtered in thousands by the climate and cannon of Europe. The man who brought the African troops to the succor of France was Blaise Diagne. He was a tall, thin Negro, nervous with energy, more patriotic in his devotion to France than many of the French. He was deputy from Senegal in the French Parliament and had been selected as the man to whom the chiefs of French West Africa would render implicit obedience. Raised to cabinet rank, he was made the official representative of the French in West Africa. The white governor who found himself subordinated to this Negro resigned in disgust, but Diagne went down the West Coast in triumph and sent a hundred thousand black soldiers to France at this critical time.

One must not forget that incident on the fields of Flanders which has been so quickly forgotten. Against the banked artillery of the magnificent German Army were sent untrained and poorly armed Senegalese. They marched at command in unwavering ranks, raising the war cry in a dozen different Sudanese tongues. When the artillery belched they shivered, but never faltered. They marched straight into death; the war cries became fainter and fainter and dropped into silence as not a single black man was left living on that field.

I was in Paris just after the armistice in 1918, and it was to Diagne that I went to ask for the privilege of calling a Pan-African Congress in Paris during the Versailles Peace Conference.

The idea of one Africa to unite the thought and ideals of all native peoples of the dark continent belongs to the twentieth century and stems naturally from the West Indies and the United States. Here various groups of Africans, quite separate in origin, became so united in experience and so exposed to the impact of new cultures that they began to think of Africa as one idea and one land. Thus late in the eighteenth century when a separate Negro Church was formed in Philadelphia it called itself "African"; and there were various "African" societies in many parts of the United States.

It was not, however, until 1900 that a black West Indian barrister, practicing in London, called together a Pan-African Conference. This meeting attracted attention, put the word "Pan-African" in the dictionaries for the first time, and had some thirty delegates, mainly from England and the West Indies, with a few colored North Americans. The conference was welcomed by the Lord Bishop of London and a promise was obtained from Queen Victoria, through Joseph Chamberlain, not to "overlook the interests and welfare of the native races."

This meeting had no deep roots in Africa itself, and the movement and the idea died for a generation. Then came World War I, and among North American Negroes at its close there was determined agitation for the rights of Negroes throughout the world, and particularly in Africa. Meetings were held and a petition was sent to President Wilson. By indirection I secured passage on the Creel press boat, the *Orizaba*, and landed in France in December 1918. I went with the idea of calling a Pan-African Congress, and to try to impress upon the members of the Peace Conference sitting at Versailles the importance of Africa in the future world. I was without credentials or influence. I tried to get a conference with President Wilson but got only as far as Colonel House, who was sympathetic but noncommittal. The *Chicago Tribune* of January 19, 1919, in a dispatch from Paris dated December 30, 1918, said:

> An Ethiopian Utopia, to be fashioned out of the German colonies, is the latest dream of leaders of the Negro race who are here at the invitation of the United States government as part of the extensive entourage of the American peace delegation. Robert R. Moton, successor of the late Booker Washington as head of Tuskegee Institute, and Dr. William E. B. DuBois, editor of the *Crisis*, are promoting a Pan-African Conference to be held here during the winter while the Peace Conference is in full blast. It is to embrace Negro leaders from America, Abyssinia, Liberia, Haiti, the French and British colonies, and other parts of the black world. Its object is to get out of the Peace Conference an effort to modernize the dark continent and in the world reconstruction to provide international machinery looking toward the civilization of the African natives.
>
> The Negro leaders are not agreed upon any definite plan, but Dr. DuBois has mapped out a scheme which he has presented in the form of a memorandum to President Wilson. It is quite Utopian, and it has less than a Chinaman's chance of getting anywhere in the Peace Conference, but it is nevertheless interesting. As

"self-determination" is one of the words to conjure with in Paris nowadays, the Negro leaders are seeking to have it applied, if possible, in a measure to their race in Africa.

Dr. DuBois sets forth that while the principle of self-determination cannot be applied to uncivilized peoples, yet the educated blacks should have some voice in the disposition of the German colonies. He maintains that in settling what is to be done with the German colonies the Peace Conference might consider the wishes of the intelligent Negroes in the colonies themselves, the Negroes of the United States, and South Africa, and the West Indies, the Negro governments of Abyssinia, Liberia, and Haiti, the educated Negroes in French West Africa and Equatorial Africa and in British Uganda, Nigeria, Basutoland, Swaziland, Sierra Leone, Gold Goast, Gambia, and Bechuanaland, and in the Union of South Africa.

Dr. DuBois' dream is that the Peace Conference could form an internationalized Africa, to have as its basis the former German colonies, with their 1,000,000 square miles and 12,500,000 population.

"To this," his plan reads, "could be added by negotiation the 800,000 square miles and 9,000,000 inhabitants of Portuguese Africa. It is not impossible that Belgium could be persuaded to add to such a state the 900,000 square miles and 9,000,000 natives of the Congo, making an international Africa with over 2,500,000 square miles of land and over 20,000,000 people.

"This Africa for the Africans could be under the guidance of international organization. The governing international commission should represent not simply governments, but modern culture, science, commerce, social reform, and religious philanthropy. It must represent not simply the white world, but the civilized Negro world.

"We can, if we will, inaugurate on the dark continent a last great crusade for humanity. With Africa redeemed, Asia would be safe and Europe indeed triumphant."

Members of the American delegation and associated experts assured me that no congress on this matter could be held in Paris because France was still under martial law; but the ace that I had up my sleeve was Blaise Diagne, the black deputy from Senegal and Commissaire-Général in charge of recruiting native African troops. I went to Diagne and sold him the idea of a Pan-African Congress. He consulted Clemenceau, and the matter was held up two wet, discouraging months. Finally we received permission to hold the Congress in Paris. "Don't advertise it," said Clemenceau, "but go ahead." Walter Lippmann wrote me in his crabbed hand, February 20, 1919: "I am very much interested in your organization of the Pan-African conference, and glad that Clemenceau has made it possible. Will you send me whatever reports you may have on the work?"

American newspaper correspondents wrote home: "Officials here are puzzled by the news from Paris that plans are going forward there for a Pan-African conference. Acting Secretary Polk said today the State Department had been officially advised by the French government that no such conference would be held. It was announced recently that no passports would be issued for American delegates desiring to attend the meeting."[4] But at the very time that Polk was assuring American Negroes that no Congress would be held, the Congress actually assembled in Paris.

This Congress represented Africa partially. Of the fifty-seven delegates from fifteen countries, nine were African countries with twelve delegates. Of the remaining delegates, sixteen were from the United States, and twenty-one from the West Indies. Most of these delegates did not come to France for this meeting but happened to be residing there, mainly for reasons connected with the war. America and the colonial powers had refused to issue special visas.

The Congress influenced the Peace Conference. *The New York Evening Globe* of February 22, 1919, described it as "the first assembly of the kind in history, and has for its object the drafting of an appeal to the Peace Conference to give the Negro race of Africa a chance to develop unhindered by other races. Seated at long green tables in the council room today, were Negroes in the trim uniform of American Army officers, other American colored men in frock coats or business suits, polished French Negroes who hold public office, Senegalese who sit in the French Chamber of Deputies. . . ."

The Congress specifically asked that the German colonies be turned over to an international organization instead of being handled by the various colonial powers. Out of this idea came the Mandates Commission.

The resolutions of the Congress asked in part:

A. That the Allied and Associated Powers establish a code of law for the international protection of the natives of Africa, similar to the proposed international code for labor.
B. That the League of Nations establish a permanent Bureau charged with the special duty of overseeing the application of these laws to the political, social, and economic welfare of the natives.
C. The Negroes of the world demand that hereafter the natives of Africa and the peoples of African descent be governed according to the following principles:
   1. *The land:* the land and its natural resources shall be held in trust for the natives and at all times they shall have effective ownership of as much land as they can profitably develop.
   2. *Capital:* the investment of capital and granting of concessions shall be so regulated as to prevent the exploitation of the natives and the exhaustion of the natural wealth of the country. Concessions shall always be limited in time and subject to State control. The growing social needs of the natives must be regarded and the profits taxed for social and material benefit of the natives.
   3. *Labor:* slavery and corporal punishment shall be abolished and forced labor except in punishment for crime; and the general conditions of labor shall be prescribed and regulated by the State.
   4. *Education:* it shall be the right of every native child to learn to read and write his own language, and the language of the trustee nation, at public expense, and to be given technical instruction in some branch of industry. The State shall also educate as large a number of natives as possible in higher technical and cultural training and maintain a corps of native teachers.
   5. *The State:* the natives of Africa must have the right to participate in the government as fast as their development permits, in conformity with the principle that the government exists for the natives, and not the natives for the government. They shall at once be allowed to participate in local and tribal government, according to ancient usage, and this participation shall gradually extend,

as education and experience proceed, to the higher offices of State; to the end that, in time, Africa be ruled by consent of the Africans. . . . Whenever it is proven that African natives are not receiving just treatment at the hands of any State or that any State deliberately excludes its civilized citizens or subjects of Negro descent from its body politic and cultural, it shall be the duty of the League of Nations to bring the matter to the notice of the civilized World.[5]

The *New York Herald* of February 24, 1919, said: "There is nothing unreasonable in the program drafted at the Pan-African Congress which was held in Paris last week. It calls upon the Allied and Associated Powers to draw up an international code of law for the protection of the nations of Africa, and to create, as a section of the League of Nations, a permanent bureau to insure observance of such laws and thus further the racial, political, and economic interests of the natives."

We were, of course, but weak and ineffective amateurs chipping at a hard conglomeration of problems about to explode in chaos. At least we were groping for light.

Not only Africa but Asia took active part in World War I on the side of the Allies. India saw for the first time a prospect of autonomy within the British Empire. Japan wanted to be recognized as the equal of white European nations, and the Chinese Republic started on its new path to modern civilization. Peace dawned, and the war came to be known as "the War to End War." But in vain, for this war had not ended the idea of European world domination. Rather it had loosened the seams of imperialism.

In Africa, Negro troops had conquered German colonies, and now British West Africa demanded a share in government. In the very midst of war came labor revolt in Russia, which Europe and North America tried to repress, but they did not succeed. There came from the colonies in Africa and Asia insistent demand for freedom and democracy. It was in 1915 that the Congress of West Africa appealed to Great Britain in these words:

In the demand for the franchise by the people of British West Africa, it is not to be supposed that they are asking to be allowed to copy a foreign institution. On the contrary, it is important to notice that the principle of electing representatives to local councils and bodies is inherent in all the systems of British West Africa.[6]

In the interval between World War I and World War II, India's determined opposition to British rule increased under the leadership of Gandhi, who sought to substitute peaceful non-co-operation for war. The answer was the massacre of Amritsar. In America organized industry rose in its might to realize fantastic profits through domination of world industry. It fought labor unions and tried to nullify democracy by the power of wealth and capital. In the very midst of this, the magnificent structure of capitalistic industry collapsed in every part of the world. Make no mistake, war did not cause the Great Depression; it was the reasons behind the depression that caused war and will cause it again.

The world tried to meet depression and unemployment and to compose differences between capital and labor. Faced by the threat of Russian Communism,

Italy, which with Spain was the most poverty-stricken country in Western Europe, seized control of the nation and of industry with the object of ruling it through an oligarchy, eliminating all democratic control. This was the answer of capitalists to the growing and threatening political power of the workers. Hitler followed, opposing the Socialist state of Weimar, with its unemployment and political chaos, with a new state and a new nationalism. The industrial leaders surrendered their power into his hands; the army followed suit; unemployment disappeared, and Hitler diverted the nation with visions of vengeance to be achieved through a new state ruled by German supermen. Simultaneously, Japan, having been rebuffed by England and America in her plea for racial equality before the League of Nations, saw an opportunity in this new order to displace Europe in the control of Asia.

Then came rumblings of World War II. The Axis wooed first England and France and then Russia. Britain made every offer of appeasement. Ethiopia was thrown to the dogs of a new Italian imperialism in Africa. Everything was offered to Hitler but the balance of power in Europe and the surrender of colonies. America, hesitating, was ready to fight for private industry against Nazism and to defend Anglo-American investment in colonies and quasi-colonial areas.

Hitler would not be appeased. So war began. Hell broke loose. Six million Jews were murdered in Germany through a propaganda which tied the small shop-keepers back of Hitler and placed unreasoning race prejudice back of war. France feared to trust colonial Africa. De Gaulle and the black Governor Eboué, with co-operation from England and France, could have established a new black France in Africa and shortened the war; but France yielded to Germany. England resisted doggedly. Russia yielded and joined hands with Germany, but not for long.

The real battle then began; the battle of the Nazi-Fascist oligarchy against the dictatorship of the proletariat. Germany determined first to crush Russia and then with Russian resources to destroy the British Empire. Japan aroused Asia, and by attacking America thus furnished the one reason, based on race prejudice, which brought America immediately into the war. India protested, China starved and struggled, the horrible world war with uncounted cost in property, life, and youth came to an end, and with it came the discovery of the use of atomic energy.

It was significant that the man who invented the phrase "White Man's Burden" and who was its most persistent propagandist, also wrote its epitaph:

> If, drunk with sight of power, we loose
>   Wild tongues that have not Thee in awe,
> Such boastings as the Gentiles use,
>   Or lesser breeds without the Law—
>
>   . . .
>
> For heathen heart that puts her trust
>   In reeking tube and iron shard,
> All valiant dust that builds on dust,
>   And, guarding, calls not Thee to guard,
> For frantic boast and foolish word—
>   Thy Mercy on Thy people, Lord![7]

NOTES

1. W. E. B. DuBois, *Darkwater* (New York: Harcourt, Brace & Howe, 1920), pp. 275–76.
2. Gustav Spiller, ed., *Papers on Inter-Racial Problems, Universal Races Congress, I* (London: P. S. King & Son, 1911), pp. 23–24.
3. *Ibid.*, p. 24.
4. *Pittsburgh [Pa.] Dispatch,* February 16, 1919.
5. Broadside published by the Pan-African Congress, Paris, 1919.
6. Memorandum of the case of the National Congress of British West Africa . . . , March 1920, p. 2.
7. Rudyard Kipling, "Recessional."

CHAPTER II

◆

The White Masters of
the World

This is an attempt to show briefly what the domination of Europe over the world has meant to mankind and especially to Africans in the nineteenth and twentieth centuries.

What are the real causes back of the collapse of Europe in the twentieth century? What was the real European imperialism pictured in the Paris Exposition of 1900? France did not stand purely for art. There was much imitation, convention, suppression, and sale of genius; and France wanted wealth and power at any price. Germany did not stand solely for science. I remember when the German professor at whose home I was staying in 1890 expressed his contempt for the rising businessmen. He had heard them conversing as he drank in a *Bierstube* at Eisenach beneath the shade of Luther's Wartburg. Their conversation, he sneered, was *lauter Geschäft!* He did not realize that a new Germany was rising which wanted German science for one main purpose—wealth and power. America wanted freedom, but freedom to get rich by any method short of anarchy; and freedom to get rid of the democracy which allowed laborers to dictate to managers and investors.

All these centers of civilization envied England the wealth and power built upon her imperial colonial system. One looking at European imperialism in 1900 therefore should have looked first at the depressed peoples. One would have found them also among the laboring classes in Europe and America, living in slums behind a façade of democracy, nourished on a false education which lauded the triumphs of the industrial undertaker, made the millionaire the hero of modern life, and taught youth that success was wealth. The slums of England emphasized class differences; slum dwellers and British aristocracy spoke different tongues, had different manners and ideals. The goal of human life was illustrated in the nineteenth-century English novel: the aristocrat of independent income surrounded by a herd of obsequious and carefully trained servants. Even today the British butler is a personage in the literary world.

Out of this emerged the doctrine of the Superior Race: the theory that a minority of the people of Europe are by birth and natural gift the rulers of mankind;

rulers of their own suppressed labor classes and, without doubt, heaven-sent rulers of yellow, brown, and black people.

This way of thinking gave rise to many paradoxes, and it was characteristic of the era that men did not face paradoxes with any plan to solve them. There was the religious paradox: the contradiction between the Golden Rule and the use of force to keep human beings in their appointed places; the doctrine of the White Man's Burden and the conversion of the heathen, faced by the actuality of famine, pestilence, and caste. There was the assumption of the absolute necessity of poverty for the majority of men in order to save civilization for the minority, for that aristocracy of mankind which was at the same time the chief beneficiary of culture.

There was the frustration of democracy: lip service was paid to the idea of the rule of the people; but at the same time the mass of people were kept so poor, and through their poverty so diseased and ignorant, that they could not carry on successfully a modern state or modern industry. There was the paradox of peace: I remember before World War I stopping in at the Hotel Astor to hear Andrew Carnegie talk to his peace society. War had begun between Italy and Turkey but, said Mr. Carnegie blandly, we are not talking about peace among unimportant people; we are talking about peace among the great states of the world. I walked out. Here I knew lay tragedy, and the events proved it; for the great states went to war in jealousy over the ownership of the little people.

The paradox of the peace movement of the nineteenth century is a baffling comment on European civilization. There was not a single year during the nineteenth century when the world was not at war. Chiefly, but not entirely, these wars were waged to subjugate colonial peoples. They were carried on by Europeans, and at least one hundred and fifty separate wars can be counted during the heyday of the peace movement. What the peace movement really meant was peace in Europe and between Europeans, while for the conquest of the world and because of the suspicion which they held toward each other, every nation maintained a standing army which steadily grew in cost and menace.

One of the chief causes which thus distorted the development of Europe was the African slave trade, and we have tried to rewrite its history and meaning and to make it occupy a much less important place in the world's history than it deserves.

The result of the African slave trade and slavery on the European mind and culture was to degrade the position of labor and the respect for humanity as such. Not, God knows, that the ancient world honored labor. With exceptions here and there, it despised, enslaved, and crucified human toil. But there were counter currents, and with the Renaissance in Europe—that new light with which Asia and Africa illumined the Dark Ages of Europe—came new hope for mankind. A new religion of personal sacrifice had been building on five hundred years of the self-effacement of Buddha before the birth of Christ, and the equalitarianism of Mohammed which followed six hundred years after Christ's birth. A new world, seeking birth in Europe, was also being discovered beyond the sunset.

With this new world came fatally the African slave trade and Negro slavery in the Americas. There were new cruelties, new hatreds of human beings, and new degradations of human labor. The temptation to degrade human labor was made vaster and deeper by the incredible accumulation of wealth based on slave labor, by the boundless growth of greed, and by world-wide organization for new agricultural crops, new techniques in industry, and world-wide trade.

Just as Europe lurched forward to a new realization of beauty, a new freedom of thought and religious belief, a new demand by laborers to choose their work and enjoy its fruit, uncurbed greed rose to seize and monopolize the uncounted treasure of the fruit of labor. Labor was degraded, humanity was despised, the theory of "race" arose. There came a new doctrine of universal labor: mankind were of two sorts—the superior and the inferior; the inferior toiled for the superior; and the superior were the real men, the inferior half men or less. Among the white lords of creation there were "lower classes" resembling the inferior darker folk. Where possible they were to be raised to equality with the master class. But no equality was possible or desirable for "darkies." In line with this conviction, the Christian Church, Catholic and Protestant, at first damned the heathen blacks with the "curse of Canaan," then held out hope of freedom through "conversion," and finally acquiesced in a permanent status of human slavery.

Despite the fact that the nineteenth century saw an upsurge in the power of laboring classes and a fight toward economic equality and political democracy, this movement and battle was made fiercer and less successful and lagged far behind the accumulation of wealth, because in popular opinion labor was fundamentally degrading and the just burden of inferior peoples. Luxury and plenty for the few and poverty for the many was looked upon as inevitable in the course of nature. In addition to this, it went without saying that the white people of Europe had a right to live upon the labor and property of the colored peoples of the world.

In order to establish the righteousness of this point of view, science and religion, government and industry, were wheeled into line. The word "Negro" was used for the first time in the world's history to tie color to race and blackness to slavery and degradation. The white race was pictured as "pure" and superior; the black race as dirty, stupid, and inevitably inferior; the yellow race as sharing, in deception and cowardice, much of this color inferiority; while mixture of races was considered the prime cause of degradation and failure in civilization. Everything great, everything fine, everything really successful in human culture, was white.

In order to prove this, even black people in India and Africa were labeled as "white" if they showed any trace of progress; and, on the other hand, any progress by colored people was attributed to some intermixture, ancient or modern, of white blood or some influence of white civilization.

This logical contradiction influenced and misled science. The same person declared that mulattoes were inferior and warned against miscegenation, and yet attributed the pre-eminence of a Dumas, a Frederick Douglass, a Booker Washington, to their white blood.

A system at first conscious and then unconscious of lying about history and distorting it to the disadvantage of the Negroids became so widespread that the history of Africa ceased to be taught, the color of Memnon was forgotten, and every effort was made in archaeology, history, and biography, in biology, psychology, and sociology, to prove the all but universal assumption that the color line had a scientific basis.

Without the winking of an eye, printing, gunpowder, the smelting of iron, the beginnings of social organization, not to mention political life and democracy, were attributed exclusively to the white race and to Nordic Europe. Religion sighed with relief when it could base its denial of the ethics of Christ and the brotherhood of men upon the science of Darwin, Gobineau, and Reisner.

It was bad enough in all conscience to have the consequences of this thought, these scientific conclusions and ethical sanctions, fall upon colored people the world over; but in the end it was even worse when one considers what this attitude did to the European worker. His aim and ideal was distorted. He did not wish to become efficient but rich. He began to want not comfort for all men, but power over other men for himself. He did not love humanity and he hated "niggers." When our High Commissioner after the Spanish War appealed to America on behalf of "our little brown brother," the white workers replied,

"He may be a brother of William H. Taft,
But he ain't no brother of mine."

Following the early Christian communism and sense of human brotherhood which began to grow in the Dark Ages and to blossom in the Renaissance there came to white workers in England, France, and Germany the iron law of wages, the population doctrines of Malthus, and the bitter fight against the early trade unions. The first efforts at education, and particularly the trend toward political democracy, aroused an antagonism of which the French Revolution did not dream. It was this bitter fight that exacerbated the class struggle and resulted in the first furious expression of Communism and the attempt at revolution. The unity of apprentice and master, the Christian sympathy between rich and poor, the communism of medieval charity, all were thrust into the new strait jacket of thought: poverty was the result of sloth and crime; wealth was the reward of virtue and work. The degraded yellow and black peoples were in the places which the world of necessity assigned to the inferior; and toward these lower ranks the working classes of all countries tended to sink save as they were raised and supported by the rich, the investors, the captains of industry.

In some parts of the world, notably in the Southern states of America, the argument went further than this: frank slavery of black folk was a better economic system than factory exploitation of whites. It was the natural arrangement of industry. It ought to be extended, certainly where colored people were in the majority. For half a century before 1861 the bolder minds of the South dreamed of a slave empire embracing the American tropics and extending eventually around the world. While their thought did not go to a final appraisement of white laboring classes, they certainly had in mind that these classes must rise or fall; must be forced into the class of employers with political power, or, like the poor whites of the South, be pushed down beside or even below the working slaves.

This philosophy had sympathizers in Europe. Without doubt, a large majority of influential public opinion in England, and possibly in both France and

Germany, favored the South at the outbreak of the Civil War and sternly set its face against allowing any maudlin sympathy with "darkies," half monkeys and half men, in the stern fight for the extension of European domination of the world. Widespread insensibility to cruelty and suffering spread in the white world, and to guard against too much emotional sympathy with the distressed, every effort was made to keep women and children and the more sensitive men deceived as to what was going on, not only in the slums of white countries, but also all over Asia, Africa, and the islands of the sea. Elaborate writing, disguised as interpretation, and the testimony of so-called "experts," made it impossible for charming people in Europe to realize what their comforts and luxuries cost in sweat, blood, death, and despair, not only in the remoter parts of the world, but even on their own doorsteps.

A gracious culture was built up; a delicately poised literature treated the little intellectual problems of the rich and well-born, discussed small matters of manners and convention, and omitted the weightier ones of law, mercy, justice, and truth. Even the evidence of the eyes and senses was denied by the mere weight of reiteration. The race that produced the ugly features of a Darwin or a Winston Churchill was always "beautiful," while a Toussaint and a Menelik were ugly because they were black.

The concept of the European "gentleman" was evolved: a man well bred and of meticulous grooming, of knightly sportsmanship and invincible courage even in the face of death; but one who did not hesitate to use machine guns against assagais and to cheat "niggers"; an ideal of sportsmanship which reflected the Golden Rule and yet contradicted it—not only in business and in industry within white countries, but all over Asia and Africa—by indulging in lying, murder, theft, rape, deception, and degradation, of the same sort and kind which has left the world aghast at the accounts of what the Nazis did in Poland and Russia.

There was no Nazi atrocity—concentration camps, wholesale maiming and murder, defilement of women or ghastly blasphemy of childhood—which the Christian civilization of Europe had not long been practicing against colored folk in all parts of the world in the name of and for the defense of a Superior Race born to rule the world.

Together with the idea of a Superior Race there grew up in Europe and America an astonishing ideal of wealth and luxury: the man of "independent" income who did not have to "work for a living," who could indulge his whims and fantasies, who was free from all compulsion either of ethics or hunger, became the hero of novels, of drama and of fairy tale. This wealth was built, in Africa especially, upon diamonds and gold, copper and tin, ivory and mahogany, palm oil and cocoa, seeds extracted and grown, beaten out of the blood-stained bodies of the natives, transported to Europe, processed by wage slaves who were not receiving, and as Ricardo assured them they could never receive, enough to become educated and healthy human beings, and then distributed among prostitutes and gamblers as well as among well-bred followers of art, literature, and drama.

Cities were built, ugly and horrible, with regions for the culture of crime, disease, and suffering, but characterized in popular myth and blindness by wide and beautiful avenues where the rich and fortunate lived, laughed, and drank tea.

National heroes were created by lopping off their sins and canonizing their virtues, so that Gladstone had no connection with slavery, Chinese Gordon did not get drunk, William Pitt was a great patriot and not an international thief. Education was so arranged that the young learned not necessarily the truth, but that aspect and interpretation of the truth which the rulers of the world wished them to know and follow.

In other words, we had progress by poverty in the face of accumulating wealth, and that poverty was not simply the poverty of the slaves of Africa and the peons of Asia, but the poverty of the mass of workers in England, France, Germany, and the United States. Art, in building, painting, and literature, became cynical and decadent. Literature became realistic and therefore pessimistic. Religion became organized in social clubs where well-bred people met in luxurious churches and gave alms to the poor. On Sunday they listened to sermons— "Blessed are the meek"; "Do unto others even as you would that others do unto you"; "If thine enemy smite thee, turn the other cheek"; "It is more blessed to give than to receive"—listened and acted as though they had read, as in very truth they ought to have read—"Might is right"; "Do others before they do you"; "Kill your enemies or be killed"; "Make profits by any methods and at any cost so long as you can escape the lenient law." This is a fair picture of the decadence of that Europe which led human civilization during the nineteenth century and looked unmoved on the writhing of Asia and of Africa.

Nothing has been more puzzling than the European attitude toward sex. With professed reverence for female chastity, white folk have brought paid prostitution to its highest development; their lauding of motherhood has accompanied a lessening of births through late marriage and contraception, and this has stopped the growth of population in France and threatened it in all Europe. Indeed, along with the present rate of divorce, the future of the whole white race is problematical. Finally, the treatment of colored women by white men has been a worldwide disgrace. American planters, including some of the highest personages in the nation, left broods of colored children who were sometimes sold into slavery.

William Howitt (1792–1879), an English Quaker, visited Australia and the East early in the nineteenth century and has left us a record of what he saw. Of the treatment of women in India he wrote: "The treatment of the females could not be described. Dragged from the inmost recesses of their houses, which the religion of the country had made so many sanctuaries, they were exposed naked to public view. The virgins were carried to the Court of Justice, where they might naturally have looked for protection, but they now looked for it in vain; for in the face of the ministers of justice, in the face of the spectators, in the face of the sun, those tender and modest virgins were brutally violated. The only difference between their treatment and that of their mothers was that the former were dishonoured in the face of day, the latter in the gloomy recesses of their dungeon. Other females had the nipples of their breasts put in a cleft bamboo and torn off. What follows is too shocking and indecent to transcribe! It is almost impossible, in reading of these frightful and savage enormities, to believe that we are reading of a country under the British government, and that these unmanly deeds were perpetrated by British agents, and for the purpose of extorting the British revenue."[1]

It would be unfair to paint the total modern picture of Europe as decadent. There have been souls that revolted and voices that cried aloud. Men arraigned poverty, ignorance, and disease as unnecessary. The public school and the ballot fought for uplift and freedom. Suffrage for women and laborers and freedom for the Negro were extended. But this forward-looking vision had but partial and limited success. Race tyranny, aristocratic pretense, monopolized wealth, still continued to prevail and triumphed widely. The Church fled uptown to escape the poor and black. Jesus laughed—and wept.

The dawn of the twentieth century found white Europe master of the world and the white peoples almost universally recognized as the rulers for whose benefit the rest of the world existed. Never before in the history of civilization had self-worship of a people's accomplishment attained the heights that the worship of white Europe by Europeans reached.

Our poets in the "Foremost Ranks of Time," became dithyrambic: "Better fifty years of Europe than a cycle of Cathay!" In home and school the legend grew of this strong, masterful giant with mighty intellect, clear brain, and unrivaled moral stamina, who was conducting the world to the last heights of human culture. Yet within less than half a century this magnificent self-worshiping structure had crashed to the earth.

Why was this? It was from no lack of power. The power of white Europe and North America was unquestionable. Their science dominated the scientific thought of the world. The only writing called literature was that of English and French writers, of Germans and Italians, with some recognition of writers in Spain and the United States. The Christian religion, as represented by the Catholic Church and the leading Protestant denominations, was the only system of belief recognized as real religion. Mohammedans, Buddhists, Shintoists, and others were all considered heathen.

The most tremendous expression of power was economic; the powerful industrial organization and integration of modern industry in management and work, in trade and manufacture, was concentrated in England, France, Germany, and the United States. All Asia and Eastern Europe was an appendage; all Africa, China, India, and the islands of the sea, Central and South America and the Caribbean area were dominated by Europe, while Scandinavia, Holland, and Belgium were silent copartners in this domination.

The domination showed itself in its final form in political power either through direct rulership, as in the case of colonies, or indirect economic power backed by military pressure exercised over the backward nations. It was rather definitely assumed in the latter part of the nineteenth century that this economic domination was but a passing phase which in time would lead to colonial absorption.

Particularly was this true with regard to Asia. India was already a part of the British Empire, and Burma. Indonesia was Dutch and Indo-China, French. The future of China depended upon how Europe would divide the land among the British Empire and the Germans, American trade, Italy, France, and Russia. It was a matter simply of time and agreement. General consent had long since decided that China should no longer rule itself.

With regard to the South American countries there was the determination that they must obey the economic rule of the European and North American system. The world looked forward to political and economic domination by Europe and North America and to a more or less complete approach to colonial status for the rest of the earth. Africa of course must remain in absolute thrall, save its white immigrants, who would rule the blacks.

The reason for this world mastery by Europe was rationalized as the natural and inborn superiority of white peoples, showing itself not only in the loftiest of religions, but in a technical mastery of the forces of nature—all this in contrast to the low mentality and natural immorality of the darker races living in lovely lands, "Where every prospect pleases, and only Man is vile!"—as the high-minded Christians sang piously. But they forgot or never were told just how white superiority wielded its power or accomplished this dominion. There were exceptions, of course, but for the most part they went unheard. Howitt, for instance, wrote from personal knowledge as well as research on the colonial question and described some phases of the pressure of Europe on the rest of the world in the centuries preceding the nineteenth. Speaking of the Indians of America, Howitt said: "All the murders and desolation of the most pitiless tyrants that ever diverted themselves with the pangs and convulsions of their fellow creatures, fall infinitely short of the bloody enormities committed by the Spanish nation in the conquest of the New World, a conquest on a low estimate, effected by the murder of ten millions of the species! After reading these accounts, who can help forming an indignant wish that the hand of Heaven, by some miraculous interposition, had swept these European tyrants from the face of the earth, who like so many beasts of prey, roamed round the world only to desolate and destroy; and more remorseless than the fiercest savage, thirsted for human blood without having the impulse of natural appetite to plead in their defence!"[2]

Howitt turned to the Portuguese in India: "The celebrated Alphonso Albuquerque made the most rapid strides, and extended the conquests of the Portuguese there beyond any other commander. He narrowly escaped with his life in endeavouring to sack and plunder Calicut. He seized on Goa, which thenceforward became the metropolis of all the Portuguese settlements in India. He conquered Molucca, and gave it up to the plunder of his soldiers. The fifth part of the wealth thus thievishly acquired was reserved for the king, and was purchased on the spot by the merchants for two hundred thousand pieces of gold. Having established a garrison in the conquered city, he made a traitor Indian, who had deserted from the king of Molucca and had been an instrument in the winning of a place, supreme magistrate; but again finding Utimut, the renegade, as faithless to himself, he had him and his son put to death, even though a hundred thousand pieces of gold, a bait that was not easily resisted by these Christian marauders, was offered for their lives. He then proceeded to Ormuz in the Persian Gulph, which was a great harbour for the Arabian merchants; reduced it, placed a garrison in it, seized on fifteen princes of the blood, and carried them off to Goa. Such were some of the deeds of this celebrated general, whom the historians in the same breath in which they record these unwarrantable acts of violence, robbery, and treachery, term an excellent and truly glorious commander! He made a descent on the isle of

Ceylon, and detached a fleet to the Moluccas, which established a settlement in those delightful regions of the cacao, the sago-tree, the nutmeg, and the clove. The kings of Persia, of Siam, Pegu, and others, alarmed at his triumphant progress, sought his friendship; and he completed the conquest of the Malabar coast. With less than forty thousand troops, the Portuguese struck terror into the empire of Morocco, the barbarous nations of Africa, the Mamelucs, the Arabians, and all the eastern countries from the island of Ormuz to China."[3]

Turning to the Dutch, Howitt continued:

"To secure the dominion of these, they compelled the princes of Ternate and Tidore to consent to the rooting up of all the clove and nutmeg trees in the islands not entirely under the jealous safeguard of Dutch keeping. For this they utterly exterminated the inhabitants of Banda, because they would not submit passively to their yoke. Their lands were divided amongst the white people, who got slaves from other islands to cultivate them. For this Malacca was besieged, its territory ravaged, and its navigation interrupted by pirates; Negapatan was twice attacked; Cochin was engaged in resisting the kings of Calicut and Travancore, and Ceylon and Java were made scenes of perpetual disturbances. These notorious dissensions have been followed by as odious oppressions, which have been practiced at Japan, China, Cambodia, Arracan on the banks of the Ganges, at Achen, Coromandel, Surat, in Persia, at Bassora, Mocha, and other places. For this they encouraged and established in Celebes a system of kidnapping the inhabitants for slaves which converted that island into a perfect hell."[4]

Howitt then turned to England in India: "Unfortunately, we all know what human nature is. Unfortunately, the power, the wealth, and the patronage brought home to them by the very violation of their own wishes and maxims were of such an overwhelming and seducing nature that it was in vain to resist them. Nay, in such colours does the modern philosophy of conquest and diplomacy disguise the worst transactions between one state and another, that it is not for plain men very readily to penetrate to the naked enormity beneath."[5]

"But if there ever was one system more Machiavellian—more appropriative of the shew of justice where the basest injustice was attempted—more cold, cruel, haughty, and unrelenting than another—it is the system by which the government of the different states of India has been wrested from the hands of their respective princes and collected into the grasp of the British power."[6]

"The first step in the English friendship with the native princes, has generally been to assist them against their neighbours with troops, or to locate troops with them to protect them from aggression. For these services such enormous recompense was stipulated for, that the unwary princes, entrapped by their fears of their native foes rather than of their pretended friends, soon found that they were utterly unable to discharge them. Dreadful exactions were made on their subjects, but in vain. Whole provinces, or the revenues of them, were soon obliged to be made over to their grasping *friends;* but they did not suffice for their demands. In order to pay them their debts or their interest, the princes were obliged to borrow large sums at an extravagant rate. These sums were eagerly advanced by the English in their private and individual capacities, and securities again taken on lands or revenues. At every step the unhappy princes became more and more embarrassed, and as the embarrassment increased, the claims of the Company became proportionably pressing. In the technical phraseology of moneylenders, 'the screw was then turned,' till there was no longer any enduring it."[7]

We may turn now to the conquest of Africa. The Portuguese, Dutch, and British decimated the West Coast with the slave trade. The Arabs depopulated the East Coast. For centuries the native Bantu, unable to penetrate the close-knit city-states of the Gulf of Guinea, had slowly been moving south, seeking pasture for their herds and protecting their culture from the encroachment of the empire-building in the black Sudan.

In the nineteenth century black folk and white—Hottentot, Bushman and Bantu, French, Dutch, and British—met at the Cape miscalled "Good Hope." There ensued a devil's dance seldom paralleled in human history. The Dutch murdered, raped, and enslaved the Hottentots and Bushmen; the French were driven away or died out; the British stole the land of the Dutch and their slaves and the Dutch fled inland. The incoming Bantu, led by Chaka, the great Zulu chieftain, fell on both Dutch and English with a military genius unique in history.

The black Bantu had almost won the wars when a mulatto native discovered diamonds. Then English and Dutch laid bare that cache of gold, the largest in the world, which the ocean thrust above the dark waters of the south five million years ago. Enough; the greed of white Europe, backed by the British Navy, fought with frenzied determination, world-wide organization, and every trick of trade, until the blacks were either dead or reduced to the most degrading wage bondage in the modern world; and the Dutch became vassals of England, to be repaid by the land and labor of eight million blacks.

Frankel, the complacent servant of capitalists and their defender, has written: "The wealth accruing from the production of diamonds in South Africa has probably been greater than that which has ever been obtained from any other commodity in the same time anywhere in the world."[8]

This was but a side enterprise of Britain. By means of its long leadership in the African slave trade to America, Great Britain in the nineteenth century began to seize control of land and labor all over Africa. Slowly the British pushed into the West and East coasts. They overthrew Benin and Ashanti. A British governor of Ashanti later admitted: "The earliest beginnings, which had their inception in the dark days of the slave trade, cannot but hold many things that modern Englishmen must recall with mingled shame and horror. The reader will find much to deplore in the public and private acts of many of the white men who, in their time, made history on the Coast; and some deeds were done which must forever remain among the most bitter and humiliating memories of every Britisher who loves his country and is jealous of its fair name."[9]

The French conquered Dahomey and the remains of the Mandingo, Haussa, and other kingdoms. The British pitted Christianity against Islam in East Africa and let them fight it out until at last Uganda became a British protectorate.

In Abyssinia the natives drove back British, Egyptians, and Italians, and the Mahdi with his black Mohammedan hordes came in from the west and drove England and Egypt out of the Sudan. The threat of the French and their possible alliance with Abyssinia brought the British back with machine guns.

It is said that Kitchener's warfare against the followers of the Mahdi was so brutal that even the British Tories were revolted. His own brother-in-law said of him: "Well, if you do not bring down a curse on the British Empire for what you have been doing there is no truth in Christianity." His desecration of the Mahdi's tomb even Winston Churchill called a "foul deed." And when Kitchener found that even the promoters of the inexcusable war could not swallow this last, he tried to put the blame of the desecration onto Gordon's nephew by making absolutely false accusations.[10] Everywhere is this sordid tale of deception, force, murder, and final subjection. We need hardly recall the Opium War in China, which the British, followed by the Americans and French, made excuse for further aggression.

The singular thing about this European movement of aggression and dominance was the rationalization for it. Missionary effort during the nineteenth and early twentieth century was widespread. Millions of pounds and dollars went into the "conversion of the heathen" to Christianity and the education of the natives. Some few efforts, as in Liberia and Sierra Leone, were made early in the nineteenth century to establish independent Negro countries, but this was before it was realized that political domination was necessary to full exploitation.

Slowly the Sudan from the Atlantic to the Nile was conquered. Slowly Egypt itself and the Egyptian Sudan passed under the control of Europe. The resistance of Nubia and Ethiopia was almost in vain down into the twentieth century. West Africa fought brilliantly and continuously. But in all this development the idea persisted in European minds that no matter what the cost in cruelty, lying, and blood, the triumph of Europe was to the glory of God and the untrammeled power of the only people on earth who deserved to rule; that the right and justice of their rule was proved by their own success and particularly by their great cities, their enormous technical mastery over the power of nature, their gigantic manufacture of goods and systems of transportation over the world. Production for production's sake, without inquiry as to how the wealth and services were distributed, was the watchword of the day.

For years the British imperial government avoided direct responsibility for colonial exploitation. It was all at first "free enterprise" and "individual initiative." When the scandal of murder and loot could no longer be ignored, exploitation became socialized with imperialism. Thus, for a century or more the West India Company, the Niger Company, the South and East Africa Companies, robbed and murdered as they pleased with no public accounting. At length, when these companies had stolen, killed, and cheated to such an extent that the facts could not be suppressed, governments themselves came into control, curbing the more outrageous excesses and rationalizing the whole system.

Science was called to help. Students of Africa, especially since the ivory-sugar-cotton-Negro complex of the nineteenth century, became hag-ridden by the obsession that nothing civilized is Negroid and every evidence of high culture in Africa must be white or at least yellow. The very vocabulary of civilization expressed this idea; the Spanish word "Negro," from being a descriptive adjective, was raised to the substantive name of a race and then deprived of its capital letter.

Then came efforts to bring harmony and co-operation and unity—among the exploiters. A newspaper correspondent who had received world-wide publicity because of his travels in Africa was hired by the shrewd and unscrupulous Leopold II of Belgium to establish an international country in central Africa "to peacefully conquer and subdue it, to remold it in harmony with modern ideas into National States, within whose limits the European merchant shall go hand in hand with the dark African trader, and justice and law and order shall prevail, and murder and lawlessness and the cruel barter of slaves shall be overcome."[11]

Thus arose the Congo Free State, and by balancing the secret designs of German, French, and British against each other, this state became the worst center of African exploitation and started the partition of Africa among European powers. It was designed to form a pattern for similar partition of Asia and the South Sea islands. The Berlin Congress and Conference followed. The products of Africa began to be shared and distributed around the world. The dependence of civilized life upon products from the ends of the world tied the everyday citizen more and more firmly to the exploitation of each colonial area: tea and coffee, diamonds and gold, ivory and copper, vegetable oils, nuts and dates, pepper and spices, olives and cocoa, rubber, hemp, silk, fibers of all sorts, rare metals, valuable lumber, fruit, sugar. All these things and a hundred others became necessary to modern life, and modern life thus was built around colonial ownership and exploitation.

The cost of this exploitation was enormous. The colonial system caused ten times more deaths than actual war. In the first twenty-five years of the nineteenth century famines in India starved a million men, and famine was bound up with exploitation. Widespread monopoly of land to deprive all men of primary sources of support was carried out either through direct ownership or indirect mortgage and exorbitant interest. Disease could not be checked: tuberculosis in the mines of South Africa, syphilis in all colonial regions, cholera, leprosy, malaria.

One of the worst things that happened was the complete and deliberate breaking-down of cultural patterns among the suppressed peoples. "Europe was staggered at the Leopoldian atrocities, and they were terrible indeed; but what we, who were behind the scenes, felt most keenly was the fact that the real catastrophe in the Congo was desolation and murder in the larger sense. The invasion of family life, the ruthless destruction of every social barrier, the shattering of every tribal law, the introduction of criminal practices which struck the chiefs of the people dumb with horror—in a word, a veritable avalanche of filth and immorality overwhelmed the Congo tribes."[12]

The moral humiliation forced on proud black people was illustrated in the British conquest of Ashanti. The reigning Asantahene had never been conquered. His armies had repeatedly driven back the British, but the British finally triumphed after five wars by breaking their word and overwhelming him by numbers and superior weapons. They promised him peace and honor, but they demanded a public act of submission.

"This, of course, was a terrible blow to Prempi's pride. It was a thing that no Ashanti king had ever done before, except when Mensa voluntarily made his submission by deputy in 1881; and was the one thing above all others that he would have avoided

if he could. For a few moments he sat irresolute, nervously toying with his ornaments and looking almost ready to cry with shame and annoyance; but Albert Ansa
came up and held a whispered conversation with him, and he then slipped off his
sandals and, laying aside the golden circlet he wore on his head, stood up with his
mother and walked reluctantly across the square to where the Governor was sitting.
Then, halting before him, they prostrated themselves and embraced his feet and
those of Sir Francis Scott and Colonel Kempster.

"The scene was a most striking one. The heavy masses of foliage, that solid
square of red coats and glistening bayonets, the artillery drawn up ready for any
emergency, the black bodies of the Native Levies, resting on their long guns in the
background, while inside the square the Ashantis sat as if turned to stone, as
Mother and Son, whose word was a matter of life and death, and whose slightest
move constituted a command which all obeyed, were thus forced to humble themselves in sight of the assembled thousands."[13]

Perhaps the worst thing about the colonial system was the contradiction which
arose and had to arise in Europe with regard to the whole situation. Extreme
poverty in colonies was a main cause of wealth and luxury in Europe. The results
of this poverty were disease, ignorance, and crime. Yet these had to be represented as natural characteristics of backward peoples. Education for colonial
people must inevitably mean unrest and revolt; education, therefore, had to be
limited and used to inculcate obedience and servility lest the whole colonial system be overthrown.

Ability, self-assertion, resentment, among colonial peoples must be represented as irrational efforts of "agitators"—folk trying to attain that for which they
were not by nature fitted. To prove the unfitness of most human beings for self-
rule and self-expression, every device of science was used: evolution was made to
prove that Negroes and Asiatics were less developed human beings than whites;
history was so written as to make all civilization the development of white people; economics was so taught as to make all wealth due mainly to the technical
accomplishment of white folks supplemented only by the brute toil of colored
peoples; brain weights and intelligence tests were used and distorted to prove the
superiority of white folk. The result was complete domination of the world by
Europe and North America and a culmination and tempo of civilization singularly satisfactory to the majority of writers and thinkers at the beginning of the
twentieth century. But it was a result that was hollow, contradictory, and fatal, as
the next few years quickly showed.

The proof of this came first from the colonial peoples themselves. Almost unnoticed, certainly unlistened to, there came from the colonial world reiterated
protest, prayers, and appeals against the suppression of human beings, against the
exclusion of the majority of mankind from the vaunted progress of the world. The
world knows of such protests from the National Congress of India, but little has
been written of the protests of Africa. For instance, on the Gold Coast, British West
Africa, in 1871, some of the kings and chiefs and a number of educated natives met
at Mankesim and drew up a constitution for self-government. These members of
the Fanti tribe were in alliance with England and had supported the British against
the Ashanti in the five long wars. They now proposed an alliance with Britain to
establish self-government. This constitution, the Mfantsi Amanbuhu Fekuw or

Fanti Confederation, agitated in 1865, organized in 1867, and adopted in 1871, consisted of forty-seven articles, many of which were subdivided into several sections. Some of the principal articles were as follows:

Article 8. That it be the object of the Confederation
§ 1. To promote friendly intercourse between all the Kings and Chiefs of Fanti, and to unite them for offensive and defensive purposes against their common enemy.
§ 2. To direct the labours of the Confederation towards the improvement of the country at large.
§ 3. To make good and substantial roads through-out all the interior districts included in the Confederation.
§ 4. To erect school-houses and establish schools for the education of all children within the Confederation and to obtain the service of efficient schoolmasters.
§ 5. To promote agricultural and industrial pursuits, and to endeavour to introduce such new plants as may hereafter become sources of profitable commerce to the country.
§ 6. To develop and facilitate the working of the mineral and other resources of the country.
Article 12. That this Representative Assembly shall have the power of preparing laws, ordinances, bills, etc., of using proper means for effectually carrying out the resolutions, etc., of the Government, of examining any questions laid before it by the ministry, and by any of the Kings and Chiefs, and, in fact, of exercising all the functions of a legislative body.
Articles 21 to 25 deal with education.
Article 26. That main roads be made connecting various provinces or districts with one another and with the sea coast. . . .
Article 37. That in each province or district provincial courts be established, to be presided over by the provincial assessors.
Article 43. That the officers of the Confederation shall render assistance as directed by the executive in carrying out the wishes of the British Government.
Article 44. That it be competent to the Representative Assembly, for the purpose of carrying on the administration of the Government, to pass laws, etc., for the levying of such taxes as it may seem necessary.[14]

This was the so-called Fanti Federation, and in punishment for daring to propose such a movement for the government of an African British colony, the participants were promptly thrown in jail and charged with treason.

This attitude toward native rights and initiative has continued right down to our day. In 1945 the colored people of South Africa, speaking for eight million Negroes, Indians, and mixed groups, sent out this declaration to the proposed United Nations:

The non-European is debarred from education. He is denied access to the professions and skilled trades; he is denied the right to buy land and property; he is denied the right to trade or to serve in the army—except as a stretcher-bearer or servant; he is prohibited from entering places of entertainment and culture. But still more, he is not allowed to live in the towns. And if it was a crime in Nazi Germany for an "Aryan" to mix with or marry a non-Aryan, it is equally a criminal offence in South Africa for a member of the Herrenvolk to mix with or marry with the slave race. . . . In the majority of instances there is a separate law for Europeans and a separate law for non-Europeans; in those rare cases where one Act legislates for both, there are separate clauses discriminating against the non-Europeans. While it is true that there are no Buchenwald concentration camps in South Africa, it is equally true that the prisons of South Africa are full to overflowing with non-Europeans whose criminality lies solely in the fact that they are unable to pay the poll-tax, a special, racial tax imposed upon them. But this law does not apply to the Aryan; for him there is a different law which makes the nonpayment of taxes not a criminal, but a civil, offence for which he cannot be imprisoned.

But if there is no Buchenwald in South Africa, the sadistic fury with which the Herrenvolk policemen belabour the non-European victim, guilty or not guilty, is comparable only to the brutality of the S.S. Guards. Moreover, the treatment meted out to the non-European in the Law Courts is comparable only to the fate of the non-Aryan in the Nazi Law Courts. But the fundamental difference in law and morality is not only expressed in different paragraphs of the Legal Statutes, it lies in the fundamentally different concept of the value of the life of a non-European as compared with the value placed upon the life of a European. The life of a non-European is very cheap in South Africa, as cheap as the life of a Jew in Nazi Germany.

From the foregoing it is clear that the non-Europeans of South Africa live and suffer under a tyranny very little different from Nazism. And if we accept the premise—as we hope the Nations of the World do—that peace is indivisible, if we accept that there can be no peace as long as the scourge of Nazism exists in any corner of the globe, then it follows that the defeat of German Nazism is not the final chapter of the struggle against tyranny. There must be many more chapters before the peoples of the world will be able to make a new beginning. To us in South Africa it is indisputable that there can be no peace as long as this system of tyranny remains. To us it is ludicrous that this same South African Herrenvolk should speak abroad of a new beginning, of shaping a new world order, whereas in actuality all they wish is the retention of the present tyranny in South Africa, and its extension to new territories. Already they speak of new mandates and new trusteeships, which can only mean the extension of their Nazi-like domination over still wider terrain. It is impossible to make a new start as long as the representatives of this Herrenvolk take any part in the shaping of it. For of what value can it be when the very same people who speak so grandiosely abroad of the inviolability of human rights, at home trample ruthlessly underfoot those same inalienable rights? It is the grossest of insults not only to the eight million non-Europeans of South Africa, but to all those who are honestly striving to shape a world on new foundations, when the highest representative of the Herrenvolk of South Africa, Field-Marshal Smuts, who has devoted his whole life to the entrenchment of this Nazi-like domination, brazenly speaks to the Nations of the World of the "sanctity and ultimate value of human personality" and "the equal rights of men and women."[15]

This does not say that all European civilization is oppression, theft, and hypocrisy; there has been evidence of selfless religious faith; of philanthropic effort for social uplift; of individual honesty and sacrifice. But this, far from answering the indictment I have made, shows even more clearly the moral plight of present European culture and what capitalistic investment and imperialism have done to it.

Because of the stretch in time and space between the deed and the result, between the work and the product, it is not only usually impossible for the worker to know the consumer; or the investor, the source of his profit, but also it is often made impossible by law to inquire into the facts. Moral judgment of the industrial process is therefore difficult, and the crime is more often a matter of ignorance rather than of deliberate murder and theft; but ignorance is a colossal crime in itself. When a culture consents to any economic result, no matter how monstrous its cause, rather than demand the facts concerning work, wages, and the conditions of life whose results make the life of the consumer comfortable, pleasant, and even luxurious, it is an indication of a collapsing civilization.

Here for instance is a lovely British home, with green lawns, appropriate furnishings and a retinue of well-trained servants. Within is a young woman, well trained and well dressed, intelligent and high-minded. She is fingering the ivory keys of a grand piano and pondering the problem of her summer vacation, whether in Switzerland or among the Italian lakes; her family is not wealthy, but it has a sufficient "independent" income from investments to enjoy life without hard work. How far is such a person responsible for the crimes of colonialism?

It will in all probability not occur to her that she has any responsibility whatsoever, and that may well be true. Equally, it may be true that her income is the result of starvation, theft, and murder; that it involves ignorance, disease, and crime on the part of thousands; that the system which sustains the security, leisure, and comfort she enjoys is based on the suppression, exploitation, and slavery of the majority of mankind. Yet just because she does not know this, just because she could get the facts only after research and investigation—made difficult by laws that forbid the revealing of ownership of property, source of income, and methods of business—she is content to remain in ignorance of the source of her wealth and its cost in human toil and suffering.

The frightful paradox that is the indictment of modern civilization and the cause of its moral collapse is that a blameless, cultured, beautiful young woman in a London suburb may be the foundation on which is built the poverty and degradation of the world. For this someone is guilty as hell. Who?

This is the modern paradox of Sin before which the Puritan stands open-mouthed and mute. A group, a nation, or a race commits murder and rape, steals and destroys, yet no individual is guilty, no one is to blame, no one can be punished!

The black world squirms beneath the feet of the white in impotent fury or sullen hate:

I hate them, O I hate them well!
I hate them, Christ, as I hate hell!
If I were God, I'd sound their knell,
This day!

The whole world emerges into the Syllogism of the Satisfied: "This cannot be true. This is not true. If it were true I would not believe it. If it is true I do not believe it. Therefore it is false!" Only an Emerson could see the paradox:

O all you virtues, methods, mights;
Means, appliances, delights;
Reputed wrongs, and braggart rights;
Smug routine, and things allowed;
Minorities, things under cloud,
Hither take me, use me, fill me,
Vein and artery, though ye kill me.

In 1945 Jan Smuts, Prime Minister of South Africa, who had once declared that every white man in South Africa believes in the suppression of the Negro except those who are "mad, quite mad," stood before the assembled peoples of the world and pleaded for an article on "human rights" in the United Nations Charter. Nothing so vividly illustrates the twisted contradiction of thought in the minds of white men. What brought it about? What caused this paradox? I believe that the trade in human beings between Africa and America, which flourished between the Renaissance and the American Civil War, is the prime and effective cause of the contradictions in European civilization and the illogic in modern thought and the collapse of human culture. For this reason I am turning to a history of the African slave trade in support of this thesis.

NOTES

1. William Howitt, *Colonization and Christianity* (London: Longman, Orme, Brown, Green & Longmans, 1838), pp. 280–81.
2. *Ibid.,* p. 61.
3. *Ibid.,* pp. 176–77.
4. *Ibid.,* p. 194.
5. *Ibid.,* p. 209.
6. *Ibid.,* p. 210.
7. *Ibid.,* pp. 213–14.
8. S. Herbert Frankel, *Capital Investment in Africa* (London: Oxford University Press, 1938), p. 52.
9. W. Walton Claridge, *A History of the Gold Coast and Ashanti* (London: John Murray, 1915), Vol. I, p. ix.
10. *Cf.* Wilfrid Scawen Blunt, *My Diaries* (New York: Alfred A. Knopf, 1921), Vol. I, pp. 311, 313, 317, 319, 322, 323–24. The brother-in-law was Sir William Butler.
11. J. Scott Keltie, *The Partition of Africa* (London: Edward Stanford, 1895), p. 132.
12. Harris, *Dawn in Africa.* p. 66.
13. Claridge, *op. cit.,* Vol. I, p. 413.
14. *Ibid.,* Vol. I, pp. 617–18.
15. A Declaration to the Nations of the World issued by the Non-European United Committee, Cape Town, South Africa, 1945.

CHAPTER III

◆

The Rape of Africa

Nothing which has happened to man in modern times has been more significant than the buying and selling of human beings out of Africa into America from 1441 to 1870. Of its worldwide meaning and effect, this chapter seeks to tell.

The rebirth of civilization in Europe began in the fifteenth century. At this time African and Asiatic civilizations far outstripped that of Europe. In the black Sudan nations, civilizations had risen and fallen even earlier. Melle, which flourished in the thirteenth and fourteenth centuries, fell before the empire of the Songhay, which in the fifteenth century became a vast, organized government two-thirds the size of the United States, with trade and commerce and cultural connections, through its University of Sankoré, with Spain, Italy, and the Eastern Roman Empire. The city-states and Atlantic culture of the West Coast of Africa had fought back triple pressure from the Sudan, the Arabs in the Nile valley, and the emigrating Bantu sweeping down on the kingdoms of the Congo.

It was here that the rape of Africa began and transformed the world. There can be little doubt but that in the fourteenth century the level of culture in black Africa south of the Sudan was equal to that of Europe and was so recognized. There is even less doubt but that Negroid influence in the valley of the Nile was a main influence in Egypt's development from 2100 to 1600 B.C.; while in East, South, and West Africa human culture had from 1600 B.C. to A.D. 1500 its monuments of a vigorous past and a growing future. What changed all this? What killed the Sudanese empires, brought anarchy into the valley of the Nile, decimated the thick populations of East and Central Africa, and pressed the culture of West Africa beneath the ruthless heel of the rising European culture?

In Europe during the thirteenth and fourteenth centuries there began to appear national integration of culture patterns, with no little inspiration from the East and from Africa. There followed in the fifteenth and sixteenth centuries increased freedom of thought and impatience with dogma; and in the seventeenth, came scientific inquiry and the beginning of a demand for democratic control of government.

But from 1400 to 1800 also came discovery, trade, and the beginnings of a new enslavement of labor. In the eighteenth century these developments leaped into opposition. The slavery of labor expanded enormously in the New World, concurrent with a new development of trade, industry, and wealth in the Old. These trends met head on with a revolutionary demand for democracy and social freedom in Europe. The clash of ideals was revealed in the nineteenth century by freedom for exploitation of slaves in America and a consequent reaction against the demands of European labor led by Napoleon and British capital. Let us follow the details of this story.

The importance of the discovery of America was not the treasure of precious metals it provided, but the new and widening market and source of supply it offered European manufacturers by the exchange of tobacco, sugar, and cotton for manufactured goods. Its first effect was to raise the mercantile system to glory and splendor. World trade increased enormously. The seventeenth and eighteenth centuries were the centuries of trade, and eventually, by the rise of capitalism, the nineteenth century became the century of production.

During the Middle Ages there had been little direct commerce between Europe and West Africa. Arabs, Berbers, and eventually Negroids like the Mandingos became intermediaries for the trade between Europe and the Sudan. Rumors filtered through the Moroccan ports regarding the Kingdom of Ghana, the Niger, "the western Nile," and the black peoples round about. The Arabs bought gold from the Negroes and sold it to the Jewish merchants in Majorca.

The demand of Europe in the fifteenth century was for new and shorter paths to the East, to the spices, silks, and other luxurious articles of the East. In this quest Spain found silver in the New World, and Portugal triumphed when she found gold in Africa. The Portuguese trade monopoly with Africa and thence to India extended over half a century. She developed an empire of tremendous wealth.

The object of Prince Henry (1394–1460) of Portugal was mainly trade to India. At the same time he hoped by union with Prester John of Ethiopia to evangelize the Negroes of all Africa and make common cause against the Mohammedans. Henry heard of the gold for which the Carthaginians had bartered at Timbuktu. Having seized Ceuta, he began to explore, and after nineteen years his seamen rounded Cape Bojador.

In 1441 Goncalves brought to Lisbon the first cargo of slaves and gold. Very shortly a flourishing trade in gold, slaves, ostrich feathers, amber, and gum opened up between Portugal and black Africa. The Portuguese tried to conceal this trade from the rest of Europe. They did not actually find the black kingdom of Ghana, but they called the coast which they did discover "Guinea," after mysterious Ghana. They heard of the empire of Melle at Timbuktu but did not actually reach it. They had commerce with the kingdom of the Jolofs and with other coast tribes. Eventually they reached the Gold Coast, or as they called it, "the Mine," where gold could be had in large quantities. They found that these Negroes were great traders who brought the gold from the interior when they could persuade the coast tribes who lived by fishing to let the gold bearers through. Eventually they came in contact with the kingdom of Benin and a mighty interior empire whose sovereign was the Ogani.

For fifty years, from 1480 to 1530, the Portuguese had a monopoly of the Guinea trade and reaped huge profits, seldom less than 50 per cent and sometimes as high as 800 per cent. Between 1450 and 1458 ten or twelve ships a year were sent to Guinea, and the amount of gold dust reached a value of over two million dollars a year, and after 1471 rapidly exceeded this.

Next to the trade in gold came the highly important importation of labor into Portugal. By the middle of the fifteenth century nearly a thousand blacks had been imported. A century later a vast majority of the inhabitants of the southernmost province were Negroids, and even up as far as Lisbon, Negroes outnumbered the whites. The two races intermingled, resulting in the Negroid characteristics of the Portuguese nation even today.[1]

The royal family became more Negro than white. John IV was Negroid; and the wife of the French ambassador described John VI as having Negro hair, nose, lips, and color.

Negro blood in the fifteenth century extended from Spain and Portugal to Italy. The Medici had colored descendants like Alessandro, first reigning duke of Florence, whose father was reported to be the Pope. This new strain of Negro blood reached Albania and Austria. Angelo Solliman, a Congo Negro, was a favorite of Joseph II and of Prince Lichtenstein in the eighteenth century. He married into the Austrian nobility, and his daughter married Baron Eduard von Feuchtersleben. Their son inherited the title. Recently in Rome a monument was dedicated to the colored consort of Garibaldi, Anita, a Brazilian.

The Guinea trade was at first mainly in gold, pepper, and other commodities, with some trading in slaves which went to Europe. In the sixteenth century, however, it began to change, and slaves began to be sent to South America. This was not at first a large trade and did not compete with legitimate commerce; but it grew, and by 1540 reached ten thousand slaves a year. The reason for this was not far to seek. Between 1480 and 1578 the peoples of Guinea enjoyed a vigorous life with economic independence based on foreign trade. Gold, ivory, and pepper were valuable as exports before the discovery of America and continued long afterward. But by the middle of the sixteenth century there was trouble in West Africa. A vast migration of black people, the Limbas, moved slowly westward from Central Africa. They were a part of the migration of the Bantu moving down from the Mohammedan invasion of the Nile Valley and the empire-building of the black kingdoms of the Sudan. They destroyed villages, massacred the inhabitants, and were soon in fierce competition with the Souzas, who possessed the most formidable native army in West Africa at that time. Migration and native wars lasted for a generation. This meant that the cheap labor of captives became available on the West Coast and opened the way for the beginning of the American slave trade. With this slave trade came trouble, not simply among native tribes but also between the Portuguese and the natives.

After 1530 the Portuguese empire in Guinea was a vast commercial enterprise, but the overhead charges, caused by difficulties with the natives and the beginning of European competition, equaled and began to exceed production. The first threat to Portuguese dominance in Guinea came from the French. By

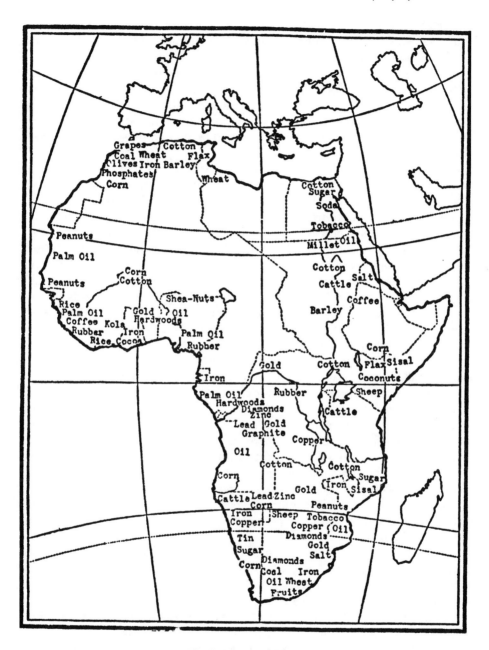

The Products of Africa

the Treaty of Crespy in 1544 the right of Frenchmen to trade in the Indies, east and west, was proposed but not ratified. French trade began to multiply after 1553; relations between Portugal and France became strained on account of the French pirates and privateers. The monopoly of the Portuguese in West Africa practically ended in 1553. The French Huguenots forced themselves into the Guinea trade after 1571, under the inspiration of Admiral Coligny. British merchants during the reign of Queen Mary became interested. Queen Elizabeth fought the monopoly claims of Portugal and Spain and herself participated in the Guinea trade.

Between 1559 and 1561 the British explorer, Martin Frobisher, took part in piracy and trade. From 1561 to 1571 the British trade increased over the French and there was direct traffic between England and Africa. "The first Englishman of note to engage in the traffic was the celebrated John Hawkins, afterwards knighted by Elizabeth and appointed Treasurer to the Navy. Froude calls him 'a peculiarly characteristic figure,' and he certainly presents that blending of piracy and piety, rascality and religion, so common in the days of Elizabeth and not altogether unknown in ours. Hawkins appears to have had his eye for a long time on the slave trade as a very lucrative business, and as the Spaniards claimed a practical monopoly, patriotic feeling—the desire to break down the Spanish claim—went, as is again not unusual, with profit. At any rate, after a reconnoitering trip, Hawkins returned to England and fitted out an expedition of five vessels, to which were later added another three. In this venture, the Earl of Leicester, the Earl of Pembroke, and others took shares. So did Queen Elizabeth. She lent the ship *Jesus,* and Hawkins drew up rules for his men, the two first of which ran: 'Serve God daily,' and 'Love one another.' The piety of the expedition was beyond reproach. So was its practice, as we read that finding the natives of Cape Verde to be of 'a nature very gentle and loving,' and 'more civil than any others,' Hawkins prepared to kidnap a number of them. After sailing for some time, 'burning and spoiling,' he landed in the Spanish American settlements and compelled the colonists to purchase the slaves at his own price. Quite fittingly, Hawkins was granted a coat of arms consisting of 'a demi-Moor in his proper colours, bound and captive,' as a token of the new trade he had opened to Englishmen."[2]

Meantime disaster overtook the Portuguese. King Sebastian attacked the Moors in North Africa and was killed. His death in 1578 changed the position of Guinea. Within two years Portugal had passed under the domination of Spain, and West Africa with some resistance submitted to Spain. Philip II of Spain (1527–1598) was able to defend to some extent his African empire, but eventually Spain was cut off from Africa by papal decree. Then came Portugal's annexation to Spain in 1581 and the loss of Spanish maritime power by the destruction of the Armada in 1588, which was a death blow to the commercial empire of Spain and Portugal.

The Protestants of England, the Huguenots of France, and the Calvinists of Holland started mortal struggle for Guinea. Eagerly the Dutch took over the Portuguese islands and settlements and formed in 1602 the East India Company.

With the seventeenth century the battle of commerce was on. The Dutch and the British fought to a finish in the Atlantic to dominate the Atlantic trade. The Portuguese, British, and Dutch fought in India. Between them they killed the trade of the German Hanseatic League and overthrew the economic dominance of Spain. Cromwell seized Jamaica as a center of British slavery and the slave trade. In Africa the kingdoms of the black Sudan moved east and displaced the Nilotic Negroes. From among these, peoples like those of the Fang and the Bambara kingdoms between the Nile and the West Coast pressed farther down upon the withdrawing Bantu.

In the seventeenth century the African slave trade to America expanded. It was not yet however a trade which made the word synonymous with Negro or black: during these years the Mohammedan rulers of Egypt were buying white slaves by the tens of thousands in Europe and Asia and bringing them to Syria, Palestine, and the Valley of the Nile. In the west, however, the character of world trade began subtly to change. While the theory of mercantilism still prevailed in academic circles and commerce continued to pour African gold into Europe, and while the Negroes and Arabs sent gold to India to bedeck the gorgeous moguls, in practical commerce the importation of gold from Africa and silver from Peru was losing its dominant attraction. What was needed was human labor; labor to raise food in Spain and Portugal; labor to raise sugar and tobacco in the West Indies and North America.

The labor situation in Europe at the time made slave labor in America peculiarly profitable. The working population of Europe in the sixteenth and seventeenth centuries was limited. The devastation of the Thirty Years' War and the demand for labor and services on the feudal estates made any large-scale exportation of labor to America unthinkable. On the other hand, sugar, cotton, and tobacco were suitable to mass production on the plantations with conventional standards of work, simple tools, and comparatively small outlay for clothing and food. The organized slave gang was more profitable on the land than the peasant proprietor. The new capitalism as a method of production and trade began to supplant the farmer and merchant at home in Europe.

In 1660 the upheaval of Civil War in England was at an end, and England was ready to embark on the slave trade for the benefit of her sugar and tobacco colonies. The British increased the import of slaves to America, raised sugar, indigo, and cotton, and began to bring these goods to England for processing. They then exported some of these processed foods to Africa to buy more slaves. Trade began to change from a gambler's search for treasure to investment for permanent income; and this income consisted of goods for sale which were in practice found more valuable than treasure for hoarding. To perfect this arrangement slaves and more slaves must be had.

At the same time, the conscience of the world began to writhe. "Modern slavery was created by Christians, it was continued by Christians, it was in some respects more barbarous than anything the world had yet seen, and its worst features were to be witnessed in countries that were most ostentatious in their parade of Christianity. It is this that provides the final and unanswerable indictment of the Christian Church."[3] There had been the splendor of the

Catholic Church under Alexander VI and Leo X, and then the revolt led by Luther, the Reformation. Thus was the growing consciousness of the dignity of the human soul brought face to face with slavery and a new slave trade. Gradually it was rationalized widely as a method of rescuing the heathen from perdition and saving his soul. However, this rationalization meant nothing when it conflicted with the profits of trade; and planters particularly, stoutly refused to release converts, and innumerable Christians often would not allow conversion. The profits of this new aspect of trade meant investment and the capitalist system.

Investment called for labor, and cheap labor, if the profit was to be high; but labor was beginning to be conscious and to revolt. This was the meaning of the Peasant War in Germany in the sixteenth century. But there was revolt and revolutionary thought not only in Europe; indeed it may be insisted that the revolt of labor against its modern degradation began in America rather than in Europe. This was the meaning of five slave revolts among the blacks in America and the beginning of the fateful dynasty of Maroons, or free Negroes, hiding in organized rebellion in the mountains of Cuba, Jamaica, and Haiti, in Mexico and Brazil. In the seventeenth century, with the increased importation of slaves, there were nine revolts, leading to pitched war in Jamaica and Barbados and Haiti and to the independent state of Palmares in Brazil.

Nevertheless, England had the bit in her teeth. "Royal adventurers trading to Africa" in 1667 had among them members of the royal family, three dukes, eight earls, seven lords, and twenty-seven knights. With the end of the civil war in England, British merchants crowded upon the landholding aristocracy for an increased share in the profits of industry. While the British were fighting ostensibly for dynastic disputes in Europe, they were really, in the War of Spanish Succession and in the Seven Years' War, fighting for profit through world trade and especially the slave trade. In 1713 they gained, by the coveted Treaty of Asiento, the right to monopolize the slave trade from Africa to the Spanish colonies. In that century they beat Holland to her knees and started her economic decline. They overthrew the Portuguese in India, and finally, by the middle of the century, overcame their last rival in India, the French. In the eighteenth century they raised the slave trade to the greatest single body of trade on earth.

The Royal African Company transported an average of five thousand slaves a year between 1680 and 1686; but the newly rich middle-class merchants were clamoring for free trade in human flesh. Eventually the Royal African Company was powerless against the competition of free merchant traders, and a new organization was established in 1750 called the "Company of Merchants trading to Africa."

In the first nine years of this "free trade," Bristol alone shipped 160,950 Negroes to the sugar plantations. In 1760, 146 ships sailed from British ports to Africa with a capacity of 36,000 slaves. In 1771 there were 190 ships and 47,000 slaves. The British colonies between 1680 and 1786 imported over two million slaves. By the middle of the eighteenth century Bristol owned 237 slave trade vessels, London, 147, and Liverpool, 89.

Liverpool's first slave vessel sailed for Africa in 1709. In 1730 it had 15 ships in the trade and in 1771, 105. The slave trade brought Liverpool in the late eighteenth century a clear profit of £300,000 a year. A fortunate slave trade voyage made a profit of £8,000, and even a poor cargo would make £5,000. It was not uncommon in Liverpool and Bristol for the slave traders to make 100 per cent profit. The proportion of slave ships to the total shipping of England was one in one hundred in 1709 and one-third in 1771. The slave traders were strong in both the House of Lords and the House of Commons, and a British coin, the guinea, originated in the African trade of the eighteenth century.

In the midst of this, a tremendous treasure from India poured into England. The Battle of Plassey gave India to the British Empire for plunder on a scale seldom seen before or since. The enormous extent of robbery of the Indians by British civil servants has been abundantly proved. Howitt referred to "the scenes and transactions in our great Indian empire—that splendid empire which has poured out such floods of wealth into this country; in which such princely presents of diamonds and gold have been heaped on our adventurers; from the gleanings of which so many happy families in England 'live at home at ease' and in the enjoyment of every earthly luxury and refinement. For every palace built by returned Indian nabobs in England; for every investment by fortunate adventurers in India stock; for every cup of wine and delicious viand tasted by the families of Indian growth amongst us, how many of these Indians themselves are now picking berries in the wild jungles, sweltering at the thankless plough only to suffer fresh extortions, or snatching with the bony fingers of famine, the bloated grains from the manure of the high-ways of their native country!"[4]

The directors of the East India Company themselves admitted: "We have the strongest sense of the deplorable state to which our affairs were on the point of being reduced, from the corruption and rapacity of our servants, and *the universal depravity of manners throughout the settlement*. The general relaxation of all discipline and obedience, both military and civil, was hastily tending to a dissolution of all government. Our letter to the Select Committee expresses our sentiments of what has been obtained by way of donations; and to that we must add, that we think the vast fortunes acquired in the inland trade *have been obtained by a scene of the most tyrannic and oppressive conduct that was ever known in any age or country!*"[5]

However this wealth was obtained and however pious the regret at the methods of its rape, there can be no doubt as to what became of it. Its owners in the main were not royal spendthrifts, nor aristocratic dilettantes; and even if some were, their financial advisers put their funds largely into the safe investment of West Indian slavery and the African slave trade. Thus an enormous amount of free capital seeking safe investment and permanent income poured into the banks, companies, and new corporations. The powerful British institution of the stock exchange was born.

It was Karl Marx who made the great unanswerable charge of the sources of capitalism in African slavery: "The discovery of gold and silver in America, the extirpation, enslavement, and entombment in mines of the aboriginal population, the beginning of the conquest and looting of the East Indies, the turning of

Africa into a warren for the commercial hunting of black-skins, signalized the rosy dawn of the era of capitalist production. These idyllic proceedings are the chief momenta of primitive accumulation. On their heels treads the commercial war of the European nations, with the globe for a theatre. It begins with the revolt of the Netherlands from Spain, assumes giant dimensions in England's anti-Jacobin war, and is still going on in the opium wars against China. . . ."[6]

"With the development of capitalist production during the manufacturing period, the public opinion of Europe had lost the last remnant of shame and conscience. The nations bragged cynically of every infamy that served them as a means of capitalistic accumulation. Read, e.g., the naïve *Annals of Commerce* of the worthy A. Anderson. Here it is trumpeted forth as a triumph of English statecraft that at the peace of Utrecht, England extorted from the Spaniards by the Asiento Treaty the privilege of being allowed to ply the Negro trade, until then only carried on between Africa and the English West Indies, between Africa and Spanish America as well. England thereby acquired the right of supplying Spanish America until 1743 with four thousand eight hundred Negroes yearly. This threw, at the same time, an official cloak over British smuggling. Liverpool waxed fat on the slave trade. This was its method of primitive accumulation. And, even to the present day, Liverpool 'respectability' is the Pindar of the slave trade which . . . 'has coincided with that spirit of bold adventure which has characterised the trade of Liverpool and rapidly carried it to its present state of prosperity; has occasioned vast employment for shipping and sailors, and greatly augmented the demand for the manufactures of the country.' Liverpool employed in the slave trade, in 1730, 15 ships; in 1751, 53; in 1760, 74; in 1770, 96; and in 1792, 132."[7]

"*Tantae molis erat*, to establish the 'eternal laws of Nature' of the capitalist mode of production, to complete the process of separation between labourers and conditions of labour, to transform at one pole the social means of production and subsistence into capital, at the opposite pole, the mass of the population into wage-labourers, into 'free labouring poor,' that artificial product of modern society. If money, according to Augier, 'comes into the world with a congenital blood-stain on one cheek,' capital comes dripping from head to foot, from every pore, with blood and dirt."[8]

The method by which slavery and capital investment were developed by Great Britain can be clearly followed: the "triangular trade" flourished. It depended first mainly upon sugar and tobacco and later on cotton. The processing of these materials turned England into a manufacturing country, and the focusing of the attention of technicians upon methods of manufacture brought an astonishing series of inventions in the latter part of the eighteenth century. The Negroes were purchased with British manufactures and transported to the plantations. There they produced sugar, cotton, indigo, tobacco, and other products. The processing of these created new industries in England; while the needs of the Negroes and their owners provided a wider market for British industry, New England agriculture, and the Newfoundland fisheries.

By 1750 there was hardly a manufacturing town in England which was not connected with the colonial trade. The profits provided one of the main streams of that capital which financed the Industrial Revolution. The West Indian islands became the center of the British Empire and of immense importance to the grandeur of England. It was the Negro slaves who made these sugar colonies the most precious colonies ever recorded in the annals of imperialism. Experts called them "the fundamental prop and support" of the Empire. The British Empire was regarded as a "magnificent superstructure of American commerce and naval power on an African foundation."[9]

William Wood said that the slave trade was the "spring and parent whence the others flow." Postlethwayt described the slave trade as "the first principle and foundation of all the rest, the mainspring of the machine which sets every wheel in motion."[10]

The triangular trade made an enormous contribution to Britain's industrial development. The profits fertilized the productive system of the country. The slate industry in Wales was revolutionized by a plantation owner. The British West Indies interest was back of the vast railway development. Cotton responded to new inventions. Between 1709 and 1787 the tonnage of British shipping in foreign trade increased fourfold. The British nobility benefited largely from the West Indian trade. The Lascelles were from Barbados, and one of their descendants is now brother-in-law of the King of England. The Earl of Chatham considered the sugar colonies as "the landed interest of this kingdom." West Indian investors bought seats in Parliament. The poetry of both Browning and Barrett with all its depth and beauty grew straight out of West Indian slavery.

While a profit of seven shillings per head per annum was sufficient to enrich a country, it was declared that each white man in the colonies brought a profit of over seven pounds. Sir Dalby Thomas declared that every person employed on the sugar plantation was a hundred and thirty times more valuable to England than one at home. Professor Pitman has estimated that in 1775 British West Indies plantations represented a valuation of fifty million pounds sterling, and the sugar planters themselves put the figure at seventy millions in 1788. In 1798 Pitt assessed the annual income from West Indian plantations at four million pounds as compared with one million from the rest of the world. As Adam Smith wrote in *Wealth of Nations:* "The profits of a sugar plantation in any of our West Indian colonies are generally much greater than those of any other cultivation that is known either in Europe or America." According to Davenant,[11] "Britain's total trade at the end of the seventeenth century brought a profit of £2,000,000. The plantation trade accounted for £600,000; re-export of plantation goods, £120,000; European, African, and Levant trade, £600,000; East India trade £500,000; re-export of East India goods, £180,000."[12]

The Napoleonic wars widened the trade empire of Great Britain and extended the market for her manufactures. After twenty-two years of fighting, British merchants surpassed in wealth the landed aristocracy, and the Reform Bill of 1832 reflected this economic fact.

We may pause here to enumerate a series of events which have been too often looked upon as separate and unconnected. They are as follows:

1500–1600: The revolt of slaves in the West Indies
1655–1738: War between the British and the Maroons

1750: British free trade in human flesh
1757: The loot of India begins
1774: American association against the slave trade
1775: The American Revolution
1789: The French Revolution
1791–1798: Revolt of Toussaint L'Ouverture
1792–1815: Reaction in France and the rise and fall of Napoleon
1800–1900: Capitalism and the factory system in England
1807: Abolition of the British slave trade
1830: The Cotton Kingdom
1833–1838: British abolition of slavery
1846: Repeal of the British Corn Laws; free trade
1863: Emancipation in America
1884: Imperial colonialism.

The slave revolts were the beginnings of the revolutionary struggle for the uplift of the laboring masses in the modern world. They have been minimized in extent because of the propaganda in favor of slavery and the feeling that the knowledge of slave revolt would hurt the system. In the eighteenth century there were fifteen such revolts: in Portuguese and Dutch South Africa, in the French colonies, in the British possessions, in Cuba and little islands like St. Lucia. There were pitched battles and treaties between the British and the black Maroons and finally there was a rebellion in Haiti which changed the face of the world and drove England out of the slave trade. A list of these revolts follows:

1522: Revolt in San Domingo
1530: Revolt in Mexico
1550: Revolt in Peru
1550: Appearance of the Maroons
1560: Byano Revolt in Central America
1600: Revolt of Maroons
1655: Revolt of 1500 Maroons in Jamaica
1663: Land given Jamaican Maroons
1664–1738: Maroons fight British in Jamaica
1674: Revolt in Barbados
1679: Revolt in Haiti
1679–1782: Maroons in Haiti organized
1691: Revolt in Haiti
1692: Revolt in Barbados
1695: Palmares; revolt in Brazil
1702: Revolt in Barbados
1711: Negroes fight French in Brazil
1715–1763: Revolts in Surinam
1718: Revolt in Haiti

1719: Revolt in Brazil
1738: Treaty with Maroons
1763: Black Caribs revolt
1779: Haitians help the United States Revolution
1780: French Treaty with Maroons
1791: Dominican revolt
1791–1803: Haitian Revolution
1794: Cuban revolt
1794: Dominican revolt
1795: Maroons rebel
1796: St. Lucia revolt
1816: Barbados revolt
1828–1837: Revolts in Brazil
1840–1845: Haiti helps Bolivar
1844: Cuban revolt
1844–1893: Dominican revolt
1861: Revolt in Jamaica
1895: War in Cuba

These revolts show that the docility of Negro slaves in America is a myth. They fall into two groups: those before the French Revolution and those after. The revolt of Maroons in Jamaica and Cuba and the Bush Negroes in South America and the repeated attempts in Haiti frightened the slaveholders and threatened the stability of the whole system. In Jamaica the Maroons "continued to distress the island for upwards of forty years, during which time forty-four acts of assembly were passed, and at least £240,000 expended for their suppression."[13] The governor of Barbados wrote: "The public mind is ever tremblingly aware to the dangers of insurrection," and the statute books all over the slave territory testified to this fact.

The next event that opposed the slave trade and slavery was the American Revolution. Not only did the colonists achieve their independence through the help of slaves and the promise of their freedom, and with the co-operation in money and men from Haiti, but they represented actual working classes rather than exploiters of labor. Finally, the French Revolution burst forth as a war against privilege based on birth and demanded freedom, especially economic freedom to trade and to enter industry without coercion.

The result was that the slave trade met distinct opposition based on humanitarian grounds; but this opposition would have been powerless to stop the trade if it had not been evident that the trade itself as a source of profit was threatened. The revolt of America confirmed the superiority of the French sugar colonies. Between 1783 and 1789 the progress of San Domingo had been amazing. At the end of the eighteenth century the British sugar planters lost their supremacy to the French colonies. French colonial exports amounted to eight millions pounds while British colonial exports amounted to five million pounds.

When the American colonies won their independence, the Caribbean ceased to be a British sea and investments began to be transferred from the West to the East Indies. In 1783 Prime Minister William Pitt showed increased interest in India and encouraged Wilberforce to propose the abolition of the slave trade.

Then came the French Revolution and eventually the revolt of Haiti. The British made every effort to seize control of this famous French sugar colony. They tried both force of arms and bribery, but at last were compelled to recognize the independence of Toussaint L'Ouverture, whom they tried to divorce from allegiance to the French.

Nevertheless, with Haiti out of the world market, the British could have retained their hold upon the sugar industry had it not been for the continued cultivation of sugar in Spanish and Portuguese colonies. So long as these colonies could obtain cheap slaves, they threatened and even destroyed the investment in slave labor already made by British capital. Looked upon as machines or "real estate," as slaves legally were, the investment in Negro labor was being undermined so long as cheaper Negro labor could be had from Africa.

To keep the prices of slaves from falling, the slave trade had to be limited or stopped. Otherwise the whole slavery investment would totter, and that is what England faced after the revolution of Toussaint. Early in the nineteenth century, therefore, she began to change, and back of philanthropists like Sharpe and Wilberforce came the unexpected support of opportunist politicians like Pitt.

Moreover, capitalism was far enough developed to produce sufficient free finance capital to effect a transfer of investment from one field to another without such losses as would cripple the system. Losses there had to be, but they were part of the anarchy of business methods, which by large-scale gambling and periodic crises rushed blindly to newer and larger fields of profit. Eventually Negro slavery and the slave trade were abandoned in favor of colonial imperialism, and the England which in the eighteenth century established modern slavery in America on a vast scale, appeared in the nineteenth century as the official emancipator of slaves and founder of a method of control of human labor and material which proved more profitable than slavery.

For a long time the fiction of the slave trade as a method of conversion to Christianity had ceased to salve the conscience of honest-thinking men. Slavery and the slave trade were pouring such treasure into England, building her cities, railways, and manufactures, and making her so powerful a country that the defense of the system was fierce. England became mistress of the seas. The empire sang "Hail Britannia, Britannia Rules the Waves."

Before the American Revolution, English public opinion accepted the view of the slavetrader: "Tho' to traffic in human creatures, may at first sight appear barbarous, inhuman, and unnatural; yet the traders herein have as much to plead in their own excuse, as can be said for some other branches of trade. . . . In a word, from this trade proceed benefits, far outweighing all, either real or pretended mischiefs and inconveniences."[14]

The cruelty and inhumanity of the slave trade was a horrible fact. A committee of the House of Commons described the "Middle Passage": "The Negroes were chained to each other hand and foot, and stowed so close that they were not allowed above a foot and a half for each in breadth. Thus rammed together like herrings in a barrel, they contracted putrid and fatal disorders; so that they who came to inspect them in a morning had occasionally to pick dead slaves out of their rows, and to unchain their carcasses from the bodies of their wretched fellow-sufferers to whom they had been fastened."[15] "During the hearing of a case for insurance, the following facts were brought out. A slave-ship, with four hundred and forty-two slaves, was bound from Guinea to Jamaica. Sixty of the slaves died from overcrowding. The captain, being short of water, threw ninety-six more overboard. Afterwards, twenty-six more were drowned. Ten drowned themselves in despair. Yet the ship reached port before the water was exhausted."[16]

The revolt against the Protestants began to appear among the Methodists, Baptists, and Quakers. Methodism condoned slavery but was sensitive to and alarmed over the slave trade. The Baptists, beginning in England in 1600, developed into an extremely democratic organization which appealed to workers and even to slaves; and the general philosophical and economic enlightenment of the eighteenth century brought men of learning and artists into a distinct anti-slavery movement.

The slave trade was abolished by England in 1807, and England undertook to make the rest of the world outlaw it too. The United States, Portugal, and Spain gave only lip service to this program, and the slave trade continued up to the middle of the nineteenth century although to a lessening extent.

With the stopping of the slave trade it was evident that investment in labor was different from investment in land, material, and machines; that labor, no matter how much it was degraded, had initiative and made demands. Revolt of the working classes, following the incentive of Haiti, spread. The spectacular and astonishing triumph of revolution in Haiti threatened the whole slave system of the West Indies and even of continental America. It was this revolt more than any other single thing that spelled doom not only of the African slave trade but of slavery in America as a basis of an industrial system. The revolt encouraged the abolition movement in the United States and in Brazil; it flamed in practically every island of the West Indies. Unless the slave worker could be pacified, income based on slave labor would be destroyed. The result was that in 1833 England abolished slavery. Similar abolition followed in the United States after civil war.

The Napoleonic wars did not ruin England; together with the African slave trade, Negro slavery, and the loot of India, they made the British government the most powerful in the world; they ruined England's industrial rivals; they left her in control of the chief sources of raw materials by colonial ownership and with the ready cash to outbid rivals; her vast store of finance capital enabled her to manufacture machinery and wait a generation for repayment; British knowledge of science and technique enabled the country to make the best machines and tools and render the whole world creditor for their purchase; Britain ruled the seas and thus monopolized transport. Even when in the earlier mad rush for profit on the new capitalism, she reduced her own labor to slavery in the factory system and faced revolution, she proved the only land able to raise wages and yet maintain high profit by shifting the burden of pauperized toil to the colonies and dominated peoples; and at the same time, although author and chief supporter of modern slavery, Great Britain could hold up her head and, by suppressing a slavery now becoming unprofitable, lead world philanthropy as the great emancipator of the slave.

But even as this role rejoiced her greater souls, the British Empire became the victim of the worst legacy of Negro slavery: the doctrine of race superiority and the color line, which in a later century made civilized man commit suicide in a mad attempt to hold the vast majority of the earth's peoples in thrall to the white race—a goal to which they still cling today, hidden away behind nationalism and power politics.

This was not a rake's progress of malevolence; it was a bitter struggle between Good and Evil—between fine and noble souls and conscienceless desire for luxury, power, and indulgence. The forces of Evil were continually reinforced by the vast power which slavery and the exploitation of men put into the hands of the betrayers of labor, making them the envied of the earth, until nations became willing to destroy the earth in order to gain it. Suppose that at any point in this Descent to Hell, Right had received help and reinforcement? Suppose that a free America had welcomed a free Haiti into a world that insisted on freedom for Africa and Asia? But no; slavery dominated the "free" republic of the west for half a century, with the slave cotton kingdom as foundation stone for British manufactures, while Great Britain seized land and labor in all the dark world. Suppose that England had freed and educated Africa, emancipated India, and joined hands with Japan to uplift China, instead of making ignorance compulsory for the majority of men even in England, in order to build up the most "comfortable" and envied aristocracy on earth? Suppose the technique and science of the nineteenth century had been used to raise the many instead of to enrich the few?

A dream? Perhaps, but even an unrealized dream would be better than the present nightmare.

The new era of capitalism dawned, springing from Calvinism: thrift, industry, honesty as the best policy, along with interest and profit. Capitalism passed into high capitalism at different periods in different nations: In England in 1846, when English capitalism needed no protective tariff, it smashed the agriculturists in Parliament and forced the adoption of free trade; in the United States invested capital passed the value of the land about 1850. The Revolution of 1848 in France revealed the power of organized labor as well as the power of capitalism, which later triumphed. In Germany capitalism began its full sway after World War I.

In the British Parliament, after the passage of the Reform Bill in 1832, capitalism was paramount. The plantation trade had formerly meant everything; but in the new capitalist system, plantation slavery had little place. Britain's mechanized might was still, however, making the whole world her footstool. She was clothing the world, exporting men and machines, and had become the world's banker. British capital, like British production, was thinking in world terms. "Between 1815 and 1830 at least fifty million pounds had been invested more or less permanently in the securities of the most stable European governments, more than twenty million had been invested in one form or another in Latin America, and five or six millions had very quietly found their way to the United States."[17] But no new capital went to the West Indies.

This then was the history of the slave trade, of that extraordinary movement which made investment in human flesh the first experiment in organized modern capitalism; which indeed made capitalism possible. It accompanied the beginnings of democracy in the modern world, but that beginning was hindered and almost stopped by the result which black slavery had on Africa itself.

In Africa a new and supplementary means of control, developed by means of the Arab trade in ivory,. led to exploration and eventual annexation under the pretense of attacking slavery. In this whole story of the so-called "Arab slave trade" the truth has been strangely twisted. Arab slave raiding was in the beginning, and largely to the end, a secondary result of the British and American slavery and slave trade and specifically was based on American demand for ivory. The Arabs had by the nineteenth century driven back the Portuguese opposite Zanzibar and had developed two profitable products of trade: ivory and slaves.

Ivory has a long history. Homer repeatedly mentions it. Ivory has been found in the ruins of Nineveh and in the days of Tuthmosis III; cargoes of ivory and ebony in addition to gold came down the Nile. In Kings and Chronicles we learn of the great throne of ivory which Solomon built and hear that once every three years ships came to Israel with gold and silver, ivory, apes, and peacocks. Ezekiel laments the ruin of Tyre with its boxwood benches inlaid with ivory. In Greece the statue by Phidias of Jupiter Olympus, one of the seven wonders of the world, was made of ivory, marble, and gold. The seats of the Roman senators were made of ivory, and large quantities of ivory poured into Rome from Africa.

By the beginning of the Christian era the trade in ivory had decreased. The herds of elephants had disappeared, and there was no organized method of gathering the ivory or of bringing it to market. Moreover, it was not until the Renaissance, in the fifteenth century, that renewed demand made search for it profitable. The Portuguese, both on the West Coast of Africa and in Mozambique, began to export it. They were so prodigal that the considerable store which the natives had collected was almost exhausted by the middle of the seventeenth century.

The Dutch began to collect ivory in South Africa, and there and in Central Africa a steady supply kept pace with the demand. By the middle of the nineteenth century, however, there came a new demand from the west. The ivory had long been carried by the slaves to the coast or down the Nile, and then instead of the bearers being returned, they were sold. Most of the ivory in the seventeenth, eighteenth, and the beginning of the nineteenth centuries went to Arabia, Persia, and India, and the slaves to the same parts of the world as soldiers and servants. The trade was small, and while the slave trade was a disrupting influence it did not transfer any large number of persons.

Ivory from about 1840 became increasingly valuable. Its gathering called for fire-arms and transport. Europe and America furnished the arms in vast quantity.

Negro porters bore the white gold over vast distances on their heads, and the traders doubled their profit by selling these Negroes into slavery in the Middle East and America. The result was an industry with huge profits, which called to service the most vicious elements of the Nile Valley with its social disintegration of centuries, aided by the efforts of Mohammed Ali, the ally of white colonial aggression.

It also called white soldiers of fortune like Selous and Lugard, who slaughtered the herds of half-human elephants in cold blood. It called the explorers who followed the hunters and slave traders. After the explorers came the missionaries. Both pointed out that the ivory-slave business was killing the goose that might lay even more golden eggs, if instead of killing valuable labor, this labor and materials were subject to political control of Europe and the abundant capital seeking investment. The missionaries like Livingstone saw in this not only a means of saving bodies and souls of human beings, but also thrift and good business, which in the folklore of early capitalism were the inevitable elements divinely conjoined for modern civilization.

The rising demand in England and America for the suppression of the slave trade in East Africa was not pure philanthropy. It was that "philanthropy and 5 per cent" which was the transition from the century of human slavery in America to the century of the transfer of capital from sugar plantations to colonial imperialism in Africa and Asia. The main end of both enterprises was profit to the owner and exploiter, mainly at the expense of poverty, ignorance, and pain for the slave and native subject.

About the middle third of the nineteenth century the situation changed abruptly. The demand for ivory increased. In America, ivory working was an early industry, especially in New England on the banks of the Connecticut, where ivory has been cut since 1820. It was processed for carving, for cutlery, billiard balls, and miniatures, and for piano keys. At Deep River and Ivoryton and Buffalo the keyboards for all the pianos in America, Canada, and Australia were made. Because of increased demand, European and American traders set up establishments for buying ivory in Zanzibar; in the thirties and forties prices increased. Arabs began to ask for arms in order to shoot elephants and coerce the natives. Increased exports of ivory to Europe and America and of slaves of Arabia and the Persian Gulf, called for increased imports of weapons and ammunition. The Germans sent thirteen thousand muskets in one year. The British and Portuguese sent thousands of the old Sepoy guns from India. The French supplied a single-barrel light weapon. American blasting powder came in ten and twenty-five-pound kegs. German cavalry sabers came and cases of percussion caps. Arabs borrowed from Indian usurers at 60 to 80 per cent, and set out for the haunts of elephants.[18]

Curiously enough it was this ivory trade that stimulated and guided travel and discovery in Central Africa. Explorers followed the ivory traders, who were the true discoverers. Burton, Speke, Livingstone, Stanley, and Cameron started from the Arab capital of Zanzibar. They followed the lines of traffic set by the Arab ivory traders. Petherick, the British ivory trader, preceded Schweinfurth, and the countries he explored were opened up by the ivory trade. Livingstone found the ivory traders on the Upper Congo. Cameron left Zanzibar in 1873 and was the first European to cross Africa from east to west along the ivory traders' routes. Stanley made his second expedition, 1874–1877, and was helped by Tippoo-Tib, the great Negro slave trader who had also helped Livingstone. The last of the great expeditions was Stanley's, in 1887–1889, when he rescued Emin Pasha and his Negro wife.

It was in this way that knowledge of the technique of the slave trade and its meaning came to Europe at a time when the slave trade from Africa to America had been largely suppressed. We had a series of first-hand descriptions of this trade.

Ivory became in the last half of the nineteenth century the scourge of Central Africa. The complete story of bloodshed and cruelty will never be known. Thousands of miles of fertile country were turned into wilderness and ruin. Hundreds of thousands of elephants were slain and thousands of human beings. It has been estimated that not more than one in five of the captives bearing the ivory ever reached the ocean. Starved and weakened by disease and the strain of marching, they lined the long paths with their dead.

"Picture, if you can, a territory nearly as large as the whole of our United States east of the Mississippi River and Illinois, terrorized and overrun in all directions with hundreds of roving bands of plundering murderers armed with invincible weapons of oppression, a land of blood and might, the nights filled with flame and destruction, the days weary with the marching of the coffles and the blood of the despairing, hopeless slaves. And this for years, *for decades*."[19]

Henry M. Stanley wrote: "Every tusk, piece, and scrap in the possession of an Arab trader has been steeped and dyed in blood. Every pound weight has cost the life of a man, woman, or child, for every five pounds a hut has been burned, for every two tusks a whole village has been destroyed, every twenty tusks have been obtained at the price of a district with all its people, villages, and plantations. It is simply incredible that, because ivory is required . . . populations, tribes, and nations should be utterly destroyed."[20]

Hamed bin Muhammed, a Negro, better known as Tippoo-Tib, was one of the greatest of slave traders. He eventually became sultan and overlord of the country of Kassongo in the very middle of Central Africa, which he made a center of ivory collecting and slave hunting. He had a thousand muzzle-loading guns. And it was not until 1905 that he died.

The credit for suppressing the slave-ivory trade must go to Livingstone who inspired it, to Kirk of East Africa who helped carry it through, and to Bargarsh, the Negroid Arab, who actually suppressed the Zanzibar trade. But these three men represent the curious interests involved: Livingstone was a humanitarian who thought that trade and commerce was the best and natural way to improve the condition of man. He would be horrified to see South Africa and Rhodesia today and realize the plight into which the natives have been forced by European trade and industrialism. Kirk was a British imperialist who foresaw the colonial era. He was no philanthropist desirous of the development and rise of the blacks. What he wanted was to expand the power of England, and he believed that could be done best by suppressing the slave trade and slave labor under the Arabs and increasing colonial ownership and serf labor under Great Britain. The Arab sultan Bargarsh was persuaded that colonial alliance with Great Britain would protect his future power and income.

The effect upon Europe was curious. European and American commerce was stimulated. The missionaries, still believing in the expanding trade of the eighteenth century, coupled commerce with missionary effort and did not see the inherent contradiction between them. The result was that the missionary and the merchant worked side by side and hand in hand. It was Livingstone who declared that he was bringing commerce and missionary effort to the natives.

Commercial companies, like the African Lakes Company, exploited and administered territories and equipped the elephant hunters. They supplied the rifles and sent the hunters, reserving the right to buy the ivory at a set price. It was thus that Sir Alfred Sharp and Lord Lugard began life as professional ivory hunters. The coming of American, British, French, German and Portuguese traders in the middle of the nineteenth century furnished the artillery for the worst period in this ivory-slave trade under the Arabs. At its height thirty thousand slaves were exported annually through Zanzibar, leaving more than a hundred thousand who had died on the way to the sea.

Then that extraordinary transformation took place in British public policy. The stopping of the expansion of the Arab slave trade in East and Central Africa became a means of building up the British Empire. All that Britain had done in establishing the new modern slavery in America was forgotten in her effort to suppress the ivory-slave trade in Africa, and that effort was only the other side of her building up of a great African colonial territory which she proposed to exploit by the use of cheap native labor, the sale of African raw materials, and the opening of markets for her merchandise. Slavery and the slave trade became transformed into anti-slavery and colonialism, and all with the same determination and demand to increase the profit of investment.

It all became a characteristic drama of capitalistic exploitation, where the right hand knew nothing of what the left hand did, yet rhymed its grip with uncanny timeliness; where the investor neither knew, nor inquired, nor greatly cared about the sources of his profits; where the enslaved or dead or half-paid worker never saw nor dreamed of the value of his work (now owned by others); where neither the society darling nor the great artist saw blood on the piano keys; where the clubman, boasting of great game hunting, heard above the click of his smooth, lovely, resilient billiard balls no echo of the wild shrieks of pain from kindly, half-human beasts as fifty to seventy-five thousand each year were slaughtered in cold, cruel, lingering horror of living death; sending their teeth to adorn civilization on the bowed heads and chained feet of thirty thousand black slaves, leaving behind more than a hundred thousand corpses in broken, flaming homes.

Quite naturally all this ivory trade centered in London. In Mincing Lane the ivory of the world was bought and sold from the time of the eighteen twenties, when the slave cotton kingdom began to pour profit from American plantations into New York and Manchester. The annual imports of ivory into London rose as follows:

1788–1798: 100 tons a year
1827:   60 tons
1845–1849: 294 tons
1870–1874: 627 tons
1880–1884: 514 tons

This meant the death of seventy-five thousand elephants a year in the heyday of the trade. An enthusiastic elephant hunter described the death of one elephant. They had killed her child. "She turned with a shriek of rage and made a furious charge. She charged three or four times. She often stood still and covered with blood faced the men as she received fresh wounds. At last with a short struggle she staggered around and sank down kneeling and dead." Far away over miles and years, on lovely keys chipped from her curving tusks, men played the *Moonlight Sonata*. Neither for the keys nor the music was the death of the elephant actually necessary.

It was this London market that supplied raw material to be made into billiard balls and piano keys and lovely little ornaments to Ivoryton, Connecticut, and also contrived through the veiled, devious ways of high finance banking to supply Arab and Negro slave raiders with powder and guns and to buy their ivory at prices which were fabulous to them. Behind the slave raiders came the explorers, who pointed out the vast resources of Africa and the possibilities of African labor; behind the explorers came the missionaries, who cried out bitterly against slavery but said nothing and knew less of the white sources of their power in London and Buffalo.

Gradually the picture changed: the captains of industry saw new opportunity for capital. They could wrench the profits of ivory from the Arabs and Negroes; they could wheel England and world religion back of imperial seizure of Africa from the Cape of Good Hope to Cairo, with not only petty profit from ivory, but vaster profits from spices, gold, diamonds, and copper; they could replace wasteful slavery with local black labor paid at wages from one-half to nine-tenths cheaper than white labor in Europe and America and make white labor like it because all this could be done to the glory of God and the superiority of the white race. And it was done.

So colonial imperialism was born. And so some of its leaders illustrated in their own individual lives its development; there was Frederick C. Selous, who began as an elephant hunter and then annexed the peoples and minerals of Mashonaland to the British Empire; there was Frederick D. Lugard, who first fought in India, Burma, and the Sudan; then as a big game hunter in East Africa, where, armed by the African Lakes Company, he murdered elephants in great numbers and became a part of the ivory-slave trade complex. Next he appeared in East Africa as a free-lance fighter against Arabs and Mohammedans and in defense of Christian missions; he reappeared as agent of the British East Africa Company and annexed Uganda to Britain. Thereupon he was recognized as a great champion of imperial England and went to West Africa to help subdue the falling remnants of Sudanese culture. Here he shrewdly realized that conquest of these peoples could most easily be accomplished if their tribal government were left undisturbed, while Britain controlled trade and foreign relations. Having thus invented "indirect rule," he became a British governor in West Africa. Eventually he retired, lived in England on a pension paid by black West Africa, was regarded as the greatest authority on Africa, and died in honor as a noble British lord.

What effect did all this have upon the dark natives of Africa? In the past we have dwelt upon physical suffering, the loss of life, and the devastation of the land, but we have not thought of the larger and deeper social disintegration. First of all, not only was the way opened from the Sahara to the Cape of Good Hope for marauding masses of Bantu warriors, but this great and long-continued movement became organized for aggression and conquest. We hear of the fierce onslaughts of wild tribes like the Yaggas, but we must also remember that there came a new sort of organization. Negro life could not settle down for political organization and empire building. It could not wait for the development of herdsmen and agriculture. It must hurry on to safer places and sheltered land and loot. "It was sorrowfully recognized that the degradation of the Negro peoples of the nearer African interior was the direct result of European slave-dealing. The savagery of Dahomey and Benin was the survival of the ferocity by which native chiefs, a century earlier, had supplied the demands of English and Dutch traders for victims for the plantations."[21]

This movement culminated in the magnificent and utterly ruthless army of a Chaka in the nineteenth century, which almost successfully battled machine guns with assagais. Then too on the West Coast came transformation: the city-states with their intricate social organization and carefully planned industry and beautiful art were pushed back and overwhelmed by newer, stronger military states, like that of Dahomey in the seventeenth century; and the Ashanti earlier had never gained in the line of peaceful industry and art as much as the new gains which they made as intermediaries of the slave traders.

The East African slave trade under Negroes like Tippoo-Tib became organized. The commercial ends and profits sought by Europe were subtly introduced into and shared by an Africa that had been foreign to this kind of life. The mild domestic slavery of the African tribes and of the Arabs and Persians, which did not preclude the son of a slave becoming a king, a statesman, or a poet, was changed into chattel slavery with hard labor and cruel tasks. The continued development of African civilization, forecast in the fourteenth and fifteenth centuries by that in the Sudan, was prevented and turned backward into chaos, flight, and death.

Decadence could be seen on the West Coast, in the shadow of fabled Atlantis, where there emerged in curious juxtaposition the blood sacrifice of the Benin juju together with the beautiful bronzes of the Benin sculptors. The great kingdoms and empires of the Sudan which fell at the battle of Tenkadibou not only suffered the incubus of a horde of Berber invaders as they moved east and became the Sudanese kingdoms of Kanem and Bornu and the realm of the

Fung; they approached the valley of the Nile and came into fierce combat with some of the worst manifestations of Mohammedanism.

Pushing farther south, the Bantu herdsmen threw themselves upon the Congo and Zimbabwe. There came to Africa an end of industry, especially industry guided by taste and art. Cheap European goods pushed in and threw the native products out of competition. Rum and gin displaced the milder native drinks. The beautiful patterned cloth, brocades, and velvets disappeared before their cheap imitations in Manchester calicos. Methods of work were lost and forgotten.

With all this went the fall and disruption of the family, the deliberate attack upon the ancient African clan by missionaries. The invading investors who wanted cheap labor at the gold mines, the diamond mines, the copper and tin mines, the oil forests and cocoa fields, followed the missionaries. The authority of the family was broken up; the authority and tradition of the clan disappeared; the power of the chief was transmuted into the rule of the white district commissioner. The old religion was held up to ridicule, the old culture and ethical standards were degraded or disappeared, and gradually all over Africa spread the inferiority complex, the fear of color, the worship of white skin, the imitation of white ways of doing and thinking, whether good, bad, or indifferent. By the end of the nineteenth century the degradation of Africa was as complete as organized human means could make it. Chieftains, representing a thousand years of striving human culture, were decked out in second-hand London top-hats, while Europe snickered.

Frobenius says in his *Civilisation Africaine:* "When they [the first European navigators of the end of the Middle Ages] arrived in the Gulf of Guinea and landed at Vaida, the captains were astonished to find streets well cared for, bordered for several leagues in length by two rows of trees; for many days they passed through a country of magnificent fields, a country inhabited by men clad in brilliant costumes, the stuff of which they had woven themselves! More to the South in the kingdom of Congo, a swarming crowd dressed in silk and velvet; great states well ordered, and even to the smallest details, powerful sovereigns, rich industries—civilized to the marrow of their bones. And the condition of the countries on the eastern coast—Mozambique, for example—was quite the same.

"What was revealed by the navigators of the fifteenth to the seventeenth centuries furnishes an absolute proof that Negro Africa, which extended south of the desert zone of the Sahara, was in full efflorescence, in all the splendour of harmonious and well-formed civilizations, an efflorescence which the European conquistadors annihilated as far as they progressed. For the new country of America needed slaves, and Africa had them to offer, hundreds, thousands, whole cargoes of slaves. However, the slave trade was never an affair which meant a perfectly easy conscience, and it exacted a justification; hence one made of the Negro a half-animal, an article of merchandise. And in the same way the notion of fetish (Portuguese *feticeiro*) was invented as a symbol of African religion. As for me, I have seen in no part of Africa the Negroes worship a fetish. The idea of the 'barbarous Negro' is a European invention which has consequently prevailed in Europe until the beginning of this century."[22]

Who now were these Negroes on whom the world preyed for five hundred years? In defense of slavery and the slave trade, and for the upbuilding of capitalistic industry and imperialistic colonialism, Africa and the Negro have been read almost out of the bounds of humanity. They lost in modern thought their history and cultures. All that was human in Africa was deemed European or Asiatic. Africa was no integral part of the world because the world which raped it had to pretend that it had not harmed a man but a thing.

In view of the present world catastrophe, I want to recall the history of Africa. I want to retell its story so far as distorted science has not concealed and lost it. I want to appeal to the past in order to explain the present. I know how unpopular this method is. What have we moderns, we wisest of the wise, to do with the dead past? Yet, "All that tread the globe, are but a handful to the tribes that slumber in its bosom," and who are we, stupid blunderers at the tasks these brothers sought to do—who are we to forget them?

I remember once offering to an editor an article which began with a reference to the experience of last century. "Oh," he said, "leave out the history and come to the present." I felt like going to him over a thousand miles and taking him by the lapels and saying, "Dear, dear jackass! Don't you understand that the past *is* the present; that without what *was*, nothing *is*? That, of the infinite dead, the living are but unimportant bits?"

So now I ask you to turn with me back five thousand years and more and ask, what is Africa and who are Negroes?

NOTES

1. Mary Wilhelmine Williams, writing on Slavery in the *Encyclopedia of the Social Sciences* (New York: The Macmillan Co., 1934) Vol. 14, p. 80.
   For other facts and allusions in this chapter, consult John W. Blake, *European Beginnings in West Africa* (New York: Longmans, Green & Co., 1937).
2. Chapman Cohen, *Christianity, Slavery and Labour* (London: Pioneer Press, 1931, issued for The Secular Society, Limited), pp. 46–47.
3. *Ibid.*, p. 44.
4. Howitt, *op. cit.*, pp. 309–310.
5. *Ibid.*, p. 262.
6. Karl Marx, *Capital*, tr. by Samuel Moore and Edward Aveling (Chicago: C. H. Kerr & Co., 1909), Vol. I, p. 823.
7. *Ibid.*, Vol. I, pp. 832–33. Marx quotes the work of Aiken (1795), p. 339.
8. *Ibid.*, Vol. I, pp. 833–34.
9. Eric Williams, *Capitalism and Slavery* (Chapel Hill, N.C.: University of North Carolina Press, 1944), p. 52.
10. *Ibid.*, p. 51.
11. Davenant was the author of *Discourses on the Publick Revenues*, published in London in 1698.
12. Eric Williams, *op. cit.*, p. 53.
13. Bryan Edwards, *The History, Civil and Commercial, of the British Colonies in the West Indies* (Philadelphia: James Humphreys, 1805), Vol. I, p. 340.
14. Eric Williams, *op. cit.*, p. 50.
15. Ingram, *History of Slavery and Serfdom* (London, 1895), p. 152.
16. Goldwin Smith, *The United Kingdom: A Political History*, Vol. II, p. 247.
17. Leland Jenks, *Migrations of British Capital to 1875* (New York: Alfred A. Knopf, 1927), p. 64.
18. E. D. Moore, *Ivory: Scourge of Africa* (New York: Harper & Brothers, 1931), p. 54.

19. *Ibid.*, p. 63.

20. Henry M. Stanley, *In Darkest Africa* (New York: Charles Scribner's Sons, 1891), Vol. I, p. 240.

21. William H. Woodward, *A Short History of the British Empire* (London: Cambridge University Press, 1924), p. 307.

22. Leo Frobenius, *Histoire de la Civilisation Africaine*, tr. from the German by Back and Ermont (Paris: Gallimard, 1936), 6th ed., p. 56. This work has never been translated into English and is therefore quoted at length, since this greatest student of Africa is now dead and German publications have ceased for the present.

CHAPTER IV

◆

The Peopling of Africa

This is the story based on science and scientific deductions from the facts as we know them concerning the physical development of African peoples.

Seers say that for full two thousand million years this world out of fiery mist has whirled about the sun in molten metal and viscous crusted ball. That crust, congealing and separating the solids from the liquids, rose and fell in bulging ridges above the boiling sea. Five times the mass of land called Africa emerged and disappeared beneath the oceans. At last, at least a thousand million years ago, a mass of rigid rock lifted its crystal back above the waters and remained. Primeval Africa stretched from the ramparts of Ethiopia to where the copper, diamonds, and gold of South Africa eventually were found. More land arose, and perhaps three hundred million years ago Africa was connected with South America, India, and Australia. As the ocean basins dropped, the eastern half of Africa was slowly raised into a broad, flat arch.

The eastern side of this arch gave way, forming the Indian Ocean, and when the roof of the arch fell in there appeared the great Rift valley. This enormous crack, extending six thousand miles from the Zambesi to Ethiopia and Syria, is said to be the only thing that Martians can descry as they look earthward of a starry night. All the great East African lakes lie in the main rift, and doubtless the Red Sea and the Sea of Galilee are also part of this vast phenomenon. Later, about ten million years ago, a second rift occurred, and rifting and tilting kept on until perhaps a hundred thousand years before our era.

Recurrent change came in geography and climate. Europe and Africa were united by land and separated. Lower Egypt was submerged, and the Mediterranean extended to Persia. Finally, what the geologists call the modern world emerged. In Egypt great rivers poured down the hills between the Red Sea, and the Nile found old and new valleys. The Sahara was crossed by a network of rivers, pouring into a vaster Lake Chad and uniting the Niger, the Congo, and the Nile.

Gondwanaland, the ancient united continent of Africa, South America, and Asia, was divided into three parts by the new changes which caused the rift valleys. The radioactivity of the inner earth made the crust break apart. We can see by the map how Africa broke from South America and Europe from North America. Changes in climate were caused by the sun, the earth's inner heat, and by two main glacial periods in Africa. The rainfall varied, bringing periods of flood between the glaciers.

The continent of Africa in its final modern form has been described as a question mark, as an inverted saucer, as the center of the world's continents. Including Madagascar, it is three times the size of Europe, four times the size of the United States; and the whole of Europe, India, China, and the United States could be held within its borders. In actual measurement it is nearly square: five thousand miles long by four thousand six hundred miles wide. But its northern half is by far the larger, with the southern half tapering off. In the middle the equator cuts across Africa, and the whole continent lies mainly within the tropics.

Of the physical aspects of Africa, its relatively unbroken coastline has had the greatest effect upon its history. Although Africa is about three times larger than Europe in area, the coastline of Europe is four thousand miles longer than that of Africa. In other words, Africa has almost no peninsulas, deep bays, or natural harbors. Its low and narrow coast, almost level, rises rapidly to a central plateau with a depression in the center. Thus the great rivers fall suddenly to the ocean, and their navigation is impeded by rapids and falls.

Its five areas include the original Great Plateau with an average elevation of over thirty-five hundred feet, where mountains crowned with snow rise from thirteen to twenty thousand feet. Over these open spaces have always roamed herds of wild animals—elephants, rhinoceroses, and buffaloes.

The second area is the Great Depression, the basin of the Congo River draining nearly a million and a half square miles. Its average altitude is a thousand feet and it is the bed of a former inland sea. As Stanley described it: "Imagine the whole of France and the Iberian peninsula closely packed with trees varying from twenty to a hundred and eighty feet in height, whose crowns of foliage interlace and prevent any view of sky and sun, and each tree from a few inches to four feet in diameter."[1] In this area lies the Belgian Congo and French Equatorial Africa, Liberia and the British West African colonies.

The fourth area is the Sahara, extending from the Atlantic to the Red Sea. It covers three and a half million square miles and is divided into desert and fertile islands. In the past the Sahara was fertile and had a large population. Its surface today is often a hundred feet below sea level. In the east is Egypt and the Egyptian Sudan. North Africa lies on the Mediterranean with Algeria and Tunisia, Libya and Egypt. There are senses in which it is true that "Africa begins at the Pyrenees," and also that "Europe ends at the borders of the Sahara."

We may distinguish in Africa equatorial and tropical climates, and then over smaller areas climates peculiar to specific areas. The equatorial climate is divided into the climate of Central Africa and that of Guinea and East Africa. The first with constant heat, much rainfall, and humidity; the second with constant heat and smaller rainfall. In both these regions there is luxuriant growth of plant life and dense forests. The East African climate is hot. There are savannahs and varied vegetation. Of the tropical climate, there is the Sudanese, with heat but less rain, and the desert type, with great heat but wide daily variation and little rain.

Besides these, there is the climate peculiar to the Mediterranean, with hot summers and rain in winter; and to the Cape district, with more moderate summers and winters and less rainfall.

This is the climate of Africa today, but it has varied, and probably greatly, in the vast stretches of past time. The changes came with the distribution of land and water, the elevation and subsidence of land, the severance of the continent from Asia and South America, and the rise of the mountains in India and Europe that affect the air and sea currents. The rim of the great inland plateau which forms most of Africa falls to sea level near the coast and falls so steeply that the valleys of the rivers draining it do not spread into broad alluvial plains inviting settled populations. The history of tropical Africa would have been far different if it had possessed a Saint Lawrence, an Amazon, a Euphrates, a Ganges, a Yangtze, or a Nile south of the Sahara. The difference of land level within the continent brings strange contrasts.

Sixty million years ago vast reptiles and dinosaurs wandered over this continent. It became, as the years passed, a zoological garden with wild animals of all sorts. Finally there came domesticated cattle, sheep, and goats and a tremendous development of insects. As Sir Harry Johnston well remarks, "Africa is the chief stronghold of the real Devil—the reactionary forces of Nature hostile to the uprise of Humanity. Here Beelzebub, King of the Flies, marshals his vermiform and arthropod hosts—insects, ticks, and nematode worms—which more than in other continents (excepting Negroid Asia) convey to the skin, veins, intestines, and spinal marrow of men and other vertebrates the microorganisms which cause deadly, disfiguring, or debilitating diseases, or themselves create the morbid condition of the persecuted human being, beasts, bird, reptile, frog, or fish."[2]

Africa is a beautiful land; not merely comely and pleasant, but haunted with swamp and jungle; sternly beautiful in its loveliness of terror, its depth of gloom, and fullness of color; its heaven-tearing peaks, its silver of endless sand, the might, width, and breadth of its rivers, depth of its lakes and height of its hot, blue heaven. There are myriads of living things, the voice of storm, the kiss of pestilence and pain, old and ever new, new and incredibly ancient.

The anthropoid ape with the great brain who walked erect and used his hands as tools developed upon earth not less than half a million years ago. Traces of him have been found in Africa, Asia, and Europe and in the islands of the sea. Many types which developed have doubtless been lost, but one species has survived, driven hither and yon by cold and hunger, segregated from time by earthquake and glacier and united for defense against hunger and wild beasts.

Groups of this species must have inbred and developed subtypes over periods of tens of thousands of years. Of the subspecies thus developed, scientists have usually distinguished at least three, all of which were fertile in their crossbreeding with one another. In course of time they have given rise to many transitional groups and intermediary types, so that less than two-thirds of the living peoples of today can be decisively allotted to one or the other of the definite subspecies. These subspecies include the long-headed dark people with more or less crinkled hair whom we know as Negroids; the broad-headed yellow people with straight and wiry hair whom we call Mongoloids; and a type between these, possibly formed by their union, with bleached skins and intermediate hair, known as the Caucasoids.

No sooner had these variant types appeared in Central Africa, on the steppes of Asia, and in Europe than they merged again. The importance of these types was not so much their physical differences and likenesses as their cultural development. As Frobenius says: "With vast and growing weight there begins to emerge today out of the microscopic spectacles of blind eyes, a new conception among living men of the unity of human culture." Inquiring search has made clear "here Greek, there old Mexican spirituality; here European economic development, there pictures of the glacial age; here Negro sculpture, there shamanism; here philosophy, there machines; here fairy tale, there politics."[3]

Was Africa the cradle of the human race? Did it witness man's first evolution from the anthropoid ape to *Homo sapiens*? We do not know. Charles Darwin thought that "it is somewhat more probable that our early progenitors lived on the African continent than elsewhere." Sir G. E. Smith agrees with this and says that Africa "may have been the area of characterization, or, to use a more homely phrase, the cradle, both of the anthropoid apes and the human family." From Africa, Negroids may have entered Asia and Europe. On the other hand, the human race originating in Asia or even in Europe may have invaded Africa and become Negroid by long segregation in a tropical climate. But all this is conjecture. Of the origin of the Negro race or of other human races, we know nothing. But we do know that human beings inhabited Africa during the Pleistocene period, which may have been half a million years ago.

A memoir presented by a well-known Belgian scientist, Alfred Rutot, just before World War I, to the scientific section of the Académie de Belgique caused some stir. It was accompanied by a series of busts, ten in number, executed under careful supervision, by M. Louis Mascré. The busts were striking. The attempt to reproduce various prehistoric types, beginning with Pithecanthropus erectus, was characterized as "audacious," and, of course, much confirmation is necessary of the facts and theories adduced.

The chief interest of the paper was the reconstruction of the Negroids of Grimaldi, so-called from the finds at Mentone, France, helped out by similar remains found in the Landes and at Wellendorff in Lower Austria. How did specimens of Negroes so intelligent in appearance find themselves in the immediate presence of Caucasians, introducing amongst them the art of sculpture which presupposes an advanced stage of civilization? Science explains this phenomenon by the successive cataclysmic changes on our planet. For the quaternary period, Sicily formed part of the Italian mainland, the Strait of Gibraltar was non-existent, and one passed from Africa to Europe on dry land. Thus it was that a race of more or less Ethiopic type filtered in amongst the people inhabiting our latitudes, to withdraw later toward their primitive habitat.

From the position of certain Negroid skeletons exhumed in France, some have concluded that this race carried and made use of the bow. This is uncertain; but it is well authenticated that these visitors brought to the white race the secret of sculpture, for their bones are almost invariably found in company with

objects sculptured on steatite or stone, in high or low relief. Some of their sculptures are quite finished, like the Wellendorff Venus, cut in a limestone block. Of
this Venus, Rutot's Negroid type of man is a replica out of mammoth ivory. The
shell net of four rows adorning the head of this artistic ancestor is a faithful
reproduction of the ornament encircling the cranium of the skeleton found in
the Grotte des Enfants at Mentone. For the ancient Negroid woman, Mascré has
gone to a figure in relief found in the excavations at Lausses (Dordogne). The
marked horn held in the right hand is that of a bison, the bracelets and armlets
are exact copies of the ornaments exhumed at Mentone.

These Negroid busts are most attractive and intelligent looking and have
no exaggerated Negro features. The Cro-Magnon man of Dordogne is a
Magdalenian, contemporary with the Negroid intrusion. The fine proportions
of the skull indicate unmistakable intellectuality. The remains left by this race in
the caves of Périgord reveal great skill in the art of sculpting and painting animals, whereas the Negroids of that time specialized in the representation of
their own species. The daggers of that epoch, described in *Reliquiae Aquitaniae*,
are engraved on reindeer horn, and the weapons underwent perhaps many practical improvements due to the effort, eventually successful, of the Magdalenians
to drive out the Negroids, their artistic rivals.[4]

"There was once an 'uninterrupted belt' of Negro culture from Central
Europe to South Africa. 'These people,' says Griffith Taylor, 'must have been quite
abundant in Europe toward the close of the Paleolithic Age. Boule quotes their
skeletons from Brittany, Switzerland, Liguria, Lombardy, Illyria, and Bulgaria.
They are universal through Africa and through Melanesia, while the Botocudos
and the Làgoa Santa skulls of East Brazil show where similar folk penetrated to
the New World.' Massey says: 'The one sole race that can be traced among the
aborigines all over the earth or below it is the dark race of a dwarf, Negrito
type.'"[5]

It seems reasonable to suppose that Negroids originating in Africa or Asia
appeared first as Negrillos. The Sahara at that time was probably covered with
rivers and verdure and North Africa was in close touch with Mediterranean
Europe. There came upon the Negrillos a wave of Negroids who were hunters
and fishermen and used stone implements. The remains of an African stone age
are scattered over a wide area with amazing abundance, and there is such a
resemblance between implements found in Africa and those in Europe that we
can apply, with few differences, the same names. The sequence in culture in
Europe resembles the sequence in Africa although they may not have been
contemporary.

The most primitive type of stone implement was found in Uganda and is
known as the pebble tool. The same pebble industry extended to Tanganyika
and the Transvaal. This gave way to the hand-ax culture, which extended over
North Africa, the Sahara, Equatorial Africa, West and South Africa. Superb
hand axes and other tools are the evidence. Then the middle Paleolithic flake-
tool culture spread over wide areas of Africa and is shown by perfect implements in South Africa and other places. The remains indicate a cave-dwelling
people with a great variety of tools as well as beads and pottery.

During the Pleistocene period came a new Stone Age, with agriculture, domestic animals, pottery, and the grinding and polishing of stone tools. Evidence of this culture is found in Egypt and North Africa, the Sahara in West Africa, East and South Africa.

The Neolithic culture is of great significance. In Egypt it is found five thousand years before Christ. A thousand years later it changed from flint to copper. The Predynastic Egyptians who represented this culture were settled folk; they hunted and fished, and cultivated grain; made clothes and baskets, used copper, and were distinctly Negroid in physique. Probably they came from the south, from what is now Nubia. Later there came to Egypt other people of the type corresponding to the modern Beja, who lived in settled communities and used copper and gold. This brown Negroid people, like the modern Beja, Galla, and Somali, mixed increasingly with Asiatic blood, but their culture was African and extended by unbroken thread up the Nile and beyond the Somali peninsula.

The first wave of Negroes were hunters and fishermen and used stone implements. They gradually became sedentary and cultivated the soil and must have developed early artistic aptitudes and strong religious feeling. They built the stone monuments discovered in Negro Africa and the raised stones and carved rocks of Gambia. They did not mix with the Negrillos nor did they dispossess them, but recognized their ancestral land rights and seized unoccupied land. Thousands of years after this first wave of Negro immigrants there came another migration. The newcomers pushed north and west, dispossessed the Negrillos, and drove them toward the central forests and the deserts. They mixed more with the Negrillos, developed agriculture, the use of cattle and domestic fowl. They invented the working of iron and the making of pottery. Also, those who advanced farthest toward the north mixed with the Mediterranean race in varying degrees, so that sometimes the resulting population seemed white mixed with Negro blood and in other cases blacks mixed with white blood. The languages were mixed in various ways. Thus we had the various Libyan and Egyptian populations. All this migration and mixture took place long before the epoch of the first Egyptian dynasty.

There exists today a fairly complete sequence of closely interrelated types of human beings in Africa, leading from Australopithecus to such known primitive African types as Rhodesian Man and Florisbad Man. If these types are affiliated with, if not actually ancestral to, Boskop Man, the common presence of all three in the southern half of Africa is presumptive evidence that they all emerged on this continent from some common ancestral stock.

The name "Negro" originally embraced a clear conception of ethnology—the African with dark skin, so-called "woolly" hair, thick lips and nose; but it is one of the achievements of modern science to confine this type to a small district even in Africa. Gallas, Nubians, Hottentots, the Congo races, and the Bantus are not "genuine" Negroes from this view, and thus we find that the continent of Africa is peopled by races other than the "genuine" Negro.

Nothing then remains for the Negro in the "pure" sense of the word save, as Waitz says, "a tract of country extending over not more than ten or twelve degrees of latitude, which may be traced from the mouth of the Senegal River to

Timbuktu." If we ask what justifies so narrow a limitation, "we find that the hideous Negro-type, which the fancy of observers once saw all over Africa, but which, as Livingstone says, is really to be seen only as a sign in front of tobacco-shops, has on closer inspection evaporated from almost all parts of Africa, to settle no one knows how in just this region. If we understand that an extreme case may have been taken for the genuine and pure form, even so we do not comprehend the ground of its geographical limitation and location. We are here in presence of a refinement of science which to an unprejudiced eye will hardly hold water."[6]

Palgrave says: "As to faces, the peculiarities of the Negro countenance are well known in caricature; but a truer pattern may be seen by those who wish to study it any day among the statues of the Egyptian rooms in the British Museum: the large gentle eye, the full but not overprotruding lips, the rounded contour, and the good-natured, easy, sensuous expression. This is the genuine African model; one not often to be met with in European or American thoroughfares, where the plastic African too readily acquires the careful look and even the irregularity of the features that surrounded him; but which is common enough in the villages and fields where he dwells after his own fashion among his own people; most common of all in the tranquil seclusion and congenial climate of Surinam plantation. There you may find, also, a type neither Asiatic nor European, but distinctly African; with much of independence and vigour in the male physiognomy and something that approaches, if it does not quite reach, beauty in the female. Rameses and his queen were cast in no other mould."[7]

What are the peoples who from vague prehistory emerged as the Africans of today? The answer has been bedeviled by the assumption that there was in Africa a "true" Negro and that this pure aboriginal race was mixed with a mythical "Hamitic race" which came apparently from neither Europe, Asia, nor Africa, but constituted itself as a "white element" in Negro Africa. We may dismiss this "Hamitic" race as a quite unnecessary assumption and describe the present African somewhat as follows:

At a period as early as three thousand years before Christ the people of the North African coastal plains were practically identical with the early Egyptians and present two types: long-headed Negroid people and broad-headed Asiatics. Among the Berber types today are tall and medium long-headed people with broad faces, swarthy skin, and dark eyes. They have many Negroid characteristics, especially toward the south. Beside these there are short, broad-headed people.

These Berbers are the ones who correspond to the ancient Egyptians and who have close relationship to the Neolithic inhabitants of France. Among them today the Negro element is widely represented. It is in every part of Mauritania, where the reigning family itself is clearly of Negro descent. A large strain of Negro blood may also be found in Algeria.

In East Africa we have the Massai, Nandi, Suk, and others, tall, slender, and long-headed. In the case of the Massai the nose is thinner and the color tinged with reddish-brown. The Bari people are tall and the Lutoko very tall. Then there are the Nilotics in the Nile valley, extending south of Khartoum to Lake

The Nations of the World
in the twelfth century A.D., according to Lambertus of the Library of Ghent

Kioga. Physically, as in the case of the Shilluk and Dinka, they are tall, very black, long-headed people, often with well-shaped features, thin lips, and high-bridged noses. The Nuba, tall, long-headed men, live in the hills of Kordofan. East of Kordofan are the Fung, with many tribes and with much Asiatic blood; and also broad-headed tribes like the Bongo and the Asande, a mixed people of reddish color with long heads.

On the other side of Africa, the lower and middle portion of the Senegal River forms a dividing line between West African types of Negroes and the Negroes of the Sudan. South of the river are the Jolofs and the Serers. With these are the Senegalese, including the Tukolor and Mandingo tribes. They are dolichocephalic with both broad and narrow noses. They are rather tall, some of them very tall, and their skin is very dark. The Mandingo, or Mandi, are among the most important groups of French Senegal and live between the Atlantic and

Upper Niger. They are tall and slender with fine features, beards, and rather lighter skin than that of neighboring Negroes.

Among the most interesting of the West African people south of the Sudan are the Fulani, stretching from the Upper Niger to the Senegal River. They are Negroids, perhaps with Asiatic blood. They are straight-haired, straight-nosed, thin-lipped and long-headed, with slender physiques and reddish-brown color. The Songhay are tall and long-headed with well-formed noses and coppery-brown color. The people of Kanem and the Bagirmi cluster around Lake Chad. They are broad-nosed and dolichocephalic and resemble the Negroes on the Nile. In the east and South Africa are the Wachagga and the Fang and especially the Swahili, mixed people whose language dominates East Africa. They have all possible degrees of physical characteristics from Arabic to Negro. In South Africa there are the Bushmen, short, yellow, with closely-curled hair. Beside them live the Hottentots, probably Bushmen with Bantu admixture and later with white Dutch admixture which gave rise to the so-called "coloured" people.

The Negroes in the neighborhood of the Gulf of Guinea can be differentiated at present chiefly by their languages, which have been called Sudanic. Three great stocks prevail: the Twi, Ga, and Ewe. Belonging to these are the Ashanti, moderately tall men, long-headed with some broad heads; the Dahomey, tall, long-headed, and black; the Yoruba, including the peoples of Benin and Ibo, dark brown or black, closely curled hair, moderate dolichocephaly, and broad-nosed. Their lips are thick and sometimes everted, and there is a considerable amount of prognathism. The Kru, hereditary sailors, are typically Negroid with fine physiques. The Haussa of the central Sudan are very black and long-headed but not prognathic and with thin noses.

Finally there are the Bantu, who are a congeries of peoples, belonging predominantly to Central and South Africa and occupying the southern two-thirds of black Africa. The Bantu are defined on purely linguistic criteria. The term "Bantu" primarily implies that the tribes included speak languages characterized by a division of nouns into classes distinguished by their prefixes (usually twelve to fifteen), absence of sex-gender in the grammar, and the existence of alliterative concord, the prefix of each class (noun-class) being repeated in some form or another in all words agreeing with any noun of that class in the sentence. It is the reappearance of the prefix in every word in agreement with the noun that gives the alliterative effect.

The southern Bantu outnumber all other groups of South Africa and are about four times as numerous as the Whites. They are divided into a large number of tribal units, each with its own distinctive name. In social organization and religious system they show broad resemblances to one another, but in details of history there are a number of important differences which permit of their being classified into four groups:

1. The Shona peoples of Southern Rhodesia and of Portuguese East Africa.
2. The Zulu-Xosa, chiefly in the coastal region south and east of the Drakensberg Mountains.

3. The Suto-Chwana occupy the greater portion of the high plateau north of the Orange River.
4. The Herero-Ovambo, in the northern half of Southwest Africa and in southern Angola.

In skin color the range is from the black of the Amaswazi to the yellowish-brown of some of the Bechuana. The prevalent color is a dark chocolate, with a reddish ground tint. The hair is uniformly short and woolly. The head is generally low and broad with a well-formed bridge and narrow nostrils. The face is moderately prognathous, the forehead prominent, cheekbones high, lips fleshy. The Negro facial type predominates in all groups, but side by side with it in the Zulu and the Thonga sections are relatively long, narrow faces, thin lips, and high noses.

The inhabitants of Natal and Zululand, divided originally into more than a hundred small separate tribes, are all now collectively known as "Zulus," a name derived from one of the tribes which, under the domination of Chaka, absorbed and conquered most of the others and so formed the Zulu nation which played so important a part in the political history of South Africa during the nineteenth century.

Tribes vary in size, some having from a few hundred to a couple of thousand members. Others are much larger, for example, the Bakwena, 11,000; the Batawana, 17,500; the Bamagwato, 60,000; the Ovandonga, 65,000; the Ovakwanyama, 55,000; the Amaswazi, again, number 110,000; while the Basuto, by far the largest of all and might be called a nation, number nearly half a million.

The area of the western Bantu includes the Cameroons (French), Rio Muni (Spanish), the Gaboon (French), French Equatoria, the Congo (Belgian), Angola (Portuguese), and Rhodesia, with the fraction of Portuguese East Africa north of Zambesi. This vast area is the true "Heart of Africa," the tropical rain forest of the Congo. Johnston enumerated over one hundred and fifty tribes in this area who speak Bantu or semi-Bantu tongues. The southern limit of the western Bantu is vague; the formation of the Lunda empire, the Yagga raids, and the subsequent encroachments of the Bajokwe (Kioko) have played havoc with tribal organization. The Bateke occupy a vast region on the right bank of the Congo which is now largely peopled by the Fang, who in their various expeditions and conquests have left their mark on most tribes north of the Ogowe River. Finally, in the midst of Africa are the Negrillos or pygmies, small men with reddish-brown or dark skin and brachiocepahalic heads.[8]

These are but a few examples of the infinitely varied inhabitants of Africa. There is thus no one African race and no one Negro type. Africa has as great a physical and cultural variety as Europe or Asia.

This is the Africa of which Langston Hughes sings:

I've known rivers:
I've known rivers ancient as the world and older than the flow of human blood
    in human veins.
My soul has grown deep like the rivers.

I bathed in the Euphrates when dawns were young.
I built my hut near the Congo and it lulled me to sleep.
I looked upon the Nile and raised the Pyramids above it.[9]

NOTES

1. Stanley, *op. cit.*, Vol. II, p. 76.
2. Harry H. Johnston, *The Negro in the New World* (London: Methuen & Co., 1910), pp. 14, 15.
3. Frobenius, *op. cit.*
4. Francis Hoggan, "Prehistoric Negroids and their Contribution to Civilization," *The Crisis*, February 1920, p. 174.
5. J. A. Rogers, *Sex and Race* (New York: published by the author, 1942—44), Vol. I, p. 32.
6. Friedrich Ratzel, *The History of Mankind*, tr. from the German by A. J. Butler (London: Macmillan & Co., 1904), 2nd ed., Vol. II, p. 313.
7. W. G. Palgrave, *Dutch Guiana* (London: Macmillan & Co., 1876), pp. 192—93.
8. In this description of African peoples, I have relied principally on C. G. Seligmann's well-known studies.
9. Langston Hughes, "The Negro Speaks of Rivers," *The Crisis*, June 1921, p. 71.

CHAPTER V

---❖---

Egypt

This is the story of three thousand years, from 5000 B.C. to 2000 B.C., and it tells of the development of human culture in the valley of the Nile below the First Cataract.

Civilization has flowed down to man along the valley of great rivers where the soil was fertile and man need not fear hunger, and where the waters carried him to other peoples who were thinking of problems of human life and solving them in varied ways. Some say that human culture started in the valley of the Yangtze and of the Hoang Ho. Some say it came up from Black Africa; some that it came west from the Euphrates; but it had begun more than four thousand years before Christ.

The development in Mesopotamia in the valley of the Tigris-Euphrates, which flows into the Persian Gulf and thence to the Indian Ocean, is striking. Before the year four thousand B.C. there is evidence that Negroid Dravidians and Mongoloid Sumerians ruled in southern Asia, in Asia Minor. and in the valley of the Tigris-Euphrates. Negroids followed them under Sargon, and Sargon boasted that "he commanded the black heads and ruled them."

But it was in the valley of the Nile that the most significant continuous human culture arose, significant not necessarily because it was absolutely the oldest or the best, but because it led to that European civilization of which the world boasts today and regards in many ways as the greatest and last word in human culture.

Despite this, it is one of the astonishing results of the written history of Africa, that almost unanimously in the nineteenth century Egypt was not regarded as part of Africa. Its history and culture were separated from that of the other inhabitants of Africa; it was even asserted that Egypt was in reality Asiatic, and indeed Arnold Toynbee's *Study of History* definitely regarded Egyptian civilization as "white," or European! The Egyptians, however, regarded themselves as African. The Greeks looked upon Egypt as part of Africa not only geographically but culturally, and every fact of history and anthropology proves that the Egyptians were an African people varying no more from other African peoples than groups like the Scandinavians vary from other Europeans, or groups like the Japanese from other Asiatics. There can be but one adequate explanation of this vagary of nineteenth-century science: it was due to the slave trade and Negro slavery. It was due to the fact that the rise and support of capitalism called for rationalization based upon degrading and discrediting the Negroid peoples. It is especially significant that the science of Egyptology arose and flourished at the very time that the cotton kingdom reached its greatest power on the foundation of American Negro slavery. We may then without further ado ignore this verdict of history, widespread as it is, and treat Egyptian history as an integral part of African history.

"The land of Egypt is six hundred miles long and is bounded by two ranges of naked limestone hills which sometimes approach and sometimes retire from each other, leaving between them an average breadth of seven miles. On the north they widen and disappear, giving place to a marshy meadow plain which extends to the Mediterranean Coast. On the south they are no longer of limestone but of granite; they narrow to a point; they close in till they almost touch; and through the mountain gate thus formed, the river Nile leaps with a roar into the valley, and runs due north towards the sea."[1]

It was a marvelous and unusual valley where a great river flowed out of the highlands of Central Africa and the mountains of the Horn, cut its way down through cliffs on either side crowned by deserts. The valley thus made was "burning and fertile, warm and smiling." Winds from the north tempered the heat of the sun so that the land was "green with meadows, golden with harvest, red with the blood of vines, a paradise of water, fruit, and flowers between two torrid deserts." The waters of the rivers rose and fell with the cumulative effect of springtime floods and summer heat. The spectacle of the inundation; the mystery of the source of the waters which was not solved until the nineteenth century, had vast effect upon mankind, Egyptians, and all who came after them.

The Negroids came as hunters and fishermen. Probably they came up from Nubia. They began to settle down and till the soil. They were the Tasians, five thousand and more years ago; the people of the Fayum and the Marimde, the Badarians, settled folk, who hunted and fished but also cultivated crops. They made cloth from flax and skins, wove baskets, fashioned pottery, and ground ax heads and vessels. They had copper and varied tools of flint capable of working timber. Ivory was used for tools.

Amratians wandered in. They were of the type of the Beja. They used copper and gold. Thus we see in the Nile valley before the reign of Menes, 3200 B.C., many groups and types of Negroids filtering in slow hesitant waves and gradually settling down in the first great experiment in human civilization.

The Nile valley may be said to have invented agriculture. It was so obvious a way to make an easy living under pleasant conditions. Fresh rich soil rolled in each year, and the waters that brought it kept it moist and fertile. Irrigation became a prime necessity, and flood control. The use of near-by building materials—wood, brick, and stone—became natural; fibers were woven into cloth; architecture followed in the attempt to honor the dead with buildings which the dry climate preserved.

Tools were invented. The first tools were stone, the eolith and the stone ax. Then came metals; copper, especially from Nubia, and then iron. Boats and ships sailed the river and the seas. The list of things which Egypt learned and handed down to us from that far day is enormous: the art of shaving, the use of wigs, the wearing of kilts and sandals, the invention of musical instruments, chairs, beds, cushions, and jewelry. The burial customs discovered in Europe came without reasonable doubt from Africa, brought by African invaders. Later the improvements made by the Egyptians were imitated in Sicily and Italy. Egyptian culture was in this way the forerunner of Greece.

In the meantime, other people, Mongoloids, filtered in from Asia. As the years passed a fixed type of Egyptian began to develop. In Egypt were all the requirements for the first long experiment in civilization in ancient times: a well-watered valley, deserts and mountains on the outskirts to keep back the enemy and the beast; a favorable warm climate and a chance for contact with foreigners which could be regulated so as to keep out the invader and trade with him in goods and ideas. The civilization of Egypt began with their invention of fixing a calendar, 4241 B.C.

There has been a great deal of contradiction and uncertainty concerning the peoples of Northwest Africa, variously called Libyans, Berbers, "Hamites," and Arabs. The Libyans or Berbers were akin to the Egyptians. They arose in prehistoric times in all probability, out of the mixture of Negroid and Mongoloid peoples, Negroids coming up from Central Africa and Mongoloids crossing from Asia. The two types of long-headed and broad-headed peoples can be distinguished even today. Toward the east and the Nile delta were the Egyptians, forefathers of the peoples today called Beja, Galla, Somali, and Danakil.

The Egyptian of predynastic times belonged then to the short, dark-haired, dark-eyed group of peoples, such as are found on both shores of the Mediterranean. The same stock extended beyond Upper Egypt into Nubia. Their physical characteristics exhibited a remarkable degree of homogeneity. Their hair was dark brown or black, and either curled or wavy. In the men there was scant growth of facial hair except on the chin, where a tuft was found. They had long, narrow foreheads and prominent occiputs. The faces were long and narrow ellipses; the noses were broader and especially flatter than those of the Europeans.

The predynastic Egyptian was short, scarcely over sixty-four inches, dolichocephalic, with a nasal index of about 50, all characteristics of a group of people known as Beja, a black people who inhabit the eastern desert of Egypt, the Red Sea province of the Anglo-Egyptian Sudan, and extend through the Italian colony of Eritrea to Abyssinia. The Beja are divisible into four groups, one of which is the "Fuzzy-Wuzzy" of the British soldier. They are the least modified of the Beja tribes and are the modern representatives of the old predynastic Egyptian stock.

In Egypt there is evidence of a gradual modification in the population from the beginning of dynastic times, so that by the Pyramid period Egyptians were of heavier build, with broader skulls and faces and heavier jaws. These are the people portrayed in such magnificent works of art of the Pyramid period as the sphinxes of Gizeh and the Louvre, and they are no doubt representative of a considerable part of the population of the Ancient Kingdom. They were the creators of the finest statuary, wall paintings, and sculptures in low relief to which Egypt attained, and the consciously archaistic Egyptians of the Twenty-sixth Dynasty endeavored to imitate their work as representing the highest development of national art. This applies only to Upper Egypt. We have no knowledge of what was happening in the delta through dynastic and predynastic times; the remains are hidden under great masses of alluvial deposits.

The type described persisted and probably increased in number through dynastic times, and it is that of the fellahin of the present day. The modern Egyptian, with a stature of about sixty-six inches, shows no great variation between Upper and Lower Egypt. He is long-headed. Moreover, in passing southward, it has been pointed out that the eye and skin color darken, that the proportion of unusually broad noses increases, and spiral and crisp hair become more frequent.

The history of civilization which began in Egypt was not so much a matter of dynasties and dates. It was an attempt to settle certain problems of living together—of government, defense, religion, family, property, science, and art. What we must remember is that in these seven lines of human endeavor, it was African Egypt that made the beginning and set the pace.

In some respects what they did has not been greatly improved upon even down to the twentieth century. In a primitive tribe, government was the family. But the valley of the Nile had to expand, rebuild, and implement this. It devised a ruler, a ruling family, and a ruling caste. It put them permanently upon a throne which became so old and stable that no man remembered when there was not an Egypt, and when there had been another world worth knowing. This government had to be built up from the family and clan, and this was accomplished through religion.

The Egyptian religion came naturally from the primitive animism of the African forest and progressed to the worship of Ra, the sun god, giver of life and beauty to the Nile valley which was the world. Opposite Ra was Osiris, god of waters and fertility, and his sister and wife Isis, the black woman. Thus from earliest times women in Egypt had singular prominence and power. The gods reflected the physical facts of the valley. The Greeks called the Egyptians "the most religious of men." There developed an oligarchy of gods and a priesthood which became a center of scientific knowledge; the laws of nature were studied and mathematical formulas devised.

The work of the nation had to be organized, the toil of planting and reaping, irrigation, burden-bearing. Work was organized so that the great mass of the laborers toiled under the whip but toiled according to plan. From their toil arose the concept of property, of wealth to be used by king and priest and noble. Power became concentrated in the hands of the Pharaoh, who headed the clans and nomes. There was a long prehistoric period when many kings fought for supremacy in the valley, but at last there came concentration and unity which existed for an extraordinary length of time.

Egypt did not remain a tyranny; an oligarchy of priests and nobles eventually took power from the Pharaoh. Then in time a popular revolution emancipated the masses. The people of Egypt were not enslaved. They have been described as a "submissive lighthearted race content with little, singing at their toil, working with taste and patience." This was the result of an unusually favorable economic organization. There was no need of starvation, exposure, or want. There was plenty in the valley if the river flow was controlled.

The first duty of government was this control of the river, which led to the power of the king, to the science of the priest, to the independence of the laborer. Egypt under the Eighteenth Dynasty, 1500 B.C., has been called the first human example of state socialism, which was developed to an astonishing degree. Nor was the Egyptian formal and conventionalized. From a stiff traditional art in the earliest days, he developed individuality in expression. His spirit inquired into fresh knowledge in this land where knowledge was "old as the world." The art of hieroglyphic writing was complete at the dawn of history, 3500 B.C., and it lasted three millenniums, until in the fourth century B.C. it was replaced by Coptic and Greek.

Beyond this was the gift of an unusual climate: the dry atmosphere with its baking sun; the chance to preserve what man delineated and carved and built, so that the art and literature of Egypt became first in the world and handed down inestimable treasure to succeeding peoples. The Egyptians studied and knew human beings; they separated their fellows into black people and brown, yellow people and white. They themselves were brown and black and so depicted themselves on their monuments. Many of the yellow peoples from the East filtered in and gradually there evolved a type which we know and would call a mulatto type, although that word brings the notion of a mixture of primary races, which was not true in Egypt. Here then, from the time that the Egyptians began history down to the birth of Christ, for five thousand years mankind evolved a pattern of human culture which became the goal of the rest of the world and was imitated everywhere. When persons wished to study science, art, government, or religion, they went to Egypt. The Greeks, inspired by Asia, turned toward Africa for learning, and the Romans in turn learned of Greece and Egypt.

It would be interesting to know what the Egyptians, earliest of civilized men, thought of the matter of race and color. Of race in the modern sense they seemed to have had no conception. On their monuments they depicted peoples by the color of their skin and their hair. The hair was treated in many ways: sometimes it was straight and Mongoloid; perhaps more often it was curled and Negroid. Now and then it was curly and hidden by wigs. The Egyptians painted themselves usually as brown, sometimes dark brown, sometimes reddish-brown. Other folk, both Egyptians and non-Egyptians, were painted as yellow. Often brown Egyptians were coupled with yellow women, either signifying less exposure to the sun or intermarriage with Mongoloids and whites. A few were painted as white, referring to some parts of North Africa and Europe.

The separation of human beings by color seemed to have had less importance among the Egyptians than the separation by cultural status: black Pharaohs and black women; brown and yellow Pharaohs and yellow women. Their attitude toward people, white or black, was based on cultural contact. Black people and yellow people were often depicted as conquered and yielding obeisance to their brown conquerors. Sometimes they appeared as equals, exchanged gifts and courtesies. Sometimes the Mongoloids and Negroids and whites were bound slaves; but in Egyptian monuments slavery was never attributed solely to black folk.

We conclude, therefore, that the Egyptians were Negroids, and not only that, but by tradition they believed themselves descended not from the whites or the yellows, but from the black peoples of the south. Thence they traced their origin, and toward the south in earlier days they turned the faces of their buried corpses.

Gradually, of course, the Egyptians became a separate inbred people with characteristics quite different from their neighbors. They were brown in color and painted themselves as such, but they recognized other colors and sorts of men. They were in continuous contact with the blacks to the south. Now and then they enslaved the blacks as they did the whites to the west and the yellow people to the east. But in the main their intercourse with the blacks consisted of trading and fighting with a people against whom they must defend themselves fiercely, but upon whom they depended for trade and for immigrants. Continually, black faces appear as Egyptian citizens. Herodotus in the fifth century B.C. described the Egyptians as black with curly hair. "The more we learn of Nubia and the Sudan," wrote Dr. D. Randall-MacIver, "the more evident does it appear that what was most characteristic in the predynastic culture of Egypt is due to intercourse with the interior of Africa and the immediate influence of that permanent Negro element which has been present in the population of southern Egypt from remotest times to our own day."[2]

Sir Flinders Petrie, in the same vein, wrote that it was remarkable how renewed vitality came to Egypt from the south.[3] Seligmann said: "On one of the great proto-dynastic slate palettes dating from circa 3200 B.C. are represented captives and dead with woolly or frizzy hair and showing the same form of circumcision as is now practiced by the Masai and other Negroid tribes of Kenya Colony. Thus, though there is not, and cannot be, any records of skin color, there is every reason to believe that these men were as much 'Negroes' as many of the East African tribes of the present day to whom this name is commonly applied. Moreover, the Archaeological Survey of Nubia has brought to light a burial— with typical Negro hair—dating to the Middle Kingdom (about 2000 B.C.), while four Negresses were found in a single cemetery, dating as far back as the late predynastic period—say about 3000 B.C."[4]

Randall-MacIver of the Department of Egyptology and Arthur Thomson, professor of Anatomy, at Oxford, in a report on what is one of the most extensive and complete surveys of Ancient Egyptian skeletal material ever made, stated that of the Egyptians studied belonging to the periods from the Early Predynastic to the Fifth Dynasty, 24 per cent of the males and 19½ per cent of the females were to be classified as Negroes. "In every character of which we have a measure they conform accurately to the Negro type."

For the period extending from the Sixth to the Eighteenth Dynasty, of the specimens studied about 20 per cent of the males and 15 per cent of the females are grouped with the Negroes. For both periods there was a goodly per cent of specimens, the "intermediates," that show some Negroid traits, but in the "intermediates" the Negro features were not sufficiently numerous or distinct enough to warrant such skeletons being classed with the Negroes.[5] In the United States all these would be legally Negroes.

According to Dr. F. L. Griffith of Oxford, writing of the Negroids of the Old Kingdom, "more than one Nubian (nh'si), dark-colored or Negroid, can be traced as holding a high position in Egypt or even in the royal court at Memphis during the Fourth and Fifth Dynasties."

There are in the Boston Museum of Fine Arts two excellent limestone portraits of an Egyptian prince and his wife dating, according to their discoverer, Dr. Reisner, from the Old Kingdom. The prince shows practically none of the features that are traditionally regarded as being distinctive of the Negro, but the princess presents every earmark of the extreme Negro type.

The famous *Stele of Una* discovered by Mariette at Abydos is "the longest narrative inscription and the most important historical document from the Old Kingdom." Dr. Breasted's interpretation of the text records among other things how Uni, an officer of King Pepi I of the Sixth Dynasty, annihilated a group of Asiatics to the north of Sinai and invaded Palestine with an army "of many tens of thousands," made up of soldiers recruited among "the Irthet Negroes, the Mazoi Negroes, the Yam Negroes, the Wawat Negroes, the Kau Negroes, and Negroes from the land of Temeh." Each of the districts here named has been identified with districts in Ethiopia. The inhabitants of Egypt were thenceforth a Negroid people in which Semitic, Nilotic, and Sudanese-Negro elements were fused.

Before the First Dynasty there must have been a long series of rulers who came out of the south, conquered the people, and consolidated their powers. Upper Egypt historically always had precedence over Lower Egypt, and the First Dynasty came from the direction of the heart of Africa. Eight kings are known in this dynasty, during which there was gradual advance in use of writing. Memphis was established as capital, and the eastern borders of the valley firmly conquered.

The First Dynasty appears to have moved up from Punt. The Third Dynasty, which led to the Fourth, shows a strongly Ethiopian face in Sa Nekht; the Twelfth Dynasty we can trace to a Galla origin; the Eighteenth Dynasty was Ethiopian paled by marriage; the Twenty-fifth Dynasty was from distant Meroe.

Among the Pharaohs of the earlier dynasties whose statues or recovered bones show them to have been deeply tinged with Negro blood are King Den of the First Dynasty, King Khasekhemui of the Second Dynasty.

Sir Harry Johnston wrote: "The Dynastic Egyptians were not far distant in physical type from the Galla of today, but they had perhaps some element of the proto-Semite; and their language is still rather a puzzle to classifiers, though mainly Kushite in its features. The Dynastic Egyptians evidently concentrated themselves in the narrow strip of fertility along the banks of the Nile, not colonizing very markedly the Red Sea coastlands. By about 8000 years ago they had become the conquerors and rulers of Lower and Upper Egypt."

Stone in the Third Dynasty began to be used for building. In the Fourth Dynasty came the great Pyramid of Gizeh, "the greatest monument that any man ever had." It contains more stone than any other building ever erected and yet is one of the earliest structures of the world. Herodotus tells us that one hundred thousand men were levied for three months at a time during the season of inundation when ordinary labor was at a standstill; and yet at this rate the building occupied twenty years. There was probably no hardship in the employment of a

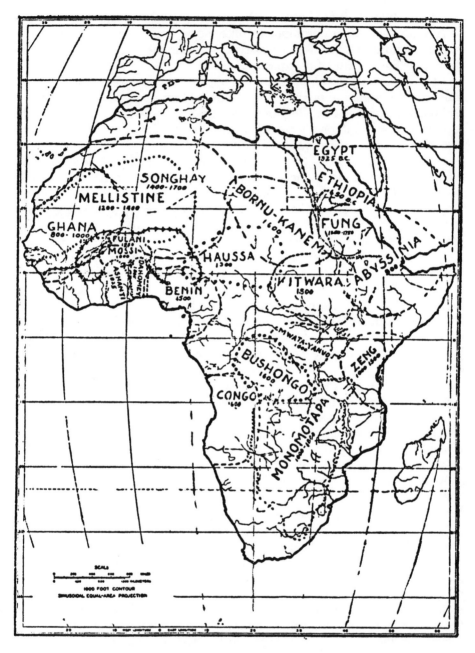

The Political and Cultural Development of Africa
1325 B.C.–A.D. 1850

(The dates indicate roughly the widest development of the different states; the lines show
approximately the boundaries of the states at the date of widest expansion.)

small percentage of the people at this work when all were idle, and the training and skill were of great advantage to the nation.

In the Fourth Dynasty was erected the well-known statue of the Sphinx with the lion's body and Negro head entirely carved in native rock. It must have been carved out of the rocky knoll of a hill. In this dynasty too there was the artistic attempt of man to rival nature. Vast buildings were placed before a background of hills or on a natural height. An artificial hill was built on which some great work of man was placed. Vast masses were used in construction. The sculptor sought to rival and even surpass nature. The painter used coloring and tints.

In the Fifth Dynasty the power of the priests was evidently growing, and religious foundations appear and with it a decline in the boldness of assertion of the earlier architecture. In the Sixth Dynasty came some of the great raids upon the Libyans to the east of Egypt. Tens of thousands of soldiers, Negroes particularly from the Sudan, beat this part of the land into subjection. Then the Pharaoh's army turned south and west and went through Nubia to force into subjection Negroes who were pressing northward upon the Egyptian state. Trading expeditions were sent to Punt. This was a time of active foreign conquest and exploration. One of the kings brought back to Egypt a dwarf from the Sudan.

The Seventh and Eighth Dynasties form an early intermediate period. The power of the kings at Memphis seems to have fallen into decay, perhaps through foreign invasion in the delta. During the Ninth and Tenth dynasties the invading race spread their rule over Upper Egypt. The Middle Kingdom began with the Eleventh Dynasty, when the Princes of Thebes became independent again. The ruler, Usertesen I, is pictured as triumphing over Asiatic and Negro. Evidently the defense of the kingdom from invaders became a serious problem when Egypt grew great and rich. A new vigor came into the administration with Amenemhat, who fought the Nubians and the Asiatics. The history of Sanehat (Sinuhi) is illustrative of the time. Because of the death of his father, he fled to Syria, where he became a ruler. "It gives a very curious view of the relation of Egypt to Syria at the beginning of the Twelfth Dynasty. A fugitive Egyptian was superior to the Syrians, and by his education and ability might rise to high power, much like some English adventurer in Central Africa at the present time."[6]

Ameny has left us a record of what a powerful noble of his day did for the workers. "I was in favour and much beloved, a ruler who loved his city. Moreover, I passed years as ruler in the Oryx nome. All the works of the king's house came into my hands. Behold he set me over the gangers of the lands of the herdsmen in the Oryx nome, and 3000 bulls of their draught stock. . . . Not a daughter of a poor man did I wrong, not a widow did I oppress, not a farmer did I oppose, not a herdsman did I hinder. There was not a foreman of five from whom I took his men for the works. There was not a pauper around me, there was not a hungry man in my time. When there came years of famine, I arose. I ploughed all the fields of the Oryx nome, to its southern and its northern boundaries. I made its inhabitants live, making provision for them; there was not a hungry man in it, and I gave to the widow as to her that had a husband: nor did I favour the elder above the younger in all that I gave. Afterward the great rises of the Nile came, producing wheat and barley, and producing all things, and I did not exact the arrears of the farm."[7]

In this dynasty the Pharaohs began to associate their successors with them so as to make less danger of change at the time of their death. The lakes of Moeris were dammed, and the overflow of the Nile was thus regulated by a vast embankment twenty miles in length.

One king of the Twelfth Dynasty, Usertesen III, was especially triumphant over the Negroes who were threatening Egypt from the south, and this Pharaoh set up a boundary across which the Nubians must not come. To celebrate this clash between the Negroid Egyptian and the Central African, we have the first specimen of Egyptian poetry extant:

> He has come to us, he has taken the land of the well,
>   the double crown is placed on his head.
> He has come, he has united the two lands,
>   he has joined the kingdom of the upper land with the lower.
> He has come, he has ruled Egypt,
>   he has placed the desert in his power.
> He has come, he has protected the two lands,
>   he has given peace in the two regions.
> He has come, he has made Egypt to live,
>   he has destroyed its afflictions.
> He has come, he has made the aged to live,
>   he has opened the breath of the people.
> He has come, he has trampled on the nations,
>   he has smitten the Anu, who knew not his terror.
> He has come, he has protected his frontier,
>   he has rescued the robbed.
> He has come . . .
>   of what his mighty arm brings to us.
> He has come, we bring up our children,
>   we bury our aged by his good favour.[8]

One can see from this poem what national fervor of delight arose in Egypt when the further aggression of Central African tribes was stopped.

The Twelfth Dynasty marks the firm organization of the country and brilliancy of development under able leaders followed by internal prosperity. Then there was a tide of foreign conquest under Usertesen III, a splendid reign under Amenemhat III, followed by a time of decay. The art work of the dynasty was fine, with great technical perfection.

From the Thirteenth to the Seventeenth Dynasties there comes a period which is obscure. During this time Egypt was conquered by the Hyksos kings, who were probably from the Arabian desert; but whether at the beginning or at the end of this period we are not certain. At the end of the kings of the Thirteenth Dynasty comes Ra-Nehesi, the king's eldest son, who is clearly called a Negro. This shows, of course, the development that had taken place in Egypt during two thousand years. There had grown up an Egyptian mulatto race differentiated in color and other physical characteristics from the Central Africans. So much so that the great triumph of Egypt was the conquest over these Africans.

But this did not mean that there were no black folk in Egypt. Despite the general development of the mulatto race, the Negro type emerges here and there and especially in the case of Ra-Nehesi. Perhaps this black Pharaoh was the last defender of Egypt against the Hyksos who came in from Syria and began the conquest of Egypt, which the historian Manetho thus described: "We had formerly a king whose name was Timaios. In his time it came to pass, I know not how, that God was displeased with us; and there came up from the East in a strange manner men of an ignoble race, who had the confidence to invade our country, and easily subdued it by their power without a battle. And when they had our rule in their hands, they burnt our cities, and demolished the temples of the gods, and inflicted every kind of barbarity upon the inhabitants, slaying some, and reducing the wives and children of others to a state of slavery."[9]

The redemption of Egypt from the Hyksos came in the Eighteenth Dynasty through an Ethiopian power. The Hyksos held Egypt perhaps five hundred years; then came Aahmes of the Thebaid. With Aahmes was associated the black Queen Nofritari, or Nefertari.

The stream of Egyptian history in the day of its proudest triumphs now merges into that of Ethiopia, the Land of the Blacks; in such wise that Ethiopian history is seen to be the main current of Negro culture, from the Mountains of the Moon to the Mediterranean, blossoming on the lower Nile, but never severed from the Great Lakes of Inner Africa.

NOTES

1. Winwood Reade, *The Martyrdom of Man* (London: John Lane Company, 1912), 20th ed., p. 1.
2. Arthur Thomson and David Randall-MacIver, *Ancient Races in the Thebaid* (London: 1905).
3. W. M. Flinders Petrie, *A History of Egypt from the Earliest Times to the XVI Dynasty* (London: Methuen & Company, 1903), 5th ed., Vol. I.
4. C. G. Seligmann, *Races of Africa* (New York, Henry Holt & Co., 1930), Ch. III. P. 52.
5. Thomson and Randall-MacIver, *op. cit.*
6. Petrie, *op. cit.*, Vol. I, p. 156.
7. *Ibid.*, Vol. I, pp. 160–61.
8. *Ibid.*, Vol. I, p. 183.
9. *Ibid.*, Vol. I, pp. 233–34.

CHAPTER VI

◆

The Land of the Burnt Faces

This is the story of fifteen hundred years in the valley of the Nile from 2000 B.C. to A.D. 500.

In Greek legend, Ethiopia, "land of the burnt faces," lay either side of the Red Sea in Africa and Asia and was inhabited by black folk. Eventually the blacks mixed with yellow Asiatics. After the fifth and fourth centuries B.C. the term Ethiopia was used usually to designate regions in Africa corresponding to what we now know as Nubia or the Egyptian Sudan. The Sudan was known to the Egyptians and Hebrews as Kash or Cush. In Hebrew folklore the descendants of Ham "were Cush and Egypt."

If efforts have been made to separate the history of Egypt from Africa and the Negro race, a similar determination with regard to Ethiopia is even more contradictory. Science for years tried to separate men into great groups called races; at first the object was to explain human history by human differences. The scientific basis of race difference, however, appeared increasingly difficult as observation and measurement became more accurate. Three, five, twenty races were differentiated, until at last it was evident that mankind would not fit accurately into any scientific delimitation of racial categories; no matter what criteria were used, most men fell into intermediate classes or had individual peculiarities. The theory of absolutely definite racial groups was therefore abandoned, and "pure" racial types came to be regarded as merely theoretical abstractions which never or very rarely existed.

On the other hand, individual variations among men were extraordinary and intriguing; and group differences in physique and cultural habits were equally interesting. It would therefore be helpful to science if the broad hypothetical division of men into three or five great groups in accord with physique and culture were provisionally maintained to facilitate, but certainly not to obstruct, further study. This was the scientific status of the race theory early in the twentieth century, and in accord with this we spoke of three "races"—Caucasoid, Negroid, and Mongoloid—as comprising mankind, knowing well that no scientifically accurate definition of these races could be made which would not leave most of mankind outside the limits.

There was, however, persistent exception to this general agreement; under Caucasoid were included men of widely different physique inhabiting Europe; the term Mongoloid was even more vague and indefinite and nearly fell into disuse. But the term "Negro," as a definite and scientific race designation, persisted, and its use was defended with bitter determination by men who otherwise ranked as leading scientists. Despite the fact that the number of human beings corresponding to the current definition of the word "Negro" was narrowed again and again in space and number to a small remnant even in Africa, nevertheless in the usage of many distinguished writers there really emerged from their thinking two groups of men: Human Beings and Negroes. And the thesis of this book is that this extraordinary result came from the African slave trade to America in the eighteenth century and the capitalistic industry built on it in the nineteenth. The facts referred to are illustrated by the treatment of Ethiopia in archaeology, anthropology, and history. The contradictions concerning this land and people would be ludicrous if the results were not so tragic.

If we follow inherent probability, ancient testimony, and legend, this would seem to have been the history of northeast Africa:

In Ethiopia the sunrise of human culture took place, spreading down into the Nile valley.

Ethiopia, land of the blacks, was thus the cradle of Egyptian civilization.

Beyond Ethiopia, in Central and South Africa, lay the gold of Ophir and the rich trade of Punt on which the prosperity of Egypt largely depended.

Egypt brought slaves from black Africa as she did from Europe and Asia. But she also brought citizens and leaders from black Africa.

When Egypt conquered Asia, she used black soldiers to a wide extent.

When Asia overwhelmed Egypt, Egypt sought refuge in Ethiopia as a child returns to its mother, and Ethiopia then for centuries dominated Egypt and successfully invaded Asia.

Neither Greece, Rome, nor Islam succeeded in conquering Ethiopia, although they pushed her back and shut her up in East and Central Africa, and hindered all contact between her peoples and the world until the day of colonial imperialism.

But this interpretation of Negro history contradicts the theory of the natural and eternal inferiority of black folk, which rendered them natural slaves and a cheap labor force for nineteenth-century industry. Those who depended on slavery and colonialism for living and luxury naturally, and often without conscious intent, sought eagerly for a science and history which would deny this interpretation of African history. They came gradually to declare vehemently that Egypt began her culture in the delta region, and Ethiopia was a far-off frontier and slave mart; that Punt and Ophir were in extreme East Africa or Asia; that the Asiatic conquest of Egypt marked her decline and the feeble efforts of Ethiopia showed an era of decadence; that even if Ethiopia showed some imitative culture, this was not due to black folk, since the Ethiopians were not Negroes!

The attitude of scientists toward these questions has thus been colored almost entirely by their attitude toward modern Negro slavery. The Frenchman Volney called the civilization of the Nile valley Negro after his visit. But such a barrage of denial from later men met him that he withdrew his earlier conclusions, not because of further investigation, but because of scientific public opinion in the nineteenth century. Reisner unearthed a civilization of black folk in Ethiopia, but hastened to declare that they were not Negroes! Reisner was born in sight of Negro slavery in America and never forgot it. Flora Shaw wrote of the blackest men of the Sudan and their brilliant civilization, but warned her readers that they were not Negroes!

So here in Ethiopia, "Land of the Blacks," country of the "Burnt Faces," we are continually faced with the silly paradox that these black folk were not Negroes. What then are Negroes? Who are Africans? Why has the whole history of Ethiopia been neglected or ascribed to white "Hamites"? And why does every historian and encyclopedist, whenever he writes of the civilization of the upper Nile, feel compelled to reiterate that these black people were "not Negroes"?

Again, the mixture of blood among the three races is always referred to as an explanation of the advance among Negroes and the retrogression among whites. Is this scientific? A "white" or Asiatic aristocracy is repeatedly adduced as accounting for the rise of the Sudan, the government of Uganda, the industry of the Bushongo, and even the art of the Ashanti. Nothing is ever said of the influence of Negro blood in Europe and Asia, yet distinct Negroid features can be seen today all over Europe. When a black Jew boasts to his fellow religionists "I am black, but comely, O ye daughters of Jerusalem," he is supposed to be tanned; when Syria and Arabia show in hair and color their Negro blood, this is completely ignored and their culture called "white." When Buddha appears all over Asia portrayed as black and curly-haired, science makes little effort to investigate or explain.

There was and is wide mingling of the blood of all races in Africa, but this is consistent with the general thesis that Africa is predominantly the land of Negroes and Negroid peoples, just as Europe is a land of Caucasoids and Asia of Mongoloids. We may give up entirely, if we wish, the whole attempt to delimit races, but we cannot, if we are sane, divide the world into whites, yellows, and blacks, and then call blacks white.

As in the case of Egypt, I shall hereafter assume that the Ethiopians were Negroids and shall try to let the facts prove their contribution to civilization.

In the eyes of the Greeks a thousand years B.C. and even in the age of Pericles, black Africans were considered equal to though different from Greeks, and superior to European and Asiatic barbarians. Significant indeed was the attitude of the early Greeks toward Africa. It was to them a land of ideals. Here in legend their gods retired to rest and recuperate. In the dawn of Greek literature, in the *Iliad,* we hear of the gods feasting among the "blameless Ethiopians."

According to mythology, the Greek people themselves came into being as the result of miscegenation. Zeus, the Father of the Gods, mates with the fair Greek maiden Io, and has a mulatto son, Epaphus, who is born in Egypt. Aeschylus says of this union, "And thou shall bring forth black Epaphus, thus named from the manner of Zeus' engendering. . . . Fifth in descent from him fifty maidens shall return to Argos [Greece], not of their choice but fleeing marriage with their cousin kin." Also, "Call this the work of Zeus, and that his race sprang from Epaphus, and thou shalt hit the truth."[1]

Two of the most illustrious writers of Greece were called Negroes—Aesop and Sappho. Planudes asserts this; Zundel, Champfleury, and others think that the "woolly-haired Negro" on the coins of Delphos was Aesop. Ovid makes it clear that the ancients did not consider Sappho white. She is compared with Andromeda, daughter of Cepheus, black King of Ethiopia. Ovid says: *"Andromede patriae fusca colore suae."* In Epistle XV of the *Heroides* of Ovid (translated by Ridley), Sappho says to Phaon, "I am small of stature but I have a name that fills all lands. I myself have produced this extended renown for my name. If I am not fair, Andromeda, the daughter of Cepheus, was swarthy though the complexion of her country was pleasing to Perseus. White pigeons, too, are often mated with spotted ones and the black turtledove is often beloved by a bird that is green."[2]

Paul Lacroix says of Sappho: "Although Plato graces her with the epithet of beautiful and although Athenaeus is persuaded of her beauty on the authority of Plato, it is more probable that Maximus of Tyre who paints her for us as little and black is in conformity with more authentic tradition."[3]

Pope's translation of Ovid reads: "Brown as I am, an Ethiopian dame."

Another Negro is mentioned in the Homeric legends, Eurybiates. Homer speaks of his "woolly hair" and "sable skin" and compares him with Ulysses, greatest of the heroes.

> Eurybiates in whose large soul alone
> Ulysses viewed an image of his own.

The Ethiopian Tithonus of Greek legend has been identified with Dedun, the Negro god of the Second Cataract.

"Of all the classical countries Ethiopia was the most romantic and the most remote. It was situated, according to the Greeks, on the extreme limits of the world; its inhabitants were the most just of men, and Jupiter dined with them twice a year. They bathed in the waters of a violet-scented spring, which endowed them with long life, noble bodies, and glossy skins. They chained their prisoners with golden fetters; they had bows which none but themselves could bend. It is certain that Ethiopia took its place among the powers of the ancient world. It is mentioned in the Jewish records and in the Assyrian cuneiform inscriptions."[4]

In Africa were great and powerful kingdoms. When Greek poets enumerated the kingdoms of the earth, it was not only natural but inevitable to mention Memnon, King of Ethiopia, as leader of one of the great armies that besieged Troy. When a writer like Herodotus, father of history, wanted to visit the world, he went as naturally to Egypt as Americans go to London and Paris. Nor was he surprised to find the Egyptians, as he described them, "black and curly-haired."

Herodotus says that the names of nearly all the Greek gods are derived from Egypt, and certainly the Greeks continually turned toward Egypt for cultural inspiration and scientific information. Homer openly borrowed from Egypt his story of Ulysses, and the islands of forgetfulness were based on Egyptian stories.

The Ethiopians are closely linked with the rising and setting of the sun. Memnon, the son of Eos, says Hesiod, is their king. Aeschylus describes the Ethiopians as dark and living near the springs of the sun. Arctinus of Melitus writes of Memnon celebrating his participation on the side of the Trojans and his victory over Antilochus, the son of Nestor, and his eventual death at the hands of Achilles. In a myth of the fifth century B.C., Andromeda was pictured as the black daughter of Cepheus and Cassiopeia, rulers of Ethiopia. She was bound to a rock and saved by Perseus on his return from his battle with the Medusa. Both Sophocles and Euripides wrote plays about Andromeda, and Perseus, Memnon, and Andromeda were worshiped as heroes in Africa and Ethiopia.

The culture of Egypt went out across the Mediterranean, lighting fires in Crete, inspiring Asia from southern Arabia to Syria and western Asia Minor. In Cretan art Negro heads appeared, and in the late Minoan Age, at the time of the expansion overseas, a black Minoan captain led Negro troops. Doubtless Minoans made use of black regiments in their final conquest of Greece, and from vases dated the latter part of the sixth century B.C. it seems clear that Ethiopians entered Greece even before the time of Xerxes. Herodotus tells that in the army of Xerxes there were Ethiopians clothed in leopard and lion skins and armed with bows and arrows. He distinguishes between oriental Ethiopians and western Ethiopians; both were black, but the hair of the former was straighter than the close curled-hair of the latter and they spoke different languages.

Herodotus reduced the races of Ethiopia to four: two native and two foreign; the native were the Ethiopians and the Libyans, and the foreign, the Phoenicians and the Greeks. Among the Libyans, Herodotus and the Egyptians distinguished between Negroids and the Mongoloids: the Negroids came from the south and the Mongoloids from the east. They had mingled in various ways so that one reads of black Getuli and white Ethiopians. The Periplus of Scilex records four Libyan populations, and Diodorus Siculus speaks of three Libyan tribes of which one is Negroid. Thus the Negroid peoples of Africa were represented in neighboring Asia and in North Africa, as well as in the valley of the Nile and Central and West Africa.

Greek culture affected Africa at an early period, and Africa in turn affected Europe. According to Frazer: "It is no longer possible to regard the rule of succession to the priesthood of Diana at Aricia as exceptional; it clearly exemplifies a widespread institution, of which the most numerous and the most similar cases have thus far been found in Africa. How far the facts point to an early influence of Africa on Italy, or even to the existence of an African population in southern Europe, I do not presume to say."[5]

It is admitted today that pre-Greek peoples assembled a considerable body of notable scientific knowledge. Individuals approached their problems with logical powers of deduction and methods of systematization. Two thousand years before Christ an Egyptian physician had made the heart the center of the human system, measured the pulse, and had written down his observations and advice.

In art no race was so interesting to the artists of Greece and Rome as the black man. Other races in the classical world were pictured far less often in Hellenistic and Roman times; the Negro was rendered with fidelity during the most idealistic period of Greek art and with full appreciation of his type of beauty. Appearing at the earliest time, the Negro type continued to be popular throughout the whole period of Greek classical art. The myths of Hercules and of Busirus are painted on a vase dating from the sixth century B.C. Hercules is represented as black and curly haired; the Egyptians of Busirus are represented as both black and yellow, and a bodyguard of five Ethiopians are marching to the defense of Busirus.

There was close and fairly frequent connection between Europe and Africa. In prehistoric times the continents were connected by land. They were separated by no obstacles which hinder migration. The large number of islands scattered through the Mediterranean served as bridges, and peninsulas stretched out from Europe toward Africa. African colonists passed over to Greece by way of the islands beginning with Crete. From Numidia they crossed into Sicily, Italy, and southern France; by Gibraltar into Spain. There is evidence of Negro blood in Asia Minor as far as the Black Sea and the Caucasus Mountains.

The history of Ethiopia consists of a prehistoric period running down to 3500 B.C., a protohistoric period from 3500 to 1723 B.C., and a historic period from 723 B.C. to A.D. 355. In prehistoric times the Ethiopians looked upon themselves as the source of Egypt and declared, according to Diodorus Siculus, that Egyptian laws and customs were of Ethiopian origin. The Egyptians themselves in later days affirmed that their civilization came out of the south, and modern research confirms this in many ways.

If, as is possible, the historic beginnings of Egyptian culture were in the delta, it was doubtless preceded by a long series of cultures streaming up from the south until they met the barriers of the sea and the desert and the invitation of the rich delta soil. Here in the Ethiopia of the Greeks culture became stationary, tied to the soil, expressing itself in agriculture and irrigation; but at the same time it was renewed and challenged by the Negroes who continued to come up from the south.

The incense needed for Egyptian worship was brought to the African coast; the logs of Sudanese ebony, so greatly prized by the Egyptians, grew along the upper course of the Blue Nile. Two trade routes can be traced from the coast of the Red Sea to the valley of the Nile. One followed the course of the Blue Nile and crossed the level plain and the Nile port of Wady Ban-Naga. The other struck across the land to the Atbara, and from there to the fertile valley which ends at Meroe. The Fourth and Fifth Cataracts were avoided by leaving the Nile and striking across the desert to Napata. To what distant date these trade routes go back may be concluded from the predynastic slates which represent the Egyptians invading the country of a woolly-haired race where giraffes browse upon the palms and the guinea-fowl abounds. The home of the giraffe and guinea-fowl since the beginning of the Neolithic period has been the neighborhood of the Blue Nile.

The history of early Egypt was that of a duel between Ethiopia and Egypt, that is, between the ancient African cultures of the Upper Nile and the settled Egyptian culture entrenched in the Nile valley. Over this long stretch of Egyptian history, biological as well as cultural differences appeared. The Egyptians became a settled race-type, brown and yellow in color, with a splendidly developed civilization.

The Ethiopians, on the other hand, were more purely Negroid, brown and black of skin and curly-haired. They were divided into various kingdoms and tribes and were continually raiding Egypt or defending themselves from Egypt, chiefly for the advantages of trade. They eventually became traders and middlemen between Egypt and Central and South-central Africa, and indirectly between Egypt and India. Their own development was in a way changed and directed by the fact that their leaders of ambition and ability were continually drawn off into the Egyptian civilization and rose in many cases to be leaders in Egypt. As Egypt expanded the Ethiopians were pushed back from the First to the Second, Third, and Fourth Cataracts.

During the middle kingdom of Egypt an independent Ethiopian culture developed, centered at Napata and Meroe, which carried on widespread trade in gold, ivory, precious stones, wood, and handicrafts. When at the end of this time the Asiatic Hyksos overthrew Egypt, Ethiopia became a refuge for the conquered Egyptians both physically and culturally. Noble Egyptian families migrated to Ethiopia and intermarried, and one such family formed the great Eighteenth Dynasty which rescued Egypt. From then on larger parts became incorporated into Egypt, and the son of a Pharaoh took the title of Royal Son of Kush. When, however, the Libyans in the Twenty-first Dynasty overthrew Egypt, the Ethiopians organized independently, and from 750 B.C. to A.D. 355 there are records of seventy-six rulers of Ethiopia.

Let us turn back to early Egypt and see the relation between its development to the fall and rise of Ethiopia. From 3115 B.C. to 2360 B.C., for a thousand years, the old kingdom of Egypt was under the stern rule of despotic kings; but with the Sixth Dynasty the power of the pyramid builders began to collapse, and during the years 2360 to 2150 the mass of Egyptian people obtained religious and political rights. During the Middle Kingdom the people began to be admitted to religious rites which were no longer the sole secret of the priesthood.

The monarchy centering at Thebes endured a thousand years, from 2160 B.C. to 1100 B.C. The courts became centers of social law, and by the time of the Eighteenth Dynasty a state socialism had been established. Egypt in these days was not a large country according to modern ideas. It had during the Theban monarchy some eight million people. In the end it was the Saiti kings from the delta who opened Egypt to a flood of foreigners. The Greeks came, and Egypt was turned into a teacher of the world; its culture spread. Alexander and the Caesars sat at its feet.

With the Eighteenth Dynasty came the New Empire, and we are on firm historical grounds as to dates. It came to power in 1580 B.C. and lasted until 1345. Its center of power was Thebes, three hundred miles from Memphis and four hundred miles south of the Mediterranean. It was less than one hundred miles from the First Cataract, the legendary southern boundary of Egypt. The power of Aahmes was probably reinforced by his marriage with an Ethiopian princess, Nefertari, or Nofritari, who was invariably painted black in Egyptian art and yet who was, as Petrie says, "the most venerated figure of Egyptian history."

Her statue in the Turin Museum represents her as having black skin. She is also painted black standing before Amenothes in the Deir el Medineh tomb, now in the Berlin Museum. This queen with a black skin has therefore been regarded as a Negress, the daughter of an Ethiopian Pharaoh, or at any rate the daughter of a chief of some Nubian tribe;[6] it was thought that Aahmes must have married her to secure the help of the Negro tribes in his wars, and that it was owing to this alliance that he succeeded in expelling the Hyksos.[7]

Naturally the legend of this black queen has caused heart-searching among white Egyptologists; they have called her "Libyan"; and Libya was certainly partly Negroid in race; but since the Libyans have usually been counted "white," why was the Libyan Nofritari black?

Nofritari reigned for a time conjointly with Amenothes, and we know that her rule was a prosperous one and that she was revered by her subjects. The remembrance of Nofritari always remained distinct in their minds, and her cult spread until it became a kind of popular religion.[8]

In the Eighteenth Dynasty all workers were organized in guilds under the state. There were scribes to guide them and voice the law. There were local assemblies to stop oppression "of the free man." Legally the Pharaoh owned all the land, but it was assigned to individuals and descended through the eldest son. The Pharaoh always kept the right of eminent domain. Soldiers were established upon freeholds and the priests had large holdings; then came lands assigned to the peasants and to tenants.

Except for the religious land for temples and burial places, the Pharaoh represented the state, held eminent domain over all land, all workers, and all renters. All sources of revenue belonged to the state, and the exploiters of the land and of trade must account to the state, usually through the head of the family. There could be no change of ownership without consent of the Pharaoh or his representative. Usually the state collected one-fifth of the crop as tax. The artisans worked in state studios. The slavery of aliens was limited by treaties with their chiefs. The state controlled all commerce.

Thebes was at the time a city of one hundred thousand and a state capital a thousand years before Rome. It was a planned city, as all Egyptian communities were planned, centering around the square with four walls, and six streets lined with workers' houses on each side. Each house had four rooms and a second story.

Aahmes reigned from 1580 B.C. to 1577 B.C., and his son, Amenophis I, from 1577 B.C. to 1536 B.C. Amenophis I finally conquered an Ethiopian Kingdom named Kerma, which had been threatening Egypt since the Twelfth Dynasty, or about 1785 B.C. Then came by marriage Tuthmosis I, the conqueror of Syria and the valley of the Euphrates, where the Egyptians probably for the first time in their history saw mountains covered with snow. Tuthmosis I pushed Egyptian domination beyond the Third Cataract. After Tuthmosis I came his son Tuthmosis II, who reigned conjointly with his half-sister Hatshepsut for two or three years, then associated upon the throne a son by a concubine, Tuthmosis III. After the death of Tuthmosis II, Hatshepsut assumed full power and was the acknowledged ruler of Egypt. The temple of Deir el Bahri, "Sublime of the Sublime," designed by Tuthmosis II was completed by her in 1500 B.C., and it represented her expedition to Punt. The king and queen of Punt are represented as of the modern Hottentot type, and the queen with the characteristic steatopygia. After Hatshepsut's death Tuthmosis III came into full power.

His granite head in the British Museum has distinct Negro features. He extended Egyptian power east and south. He conquered Syria in seventeen campaigns and crossed the Euphrates. He fought in Libya and in Ethiopia. His reign was without doubt, as Petrie said, "one of the grandest and most eventful in Egyptian history." He repressed robbery and injustice, did much building and adorning of temples with the labor of his captives; and by taking the children of subdued kings in Asia as hostages to Egypt, established his empire on a sound basis perhaps for the first time in history. His empire extended from Napata to the Euphrates. The Assyrians and Babylonians sent their daughters to him in marriage, and the descendants of Syrian rulers, conquered by his father and educated in Egypt, ruled as slaves of the Pharaoh. Tribute poured into Egypt. He reigned thirty-six years until the Hittites from the north and the Khabiri from the east began to press down upon Syria. His son Amenophis II, whom he had associated on his throne, reigned twenty-six years, leaving his throne to Tuthmosis IV.

This monarch married a black woman, Mutemua. Their son, Amenophis III, succeeded about 1400 B.C. He built the temple of Luxor at Karnak. He inherited his mother's Negroid features and married the brilliant Taia. It is possible that the Greeks derived the name of "Memnon, king of the Ethiopians," from this Pharaoh. J. G. Wilkinson says of Amenophis III: "The features of this monarch cannot fail to strike everyone who examines the portraits of Egyptian kings as having more in common with the Negro than those of any other Pharaoh."[9] Anna Graves says: "Amenophis, or Amenhotep, III (1411–1375 B.C.) was evidently what, south of Mason and Dixon would be called a 'colored man,' and his chief queen Taia must have had much more Negro blood than her husband. Indeed, judging from her portrait bust in the Berlin Gallery . . . she may have been very nearly pure Nubian. Their son, Amenophis, or Amenhotep, IV (1375–1358 B.C.), who later took the name Akhnaton, or Akhenaton, though less Negroid than his mother was more of the mulatto type than his father, and the portrait bust of his daughters show them all to be beautiful quadroons, though perhaps octoroons. And this mulatto Pharaoh, Akhenaton, was not only the most interesting Pharaoh in all the long lines of the many dynasties; but he was in many ways one of the most remarkable human beings who ever lived."[10]

It was this ruler who brought profound revolution in the religion of Egypt, changed it to an imperial monotheism, and introduced a philosophical worship of the powers of nature. The great hymn to the sun came from this reign:

> In the hills from Syria to Kush, and the plain of Egypt,
> Thou givest to every one his place, thou framest their lives;
> To every one his belongings, reckoning his length of days;
> Their tongues are diverse in their speech,
> Their natures in the colour of their skin.
> As a divider, thou dividest the strange peoples.[11]

Along with this religious change went a change in ethics, and the glorifying of war almost disappeared. "Living in truth" was made characteristic of the Pharaoh and domestic affection the ideal of life. In art there was a direct study of nature and drawing away from convention.

Universal humanitarianism arose under the reforms of Amenophis IV:

> Thou didst create the earth in thy heart, the earth with people, herds, and floods . . .
> the foreign lands: Syria, Nubia, Egypt. Thou settst every man in his place. . . . They
> speak in diverse tongues, they are varied in form and color of skin.[12]

During the reign of his successor Tutankhaton, or Tutankhamen, whose tomb
was found by Lord Carnarvon and Howard Carter, there was a reaction toward
the older forms of religion, until in a succeeding reign Akhenaton was reviled
as a criminal.

The founder of the Nineteenth Dynasty, Rameses I, and his son, Seti I, became
great builders of temples at Karnak and elsewhere. Then came the long reign of
sixty-seven years of Rameses II, the Conqueror, who built monuments all over
Egypt and Nubia and fought against the Libyans, Syrians, and Hittites. His conquests eventually exhausted the nation, which became prey to the Libyans and
the peoples pressing down from the delta.

It was around 2500 B.C. that the Hebrew nation had begun to arise. It became
enslaved in Egypt, perhaps in the time of Rameses I. Its history touched Ethiopia
at many points, and Jews showed the blacks the highest respect.

In personal relations there were repeated bonds between Jews and Ethiopians.
A black minister of state, Ebedmelech, rescued the prophet Jeremiah from prison:

> Now when Ebedmelech the Ethiopian, one of the eunuchs which was in the king's
> house, heard that they had put Jeremiah in the dungeon; the king then sitting in the
> gate of Benjamin; Ebedmelech went forth out of the king's house, and spake to the
> king, saying, My lord the king, these men have done evil in all that they have done
> to Jeremiah the prophet, whom they have cast into the dungeon; and he is like to
> die for hunger in the place where he is: for there is no more bread in the city. Then
> the king commanded Ebedmelech the Ethiopian, saying, Take from hence thirty
> men with thee, and take up Jeremiah the prophet out of the dungeon, before he die.
> So Ebedmelech took the men with him, and went into the house of the king under
> the treasury, and took thence old cast clouts and old rotten rags, and let them down
> by cords into the dungeon to Jeremiah. And Ebedmelech the Ethiopian said unto
> Jeremiah, Put now these old cast clouts and rotten rags under thine armholes under
> the cords. And Jeremiah did so. So they drew up Jeremiah with cords, and took him
> up out of the dungeon: and Jeremiah remained in the court of the prison.[13]

Moses married a black woman:

> And Miriam and Aaron spake against Moses because of the Ethiopian woman
> whom he had married: for he had married an Ethiopian woman.[14]

Jehovah is said to have punished these protests by making Miriam a leper.
Aaron admitted:

> We have done foolishly.

The writer of the Song of Solomon defended the color of the Ethiopians:

> I am black but comely, O ye daughters of Jerusalem!

Jewish writers pictured Ethiopia as one of the most powerful countries of their day, equal in strength to Egypt, Persia, Assyria, and Babylon:

> Ethiopia and Egypt were her strength, and it was infinite; Put and Lubim were thy helpers.[15]
> With twelve hundred chariots, and threescore thousand horsemen: and the people were without number that came with him out of Egypt; the Lubims, the Sukkiims, and the Ethiopians.[16]

The prophet Isaiah wrote the well-known appeal to Ethiopia:

> Ah! Land of the buzzing wings,
> Which lies beyond the rivers of Ethiopia,
> That sends ambassadors by sea,
> In papyrus vessels on the face of the waters:
> To a nation tall and sleek,
> To a nation dreaded near and far,
> To a nation strong and triumphant.[17]

Jews hoped that Ethiopia might turn to the Jewish faith:

> Princes shall come out of Egypt; Ethiopia shall soon stretch out her hands unto God.[18]
> Are ye not as children of the Ethiopians unto me, O children of Israel? saith the Lord. Have not I brought up Israel out of the land of Egypt? and the Philistines from Caphtor, and the Syrians from Kir?[19]
> For I am the Lord thy God, the Holy One of Israel, thy Saviour: I gave Egypt for thy ransom, Ethiopia and Seba for thee.[20]
> The sons of Ham; Cush, and Mizraim, Put, and Canaan.[21]
> And the sons of Ham; Cush, and Mizraim, Put, and Canaan.[22]

Shabaka of Ethiopia or "So, King of Egypt," as the Jews called him,[23] was the cause of the overthrow of Hoshea, last king of Israel. Isaiah summoned the Ethiopians in the struggle against Sennacherib. Repeatedly the Jews made alliance with the Ethiopians.

> And he heard say concerning Tirhakah king of Ethiopia, He is come forth to make war with thee. And when he heard it, he sent messengers to Hezekiah. . . .[24]

He was assured that with this mighty ally the God of Israel would overthrow the Assyrians.

Taharqa joined battle against Sennacherib in accordance with the treaty made with Hezekiah. Sennacherib's army was destroyed miraculously, as the Jews believed, and Taharqa recovered the cities of Palestine which had formerly belonged to Egypt.

The Jews envied the resources of Ethiopia:

> Come up, ye horses; and rage, ye chariots; and let the mighty men come forth; the Ethiopians and the Libyans, that handle the shield; and the Libyans, that handle and bend the bow.[25]
>
> But he shall have power over the treasures of gold and of silver, and over all the precious things of Egypt: and the Libyans and the Ethiopians shall be at his steps.[26]

They threatened that great as Ethiopia was, the Lord of Israel would eventually overcome them and other enemies:

> Thus saith the Lord, The labour of Egypt, and merchandise of Ethiopia and of the Sabeans, men of stature, shall come over unto thee, and they shall be thine: they shall come after thee; in chains they shall come over, and they shall fall down unto thee, they shall make supplication unto thee, saying Surely God is in thee; and there is none else, there is no God.[27]
>
> And the sword shall come upon Egypt, and great pain shall be in Ethiopia, when the slain shall fall in Egypt, and they shall take away her multitude, and her foundations shall be broken down. Ethiopia, and Libya and Lydia, and all the mingled people, and Chub, and the men of the land that is in league, shall fall with them by the sword.
>
> Persia, Ethiopia, and Libya with them; all of them with shield and helmet. . . .[28]

Rameses III represented the decadence of Egypt and concentration of land ownership in the hands of the priests. The end of this dynasty came in 1100 B.C., and from then on Egypt declined. First there were the Libyan dynasties in the delta from 1100 to 945. The Twenty-second and Twenty-third Dynasties had rival princes fighting among themselves and seeking to re-establish their control over Egypt. But in the meantime Ethiopia arose, and the Ethiopian, Piankhi, became head of the Twenty-fifth Dynasty, 712 B.C.

When the New Empire began to decline, a governor-general rebelled and the kingdom of Ethiopia was established. It was a dominion composed of brown men and black men, shepherds and savages, Egyptians and Negroes, ruled over by a king and a college of priests. It was enriched by annual excursions into the black country, and by the caravan trade in ivory, gold dust, and gum. It also received East Indian goods and Arabian produce through its ports on the Red Sea. Meroe, its capital, attained the reputation of a great city; it possessed temples and pyramids like those of Egypt, only on a smaller scale. The Ethiopian empire, in its best days, comprised the modern Egyptian provinces of Kordofan and Senaar, with the mountain kingdom of Abyssinia as it existed under Theodore.

The first capital of the Sudan was Napata. Here Amenophis II of the Eighteenth Dynasty brought one of the rebellious princes of northern Syria, and, after putting him to death, hung his body on the walls of the city as a warning to the Sudanese tribes. How much older than the Eighteenth Dynasty Napata may have been is uncertain.

As long as the Sudan continued as part of the Egyptian empire, it was ruled by Egyptian viceroys. The name and worship of Ammon, the god of Thebes, were carried southward, and it is possible that Napata, of which Ammon became the supreme divinity, was under Theban priests. When the Libyan Shishak usurped the throne of the Pharaohs in the tenth century B.C., the descendants of the Theban priest-kings of the Twenty-first Dynasty are believed to have retreated to Napata and there established a theocratic monarchy. The decline of the Bubastite dynasty enabled one of these, Piankhi, to assert once more the claim of his family to the throne of Egypt, and to overrun the valley of the Nile almost as far as the Mediterranean. He led the Ethiopians against the Libyans and overthrew them; and he made Egypt a dependency of Ethiopia. The heir to the throne was called "Prince of Egypt." At his death in 710 B.C., Shabaka became king of the two lands. Herodotus said that he abolished capital punishment in Egypt. Kashto, Sahbatok, Taharqa, and Tanut-Amon, succeeded Piankhi and founded the Ethiopian dynasty which governed Egypt from 715 B.C. onward, until they were driven back to Ethiopia by the Assyrians.

Their names show that the ruling caste in the Sudan was Ethiopian, and they were hailed in Upper Egypt as the rightful lords of the country and as the successors of the ancient Pharaohs. On a stela of the Assyrian king Esar-haddon, Taharqa is depicted as a Negro with a ring through his lip; but Taharqa was never a prisoner in Assyrian hands. We see now that out of the remote regions of the Upper Nile the Ethiopians emerged and attempted in the world an imperial role, but they faced in the years from 750 B.C. to 500 B.C. the empire building in western Asia.

The history of western Asia and Asia Minor during this period is difficult to summarize, but in earliest times we find Sumerians in the Tigris-Euphrates area, evidently Mongoloids. They attempted development there similar to the development in the Nile valley. Then out of Arabia began to stream a series of peoples. The Babylonians appeared more than three thousand years B.C. In the eighth century before Christ the Hittites moved eastward from Asia and threatened Egyptian power until Rameses II defeated them at Kadesh. Then from the mountain lands northeast of the Euphrates the Assyrians came down, "like a wolf on the fold." They overthrew Nineveh in 612 B.C. and themselves bowed before the Scythians and the Medes. A new Babylonian imperialism followed, and then came Cyrus, the Persian. In the sixth century B.C. Sardis fell, and soon the cry "Babylon is fallen, is fallen," went throughout the East.

Asia precipitated itself upon Africa. Egyptian civilization fell before the Mongoloid intruder. The Nile valley was swept by vast forces just as the renewed Ethiopian kingdom came to power. It was the heyday of Negro imperialism. Black Africa was still pressing up from the center of the continent, as it had for thousands of years. Yellow Asia was bearing down on Egypt in flood after flood of differing oncoming peoples. Phoenicia was inspiring Carthage and beginning North African development, which pressed on western Egypt. In the center of these forces the Egyptian empire, incredibly ancient, had fallen, first before the Hyksos, and then later before other eastern Asiatic tribes. Ethiopia had restored her, but the situation in the closed valley of the Nile did not invite or encourage expansion in face of the increased might of armed enemies. Ethiopian imperialism, therefore, while striking and effective, lasted but two centuries.

The Assyrians defeated the forces of Egypt and drove back the Ethiopians until at last, from 688 B.C. to 663 B.C., came the greatest of the Ethiopian kings, Taharqa.

His reign was an era of prosperity and cultural advancement. Weigall called his reign "that astonishing epoch of nigger domination"; and Randall-MacIver said: "It seems amazing that an African Negro should have been able with any sort of justification to style himself Emperor of the World." Taharqa ascended the throne in 688 B.C. at the age of about forty-two. For fifteen years he fostered the economic, cultural, and religious life of Ethiopia and Egypt. The trade of the country increased, and there was money to repair the ancient temples and build new ones. Taharqa established friendly alliances with western Asia and with Assyria. The Hebrew Bible chronicles this in the downfall of Sennacherib, and notes Ethiopia's trade.[29]

Taharqa's building at Karnak was planned as one of the most striking in the ancient world. The temple built at Thebes had a relief representing the four courts of the four quarters of the Nilotic world: Dedun, the great God of Ethiopia, represents the south; Sopd, the eastern desert; Sedek, the western desert; and Horus, the north. According to Petrie: "This shows how southern was the center of thought when the whole of Egypt is reckoned as the north. Some writers say that Taharqa led expeditions as far as the Strait of Gibraltar."[30]

Eventually the Assyrians were too strong for Taharqa and he had to give up Egypt and retire into Ethiopia and the "night of death." Tanutamen, his successor, held back the Assyrian storm for awhile,[31] but Ethiopian and Egyptian strength were eventually dashed to pieces. Egyptian temples were wrecked, and the conqueror, Ashurbanipal, declared: "I captured Thebes like a flood. . . ."

Aspeluta, a full-blooded Negro, ruled probably from 593 B.C. to 567 B.C. In 524 B.C. Cambyses, the Persian, having conquered Egypt, tried to invade Nubia, but was defeated and his fleet destroyed. Horsiatef (c. 372–361 B.C.) made nine expeditions against the warlike tribes south of Meroe, which was attacked unsuccessfully by the Rehrehsa under their chief Arua. One successor was Nastasen (c. 328–308 B.C.), who removed the capital from Napata to Meroe, although Napata continued to be the religious capital and the Ethiopian kings were still crowned on its golden throne. Nastasen was saluted king by the priests of Ammon from both Meroe and Napata. He called himself king of To-Kenset (or Nubia, including Dongola), and of the city of Alut. Alut was an alternative name of Meroe.

Meroe, between the Atbara River and the Blue Nile, was founded later than Napata, probably around the eighth century B.C. The site of the town was well chosen. It stood on the bank of the Nile, between the Fifth and Sixth Cataracts, and at the end of a valley which extended for many miles into the interior. During the rainy season the valley afforded an easy road for caravans coming across the Atbara from the Red Sea. The city of Meroe was the natural outlet on the Nile of the more northern prehistoric trade route from the East. Immediately to the north of it were hills containing the extensive quarries where stones used in the construction of its buildings were worked. Northward there was navigation down the Nile to Berber, where the desert road to Napata left the river.

The mission sent by Nero to discover the sources of the Nile reported that Meroe was three hundred and sixty Roman miles from Napata, and seventy miles south of the Atbara. Opposite the city was the island of Tadu, which sheltered the harbor from the northwest wind. At the time of the visit of the Romans the town seems to have fallen into decay in consequence of its capture and partial destruction by some enemy, but it was said to have once supported two hundred thousand soldiers and four thousand artisans. It was then ruled, according to Pliny, by a queen named Candace, who had had forty-four predecessors on the throne.

During the period from 308 B.C. to 225 B.C., there were ten rulers, five reigning at Napata and five at Meroe. The Ptolemies did not invade Nubia but tried to obtain trade by peaceful inroads. Ergamenes (225–200 B.C.) who was brought up at the court of Ptolemy II, united the "nine nations" of Ethiopia. Six kings reigned over the whole of Ethiopia; then came nine kings, of whom four reigned at Meroe, and five at Napata. These were succeeded by three kings ruling over a united Ethiopia. A great builder, Netekamane, appeared, who with his queen Amanetari is depicted on temples at many points up the Nile.

This history of Ethiopia[32] means that out of the south for many thousands of years migrations streamed northward for settlement and for trade, to furnish soldiers for the armies of the Pharaohs and to reach a better climate and opportunities for defense. Down toward the hot center of Africa human culture had to fight the insects and disease and found no natural barriers to protect them against oncomers. There were probably movements south and west from the Great Lakes, but the lure of Egypt attracted the larger streams, and, as Chamberlain has said, this migration was at once advantageous and detrimental to Central Africa. It continually siphoned off the able and the adventurous into the great opportunities of Egypt. Egypt profited and grew on these new resources of inspiration. Individual Negroes became Egyptians and occupied high places, but left their own southern brethren the poorer from this continuous loss of ability and strength.

Books were written about Ethiopia by Dalion, Aristocreon, Basilis, Bion, and Simonides the Younger, the last of whom resided for five years in Meroe.[33] As early as 431 B.C. the trade of Egypt was well known in Athens. Sails and papyrus rolls came from Egypt and ivory from Libya. The slaves were usually not from Africa but from Asia.

It was natural that Alexander, seeking to conquer the world, should bring his conquest to a triumphant end by overthrowing Egypt and establishing there his capital, Alexandria. Alexander had Negroes in his armies. One of the most illustrious was Clitus, his best beloved, whom he made King of Bactria and commander of his cavalry. Clitus' mother, Dropsica, was Alexander's nurse, and Clitus is mentioned by Plutarch and others as Clitus Niger, that is, "Clitus the Negro."[34]

There are legends of the visit of Alexander the Great to Candace, Queen of Meroe. Fabulous perhaps, but they show her fame. It is said that Candace would not let Alexander enter Ethiopia and warned him not to scorn her people because they were black, for they were whiter in soul than his white folk. "She sent him gold, maidens, parrots, sphinxes, and a crown of emeralds and pearls. She ruled eighty tribes, who were ready to punish those who attacked her."[35] The Ptolemies were in contact with the Abyssinians. The earliest Ptolemies were white; but as time went on they changed more and more toward the Negroid. "The Negro strain in Alexander II is apparent, and still more so in Ptolemy XIII, the flute-playing father of the most celebrated of the Cleopatras. Ptolemy's mother was a slave. Cleopatra herself is known through tradition as having been of a tawny, or mulatto color."[36]

From 332 B.C., when Alexander the Great conquered Egypt, down to the conquest of Egypt by Rome after the birth of Christ, Egyptian civilization was subject to increasing Grecian influences and Grecian migration. During the time of Augustus Caesar a club for women existed in the Egyptian capital, Alexandria. About 240 B.C. there was said to have been four hundred and ninety thousand rolls of manuscript in the Alexandria library. The directors of this library were distinguished literary and scientific figures.

When Greece fell under the domination of expanding Rome, the greatest prize of the new empire was Egypt, not simply the valley of the Nile, but the whole of North Africa from the Strait of Gibraltar east and across the Red Sea. The Romans called the district about Carthage, Africa. It held not only Caucasoids from Europe and Mongoloids from Asia, but brown Moors and black Numidians. Roman expeditions went south toward the center of Africa where other black folk and great beasts like the rhinoceros were discovered. There was an expedition under the Romans led by Julius Maternus under the Emperor Domitian in A.D. 80, which searched for gold mines in the Sudan.

The duel between Europe and Africa came with the Punic Wars: the first from 264 to 241 B.C.; the second from 218 to 201 B.C.; and the final one from 149 to 146 B.C. These wars started as efforts to defend Italy against migration and conquest from Africa, where Mongoloids and Negroids with some infiltrating of Europeans had built the city of Carthage. Within this city all races were represented, and Carthage secured a stronghold in Sicily which the first Punic War was fought to break.

The second Punic War began with the invasion of Spain by Carthage and the eruption of the Carthaginian army into Italy. The leader, Hannibal, was finally driven back into Africa. Hannibal and his African troops must have brought a strong Negro strain into the Roman population. For thirteen years they dominated the peninsula from Naples to the Alps. Hannibal himself, if we believe his coins, may well have been a Negro with woolly hair. His wife was Spanish.[37] In Rome the spread of the plantation system after the second Punic War led to the wide use of slaves, but these slaves were from Greece and from Spain.

It was during the next fifty years that the cry raised by Cato the Elder, "Carthage must be destroyed," spread through Rome, making common cause with the black rebel, Massinissa. The Romans attacked again and Carthage fell. Fifty thousand Carthaginians were sold into slavery. Massinissa died in 143 B.C. and was succeeded by his son Micipsa, and his grandson Jugurtha. It was Jugurtha who called Rome "a city for sale and doomed to perish as soon as it finds a purchaser." The war was renewed in Africa, but finally Jugurtha fell into an ambush and was carried as a prisoner to Rome. He and his two sons figured in the triumphs of Marius. He was murdered in prison beneath the capitol.

In Numidia, Rome found itself opposed by the Negroid king Cyphax. Under Diocletian, Numidia was separated from Africa and became one of the seven provinces of the continent. It reached under Constantine a high degree of civilization, but was overthrown by the Vandals in A.D. 428 and again by the Arabs in the eighth century.

On the death of Cleopatra, Egypt became a province of the Roman Empire and Augustus sent a prefect there. The power of Ethiopia had already declined before black invaders from the west. The prefect Gallus summoned these chiefs and granted them their independence under the power of Rome in A.D. 29. After his death the blacks revolted and advanced northward. The Romans sent a great army of ten thousand infantry and eight hundred cavalry to suppress thirty thousand rebels. The Romans were victorious and advanced on the Ethiopians at Napata, where a Candace, "a masculine woman with one eye," was reigning. She is probably the "Candace" mentioned in Acts 8:27:

> And he arose and went; and, behold, a man of Ethiopia, an eunuch of great authority under Candace queen of the Ethiopians, who had charge of all her treasure, and had to come to Jerusalem for to worship, Was returning and sitting in his chariot. . . .

Petronius captured Napata, and a thousand prisoners were sent to Caesar as slaves and many were sold at auction. Nevertheless, as soon as Petronius left, Candace attacked the Roman garrison. The Ethiopians demanded the right to lay their case before Caesar, which was granted, and Caesar remitted the tribute.

In this era there was born in the Egypto-Syrian area, with its Mongoloid and Negroid elements, a social reformer called Jesus Christ. Nordics who have never accepted his doctrine of submission to evil, repudiation of riches, and love for mankind, have usually limned him as Caucasoid. He was probably a swarthy Syrian Jew, with hooked nose and curled hair; perhaps he even inherited Ethiopian blood. He probably looked like that Jew at whom Hitler stared in Vienna: "One day when I was walking through the inner city, I suddenly came upon a being clad in a long caftan, with black curls."[38] From that day dates his active anti-Semitism. Jesus tried to make men better, simpler, truer; he did not succeed. He was charged with blasphemy and treason, and hanged on nails until he was dead. Around legends of his person and ideals have been built creeds, churches, inquisitions, and dreams. Finally there arose the organized and institutionalized Christian Church.

The Roman Emperor Nero, A.D. 54–68, planned to invade Ethiopia and sent some scouts to report. They penetrated as far as the region of the Saad. For the next two hundred years the Nubians and other desert tribes did as they pleased; the power of Ethiopia continued to decline. From the beginning of the third century tribes from the eastern desert, probably the modern Beja, invaded Egypt and plundered; they became masters of southern Egypt during the reign of Aurelian. The Romans continued to have so much trouble with their Ethiopian frontier that finally, when the Abyssinians appeared in the east, the Emperor Diocletian invited the Nubians from the west to repel them. These Nubians finally embraced Christianity, and northern Ethiopia came to be known as Nubia. The Roman garrisons were withdrawn and the Romans depended upon the Nubians from Darfur and Kordofan to protect their interests. Diocletian gave these Nubians land and a yearly subsidy and also subsidized the Beja. During the reigns of Theodosius and Justinian these tribes again and again broke into uneasy revolt.

Black Africa widely influenced Rome. Many of her great men were called "African" because of their birth, and some of these had Negro blood. Terentius Afer (Terence the African) was an ex-slave whose complexion was described by Suetonius, as *fuscus,* or dusky. Terence was the greatest of the Latin stylists, the author of six plays. He is famous mostly, however, for his *"Homo sum; humani nihil a me alienum puto"*—"I am a man and nothing human is alien to me."

Virgil mentions a beautiful black boy:

quamvis ille niger, quamvis tu candidus esses
o formose puer,
nimium ne crede colori:
alba ligustra cadunt, vaccinia nigra leguntur.

Two Latin epigrams praised the Egyptian hunter Olympius:

Nil tibi forma nocet nigro fuscata colora. . . .

Vivet fama tui post te longaeva decoris
Atque tuum nomen semper Karthago loquetur.

In A.D. 330 the Eastern Roman Empire was established at Constantinople. It became Greek rather than Roman, and Christian even before Rome was Christian. This empire had strong connections with Africa: it traded not only with the valley of the Nile but even with the West Coast of Africa. As Mommsen said: "It was through Africa that Christianity became the religion of the world. Tertullian and Cyprian were from Carthage; Arnobius from Sicca Veneria; Lactantius, and probably in like manner Minucius Felix, in spite of their Latin names, were natives of Africa, and not less so, Augustine. In Africa the Church found its most zealous confessors of the faith and its most gifted defenders."[39]

Origen, Athanasius, and Saint Cyril were from the Nile valley. At the head of the Catholic hierarchy at Rome, three popes were African by birth: Victor I (187–198), who defended the Roman date for Easter; Miltiades (311–314), who was pope when the Emperor entered Rome as a Christian; and Gelasius I (492–496), who defended the rights of the papacy against the state.

The Africa here referred to was the Africa above the Sahara Desert; there, as we have seen, Negroid blood was widespread, and in the valley of the Nile the Coptic Church, representing black Africa more directly, was organized. The patriarchate had a hundred bishoprics in the fourth century. In 330 Saint Athanasius, bishop of Alexandria, consecrated Fromentius as Bishop of Ethiopia.

On the highlands of Ethiopia, Negroid and Mongoloid peoples had united to found a center of trade and government more than a thousand years before Christ. From this Axumite Kingdom came the legend of the Queen of Sheba. As

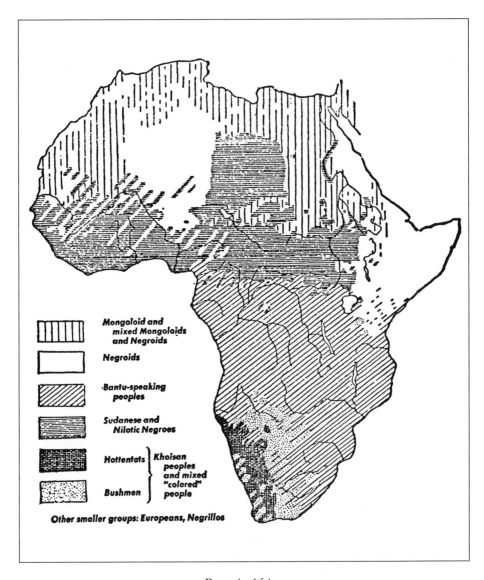

Races in Africa

From *Les Races de L'Afrique*. Paris. Payot. 1935.

early as 1800 B.C. the descendants of Jokdan, seafaring Arabs, had conquered the shores of the Red Sea opposite Abyssinia and founded Yemen. It was along this route that Pharaoh Necho's expedition went around Africa from east to west. The Periplus of the Erythraean Sea, dated from A.D. 60 to 80, shows the increasing commerce around this eastern horn to Africa.

Abyssinia for a time controlled both its own country and Yemen, and King Kaleb conquered Yemen in 525 and held it fifty years. Eventually the Abyssinians were expelled from Arabia and shut themselves up on their highlands where, as Gibbon said, "encompassed by the enemies of their religion, the Ethiopians slept for nearly a thousand years forgetful of the world by whom they were forgotten." Throughout the Middle Ages the legend of this Christian kingdom under Prester John persisted. At one time the Abyssinians established themselves at Meroe, but were driven back by the Nubians who had made league with Rome.

Finally in A.D. 450 the Nubians under Silko embraced Christianity and made old Dongola their capital. This city replaced Napata and Meroe, and by the twelfth century had churches and brick dwellings.

In A.D. 525 there was considerable trade between Abyssinia and Central Africa. Spices and gold were imported in return for cattle, salt, and iron.

Thus the flood of Mohammedanism as it pressed up the Nile valley was held back for two centuries by a solid Christian phalanx in Abyssinia and Nubia. For years the dream of the Europeans was to make contact and alliance with the forces of Prester John and the other African Christians. It was not until 1270 that Saladin crushed the Nubians and annexed Nubia. The Christian kingdom of the Nubians finally fell in the sixteenth century.

NOTES

1. Aeschylus, *Prometheus Bound*, line 850; *The Suppliant Maidens*, line 859.
2. Rogers, *op. cit.*, Vol. I, p. 84.
3. Paul Lacroix, *History of Prostitution* (New York: Covici, Friede, 1931), p. 150.
4. Reade, *op. cit.*, pp. 37–38.
5. James George Frazer, *The Golden Bough* (New York: The Macmillan Co., 1940), Vol. I, pp. vi, vii.
6. Edward Meyer, *Geschichte des Alten Aegypten* (1887), p. 224, note 1.
7. G. C. G. Maspero, *Struggle of the Nations*, ed. by A. H. Sayce, tr. by M. L. McClure (New York: D. Appleton and Company, 1897), pp. 98–99.
8. Maspero, *op. cit.*
9. J. G. Wilkinson, *The Ancient Egyptians* (London: 1878), quoted in Rogers, *op. cit.*, Vol. I, p. 42, 54.
10. Anna M. Graves, *Benvenuto Cellini Had No Prejudice against Bronze* (Baltimore: Waverly Press, 1943), p. xix.
11. Petrie, *op. cit.*, Vol. II, p. 216.
12. *Cf.* translations by James H. Breasted, *History of the Ancient Egyptians* (New York, 1908), p. 275; Arthur Weigall, *Life and Times of Akhnaton* (London, 1922), p. 132.
13. Jeremiah 38:7–13.
14. Numbers 12:1.
15. Nahum 3:9.
16. II Chronicles 12:3.
17. Smith and Goodspeed, *The Complete Bible* (Chicago: University of Chicago Press, 1944).
18. Psalms 68:31.
19. Amos 9:7.
20. Isaiah 43:3.

21. I Chronicles 1:8.
22. Genesis 10:6.
23. II Kings, 17:4.
24. Isaiah 37:9.
25. Jeremiah 46:9.
26. Daniel 11:43.
27. Isaiah 45:14.
28. Ezekiel 30:4, 5; 38:5.
29. Isaiah 18:2, 37:9.
30. Petrie, *op. cit.,* p. 301.
31. Nahum, 3:1–19.
32. For the history of Ethiopia I have leaned heavily on ms. material furnished me by Professor Leo Hansberry of Howard University.
33. J. Garstand, A. H. Sayce, and F. L. Griffith, *Meroe* (Oxford: Clarendon Press, 1911), pp. 4–5.
34. Plutarch, *Alexander the Great;* Diodorus Siculus, Book XVII, Ch. 2.
35. W. E. B. DuBois, *Black Folk: Then and Now* (New York: Henry Holt & Company, 1939), pp. 32, 33.
36. Rogers, *op. cit.,* Vol. I, p. 57.
37. P. R. Garrucci, *La Monete dell' Italia Antica* (Rome: 1885), Part II, p. 58; Plate No. LXXV, Coin Nos. 11, 12, 13, 14, 15.
38. Hitler, *Mein Kampf,* p. 73.
39. Theodor Mommsen, *The Provinces of the Roman Empire,* tr. from the German by Dickson (London: Bentley, 1886), Vol. II, p. 345.

CHAPTER VII

---◆---

Atlantis

This is the story of the West Coast of Africa and its relation to the development of the world from A.D. 500 to 1500.

It has long been the belief of modern men that the history of Europe covers the essential history of civilization, with unimportant exceptions; that the progress of the white race has been along the one natural, normal path to the highest possible human culture. Even in its collapse today, the dominant opinion is that this is but an unfortunate halting on the way; the same march must and will be resumed after a breathing space for recovery.

On the other hand, we know that the history of modern Europe is very short; scarcely a moment of time as compared with that of eternal Egypt. The British Empire is not more than two hundred and fifty years old; France in her present stature dates back three hundred years; the United States was born only a hundred and seventy years ago; and Germany less than one hundred years. When, therefore, we compare modern Europe with the great empires which have died, it is not far different in length of days from the empires of Persia, Assyria, the Hittites, and Babylon. Ethiopia ruled the world longer than England has.

It is surely a wider world of infinitely more peoples that Europe has ruled; but does this reveal eternal length of rule and inherent superiority in European manhood, or merely the temporary possession of a miraculously greater brute force? Mechanical power, not deep human emotion nor creative genius nor ethical concepts of justice, has made Europe ruler of the world. Man for man, the modern world marks no advance over the ancient; but man for gun, hand for electricity, muscle for atomic fission, these show what our culture means and how the machine has conquered and holds modern mankind in thrall. What in our civilization is distinctly British or American? Nothing. Science was built on Africa and Religion on Asia.

Was there no other way for the advance of mankind? Were there no other cultural patterns, ways of action, goals of progress, which might and may lead man to something finer and higher? Africa saw the stars of God; Asia saw the soul of man; Europe saw and sees only man's body, which it feeds and polishes until it is fat, gross, and cruel.

Let us turn to West Africa, where man tried a different way for a thousand years. First we face the query: how do we know what man did in West Africa, since black Africa has no written history? This brings the curious assumption that lack of written record means lack of matter and deed worth recording. The deeds of men that have been clearly and accurately written down are as pinpoints to the oceans of human experience. To recall that experience we must rely on written record, varying from direct narrative to indirect allusion and confirmation; we must rely also on memory—the memory of contemporary onlookers, of those who heard their word, of those who over a lapse of years interpreted it and handed it on; we must rely on the mute but powerful testimony of habits, customs, and ideals, which echo and reflect vast stretches of past time. Finally, we agree upon as true history and actual fact any interpretation of past action which we today believe and want to believe is true. The relation of this last historical truth to real truth may vary from fact to falsehood.

Climate, with sun and ice, gave Europe opportunity to expand vastly the Asiatic and African invention of written records. Heat and rain made written record in West Africa almost impossible and forced that land to rely on the memories of men, developed over the centuries to a marvelous system of folklore and tradition. But back of both methods lay real human history recorded in cultural patterns, industry, religion, and art.

One of the extraordinary developments of civilization in Africa was on the West Coast around the great Gulf of Guinea. Frobenius has fancifully called this "Atlantis" and regards it as possibly a development of the culture of that fabled island in the Atlantic. Whatever its origin, there grew up on the West Coast of Africa a peculiarly African state. How far back its development extends, no man knows. We have a fairly authentic history from the seventeenth century on, creditable but discontinuous reports in the sixteenth and fifteenth, and before that only customs, tradition, and legend.

On a coast protected from inland by mountain, forest, and desert, and on the west by the ocean, there grew up an agricultural culture centering in the village. On this was developed in time, industry and art. Industry discovered division of labor between cities; each town had its own peculiar industry and then traded its surplus with the other towns. The towns were united in a loose confederacy with councils and chiefs.

Six hundred years before Christ, Phoenicians traded on the West Coast of Africa and a century later the Carthaginians. From prehistoric times this coast was peopled by the black West African type of Negro. The center of their culture lay above the Bight of Benin, along the slave coast, and reached east and north. It can be traced in stone monuments, architecture, works of art, and especially patterns of culture.

The fabrication of cloth and tools was widespread and leisurely, as befitted a tropical sun. For there was here the fierce fight with the mosquito, just as in the Congo, and east there was the duel with the tsetse fly; and this battle with malaria, sleeping-sickness, and a dozen enemies of man was as much a part of the struggle for life and happiness as any of man's activities. Despite this, not only the making of cloth, the fashioning of garments, and the welding of iron reached a high development but there grew up also an art, primitive but of exceptional power, which has influenced the modern world and deserves to be called one of the three or four original art forms of this earth. Agriculture and fishing, manufacturing and pottery, the welding and processing of metal, the development of painting and art, characterize this Negro culture.

In Ashanti weaving was done with simple tools, calling for great skill, and resulted in cloth artistically beautiful. There was wood-carving, divided into many separate branches; carvers made fetishes and drums and figures which were individual and original. "Regarded in the light of certain modern aesthetic tendencies, they possess an individuality and peculiar merit which astonish many people who see them for the first time. Love and appreciation of what is artistic and beautiful are attributes which cannot be said to be the prerogative of all of us. In Ashanti, however, such traits seem to be possessed by what we should call 'the uneducated masses.' There is hardly any object capable of artistic treatment which is not made the medium for some ornamental design which gives aesthetic delight to the African's mind and eye; such as stools, spoons, combs, wooden plates, calabashes, doors, sticks, staves of office, canoes, *wari* boards, knives, mortars, drums, ivory tusks, pots, pipes, weights and scales, metal work of every description, walls of temples and dwellings, and textiles of every kind. Even the tools and appliances used to obtain these effects, the forge itself, the shuttle, the mesher used for making nets, are ornamental, being decorated with artistic effects, which, however crude, are never vulgar and inartistic."[1]

The true West African showed great skill in plastic art; he carved ivory and wood, and the bronzes of Benin are among the most noteworthy remains of artistic effort in the world. When the state was seized by the British in 1897, they found carved elephant tusks, bronzes cast by the *cire-perdue* process, including the well-known bronze head of a Negress, now in the British Museum, a masterpiece of art.

A bronze head was discovered by Frobenius in Nigeria in 1910–1912. In this remarkable figure we have what is perhaps the finest known example of African achievement in the realm of the plastic arts. In the words of its discoverer, "the setting of the lips, the shape of the ears, the contour of the face, all prove, if separately examined, the perfection of a work of true art which the whole of it obviously is. . . . It is cast in what we call the 'cire perdue,' or the hollow cast, and is very finely chased, indeed like the best Roman examples."[2]

Considerations growing out of the study of this and terra-cotta specimens, supplemented by many other findings reported by previous investigators, led Frobenius to the daring conclusion that this art belongs to the old order of Central African civilization whose beginnings go back perhaps to the second millennium before Christ. He was also of the opinion that there is sufficient evidence to warrant the assumption that there were important links between this ancient culture and some of those famous and widely heralded civilizations which flourished along the banks of the Nile and in the Mediterranean Basin in the Classical and pre-Classical Ages.

The oldest art is that of pottery, of which there are endless remains in West Africa. Traces of pottery-making go back certainly five hundred years and possibly a thousand years on the West Coast. It is done chiefly by women and is a hereditary craft handed down from mother to daughter.

It may well be that the West Coast Negroes first gave to civilization the art of welding iron which spread over all Africa and then eventually into Europe and Asia. It is of course possible that iron welding was discovered on other continents independently of Africa, but no continent had so wide a use of iron in earliest times.

According to Boas: "It seems likely that at times when the European was still satisfied with rude stone tools, the African had invented or adopted the art of smelting iron. Consider for a moment what this invention has meant for the advance of the human race. As long as the hammer, knife, drill, the spade, and the hoe had to be chipped out of stone, or had to be made of shell or hard wood, effective industrial work was not impossible, but difficult. A great progress was made when copper found in large nuggets was hammered out into tools and later on shaped by melting; and when bronze was introduced; but the true advancement of industrial life did not begin until the hard iron was discovered. It seems not unlikely that the people who made the marvelous discovery of reducing iron ores by smelting were the African Negroes. Neither ancient Europe, not ancient western Asia, nor ancient China knew iron, and everything points to its introduction from Africa. At the time of the great African discoveries toward the end of the past century, blacksmiths were found all over Africa from north to south and from east to west. With his simple bellows and a charcoal fire he reduced the ore that is found in many parts of the continent and forged implements of great usefulness and beauty."[3]

Torday has argued: "I feel convinced by certain arguments that seem to prove to my satisfaction that we are indebted to the Negro for the very keystone of our modern civilization and that we owe him the discovery of iron."[4] Togoland is perhaps the oldest and most famous iron-working area in Africa.

According to Reclus, "The smelting and working of iron, most useful of all metallurgic discoveries, has been attributed to the Negroes as well as to the Chalybes of Asia Minor; and the Bongos of the White Nile, as well as some other African tribes, have constructed furnaces of a very ingenious type. Their smelters and forgers are, for the most part, satisfied with rude and primitive implements, in the use of which they, however, display marvelous skill. The Fangs of the Ogowe basin produce excellent iron, whose quality is scarcely equalled by Europeans themselves. In most of the native tribes the smiths constitute a special caste, much respected and even dreaded for their reputed knowledge of the magic arts."[5]

Concerning West African art in general, Sir Michael Sadler said: "West Africa has made its own characteristic contribution to the artistic treasures of the world." Sir William Rothenstein added: "I know nothing of the culture which produced these noble pieces, nor what influences, native or alien, inspired them. I know only that they are superb works of art, worthy to be set beside the best examples of sculpture of any period." According to J. J. Sweeney, the American critic: "As a sculptural tradition, African art has had no rival."[6]

Professor Roger Fry, distinguished British art critic, said: "We have the habit of thinking that the power to create expressive plastic form is one of the greatest of human achievements, and the names of great sculptures are handed down from generation to generation, so that it seems unfair to be forced to admit that certain nameless savages have possessed this power not only in a higher degree than we at this moment, but than we as a nation have ever possessed it. And yet that is where I find myself. I have to admit that some of these things are great sculpture, greater, I think, than anything we produced even in the Middle Ages. Certainly they have the special qualities of sculpture in a higher degree. They have indeed complete plastic freedom; that is to say, these African artists really conceive form in three dimensions. Now this is rare in sculpture."[7]

In drum and strings African music reached a high degree of originality and perfection. The development of the drum language by intricate rhythms enabled the natives not only to lead in dance and ceremony, but to telegraph all over the continent with a swiftness and precision hardly rivaled by the electric telegraph. Von Hornbostel said of African music, particularly in Togo: "The African Negroes are uncommonly gifted for music, probably, on an average, more so than the white race. This is clear not only from the high development of African music, especially as regards polyphony and rhythm, but a very curious fact, unparalleled, perhaps, in history, makes it even more evident; namely, the fact that Negro slaves in America and their descendants, abandoning their original music style, have adapted themselves to that of their white masters and produced a new kind of folk music in that style. Presumably no other people would have accomplished this. In fact, the plantation songs and spirituals and also the blues and ragtimes which have launched or helped to launch our modern dance music, are the only remarkable kinds of music brought forth in America by immigrants."[8]

Professor von Luschan considered the craftsmanship of Benin workers equal to the best that was ever produced by Cellini. Yet at the time they were creating, "in 1550, not a single peasant's house in Scandinavia had a window; and as late as 1773 Dr. Johnson and Boswell entered during their tour of the Hebrides, a hovel which 'for a window had only a small hole, which was stopped with a piece of turf, that was taken out occasionally to let in light.' In Berlin at the time of the Great Elector (1681), many houses in the capital had pigsties immediately below the front windows."[9]

Frobenius wrote of West African cultures: "What these old captains recounted, these chiefs of expeditions—Delbes, Marchais, Pigafetta, and all the others, what they recounted is true. It can be verified. In the old Royal Kunstkammer of Dresden, in the Weydemann collection of Ulm, in many another 'cabinet of curiosities' of Europe, we still find West African collections dating from this epoch. Marvellous plush velvets of an extreme softness, made of the tenderest leaves of a certain kind of banana plant; stuffs soft and supple, brilliant and delicate, like silks, woven with the fibre of a raffia, well prepared; powerful javelins with points encrusted with copper in the most elegant fashion; bows so graceful in form and so beautifully ornamented that they would do honor to any museum of arms whatsoever; calabashes decorated with the greatest taste; sculpture in ivory and wood of which the work shows a very great deal of application and style.

"And all that came from the countries of the African periphery, delivered over after that to slave merchants. . . .

"But when the pioneers of the last century pierced this zone of 'European civ-ilization' and the wall of protection which had, for the time being raised behind it—the wall of protection of the Negro still 'intact'—they found everywhere the same marvels which the captains had found on the coast.

"In 1906 when I penetrated into the territory of Kassai-Sankuru, I found still, villages of which the principal streets were bordered on each side, for leagues, with rows of palm trees, and of which the houses, decorated each one in charm-ing fashion, were works of art as well.

"No man who did not carry sumptuous arms of iron or of copper, with inlaid blades and handles covered with serpent skin. Everywhere velvets and silken stuffs. Each cup, each pipe, each spoon was an object of art perfectly worthy to be compared to the creations of the Roman European style. But all this was only the particularly tender and iridescent bloom which adorns a ripe and marvel-lous fruit; the gestures, the manners, the moral code of the entire people, from the little child to the old man, although they remained within absolutely natu-ral limits, were imprinted with dignity and grace, in the families of the princes and the rich as in the vassals and slaves. I know of no northern people who can be compared with these primitives for unity of civilization. Alas these last 'Happy Isles'! They, also, were submerged by the tidal wave of European civi-lization. And the peaceful beauty was carried away by the floods.

"But many men had this experience: the explorers who left the savage and warrior plateau of the East and the South and the North to descend into the plains of the Congo, of Lake Victoria, of the Ubangi: men such as Speke and Grant, Livingstone, Cameron, Stanley, Schweinfurth, Junker, de Brazza—all of them—made the same statements: they came from countries dominated by the rigid laws of the African Ares, and from then on they penetrated into the coun-tries where peace reigned, and joy in adornment and in beauty; countries of old civilizations, of ancient styles, of harmonious styles."[10]

All this industry in West Africa was developed around the Africans' ideas of religion: the worship of souls of trees and plants of animals; the use of the fetish; the belief in fairies and monsters. Along with this went training for medicine men and chiefs, and careful rules for birth, marriages, and funerals.

Of religion Frobenius said: "There is, among the deities possessed by all the other dark-skinned African nations combined, not one who can equal Shango, the [West African] Yoruban God of Thunder, in significance. This country's first royal ruler sprang, as its people believe, from his loins. His posterity still have the right to give the country its kings.

"Myth relates that Shango was born of the All-Mother, Yemaya. Powerful, warlike, and mighty, he was as great a God as was ever created in the minds of a nation striving for self-expression. He was the Hurler of Thunderbolts, Lord of the Storm; a God who burns down cities and rends trees. He is cruel and sav-age, yet splendid and beneficent.

"The floods which he pours give life to the soil and gladden the fields. Mankind fears him, yet loves him. Terrified by his wrath, they pray for his pres-ence. They picture him riding a ram. They represent him with his hands full of thunderbolts, surrounded by his wives, the Lakes and the Rivers. He lives in a palace of brass, which is dazzlingly bright, and whence lightning shoots forth. He has a mighty 'medicine,' which he takes through his mouth, and fire comes out when he opens it."[11]

The architecture of the West Coast was strikingly integrated with climate, physiography, and culture. The lovely buildings of Benin and Ashanti have been described. A traveler in 1835 described the palace of a chief in Togoland: "Glele's palace was enormous—it had housed in its time more than two thousand people—but the greater part is falling into ruins. . . . This palace is by far the largest and most elaborate piece of Negro architecture I have seen; it was with that of Great Benin I imagine the most important in West Africa."[12]

In 1787 the Chevalier de Boufflers, writing to the Comtesse de Sabran, spoke of his enthusiastic admiration of the beauty and cleanness of the townships in the Senegal.

The climate and physical surroundings conditioned much of this human development. There was lacking here the stone and dry climate which made it easy to preserve records in the Nile valley. Material on the West Coast disappeared before the dampness and the hosts of insects. This made the art of memory recording, of tradition handed down, of unusual importance, and here it was developed to an astonishing extent. The population invented systems of writing of which at least two on the Guinea Coast and the Cameroons have come down to our day. There were probably others. Thus alphabets which were never invented in Europe came to the world through Asia and Africa.

Certain states on the West Coast were politically noteworthy. Among these were the Mossi states, two of which still exist. Each state consisted of several kingdoms of which one had the leadership. According to Delafosse: "This organization, which still functions in our day at Wagadugu and at Yatenga, strangely resembles that which, according to what has been told us by Arab authors and the writers of Timbuktu, existed at Ghana, at Diara, at Gao, and at Mandingo, as well as what could formerly be observed at Coomassie, at Bonney, in certain states of subequatorial Africa, and also what can be studied in some of the little kingdoms of the Senegal, principally the Jolof, and elsewhere."[13]

This seems to constitute the type, perhaps more perfected at Mossi than elsewhere, of all the states worthy of that name, great or small, that have been developed all across Negro Africa since the most remote antiquity. "If the Mandingo empire, founded and directed by Negroes of probably pure race, could nevertheless have benefited by some foreign influence through the canal of Islamism, if the kingdoms of Ashanti and Dahomey, as those of the Senegal and of the Congo, might have received some inspiration from the Europeans, it seems very certain that the Mossi empires have always been sheltered from all non-Negro interference as well as non-Negro influence, and consequently the political institutions which characterize them and which are found almost all over Negro Africa are of indigenous origin."[14]

The Mossi state did not make territorial conquests and always constituted a rampart against the extension of Mohammedanism. In its integrity it represented a civilization uniquely and really Negro.

Secret societies have always played an important part in West Africa. They include a large variety of associations, of which the majority are mutual benefit clubs. Membership confers social distinction and are methods of bestowing charity. Some have six or seven grades and judicial functions, with execution for recalcitrants. One which was perhaps known to Ptolemy, the geographer of the second century, is associated with the leopard and has made difficulties for administrators in modern times. The secret societies used masks and ceremonies and are peculiarly West African.

The whole culture complex of the African West Coast is native and original. It is a picture of the development of human institutions unique in the history of mankind, and we can only lament that we know so little of it and have studied it so imperfectly. This body of culture grew up strong and self-contained upon the West Coast and met in time the sudden impact of two outer forces: Islam from the north and Christianity from the west.

"West Africans are still today in the period of integral collectivism, known to our ancestors before the Middle Ages, while we have arrived at individualism. The question which presents itself is to know whether indeed we have made definitive progress in this line, since many of our thinkers, of the so called advance guard, demand, as a benefit, the return to collectivism, although of a somewhat different form. This proves that the peoples of Negro Africa have not marched at the same rate of speed as the peoples of Europe, but in nowise proves that the former are inferior to the latter. Who knows, indeed, whether the latter have not gone too fast?"[15]

Among the groups which showed striking intellectual development were the Abron, whose state dates from the fifteenth century; the Akan people, including the Ashanti, whose known history goes back beyond 1600. In addition there were the Ewe, Yoruba, people of Benin, Dahomey, and Nubia. Benin was among the oldest of the states and has a legendary history going back to A.D. 880 or perhaps earlier. It was a carefully organized state with a remarkable native culture. It was with Benin that the Portuguese made contact in the fifteenth century and traded in slaves and other produce. The people of Yoruba, with a notable culture, moved westward as the kingdoms of the Sudan began to expand, and attacked Dahomey.

Dahomey has a known history that dates from before the sixteenth century; it had a well-organized state with farmers and artisans, but they became middlemen in the slave trade. In the nineteenth century they made a treaty with the French, but finally war broke out and the country became a French protectorate.

The Ashanti played a notable part in West Africa. They conquered the Fanti people and fought six wars with England between 1803 and 1874; they were finally subdued in 1894. Their king, Osai Tutu Quamina, was a man of intelligence and character who would have made advantageous contact between whites and Negroes if he had been treated fairly. But the English during these days were wavering between two ideas: between the suppression of the slave trade to America and emancipation of the slaves in the West Indies, and the newer idea of reducing West Africa to colonial status. For a time they hesitated, even setting up the Negro state of Sierra Leone to be ruled by free slaves, and co-operating with the similar American experiment in Liberia. Finally, however, when the clear meaning of colonial imperialism began to be understood, they turned to definite conquest. The Fanti people who had helped the English conquer the Ashanti attempted to organize their relation to England by a federation, but the constitution that they adopted was regarded as treasonable and those who drafted it were put in jail, although afterward released by the Home Secretary.

The whole European situation was changing in the late nineteenth century. The Franco-Prussian war had been fought, Germany was a great power, and England was consolidating a wide colonial empire. The native culture on the West Coast underwent various consecutive changes. The powerful states of earlier days had been pressed back by the developments in the Sudan and even in the Nile valley. They found prosperity and encouragement in the new trade to the West, which developed and degenerated into man-hunting; most of the black kingdoms on the coast became intermediaries. The slaves and prisoners captured during the internal wars became no longer incidents of these wars, but the wars became deliberate efforts to gather slaves for trade and export.

The character of culture on the slave coasts slowly changed; an element of cruelty crept into states like Benin and Dahomey, although other states, like that of the Yoruba, seem to have resisted to some extent. But the ancient culture of the Atlantic coast was ruined by the trade in slaves, by the importation of gin, and by the European trade; European goods drove out native art and artistic industry.

Of all this West African cultural development our knowledge is fragmentary and incomplete, jumbled up with the African slave trade. There has been no systematic, general study of the history of humanity on this coast. Nearly all has disappeared in the frantic effort to paint Negroes as apes fit only for slavery and then to forget the whole discreditable episode, wipe it out of history, and emphasize the glory and philanthropy of Europe. The invaluable art treasure which Britain stole from Benin has never been properly classified or exhibited, but lies in the British Museum.

Yet on the West Coast was perhaps the greatest attempt in human history before the twentieth century to build a culture based on peace and beauty, to establish a communism of industry and of distribution of goods and services according to human need. It was crucified by greed, and its very memory blasphemed by the modern historical method.

There can be no doubt but that the level of culture among the masses of Negroes in West Africa in the fifteenth century was higher than that of northern Europe, by any standard of measurement—homes, clothes, artistic creation and appreciation, political organization and religious consistency. "Throughout the whole of the Middle Ages, West Africa had a more solid politico-social organization, attained a greater degree of internal cohesion and was more conscious of the social function of science than Europe."[16] What stopped and degraded this development? The slave trade; that modern change from regarding wealth as being for the benefit of human beings, to that of regarding human beings as wealth. This utter reversal of attitude which marked the day of a new barter in human flesh did not die with the slave, but persists and dominates the thought of Europe today and during the fatal era when Europe by force ruled mankind.

NOTES

1. Robert S. Rattray, *Religion and Art in Ashanti* (Oxford: Clarendon Press, 1927), pp. 269–70.
2. Frobenius, *op. cit.*
3. Atlanta University Leaflet, No. 19.
4. *Journal of Royal Anthropological Institute*, Vol. XLIII, p. 14.
5. Elisée Reclus, *The Earth and Its Inhabitants, Africa* (New York: D. Appleton & Co., 1882–1895), p. 22.
6. J. J. Sweeney. *African Negro Art* (New York: Museum of Modern Art, 1935). Sir Michael Ernest Sadler, *Arts of West Africa* (London: Oxford University Press, 1936), p. 2.
7. Roger Eliot Fry, *Vision and Design* (London: Chatto and Windus, 1920), pp. 65–66.
8. Memorandum IV, International African Institute, London, p. 33.
9. R. F. G. Armattoe, *The Golden Age of Western African Civilization* (Londonderry: Lomeshie Research Center, 1946), p. 41.
10. Frobenius, *op. cit.*
11. *Ibid.*
12. Armattoe, *op. cit.*, p. 29.
13. Maurice Delafosse, *The Negroes of Africa*, tr. from the French by F. Fligelman (Washington, D.C.: Associated Publishers, 1931), p. xxxii.
14. *Ibid.*, pp. 69–70.
15. *Ibid.*, p. xxxii.
16. Armattoe, *op. cit.*, pp. 33, 35.

CHAPTER VIII

◆

Central Africa and the March of the Bantu

The story of Central Africa, the Congo valley, the region of the Great Lakes and the South-central lands, together with their invaders.

The story of the Congo valley and the Great Lakes region has never been written save from the piecemeal points of view of special interests: the explorers, the travelers, the missionaries, the slave raiders, the hunters for ivory, game, gold, and territory. There is practically no coherent account of the millions of human beings who have lived here for thousands of years, nor any body of study to guide the sociologist or historian.

Yet this is the Africa whence all the other Africas have emerged; this is the hot heart of that mighty land which probably first gave birth and sustenance to human beings, and from which they crept, crawled, and marched to the conquest of the earth. Later, in the vast upheavals of the land and the vaster stirrings of nations, groups, and peoples, the folk of this area streamed back and forth, marched up and down and across, in refuge and pursuit, in quest and conquest, until in the last fateful and far-reaching march of the Bantu they settled in something like the present distribution of African peoples. Around this march and countermarch, this endless battle and strife, circled the fate of the whole earth, its labor, its trade, its jewels and gold, its conquest, mastery, slavery, power, and fall. It should be worth a study which it never has received.

Journeying south from Egypt, one finds on the left the highlands of Abyssinia; on the right, the River Nile and what is now the Anglo-Egyptian Sudan leading south to the Great Lakes and the Congo valley. It was out of these lakes, forests, and valleys that the trade of Egypt came: the gold and ivory, the ostrich feathers, the gum and incense, and all the vast body of goods which made the connection so strong between Egypt and the south. It has been a matter of long dispute as to how far south this trade reached. Logically it seems that gold must have been brought from the same South African reefs which still furnish the largest supply in the world; but some might have come from mine- and placer-digging on the way, and even from West Africa.

The organization of human beings here varied from millennium to millennium and from century to century. Probably the first settlers or autochthonous inhabitants of the Lake region of Africa were the little Negrillos. Upon these in the long course of time descended the tall, black Africans, possibly from Asia, or from the land connecting Asia and Africa, possibly from neighboring parts of Africa. These Africans moved from the Great Lakes northward, pushing the pygmies before them. The Sahara at that time was not yet a desert, but abounded with rivers and forests, inviting invaders even to the shores of the Mediterranean. These users of stone implements gradually became agriculturalists and developed art and religion.

Thousands of years after this first wave of Negro immigrants there came another migration. The newcomers pushed north, west, and south, dispossessed the remaining Negrillos of the soil and greedily drove them toward the central forests and the deserts. They developed agriculture, the use of cattle and domestic fowls. They invented the working of iron and the making of pottery. Also, those who advanced farthest toward the north mixed with the Europeans and Asiatics in varying degrees so that sometimes the resulting population seemed now white and yellow mixed with Negro blood, and in other cases blacks mixed with white and yellow blood. The languages were mixed in similar ways. Thus arose the various Libyan and Egyptian populations. All this migration and mixture took place long before the epoch of the First Egyptian Dynasty.

As Egypt developed, the peoples of Central Africa as well as those in North Africa set out toward the Nile valley. Over thousands of years a stream of Negroes passed down the Nile, as migrants, as traders, as soldiers, as slaves. They further developed that Ethiopia whence Egypt sprang and which later conquered the Nile valley and the world.

Later the peoples from West and North Africa as well as Asia began to press down upon Ethiopia, as Nubia and Dongola rose to power. Abyssinia, turning back from Asia, encroached on Ethiopia from the south. These developments must have turned the tide of migration from Central Africa south toward the Cape of Good Hope. Hottentots and Bushmen, people formed by mixture of the tall tribes and the Negrillos and by absorption of other strains, left the Great Lakes region and migrated to South Africa more than a thousand years before Christ. South Africa was already occupied by peoples who had come there from thirty thousand to fifty thousand years before, possibly from Asia, and who, living long in a temperate climate, were less Negroid than the invaders. The Bushmen exhibited a marvelous gift for drawing and engraving and left their pictures not only in South Africa but in North Africa and Europe, raising the baffling question of their origin and wanderings.

Meantime the so-called Bantu began to develop. Various black tribes began to be pushed west and south by the developments in the Nile valley and the western Sudan, as well as by the strong defense and even aggression from the West Coast, which threw out arms of trade and cultural contact to Egypt, Greece, and Rome. With the coming of Islam into Africa in the seventh century their march became a steady but slow movement lasting several hundred years. In their path were a large number of different tribes and nations, in various stages of cultural development. Gradually these peoples, some conquering, some overcome by conquest and infiltration, came to be known as Bantu, from the languages they used, adopted, and rebuilt.

The migration and formation of the Bantu peoples was a long slow movement beginning a thousand years or more before Christ and extending to the nineteenth century of our era with periods of stoppage and acceleration.

The oldest of these languages were formed around the headwaters of the Nile in the Great Lake region of Equatorial Africa. Thence the Bantu apparently spread south across the mountains and plateaus of southern Congoland to the Atlantic, east and south to the Indian Ocean, and south across the Zambesi to South Africa.

In Africa before them had been inhabitants for many thousands of years: the pygmies and perhaps other forest and Sudanese Negroes. In South Africa, however, when the Bantu crossed the Zambesi, perhaps around 700 B.C., they found the land occupied by the Bushmen and the Hottentots.

This movement of the Bantu south led to the barrier of the wide sea, a new contact with the European slavery, and a new approach toward Asia over the ramparts through which the Zambesi had to force its way. The great rift opposed its mountains and valleys. There must have come in these thousand years all sorts of cultural events: the overthrow of well-developed kingdoms and cultures; the wild forays on established centers of life, like that of the Jaggas, of whom we continually hear, east and west; the more or less increased mingling of people of different origins and cultures, until at last there emerged new languages and one dominant Bantu tongue.

Sir Harry Johnston wrote: "What are the Bantu languages? And why should they have been preferred as a special subject of interest in philological research to a degree far exceeding that of other language families of purely African location? They constitute a very distinct type of speech which, as contrasted with others amongst the groups of Negro tongues, is remarkable as a rule for the Italian melodiousness, simplicity and frequency of its vowel sounds, and the comparative ease with which its exemplars can be acquired and spoken by Europeans. The Bantu languages are attractive to the explorer, not only from the harmonious adjustment of vowels and consonants, but from the logic of their grammatical structure, which, in the majority of these tongues, provides for a wide range and a nice discrimination in the expression of ideas."[1]

The result of this march of the Bantu was extraordinary, but it is difficult for the student today to distinguish between pre-Bantu and Bantu cultures. Or perhaps it would be clearer to say that we do not know when and how particular cultures became Bantu-ized, and just what they were before the Bantu influx and influence.

Possibly the first of the ancient Bantu tribes moved eastward toward the mountain Nile and the Great Lakes from the valley north of the Albert Nyanza. They remained in the southwestern part of what is now the Anglo-Egyptian Sudan until 300 or 400 B.C. when they started south. Probably at the beginning of the Christian era the Bantu were settled on the Indian Ocean, and there the Arab traders cultivated relations with them and mingled their blood. Eventually the

Bantu invaded the Congo basin, already possibly inhabited by Negroes of the West African type and by pygmies. First the Bantus went round and not through the forests, but finally they broke through the forests and sent migrants across Congoland as far as the coast, where they met the West African Negro culture.

These Bantu peoples were of many types. Livingstone, Stanley, and others were struck with the Egyptian features of many of the tribes of Africa, and this is true of many of the peoples between Central Africa and Egypt, so that some students have tried to invent a "Hamitic" race to account for them—an entirely unnecessary hypothesis. The Bantu cultures included the herdsman craft, agriculture with the hoe, knowledge of iron and copper. It is quite possible that the Bantu invasion was facilitated by their iron weapons.[2]

It is difficult to rebuild today a picture of civilization in Central Africa in these times. We have notes by travelers of numbers of centers of culture: north of the kingdom of the Congo lay the kingdom of Ansika; the kingdoms of Luanda, including Katanga and other states, founded by the Luba-lunda people, extended into the valley of the Kasai and the Zambesi. Here also was the realm of the celebrated Muata Yanvo, the last of fourteen rulers, who was lord of three hundred chiefs two million inhabitants spread over a hundred thousand square miles.

The Portuguese came on their way to India and occupied the East African Coast as a stopping point on the way to India. They became excited by the tales of African kingdoms and especially by that of gold in Sofala. By 1506 the Portuguese were participating in the wealth of these gold mines. They mentioned the kingdom of Velanga and especially the empire of the Monomotapa. Vasco da Gama found prosperous and busy cities, some built of stone and mortar. The Portuguese established themselves on the coast but could not penetrate into the Bantu interior.

When the Portuguese arrived on the West Coast in the fifteenth century, a large state known as the kingdom of the Congo had already been in existence for centuries and extended over modern Angola as far east as the Kasai and the upper Zambesi Rivers. Its emperor was converted to Christianity and his sons were educated in Portugal. Several Congolese became priests and one became a bishop.

In its capital, San Salvador, were numerous cathedrals. "Early in the sixteenth century it became a Christian land, whose wealth and pomp dazzled all Christendom. Its emperors and courtiers vied in their splendour with the grandees of Spain and Portugal and its native prelates were ordained by Rome. Never again will an African kingdom exhibit so much refinement and so much grace. We have it on the authority of the ancient chroniclers that in their deportment and attire, in their manners, and in their conversation, they had nothing to learn from the illuminati of Europe.

"Then came the seventeenth century when the power of the court began to wane and a mere parish priest from Europe could threaten to depose the Emperor. With the eighteenth century came the decline, and towards its end, the very memory of what it once was had been lost upon the new generation."[3]

Duarte Lopes, whom Philip II of Spain and Portugal sent to the Congo, related his experiences to Filippo Pigafetta, a papal official, who published his accounts in Rome in 1591. In 1574 Paulo Diaz, grandson of Bartolomeo, the explorer, visited Angola and was deeply impressed by the high culture of the inhabitants.

Upon these old centers of culture moved slowly the oncoming Bantu from the Nile valley and the Sudan and the Lake regions. They established new kingdoms, of which one was that of the Bushongo. This organized state instituted or adopted a new industrial political system; it was ruled by a national council containing representatives of the various arts and crafts as well as representatives from territorial divisions. The Bushongo made remarkable damask embroidery and velvets and had skilled social leadership.

Of some Negro states we know only that they existed and had power, but little of their history. There was for instance the Kitwara empire, whose greatness is attested to by the fact that out of it grew Uganda, one of the best organized states of Africa in the Middle Ages. Of the origin of Kitwara we have only legend, which says that the common founder and first ruler, Kintu, came from the north, bringing with him a single cow, goat, chicken, banana root, and sweet potato; these, increasing miraculously, soon stocked the country, the potato being especially apportioned to Banyoro and the banana to Uganda. Presently Kintu became weary of his people's stupidities and blood-shedding and disappeared, but since it was known that he did not die, it became traditional for his successor to seek for him. At last he was found by a king, Ma'anda, as an aged man, seated on a throne in the forest, his beard white with age and his followers white-skinned and clothed in white robes. The story tells how Ma'anda committed some act of bloodshed, whereupon Kintu and his followers vanished and have been seen no more.

The kingdom of Kitwara, the vaster empire of the Monomotapa, the kingdom of the Congo, and the various organizations of the Lunda people in the Congo valley, probably predated and at the same time were the results and remains of the migration of the Bantu. For two reasons the history of this movement and clash of cultures have been lost: first, the climate, which records could not withstand; and second, because the movement of these people was toward a dead end in a slave-ridden South, differing from similar movements in Asia which led toward the Islamic culture of Bagdad and to Egypt; and movements in Europe which led toward Rome.

The Bantu nations thus formed, found, or transformed a multitude of kingdoms and cultures, and with our present knowledge we cannot say just how a given culture fits into the picture, whether as a civilization existing prior to the coming of the Bantu or as a state which the invaders transformed.

Certain it is that the greatest kingdom of Central Africa was that of the Monomotapa, and the greatest cultural remains of the Monomotapa are the celebrated ruins of Zimbabwe. An early Negro migration, some thousand years before Christ, had come upon or founded the remarkable civilization which we know as that of Zimbabwe. By the tenth century a later Bantu migration had overthrown and reorganized it, establishing among the Maka-langa, Matabele, and Mashona, a line of rulers called the Monomotapa.

Zimbabwe was an extensive state. In the seventeenth century it stretched from the Zambesi River down to the Fish River, ran seven hundred and fifty miles inland, and was approximately the size of Mexico. Frobenius regarded it as undoubtedly a "very great kingdom"; the king was powerful and conducted courts of justice in spring and fall. After seven years the reigning king was killed by the people and a new king crowned. The name itself means "prince of the mine," and the area was a mineral center from which came gold, diamonds, and rubies long before modern times.

The ruins of Zimbabwe show today an extraordinary cultural past, presenting certain phenomenal remains not to be found anywhere else in Africa south of the Great Lakes. Among these are extensive gold mines sunk to a depth in rock; scores of colossal stone buildings; forms of ceremonial not common among present Bantu people; impressions of some Asiatic influence; and the presence of many nonindigenous plants and trees.

Unfortunately, any reconstruction of this ancient African culture and history must be pursued today mainly in the Negro-hating atmosphere and amid the color-caste system of South Africa. Despite some eminent and fair scholars, the main situation is like setting Nazis to study Jews.

The area of these prehistoric mines is strewn over large tracts of territory, measuring over forty thousand square miles. Only a few of these tracts have yet been explored, but the partial exploration has already yielded relics of birds of stone, phalli, great soapstone bowls, and gold ornaments.

It is evident that the vast amount of gold extracted from prehistoric Rhodesia, as indicated in the Hebrew Scriptures and by ancient historians before the commencement of the Christian era, exceeded that obtained within historic times.

Gold mines discovered in the northern part of Rhodesia show that gold was mined and used in Africa in the Stone Age. Caton-Thompson has assured us that the belief that the natives of earlier days knew nothing about depth mining is quite untrue. The Africans, even in modern times, were so resentful of European exploitation that they prevented the whites as far as possible from learning the whereabouts of the mines. In the nineteenth century English explorers found natives gold mining at depth, with buckets, ropes, axes, and charcoal.

It is not difficult to account for the gold mined between the ninth and sixteenth centuries. Probably the bulk of it went to India. The wealth of the Hindu kings in the fourteenth century was astonishing. Firishtah, the Persian historian in A.D. 1311 recorded a hoarding of gold worth a hundred million pounds sterling. In the sixteenth century a Portuguese correspondent described the immense revenue, the gold-covered furniture, and trappings of the kings of Vijayanagar and of the religious institutions.[4]

"The interest in Zimbabwe and the allied ruins should to all educated people be enhanced a hundredfold; it enriches, not impoverishes, our wonderment at their remarkable achievement: it cannot detract from their inherent majesty: for the mystery of Zimbabwe is the mystery which lies in the still pulsating heart of native Africa."[5]

What was it that overthrew this civilization? Undoubtedly the same sort of raids of barbarous warriors that we have known in our day. For instance, in 1570 there came upon the country of Mozambique, farther up the coast, "such an inundation of Pagans that they could not be numbered. They came from the part of Monomotapa where is the Great Lake from which spring these great rivers."[6] In later days throng upon throng of herdsmen invaders overthrew Bantu settlers and were in turn overwhelmed.

That Asiatic and even Chinese influences were present at times in this remarkable cultural development, with its irrigation and fortresses, is not improbable. The trade between Asia and Africa by way of the East Coast dates back to prehistory and was especially rife when Mohammedans took refuge there in the seventh, eighth, and ninth centuries. But just as neither Arabs, Persians, nor Portuguese ever dominated the blacks here in historic times, so the culture of Zimbabwe was without doubt always dominantly Negro, with that cultural inspiration that everywhere comes with foreign contacts.

There is continued difficulty in disentangling the threads of African culture in this region of the continent, but that it is authentically and indubitably African there can be no doubt. Schweinfurth said: "Not a custom, not a superstition is found in one part which is not more or less accurately repeated in another; not one contrivance of design, not one weapon of war exists of which it can be declared that it is exclusive property of any one race. From north to south, and from sea to sea, in some form or other, every invention is sure to be repeated; it is 'the thing that has been.' If we could at once grasp and set before our minds facts that are known (whether as regards language, race, culture, history, or development) of that vast region of the world which is comprehended in the name of Africa, we should have before us the witness of an intermingling of races which is beyond all precedent. And yet, bewildering as the prospect would appear, it remains a fact not to be gainsaid, that it is impossible for any one to survey the country as a whole without perceiving that high above the multitude of individual differences there is throned a principle of unity which embraces well-nigh all the population."[7]

ANCIENT ITALIAN COINS OF THE THIRD OR SECOND CENTURY BEFORE CHRIST

To the final eruption of the Bantu into South Africa and their contact with the Dutch and British we have already alluded. It leaves there today perhaps the worst interracial situation in the world, with caste, ignorance, cruelty, and dogmatic religious hypocrisy. Together with the southern United States, it forms the most backward section of the world in race relations.

NOTES

1. Harry H. Johnston, *A Comparative Study of the Bantu and Semi-Bantu Languages* (Oxford: Clarendon Press, 1919), Vol. I, p. 15.
2. See map of Bantu language migrations, Johnston, *ibid.*, Vol. II, frontispiece.
3. Armattoe, *op. cit.*, p. 30.
4. G. Caton-Thompson, *The Zimbabwe Culture* (Oxford: Clarendon Press, 1931), pp. 194, 195, 198.
5. *Ibid.*, p. 199.
6. DuBois, *Black Folk*, p. 75.
7. Georg A. Schweinfurth, *Heart of Africa*, tr. from the German by Ellen E. Frewer (London: Sampson, Low, Marston Low & Searle, 1873), Vol. I, p. 313.

CHAPTER IX

◆

Asia in Africa

The story of the outpouring of Asia into Africa from A.D. 500 to 1500, and the effect which the interaction of these two continents had on the world.

The connection between Asia and Africa has always been close. There was probably actual land connection in prehistoric times, and the black race appears in both continents in the earliest records, making it doubtful which continent is the point of origin. Certainly the Negroid people of Asia have played a leading part in her history. The blacks of Melanesia have scoured the seas, and Charles Taüber makes them inventors of one of the world's first written languages: thus "this greatest of all human inventions was made by aborigines whose descendants today rank among the lowest, the proto-Australians."[1]

The ethnic history of India would seem to be first a prehistoric substratum of Negrillos or black dwarfs; then the pre-Dravidians, a taller, larger type of Negro; then the Dravidians, Negroes with some mixture of Mongoloid and later of Caucasoid stocks. The Dravidian Negroes laid the bases of Indian culture thousands of years before the Christian era. On these descended through Afghanistan an Asiatic or Eastern European element, usually called Aryan.

The *Rig Veda*, ancient sacred hymns of India, tells of the fierce struggles between these whites and blacks for the mastery of India. It sings of Aryan deities who rushed furiously into battle against the black foe. The hymns praise Indra, the white deity, for having killed fifty thousand blacks, "piercing the citadel of the enemy" and forcing the blacks to run out in distress, leaving all their food and belongings. The blacks under their renowned leader Krishna, that is, "The Black," fought back with valor. The whites long held the conquered blacks in caste servitude, but eventually the color line disappeared before commerce and industry, intermarriage, and defense against enemies from without.

In the Gangetic region caste disappeared. The whites enlisted in the service of the blacks and fought under Negro chiefs. In the famous battle of the Ten Kings, one of the leading Aryan chiefs was a Negro. Nesfield said: "The Aryan invader, whatever class he might belong to, was in the habit of taking the women of the country as wives, and hence no caste, not even that of the Brahman, can claim to have sprung from Aryan ancestors."[2] Today some of the Brahmans are as black and as flat-nosed as the early Negro chiefs. Max Müller said that some Brahmans are "as black as Pariahs."[3]

The culture of the black Dravidians underlies the whole culture of India, whose greatest religious leader is often limned as black and curly-haired. According to Massey: "It is certain that the Black Buddha of India was imaged in the Negroid type. In the black Negro God, whether called Buddha or Sut-Nahsi, we have a datum. They carry their color in the proof of their origin. The people who first fashioned and worshipped the divine image in the Negroid mould of humanity must, according to all knowledge of human nature, have been Negroes themselves. For blackness is not merely mystical, the features and hair of Buddha belong to the black race and Nahsi is the Negro name. The genetrix represented as the Dea Multimammia, the Diana of Ephesus, is found as a black figure, nor is the hue mystical only, for the features are Negroid as were those of the black Isis in Egypt."[4]

Of the thirty apostles who took Buddhism to China, ten are represented as yellow, ten brown, and ten black. The Indian blacks, mingling with the straight-haired yellow Mongoloids, tended to have straighter hair along with their dark color than Africans, although this was not true in the case of the island Negroes.

According to Balfour: "Ethnologists are of the opinion that Africa has had an important influence in the colonization of Southern Asia, of India, and of the Easter Islands in time prior to authentic history or tradition. The marked African features of some of the people in the extreme south of the Peninsula of India, the Negro and Negrito races of the Andamans and Great Nicobar, the Semang, Bila, and Jakun of the Malay Peninsula, and the Negrito and Negro, Papuan and Malagasi races of the islands of the Indian Archipelago, Australia, and Polynesia, indicate the extent which characterizes their colonization. . . . The spiral-haired Negro race seem to have preceded the lank-haired brown race. . . . When we consider the position of India between the two great Negro provinces, that on the west being still mainly Negro, even in most of its improved races, and that on the east preserving the ancient Negro basis in points so near India as the Andamans and Kedah, it becomes highly probable that the African element in the population of the Peninsula has been transmitted from an archaic period before the Semitic, Turanian, and Iranian races entered India and when the Indian Ocean had Negro tribes along its northern as well as its eastern and western shores. . . . Perhaps all the original population of southern Arabia, and even of the Semitic lands, generally was once African."[5]

Widney has said: "They [the Negroes] once occupied a much wider territory and wielded a vastly greater influence upon earth than they do now. They are found chiefly in Africa, yet traces of them are to be found through the Islands of Malaysia, remnants, no doubt, of that more numerous black population which seems to have occupied tropical Asia before the days of the Semites, the Mongols, and the Brahminic Aryan. Back in the centuries which are scarcely historic, where history gives only vague hintings, are traces of a widespread, primitive civilization, crude, imperfect, garish, barbaric, yet ruling the world from its seats of power in the valley of the Ganges, the Euphrates, and the Nile, and it was of the

Black races. The first Babylon seems to have been of a Negroid race. The earliest Egyptian civilization seems to have been Negroid. It was in the days before the Semite was known in either land. The Black seems to have built up a great empire, such as it was, by the waters of the Ganges before Mongol or Aryan. Way down under the mud and slime of the beginnings . . . is the Negroid contribution to the fair superstructure of modern civilization."[6]

H. Imbert, a French anthropologist, who lived in the Far East, has said in *Les Negritos de la Chine:* "The Negroid races peopled at some time all the south of India, Indo-China, and China. The south of Indo-China actually has now pure Negritos as the Semangs, and mixed as the Malays and the Sakais. . . . In the first epochs of Chinese history, the Negrito type peopled all the south of this country and even in the island of Hai-Nan, as we have attempted to prove in our study on the Negritos, or Black Men, of this island. Skulls of these Negroes have been found in the island of Formosa and traces of this Negroid element in the islands of Liu-kiu to the south of Japan. In the earliest Chinese history several texts in classic books spoke of these diminutive blacks; thus the Tcheu-Li, composed under the dynasty of Tcheu (1122–249 B.C.), gives a description of the inhabitants with black and oily skin. . . . The Prince Liu-Nan, who died in 122 B.C., speaks of a kingdom of diminutive blacks in the southwest of China."

Additional evidence of Negroes in China is given by Professor Chang Hsing-land in an article entitled, "The Importation of Negro slaves to China under the T'ang Dynasty, A.D. 618–907": "The Lin-yi Kuo Chuan (Topography of the Land of Lin-yi) contained in Book 197 of the Chiu T'ang Shu (Old Dynastic History of T'ang) says: 'The people living to the south of Lin-yi have woolly hair and black skin.'" Chinese folklore speaks often of these Negroes, he says, and mentions an empress of China, named Li (A.D. 373–397), consort of the Emperor Hsiao Wu Wen, who is spoken of as being a Negro. He adds that according to the writings of a later period—the seventh to the ninth century—Negro slaves were imported into China from Africa.[7]

According to Professor Munro, one of the foremost students of Japanese life and culture: "The Japanese are a mixture of several distinct stocks—Negrito, Mongolian. . . . Breadth of face, intraorbital width, flat nose, prognathism, and brachycephaly might be traced to the Negro stock."[8]

The Asiatic and African blacks were strewn along a straight path between tropical Asia and tropical Africa, and there was much racial intermingling between Africa and western Asia. In Arabia particularly the Mongoloids and Negroids mingled from earliest times. The Mongoloids invaded North Africa in prehistoric times, and their union with the Negroids formed the Libyans. Later there was considerable commerce and contact between the Phoenicians of North Africa, especially Carthage, and the black peoples of the Sudan.

Speaking of the mixture that went on in this area between Elamite black and Aryan white, Dieulafoy has said: "The Greeks themselves seemed to have known these two Susian races, the Negroes of the plains and the Scythian whites of the mountains. Have not their old poets given to the direct descendants of the Susian, Memnon, the legendary hero who perished under the walls of Troy, a Negro father, Tithon, and a white, mountain woman as mother—Kissia? Do they not also say that Memnon commanded an army of black and white regiments? 'Memnon went to the succor of Priam with ten thousand Susians and ten thousand Ethiopians.' . . . I shall attempt to show to what distant antiquity belongs the establishment of the Negritos upon the left bank of the Tigris and the elements constituting the Susian monarchy. . . . Towards 2300 B.C., the plains of the Tigris and Anzan-Susinka were ruled by a dynasty of Negro kings.

"The coming of this dynasty of Medes corresponded perhaps to the arrival in the south of an immense Scythian invasion. Pushed back by the black Susians after having taken possession of the mountains, the whites poured into the plains of the Tigris and remained master of the country until the time when Kudur Nakhunta subdued Chaldea and founded Anzan-Susinka. He added to the territory of the blacks—Nime, Kussi, Habardip—all the mountainous districts once inhabited by the whites of the Scythian race."[9]

Herodotus, who visited this region in the fifth century B.C., mentioned the dark skins of the people. He called them Ethiopians, but said their hair was straighter than those of the western Ethiopians, who had woolly hair. The Elamites, however, seemed rather to have belonged to the more Negroid stock of the west; their hair, as seen on the monuments, is short and woolly. "The Elamites," said Sir Harry Johnston, "appear to have been a Negroid people with kinky hair and to have transmitted this racial type to the Jews and Syrians. There is curliness of the hair, together with a Negro eye and full lips in the portraiture of Assyria which conveys the idea of an evident Negro element in Babylonia. Quite probably the very ancient Negro invasion of Mediterranean Europe (of which the skeletons of the Alpes Maritimes are vestiges) came from Syria and Asia Minor on its way to Central and Western Europe."[10]

Professor Toynbee also says, "The primitive Arabs who were the ruling element of the Omayyad Caliphate called themselves 'the swarthy people' with a connotation of racial superiority, and their Persian and Turkish subjects, 'the ruddy people,' with a connotation of racial inferiority, that is to say, they drew the distinction that we draw between blonds and brunets but reversed the value."[11]

Carthage especially traded with the Sudan for gold dust, ostrich feathers, and ivory in exchange for textiles, cloth, copper, and beads. Often the Carthaginians settled among the Negroes and the Negroes among them. As a result the horse became known in the Sudan, textiles were made from cotton, and gold was gathered and worked. The glass industry was born and spread. The Libyans, or Berbers, were descendants from the populations of North Africa which consisted of an Asiatic element that came in prehistoric times and mixed with the Negroids. From these mixed races came the Sudan stone houses and the cemented wells and the spread of cattle-raising and gardening.

The whole population becomes darker and darker toward the south, until it merges into the blacks of the Sudan. The divisions, especially the political units—Tripoli, Tunisia, Algeria, and Morocco—have no anthropological significance and do not correspond to any ethnic division. There are many striking groups: the Negroid Tuareg, or people of the Veil; the Tibu, or rock people, Negroids with mixed Mongoloid or Caucasoid blood; the dark Fulani, scattered all over North Africa from the Upper Niger to the Senegal and forming often the dominant political power in the lands toward the coast.

Mohammedanism arose in the Arabian deserts, starting from Mecca which was in that part of the world which the Greeks called Ethiopia and regarded as part of the African Ethiopia. It must from earliest time have had a large population of Negroids.

The two greatest colored figures in the history of Islam are Bilal-i-Habesh (Bilal of Ethiopia) and Tarik-bin-Ziad: "Bilal-i-Habesh was Mohammed's liberated slave and closest friend to whom he gave precedence over himself in Paradise. The Prophet liberated all his slaves, and they were all well-known figures in the early Islamic history. He adopted as his own son another Negro, Zayd bin Harith, his third convert, who rose to be one of his greatest generals. Later, to show his regard for Zayd, he took one of Zayd's wives, the beautiful Zainab, as his own. But Bilal stands out in greatest relief. Apart from his services in the cause of Islam, it was through him that the Moslems decided to use the human voice instead of bells to call the Moslems to prayer. He had evidently a marvelous voice and was the first who called for prayers in Islam.

"Tarik-bin-Ziad also was a slave and became a great general in Islam and was the conqueror of Spain as the commander of the Moorish Army which invaded Spain. Jebel-u-Tarik (the mount of Tarik), that is, Gibraltar, is named after him. One of the greatest Turkish classics is called 'Tarik-bin-Ziad' and has him as its hero. It was written by Abdul-Hak-Hamid, our greatest poet (alive though 84) and equals any tragedy of Corneille. I do hope that some time the biographies of these great figures will be written in English."[12]

The Mohammedans organized for proselyting the world, overthrew Persia, and took Syria and eventually Egypt and North Africa from the Eastern Roman Empire. They went east as far as India and west to Spain, and eventually the Golden Horde, as the Russian Mongols had come to be called, became followers of Islam and thus religious brothers of the Mohammedan Arabs.

The Arabs brought the new religion of Mohammed into North Africa. During the seventh century they did not migrate in great numbers. Spain was conquered not by Arabs, but by armies of Berbers and Negroids led by Arabs. Later, in the eleventh century, another wave of Arabs came, but the number was never large and their prestige came from their religion and their language, which became a *lingua franca* for the peoples north and south of the Sahara. The total substitution of Arabian for Berber or Negro blood was small.

Anyone who has traveled in the Sudan knows that most of the "Arabs" he has met are dark-skinned, sometimes practically black, often have Negroid features, and hair that may be almost Negro in quality. It is then obvious that in Africa the term "Arab" is applied to any people professing Islam, however much race mixture has occurred, so that while the term has a cultural value it is of little ethnic significance and is often misleading.

The Arabs were too nearly akin to Negroes to draw an absolute color line. Antar, one of the great pre-Islamic poets of Arabia, was the son of a black woman; and one of the great poets at the court of Harun-al-Rashid was black. In the twelfth century a learned Negro poet resided at Seville.

The Mohammedans crossed the Pyrenees in A.D. 719 and met Charles Martel at Poitiers; repulsed, the invaders turned back and settled in Spain. The conflict for the control of the Mohammedan world eventually left Spain in anarchy. A prince of the Omayyads arrived in 758. This Abdurahman, after thirty years of fighting, founded an independent government which became the Caliphate of Cordova. His power was based on his army of Negro and white Christian slaves. He established a magnificent court and restored order, and his son gave protection to writers and thinkers.

Eventually rule passed into the hands of a mulatto, Almanzor, who kept order with his army of Berbers and Negroes, making fifty invasions into Christian territory. He died in 1002, and in a few years the Caliphate declined and the Christians began to reconquer the country. The Mohammedans looked to Africa for refuge.

In the eleventh century there was quite a large Arab immigration. The Berbers and some Negroes by that time had adopted the Arab tongue and the Mohammedan religion, and Mohammedanism had spread slowly southward across the Sahara.[13]

The invasions of the eleventh century were launched in 1048 by the Vizier of Egypt under the colored Caliph Mustansir. Each man was provided with a camel and given a gold piece, the only condition being that he must settle in the west. In two years they pillaged Cyrenaica and Tripoli and captured Kairwan. The invaders for the most part settled in Tripoli and Tunis, while their companions pressed on westward into Morocco. This exemplifies the process of arabization in North Africa, and it was to a large extent a reflex from the invasion that had most to do with the arabization of the Nile valley. It is thus responsible for much of the present-day distribution of the "Arab" tribes of the Sudan.

The Arabs invaded African Egypt, taking it from the Eastern Roman Emperors and securing as allies the native Negroid Egyptians, now called Copts, and using Sudanese blacks, Persians, and Turks in their armies. They came in 639 under Amr-ibn-el-Asr, partly as friends of Egyptians against the tyranny of the Eastern Roman Empire, partly even as defenders of the heretical Coptic Church. It must be remembered that they were related by blood and history to the Negroid peoples. One of Mohammed's concubines was a dark curly-haired Coptic woman, May; and Nubians from the Sudan took frequent part in these wars. Alexandria surrendered in 642, and ten years later the Arabs invaded Nubia and attacked Dongola crying, "Ye people of Nubia, Ye shall dwell in safety!"[14]

For two centuries from 651 there were ninety-eight Mohammedan governors of Egypt under Caliphs of Medina, Damascus, and Bagdad. The Copts, representing the majority of the Egyptians, for the most part submitted to this rulership, but the black Nubians continued to be unruly and even came to the defense of the Copts. In 722 King Cyriacus of Nubia marched into Egypt with one hundred thousand soldiers and secured release of the imprisoned Coptic patriarch. There is an intriguing story of a black virgin whom the Mohammedans had seized and who promised them an unguent to make them invulnerable. To prove it she put it on her own neck, and when the Arab soldier swept his sword down upon her, her head fell off as she had intended.[15]

The change from the Omayyad to the Abasid Caliphs took place in Egypt peacefully in the middle of the eighth century. By 832 Egypt had become almost entirely Mohammedan, by conversion of the Copts through economic and social pressure. In 852 the last Arab governor ruled in Egypt, and in 856 the Turks began to replace the Arabs and to favor the Copts. There was much misrule, and from 868 to 884 Ahmad-ibn-Tulun, a Turkish slave, ruled. The Berga people of the Sudan refused further tribute of four hundred slaves annually and revolted in 854; the army of Ali Baba, "King of the Sudan," led the revolt, but spears and shields strove against mail armor and Arab ships, and failed.

We know that in 850 four hundred black East Africans had been enrolled in the army of Abu'l Abbas, ruler of Bagdad, and that they rose in revolt with a Negro, called "Lord of the Blacks," at their head. In 869 the Persian adventurer, Al Kabith, summoned the black slaves to revolt, and they flocked to his side in tens of thousands. In 871 they captured Basra and for fourteen years dominated the Euphrates delta. When Masudi visited this country fourteen years later, he was told that this conquest by famine and sword had killed at least a million people.

Syria was annexed to Egypt in 872, and from that time until the eleventh century Egypt, Syria, Palestine, and Mesopotamia form one realm, more or less closely united. When Syria was first annexed, Egypt ruled from the Euphrates to Barka and Aswan, and the famous black cavalry of ten thousand or more took part in the conquest. In 883 the Zeng Negroes of East Africa revolted, and some settled in Mesopotamia. The Tulum dynasty finally ended in 905, and there were thirty years of unsettled rule in Egypt under the suzerainty of weak caliphs. From 935 to 946 Ikshid was governor of Egypt.

He was succeeded by a black Abyssinian eunuch, Abu-l-Misk Kafur, "Musky Camphor," for whom Ikshid named a celebrated garden in Cairo. Kafur was a clever man of deep black color with smooth shiny skin, who had been guardian of the sons of Ikshid. He read history and listened to music and was lavish with his vast wealth. Daily at his table there were served two hundred sheep and lamb, seven hundred and fifty fowls, and a thousand birds and one hundred jars of sweetmeats. He attracted men of learning and letters and began an era of art and literature which placed Egypt as a cultural center next to Bagdad, Damascus, and Cordova.[16] The poet Muttanabi praised him as "The Moon of Darkness."

Kafur ruled Egypt for twenty-two years, from 946 to 968; he was regent for nineteen years, but the two sons of Ikshid who were nominally on the throne were playboys without power. Kafur ruled three years alone, from 965 to 968. He conquered Damascus and Aleppo and incorporated Syria under Egyptian rule. Trouble arose from time to time in Syria, while in Egypt there were earthquakes, bad Nile seasons, and a Nubian revolt. Nevertheless, in general good order was maintained. He died in 968 and was succeeded by a child, then by the Caliph Hoseyn, and finally by Moizz.

The Shiites or Fatimids from Morocco, under the man who called himself the Mahdi, now began to war on Egypt and conquered it. They sent an embassy to George, King of Nubia; reconquered Syria and became rich with gold and jewelry, ivory and silk. By the middle of the twelfth century the Mohammedan empire included North Africa, Syria, Sicily, and Hejaz; Turkish slaves and Sudanese troops held the empire.

Moizz was helped by Killis, a Jew who had been Kafur's righthand man; and had a bodyguard of four thousand young men, white and black. By the help of Negro troops another Syrian revolt was quelled. Then came the reign of mad Hakim and finally Zahir.

Zahir ruled Egypt from 1021 to 1026. His wife was a black Sudanese woman, and after the death of her husband largely influenced the rule of her son, who came to the throne in 1036 and ruled until 1094, the longest reign in the dynasty. This son, M'add, took the name of Mustansir and is regarded as the best and ablest of the rulers of his time. He loved and encouraged learning and had a library of a hundred and twenty thousand volumes. The Black Dowager, who had great influence over him, sailed the Nile in her silver barge and imported additional Negro troops from the south, until Mustansir had in his escort fifty thousand black soldiers and swordsmen, twenty thousand Berbers, ten thousand Turks, and thirty thousand white slaves. For years all Upper Egypt was held by black regiments.

Mustansir had enormous wealth, including his celebrated golden mattress. Makrizi described his jewels, gold plate, and ivory. Cairo consisted at this time of twenty thousand brick houses; there was art in pottery and glass work, and a beautiful "Lake of the Abyssinians." Mustansir had difficulties with Syria and nearly lost his power in 1068; his library was destroyed and the Black Dowager had to flee to Bagdad for sanctuary. Through the aid of Bedar, his prime minister, he regained power and restored Syria to Egyptian rule.

Then the Seljukian Turks appeared. They subdued Persia, captured Bagdad, and attacked Syria. Jerusalem was captured in 1071, and this became the excuse for the European Crusades which began in 1096, two years after Mustansir died. The Europeans took Jerusalem in 1099 and later seized most of Syria, but Egypt, with the aid of the black veterans of Mustansir's former army, eventually defeated Baldwin in 1102. From 1169 to 1193 Saladin, the Kurd, ruled Egypt and the East.

After Saladin's accession, black Nubian troops attacked Egypt, and the rebellion continued for many years. Gradually Saladin asserted his power in Nubia, and peace was made with the African Zeng in Mesopotamia. Mesopotamia had been ruined by the Mongols, and Cairo now became the greatest cultural center in the Orient, and indeed in the world, from 1196 to 1250. Saint Francis of Assisi preached there in 1219, and world trade centered in Alexandria.

Artists flocked to Egypt from Asia Minor. Men of culture lived at court, poets and writers. The Thousand and One Nights stories were collected. Indian stories and European romances were combined with Egyptian materials. A companion collection of poems made at this time were those of Antar-bin-Shaddad. He was born about A.D. 498, the son of a black slave girl, Zebbeda, and of Shaddad, a nobleman of the tribe of Abs. Antar is famous. One of his works is found as the sixth poem of the Mo'allaqat—the "golden verses"—which are considered in Arabia the greatest poems ever written. The story is that they were hung on the Ka'bah at the Holy Temple at Mecca so that all the pilgrims who came there might know them and do obeisance to them. The Mo'allaqat belongs to the first school of Arabian poetry—to the "Gahilieh"—"time of ignorance." The Antar poem belongs to the time of the war of Dahis, and, like the five poems which preceded it in the epic, it lauds the victors of the battlefield, describes the beauties of nature, and praises the camel of the desert. The main theme, however, is love.

Rimski-Korsakov's Symphony *Antar*, with its wealth of barbaric color and oriental fire has been deservedly popular. The libretto is drawn from the voluminous work known as *The Romance of Antar*, which was published in Cairo in thirty-two volumes and has been translated in sections from the Arabic by various scholars. There are two editions of the work—one known as the *Syrian Antar*, the other as the *Arabian Antar*. The abridged work was first introduced to European readers in 1802; a translation was made and issued in four books by Terrick Hamilton in 1819. the *Romance* is a companion piece to the *Arabian Nights* and is a standard Arabian work. The seemingly numberless tales that are incorporated in *The Romance of Antar* are traditional tales of the desert that were retold and preserved by Asmai during the reign of Harun-al-Rashid.

As autocratic power grew among the Mohammedans, a number of religious and political malcontents migrated down the eastern coast of Africa. They filtered through for a number of centuries, not as conquerors, and they were permitted to live and trade in limited areas and mingled and intermarried with the black Bantu. An Arab settlement was made about A.D. 684 under a son-in-law of Mohammed. Then came another migration in 908, and many of the Arabs wandered inland. Cities were established and soon were trading with the gold-mining peoples of Sofala. Masudi, an Arab geographer, visited this part of Africa in the tenth century and described the gold trade and the kingdom of the Waklimi. Marco Polo, writing in 1298, described the island of Madagascar and Zanzibar as peopled with blacks.

There are indications of trade between Nupe in West Africa and Sofala on the East Coast, and certainly trade between Asia and East Africa dates back earlier than the beginning of the Christian era. Asiatic traders settled on the East coast, and by means of mulatto and Negro merchants brought Central Africa into contact with Arabia, India, China, and Malaysia.

Zaide, great-grandson of Ali, nephew and son-in-law of Mohammed, was banished from Arabia. He passed over to Africa and formed settlements. His people mingled with the blacks, and the resulting mulatto traders, known as the Emoxaidi, seem to have wandered as far south as the equator. Other Arabian families came over on account of oppression and founded the towns of Magadosho and Brava, both not far north of the equator. The Emoxaidi, whom the later immigrants regarded as heretics, were driven inland and became the interpreting traders between the coast and the Bantu. Some wanderers from Magadosho came into the port of Sofala and there learned that gold could be obtained. This led to a small Arab settlement at that place.

Seventy years later, and about 150 years before the Norman conquest of England, certain Persians settled at Kilwa in East Africa, led by Hasan-ibn-Ali, who was the son of a black Abyssinian slave mother, and accompanied by his own six sons.

Ibn Batuta, who was acquainted with Arab life on the Mediterranean coast and at Mecca in the fourteenth century, was surprised by the wealth and civilization of East Africa. Kilwa he describes as "one of the most beautiful and best built towns." Mombasa is a "large" and Magadosho an "exceedingly large city."

Duarte Barbosa, visiting the coast ten years later, described Kilwa as "a Moorish town with many fair houses of stone and mortar, with many windows after our fashion, very well laid out in streets, with many flat roofs. The doors are of wood, well carved, with excellent joinery. Around it are streams and orchards and fruit-gardens with many channels of sweet water. . . . And in this town was great plenty of gold, as no ships passed to or from Sofala without coming to this island." Of the Moors, he continued: "There are some fair and some black: they are finely clad in many rich garments of gold and silver in chains and bracelets . . . and many jeweled ear-rings in their ears." Mombasa, again, is "a very fair place, with lofty stone and mortar houses, well lined in streets. . . . Their women go very bravely attired."[17]

It is probable that Chinese ships traded directly with Africa from the eighth to the twelfth centuries. When the Portuguese came they found the Arabs intermarried and integrated with the Bantu and in control of the trade.

One of the most astonishing developments in Africa was the rule of the Mameluke slaves in Egypt for six centuries, from 1193 to 1805. There has been no exact parallel to this in history, and yet students have neglected this period with singular unanimity. The Mamelukes were white slaves bought by the thousands in the Balkans, Greece, Turkey, and the Near East. They were used mainly as soldiers and shared in the conquests of Islam and especially in the capture and holding of the Nile valley. At first they were auxiliary troops under strong and ambitious sultans, several of whom were of Negro descent. Then at the time of the Mongols and Christian Crusades, the Mamelukes, organized by groups of hundreds, began to choose their own chiefs and even raised them to the sultanate. Usually such sultans ruled but short periods, averaging five years. Strong men, like Saladin, held the Mamelukes in control and imposed their policies upon them. Other such powerful rulers were Bibars, who became sultan in 1260; and Kala'un, 1272, whose "Golden Age" was praised by Machiavelli. But gradually the level of culture declined, and instead of the literature and art of Saladin came the brawling, raping, and thieving of ignorant demagogues.

At first these white slaves served side by side with black Sudanese, and even under Negroid rulers. But as the Egyptian sultans tried in vain to conquer Nubia and the south, the Mamelukes found themselves in opposite camps, and white slave rule with few Negroids prevailed in the north, while in the south the Negroes stubbornly held their ground down to the nineteenth century.

The contrast between this white slavery and black American slavery was striking. It involved no inborn racial differences, and because of this Nordic historians have neglected white slavery and tied the idea of slavery to Negroes. The difference between the two groups of slaves was clear: the white slaves, under leadership like that of the colored Mustansir and Saladin the Kurd, opened the way to civilization among both white and black. Had it not been for the attack on this culture by the heathen East and Christian West, the flowering of civilization in Africa might have reached great heights and even led the world.

Napoleon Bonaparte explained the difference between slavery in the East and West:

"These countries were inhabited by men of different colors. Polygamy is the simple way of preventing them from persecuting one another. The legislators have thought that in order that the whites be not enemies of the blacks, the blacks of the whites, the copper-colored of the one and the other, it was necessary to make them all members of the same family and struggle thus against a penchant of man to hate all that is not like him. Mohamet thought that four women were sufficient to attain this goal because each man could have one white, one black, one copper-colored, and one wife of another color. . . .

"When one wishes to give liberty to the blacks in the colonies of America and establish a perfect equality, the legislator will authorise polygamy and permit at the same time a white wife, a black one, and a mulatto one. Then the different colors making part of the same family will be mixed in the opinion of each. Without that one would never obtain satisfactory results. The blacks would be more numerous and cleverer and they would hold the whites in abasement and vice versa.

"Because of the general principle of equality that polygamy has established in the East there is no difference between the individuals composing the house of the Mamelukes. A black slave that a bey had bought from an African caravan became katchef and was the equal of a fine white Mameluk, native of Circassia; there was no thought even of having it otherwise.

"Slavery has never been in the Orient what it was in Europe. The customs in this respect have remained the same as in the Holy Scriptures; the servant marries with the master. In Europe, on the contrary, whoever bore the imprint of the seal of slavery remained always in the last rank. . . ."[18]

According to W. G. Palgrave: "Negroes can without any difficulty give their sons and daughters to the middle or lower class of Arab families, and thus arises a new generation of mixed race. . . . Like their progenitors, they do not readily take their place among the nobles or upper ten thousand; however, they may end by doing even this in process of time; and I have myself, while in Arabia, been honoured by the intimacy of more than one handsome 'Green-man' (mulatto) with a silver-hilted sword at his side and a rich dress on his dusky skin but denominated Sheik, or Emeer, and humbly sued by Arabs of the purest Ishmaelitish or Kahtanic stock. . . . All of this was not by Act of Parliament but by individual will and feeling."[19]

There arose numbers of cases of ruling blacks and mulattoes in the Near East. Nedjeh, a Negro slave, and his descendants ruled Arabia from 1020 to 1158. Again in 1763 Abbas, called "El Mahdi," black, thick-lipped and broad-nosed, ruled Yemen.

The Crusades and Mongols distracted the paths of leaders and left Africa and the Middle East to the ravages of the leadership of the degenerate Mamelukes of the eighteenth century. The black slaves taken to America became after a short period of hesitancy part of a new system of industry. They were chained to hard labor, kept in ignorance, and given no chance for development. Their one goal became freedom, and the Maroons were the nearest counterpart to the Mamelukes. Toussaint in Haiti was the first successful black sultan of the West. Byano and Palmares cleared his way.

There were twenty-five sultans of the Bahrite Mamelukes dynasty; among them was Bibars, who restored Syria to Egypt and attacked the Negroes of the Sudan between 1272 and 1273. Nubia regained its independence in 1320, and there was strife between Nubia and Egypt in 1366, 1385, and 1396. Nubia became practically independent after 1403.

Most scientists agree that the modern Beja are nearest the Egyptian type. Ibn Batuta described them in the fourteenth century. "After fifteen days' travelling we reached the town of Aydhab, a large town, well supplied with milk and fish; dates and grain are imported from Upper Egypt. Its inhabitants are Bejas. These people are black-skinned; they wrap themselves in yellow blankets and tie headbands about a finger-breadth wide around their heads. They do not give their daughters any share in their inheritance. They live on camels' milk and they ride on Meharis (dromedaries). One-third of the city belongs to the Sultan of Egypt and two-thirds to the King of the Bejas, who is called al-Hudrubi. On reaching Aydhab we found that al-Hudrubi was engaged in warfare with the Turks (i.e., the troops of the Sultan of Egypt), that he had sunk the ships and that the Turks had fled before him."[20]

A new dynasty of the Circassian Mamelukes reigned in Egypt from 1382 to 1517 and included twenty-three sultans. Literature and architecture still were cultivated, but there was license and fighting and slave purchases of Mongolians.

Nizir ruled from 1310 to 1341 in Egypt and exchanged embassies with the Mongols of Kepchak, with the Syrians, with the kings of Yemen and Abyssinia, and with West Africa, as well as with the emperors at Constantinople and the kings of Bulgaria.

Africans later were imported into India. King Rukn-ud-din-Barbak, who ruled at Gaur from 1459 to 1474, possessed eight thousand African slaves and was the first king of India to promote them in large numbers to high rank in his service. In 1486 these slaves rebelled, killed Fath Shah, and set their leader on the throne with the title Barbah Shah. Another African, Indil Khan, remained loyal to Fath and, returning from a distant expedition, killed Barbah and accepted the crown under the title of Saif-ud-din-Firuz. Firuz quelled the disorders of the kingdom and restored the discipline of the army. He was succeeded in 1489 by Fath Shah's young son under a regency exercised by another African; but before a year was out still another Negro, Sidi Badr, murdered both child-king and regent and usurped the throne. He reigned three years. In 1493 he was killed at the head of a sortie against rebel forces that were besieging Gaur, and with his death this remarkable Negro regime in Bengal came to an end. An Asiatic from the Oxus country was elected to the throne, and one of his first acts was to expel all the Africans from the kingdom. The exiles, many thousands in number, were turned back from Delhi and Jaunpur and finally drifted to Gujarat and the Deccan, where the slave trade had also created a considerable Negro population.[21]

In the fourteenth century Islam in the West had been shorn of its outposts in Spain and Sicily, but in the East had been extended into India and Malaysia. It had beaten back the Crusaders, but nevertheless signs of weakness appeared. For two centuries Islam had struggled against the Europeans, and the rule in the Mohammedan world had passed from the Arabs and Persians to the Turks. After the year one thousand, Turkish generals and chieftains had torn the body of Islam, had devastated its land, until at length the heathen Mongols from Central Asia started west against the Turks and in 1258 made the eastern lands of Islam a province of the Mongol empire. Timur the Lame took Bagdad in 1393.

The history of the Nile valley from the time of Saladin to the nineteenth century reads like a phantasmagoria. The promise of high and delicate culture was there; but toward the east rose menacingly the threat of Turkey, forming the right wing of Islam and ready to overwhelm Egypt. If it had not, the history of Europe might have been the history of Egypt. From the west came the steady pressure of a new and virile Negro culture, but one destined to be suddenly arrested by the repulse of the left wing of Islam in Spain, the record of the Sudan, the stubborn resistance of Atlantis overwhelmed by the slave trade to America, and the march of the Bantu toward the Great Lakes.

The effort of this ancient land of Egypt to achieve a new independence and a renewed culture depended on a fusion of Syria and Nubia with Egypt. But the rough and ignorant white slaves, who had lost all culture patterns and learned no new ones, and who nonetheless held all power of government, stifled the budding culture which might have been an African Renaissance and led to futile efforts to conquer Nubia. This distraction of power lost Egypt control of Syria.

Nubia gained independence in 1403, and from the west came the Fung and the people of Darfur, while farther down the Shilluk and Central Africa still resisted. It was in vain that Bibars and Kala'un revived Egypt; most of the fourteenth and fifteenth centuries were filled with struggles of weak and degenerate leaders. Then Selim the Great of the Ottoman empire conquered and annexed Egypt in 1517. Egypt was divided into twenty-four districts, each under Mameluke beys and all under a Turkish pasha. Degeneration set in after the seventeenth century.

Thefts and mutinies filled the sixteenth and seventeenth centuries, and in the eighteenth century the French Revolution tried to unload Napoleon on Egypt and Asia. England thwarted him in far-flung defense of India. In 1811 came Mehemet Ali, a Rumelian, who rid Egypt of the Mameluke beys by deliberate murder and set about the conquest of the Sudan. He overran Nubia in 1820, but lost his son in the mad resistance of the blacks. Meantime he courted Europe by trade and political alliance and tried to share in the profits of the ivory-slave trade. He provoked resistance and rebellion and died a madman in 1849.

His successor, Ishmael, fell into the snare of colonial imperialism, baited by Lord Beaconsfield. Britain saw in the Suez Canal, once conceived by the Pharaohs and dug by the French thousands of years later, a link to unite the British Empire, guard her Indian investment and consolidate her control of trade. Beaconsfield bought the canal from Ishmael after the British and French had involved him hopelessly in debt. When France declined to enter what was to her a doubtful partnership, England practically annexed Egypt to the British Empire.

Why was this? Was it "race"? "Surely," answered the nineteenth century, fattening on the results of Negro slavery and sneering at the mongrels of the Nile valley. But the answer was nothing so simple as the color of a man's skin or the kink of his hair. It was because Egypt during centuries of turmoil and foreign control could achieve no nationhood; because her ancient sources of self-support failed under exploitation, and her ancient culture patterns were submerged and could no longer be renewed from Central Africa by reason of the persistent and continued effort to conquer Nubia. Her new flowering of art in the thirteenth century had died. No democracy could arise in the years from Saladin to Mehemet Ali, and by that time the slave trade for ivory, succeeding the slave trade for sugar, backed by the same demand from Europe and America, had put all Africa beyond the pale of civilization.

One result of Egyptian pressure on Central Africa and its connection with modern colonization is shown by the history of Kilwara in East Africa. The empire was dismembered, the largest share falling to Uganda. When King Mutesa came to the throne of Uganda in 1862, he found Mohammedan influences in his land and was induced to admit Protestants and Catholics. The Protestants, representing British imperialism, tried to convert the king, and the Catholics, representing French imperialism, tried to make him a Catholic. In the midst of this more Mohammedans appeared, seeking also to convert Mutesa. He refused all these faiths and died a rugged pagan.

He was succeeded by his son Mwanga, who distrusted the whites. He ordered the eastern frontier closed against Europeans, and when the Protestant Bishop Hannington attempted to cross in 1885, he had him killed. The Protestants organized against Mwanga, and he banished both Protestants and Catholics. The Mohammedans became the power behind the throne. The Protestants withdrew from Buganda into Angola and organized a united front of Christians against Mohammedans and Mwanga. They captured Mwanga's capital and divided it between Protestants and Catholics. The Mohammedans began to fight back, and finally the Protestants appealed to the British East Africa Company. In 1889 the company dispatched a military mission to Uganda which was later joined by Lugard. Open civil war ensued between Catholics and Protestants.

"At the head of a considerable military force, Captain Lugard, of the Imperial British East Africa Company (Ibea), penetrated as far as Mengo, the residence of King Mwanga, and forced upon him a treaty of protectorate; then, turning against the Catholics, he attacked them on some futile pretext, and drove them onto a big island in Lake Victoria. There, around the king and the French missionaries, had gathered for refuge a considerable multitude of men, women, and children. Against this helpless and defenseless population Captain Lugard turned his guns and maxims. He exterminated a large number and then, continuing his work of destruction, he gave full rein to his troops and adherents, who burnt all the villages and stations of the White Fathers, their churches and their crops."[22] The British Protestant version of this story varies from this in many particulars.

Mwanga was finally defeated in 1899, taken prisoner and deported. Uganda then became a British protectorate.

So for a thousand years Asia and Africa strove together, renewing their spirits and mutually fertilizing their cultures from time to time, in West Asia, North

Africa, the Nile valley, and the East Coast. But at last Europe encompassed them both. In Africa she came to the south as settlers, to the west as slave traders, and to the east as colonial imperialists. Africa slept in bloody nightmare.

NOTES

1. Charles Taüber, *Seafarers and Hieroglyphs* (American Documentation Institute, Washington, D.C.).
2. Rogers, *op. cit.*, Vol. I, p. 62.
3. *Ibid.*, p. 63.
4. G. Massey, *A Book of the Beginnings* (London: Williams & Norgate, 1881), Vol. I, pp. 18, 218.
5. Edward G. Balfour, ed., "Negro Races," *Cyclopaedia of India* (London: Quaritch, 1885), 3rd ed. Vol. II, p. 1073.
6. Joseph P. Widney, *Race Life of the Aryan Peoples* (New York: Funk and Wagnalls, 1907), Vol. II, pp. 238–39.
7. Quoted in Rogers, *op. cit.*, Vol. I, p. 67.
8. Munro, *Prehistoric Japan* (Yokohama: 1911), pp. 676–78.
9. Marcel A. Dieulafoy, *L'Acropole de Suse* (Paris: Hachette et Cie, 1893), pp. 27, 44, 46, 57–86, 102, 115.
10. Harry H. Johnston, *The Negro in the New World*, pp. 24–27.
11. Arnold J. Toynbee, *A Study of History* (London: 1934), Vol. I, p. 226.
12. A letter to J. A. Rogers, December 15, 1933, quoted in Rogers, *op. cit.*, Vol. I, p. 286.
13. *See* DuBois, *Black Folk*, pp. 41–53.
14. E. Stanley Lane-Poole, *History of Egypt in Medieval Times*, edited by W. M. Flinders Petrie (London: Methuen & Co., 1914), Vol. VI, pp. 22, 28, 89.
15. *Cf.*, *ibid.*, p. 28.
16. *Cf. ibid.*, p. 89.
17. *The Book of Duarte Barbosa*, tr. from the Portuguese by M. L. Davis (London: Hakluyt Society, 1918), Vol. I, pp. 11–13, 18–20.
18. *Memoirs of the History of France* (London: Colburn, 1823–24), 2nd ed., Vol. III, pp. 152–54, 259–76.
19. W. G. Palgrave, *Narrative of a Year's Journey Through Central and Eastern Arabia* (London: 1866), Vol. I.
20. Ibn Batuta, *Travels in Asia and Africa, 1325–1354*, tr. by H. A. R. Gibb (London: G. Routledge & Sons, 1929), pp. 53, 54, 321, 322, 328, 329, 330.
21. Reginald Coupland, *East Africa and Its Invaders* (Oxford: Clarendon Press, 1938), pp. 32–33.
22. Leonard Woolf, *Empire and Commerce in Africa* (London: Allen and Unwin, n.d.), p. 288.

CHAPTER X

◆

The Black Sudan

How civilization flamed in the Sudan in a culture which was African and not Arabian and which helped light a renaissance of culture in Europe.

Early in the seventh century Islam had entered North Africa and proselyted among the Berbers and Negroes. Aided by black soldiers, the Moslems crossed into Spain; in the following century, repulsed in Europe, they crossed the west end of the Sahara and came to Negroland. Later, in the eleventh century, Arabs penetrated the Sudan and Central Africa from the east, filtering through the Negro tribes of Darfur, Kanem, and neighboring regions.

Frobenius reminded us that the ensuing culture was not Arab but Negro: "The revelations of fifteenth and seventeenth century navigators furnish us with certain proof that Negro Africa, which extended south of the Sahara desert zone, was still in full bloom, in the full brilliance of harmonious and well-formed civilizations. In the last century the superstition ruled that all high culture of Africa came from Islam. Since then we have learned much, and we know today that the beautiful turbans and clothes of the Sudanese folk were already used in Africa before Mohammed was even born or before Ethiopian culture reached inner Africa. Since then we have learned that the peculiar organization of the Sudanese states existed long before Islam and that all of the art of building and education, of city organization and handwork in Negro Africa, were thousands of years older than those of Middle Europe.

"Thus in the Sudan old real African warm-blooded culture existed and could be found in Equatorial Africa, where neither Ethiopian thought, Hamitic blood, or European civilization had drawn the pattern. Everywhere when we examine this ancient culture it bears the same impression. In the great museums—Trocadero, British Museum, in Belgium, Italy, Holland, and Germany—everywhere we see the same spirit, the same character, the same nature. All of these separate pieces unite themselves to the same expression and build a picture equally impressive as that of a collection of the art of Asia. The striking beauty of the cloth, the fantastic beauty of the drawing and the sculpture, the glory of ivory weapons; the collection of fairy tales equal to the Thousand and One Nights, the Chinese novels and the Indian philosophy.

"In comparison with such spiritual accomplishment the impression of the African spirit is easily seen. It is stronger in its folds, simpler in its richness. Every weapon is simple and practical, not only in form but fantasy. Every line of carving is simple and strong. There is nothing that makes a clearer impression of strength, and all streams out of the fire and the hut, the sweat and grease-treated hides and the animal dung. Everything is practical, strong, workmanly. This is the character of the African style. When one approaches it with full understanding, one immediately realizes that this impression rules all Africa. It expresses itself in the activity of all Negro people even in their sculpture. It speaks out of their dances and their masks; out of the understanding of their religious life, just as out of the reality of their living, their state-building, and their conception of fate. It lives in their fables, their fairy stories, their wise sayings, and their myths. And once we are forced to this conclusion, then the Egyptian comes into the comparison. For this discovered culture form of Negro Africa has the same peculiarity."[1]

It was Asia and Africa which in the thirteenth century prepared Europe for the Renaissance through Genghis Khan and the Crusades. Negroes were building then in the Sudan the beginnings of the great states which flourished in the fourteenth century and which became an integral part of the cultural complex of the Middle Ages. For a century Ghana had been trading across the sands with Europe. Already the power of the Mandingos was being felt in West Africa, which in another century would build the great kingdom of Melle known to all Europe. In Asia, the black slaves from Africa had revolted, seizing power and becoming great rulers. The Almoravides, Berbers with Negro blood, and hosts of pure Negro adherents had invaded and seized Morocco. On the African East Coast, Arabs and Persians with troops of Negroid mulattoes had built large and beautiful cities and were trading not only with the black kingdoms of the interior but with China and India. The Crusades, beginning in the eleventh century and extending through the thirteenth, had brought crude Europe into close touch with the civilization of the Orient and led to a desperate effort to ally the Christian Church of Rome with black Prester John of Ethiopia in an attack upon Islam.

Sidjilmessa, the last town in Lower Morocco toward the desert, was founded in 757 by a Negro who ruled over the Berber inhabitants. Indeed, many towns in the Sudan and the desert were thus ruled and felt no incongruity in this arrangement. They say, to be sure, that the Moors destroyed Howdaghost because it paid tribute to the black town of Ghana, but this was because the town was heathen and not because it was black. There is a story that a Berber king overthrew one of the cities of the Sudan and all the black women committed suicide, being too proud to allow themselves to fall into the hands of white men.

In the west the Moslems first came into touch with the Negro kingdom of Ghana. Here large quantities of gold were gathered in early days, and we have the names of seventy-four rulers before A.D. 300, running through twenty-one generations. This would take us back approximately a thousand years, to 700 B.C., or about the time that Pharaoh Necho of Egypt sent out the Phoenician expedition which circumnavigated Africa; and possibly before the time when Hanno, the Carthaginian, explored the West Coast of Africa.

By the middle of the eleventh century Ghana was the principal kingdom in the western Sudan. Already the town had a native and a Mussulman quarter, and was built of wood and stone with surrounding gardens. The king had an army of two hundred thousand. The wealth of the country was great. A century later the king had become Mohammedan in faith. He had a palace with sculptures and glass windows. There was a prosperous desert trade. Gold, skins, ivory, kola nuts, gums, honey, wheat, and cotton were exported, and the whole Mediterranean coast traded in the Sudan. Other and lesser black kingdoms like Tekrou, Silla, and Masina surrounded Ghana.[2] Semitic immigrants, who probably invaded this part of Africa before the Arabs, settled as farmers and shepherds and had a culture inferior to that of the surrounding Negroes with whom they mingled.

Under the black rulers of Ghana the state attained its highest civilization. Bekri, Yakut, and Ibn Kaldoun testify that it ruled over the Berbers in what is now Mauritania. The Berber capital, Howdaghost, paid tribute to the king of Ghana. On the south its dependencies stretched beyond the Senegal River to the gold mines of the Faleme and the Bambuk. It touched the Mandingo on the Upper Niger. Toward the east it extended almost as far as Timbuktu. It was known in Cairo and Bagdad.

Around 1040 a movement of Mohammedan propaganda started among the Berbers and Negroes. They formed the famous sect of the Almoravides and began waging war from the Sudan into Spain. "The Almoravides . . . were Berbers and were largely mingled with pure Negroes. Yusuf, their leader, was himself a Negro. The 'Roudh-el-Kartas,' a Moorish work, describes him as having 'woolly hair' and being 'brown' in color. Yusuf's favorite concubine was a white captive, Fadh-el-Hassen (Perfection of Beauty). She was the mother of Yusuf's successor, Ali. Alphonso VI, the white Spanish King, who was often defeated by Yusuf, had, in turn, a Moorish Queen, the lovely Zayda, who was the mother of his favorite son, Sancho. It was the latter's death in battle that hastened the aged Alphonso's death."[3]

The Almoravides converted numbers of Sudanese Negroes but gained no political control over them. They tried to subdue the kings of Ghana; in 1051 Howdaghost was taken and pillaged. Some of the Negroids migrated south while others, attracted by the new religion, joined the Almoravides. Among the converts was the king of the Mandingos. A number of such kings and chieftains were converted, but the mass of people changed their religion slowly. Finally under the Sarkolle chiefs the Mohammedanized Negroes moved toward the Gulf of Guinea, founding cities and becoming rich from commerce in kola nuts, cattle, cloth, and gold. Habits of intellectual research were introduced which have continued until today.

In 1076 the Almoravides captured Ghana and in 1087 Seville was taken. This made the Almoravides masters of Spain as well as of Morocco. Consisting not simply of Berbers but of numbers of converted blacks, the Almoravides set up a kingdom in Spain, but were finally defeated in 1620. They were followed by the

Almohades, who held the Mohammedan part of Spain against the Christians. Under their influence Moorish power in Spain reached its highest peak of grandeur, and reared such monuments of artistic splendor as the Alhambra and the Mosque at Cordova.

In the ninth and tenth centuries Ghana flourished, but toward the middle of the eleventh century began to decline, probably because of the encroachment of the desert and the attack of the Almoravides. Ghana ceased to exist about the middle of the thirteenth century. Its site was excavated in 1914 and vestiges of a great city were found, with ruins of hewn stone construction, and some sculpture.

In the meantime, various tribes freed themselves from the overlordship of Ghana and became independent. The Diawara dynasty, founded in 1270, maintained its power until 1754. The great Songhay state, founded about 690, began to develop but was overshadowed by the kingdom of Melle. Melle was the kingdom of the Mandingos where there ruled and still rules what Delafosse called "probably the most ancient dynasty of the world." For seven hundred years the little village on the Upper Niger was the principal capital of one of the largest kingdoms in Africa, the empire of the Mandingos, or Melle. For several centuries the Mansas, or kings of the Mandingos, ruled their little village. When in 1050 the king was converted to Islamism by the Almoravides, he made a pilgrimage to Mecca and established relations with neighboring states.

"As to the people of Mali [Melle], they surpassed the other blacks ... in wealth and numbers. They extended their dominions and conquered the Susu, as well as the kingdom of Ghana in the vicinity of the ocean towards the west. The Mohammedans say that the first King of Mali was Baramindanah. He performed the pilgrimage to Mekkah, and enjoined his successors to do the same."[4]

The territory of Melle lay southeast of Ghana and some five hundred miles north of the Gulf of Guinea. Its kings were known by the title of Mansa, and from the middle of the thirteenth century to the middle of the fourteenth, the Mellestine, as its dominion was called, was the leading power in the land of the blacks. The state was partially overthrown by the king of Sosa but was restored by Sandiata who captured Ghana in 1240. He introduced the raising and weaving of cotton and made his kingdom secure. His successor increased it. The empire reached its greatest power between 1307 and 1332. Its greatest king, Mari Jalak (Mansa Musa), made his pilgrimage to Mecca in 1324 with a caravan of sixty thousand persons including twelve thousand young slaves gowned in figured cotton and Persian silk. He took eighty camel loads of gold dust (worth about five million dollars) to defray his expenses, and greatly impressed the people of the East with his magnificence. During his reign was erected the brick mosque at Gao with crenelated flat roof and pyramidal minaret, a type of architecture which was extended through the Sudan. This type of construction was said to have been originated by an architect hired by Mansa Musa, who rewarded him with fifty-four kilograms of gold according to Ibn Kaldoun.

We must remember that at the time of the development of these Negro kingdoms, Europe was just emerging from the Dark Ages and was full of "robbers, fetishmen, and slaves."[5] The Mandingan empire of Melle occupied nearly the whole of what is now French Africa and part of British West Africa. Its rulers were in close communication with the rulers of the shores south and north of the Mediterranean.

Ibn Batuta visited Melle in 1352 and wrote: "My stay at Iwalatan lasted about fifty days; and I was shown honour and entertained by its inhabitants. It is an excessively hot place, and boasts a few small date-palms, in the shade of which they sow watermelons. Its water comes from underground waterbeds at that point, and there is plenty of mutton to be had. The garments of its inhabitants, most of whom belong to the Massufa tribe, are of fine Egyptian fabrics. Their women are of surpassing beauty, and are shown more respect than the men. The state of affairs amongst these people is indeed extraordinary. Their men show no signs of jealousy whatever; no one claims descent from his father, but on the contrary from his mother's brother. A person's heirs are his sister's sons, not his own sons. This is a thing which I have seen nowhere in the world except among the Indians of Malabar. But those are heathens; *these* people are Muslims, punctilious in observing the hours of prayer, studying books of law, and memorizing the Koran.

"I was at Malli during the two festivals of the sacrifice and the fast-breaking. On these days the sultan takes his seat on the *pempi* after the mid-afternoon prayer. The armour-bearers bring in magnificent arms—quivers of gold and silver, swords ornamented with gold and with golden scabbards, gold and silver lances, and crystal maces. At his head stand four amirs driving off the flies, having in their hands silver ornaments resembling saddle stirrups. The commanders, *qadi,* and preachers sit in their usual places. The interpreter Dugha comes with his four wives and his slave-girls, who are about a hundred in number. They are wearing beautiful robes, and on their heads they have gold and silver fillets, with gold and silver balls attached. A chair is placed for Dugha to sit on. He plays on an instrument made of reeds with some small calabashes at its lower end, and chants a poem in praise of the sultan, recalling his battles and deeds of valour. The women and girls sing with him and play with bows. Accompanying them are about thirty youths, wearing red woolen tunics and white skull-caps; each of them has his drum slung from his shoulder and beats it. Afterwards come his boy pupils, who play and turn wheels in the air, like the natives of Sind. They show a marvellous nimbleness and agility in these exercises and play most cleverly with swords. Dugha also makes a fine play with the sword. Thereupon the sultan orders a gift to be presented to Dugha and he is given a purse containing two hundred *mithqals* of gold dust, and is informed of the contents of the purse before all the people.

"The Negroes possess some admirable qualities. They are seldom unjust, and have a greater abhorrence of injustice than any other people. Their sultan shows no mercy to anyone who is guilty of the least act of it. There is complete security in their country. Neither traveller nor inhabitant in it has anything to fear from robbers or men of violence. They do not confiscate the property of any white man who dies in their country, even if it be uncounted wealth. On the contrary, they give it into the charge of some trustworthy person among the whites, until the rightful heir takes possession of it.

". . . one has the impression that Mandingo was a real state whose organization and civilization could be compared with those of the Musselman kingdoms or indeed the Christian kingdoms of the same epoch."[6]

Cooley has told us: "Ibn S'aid, a writer of the thirteenth century, has enumerated thirteen nations of blacks extending across Africa, from Ghana in the west, to the Beja on the shores of the Red Sea in the east."[7]

Professor Leo Hansberry of Howard University gives me the following list of rulers and the various Sudanese countries:

SOME KINGDOMS AND EMPIRES IN WEST AFRICA IN THE MIDDLE AGES

1. The kingdom of Ghana
2. The kingdom of Melle
3. The Mellestine empire
4. The kingdom of Songhay
5. The empire of Songhay
6. The kingdom of Borgu
7. The kingdom of Mossi
8. The kingdom of Nupe
9. The kingdom of Yoruba
10. The kingdom of Benin

SOME KINGS OF MELLE AND THE MELLESTINE FROM 1213 TO 1464

1. Mausa Allakoy
2. Mausa Jatah
3. Mausa Wali I
4. Mausa Wali II
5. Mausa Khalifa
6. Mausa Abu Bekr
7. Mausa Sakura
8. Mausa Gongo-Mussa I
9. Mausa Suleiman
10. Mausa Magha
11. Mausa Mussa II
12. Mausa Mahmud

SOME RULERS OF SONGHAY FROM 679 TO 1592

1. Za Alayaman
2. Za Zakoi
3. Za Takoi
4. Za Akoi
5. Za Kou
6. Za Alifoi
7. Za Biyai
8. Za Biyai
9. Za Karai
10. Za Yama I
11. Za Yama II
12. Za Yama III
13. Za Koukorai
14–32. Nineteen Others of this Dynasty
33. Sonni Ali-Kolon
34. Sonni Selman Nare
35–51. Sixteen Others of this Dynasty
52. Sonni Ali
53. Askia El Hadj or Askia the Great
54. Askia Moussa
55. Askia Mohammed-Beukan
56. Askia Isma'il
57. Askia Ishaq I
58. Askia Daoud
59. Askia El Hadj II
60. Askia Mohammed-Bano
61. Askia Ishaq II

The greatest development of civilization in Africa, after Egypt, arose late in the fifteenth century in the empire of the Songhay, east of the Mellestine. The story is that a king of Melle, returning from a pilgrimage to Mecca, stopped at Timbuktu, where a black and ancient dynasty was ruling. He seized two young princes and carried them home to educate them and bring them up subservient to his power. Eventually they escaped, returned home, and founded the Songhay state. It expanded rapidly; first westward, where it absorbed the Mellestine and the remains of ancient Ghana. Then it turned south and drove the peoples of the Mossi and the city-states of the coast south, beyond the Kong mountains. Under the victorious Sonni Ali, the Songhay began to expand east toward the Nile valley, starting ever-widening centers of culture among the Haussa, the peoples of Bornu; and centuries later among the Fung and the folk of Kanem until in the nineteenth century this western culture came in contact with Mehemet Ali in Egypt and the Nubians of the Sudan.

The organized Songhay state at the height of its power under the black Mohammedan Askia the Great was a remarkable state from any point of view. Its organized administration, its roads and methods of communication, its system of public security, put it abreast of any contemporary European or Asiatic state. It was as large as Europe. The emperor "was obeyed with as much docility on the farthest limits of his empire as in his own palace." Gao, Timbuktu, and Jenne were intellectual centers, and at the University of Sankoré gathered thousands of students of law, literature, grammar, geography, and surgery. A literature began to develop in the sixteenth and seventeenth centuries. The University was in correspondence with the best institutions on the Mediterranean coast.

Art, especially in building and manufacture, reached a high level. The system of labor rested in part on domestic slavery, but that slavery not only protected the slave from exploitation and poverty, but left the way open, with no barrier of class or color, for him to rise to high positions of state. The clan organization of the artisans gave each one a chance for individual taste in his work and no fear of hurry or hunger.

Leo Africanus describes the kingdom of Songhay under the Askias in the fifteenth century: "Corne, cattle, milke, and butter this region yeeldeth in great abundance: but salt is verie scarce here; for it is brought hither by land from Tegaza, which is fiue hundred miles distant. When I my selfe was here, I saw one camels loade of salt sold for 80 ducates. The rich king of Tombuto hath many plates and sceptres of gold, some whereof weigh 1300 poundes: and he keepes a magnificent and well-furnished court. . . . Here are great store of doctors, iudges, priests, and other learned men, that are bountifully maintained at the kings cost and charges. And hither are brought diuers manuscripts or written bookes out of Berbarie, which are sold for more money than any other merchandize. . . ."[8]

It is a matter for reflection to ask what influence Africa might have had on the world if the Songhay state had been able to fulfill its promise. But a singular fate overtook it. First came the Mongol and the Turk from Asia. The Turk seized the Eastern Roman Empire and in the west drove Arab and Berber from the coast down into Africa and below the barrier of desert sand. Armed with gunpowder, these fugitives fell upon the Songhay and overthrew their state and culture at Tenkadibou in 1591. Shutting themselves up in North Africa, they degenerated and dragged the Songhay with them, leaving only the eddies of their culture to move farther east. If the culture of Ethiopia had not been imprisoned by the desertion of European Christianity, it might have expanded under another Taharqa and rescued the Songhay culture. On the contrary, it was nullified by the decline of the Mamelukes after the brilliant age of Saladin.

For one hundred and twenty years after 1660 these pashas of mixed Turkish, Berber, and Negro blood ruled Timbuktu, paying tribute to the black Bambara kings and bribing the Tureregs. Finally in 1894 the city was taken by Marshal Joffre of France.

East of the Songhay there developed two powerful states. The Haussa states were formed of seven cities, among which were Kano and Katsina. They were centers of cotton and leather manufactures, agriculture and trade, smelting, weaving and dyeing. Katsina in the middle of the sixteenth century was thirteen miles in circumference and divided into quarters for the different trades and industries. The Haussa fell under the control of other rulers and finally was governed by Mohammed Bello in the eighteenth century. Bello was a noted man of letters. The Haussa states were occupied by the British in 1904.

Still farther east was the domain called Bornu in the west and Kanem in the east. The population occupied a large territory and was of mixed Negro and Berber descent. The first ruler was Saefe, and the kings took the title of Mai. Mai Idris I (1352–1376) was visited by Ibn Batuta, who found copper mines in full operation, the Negro custom of concealing the king behind a curtain, and the use of drums to send messages.

In the political development of the western Sudan the kingdom of Bornu played a notable part and has a recorded history as far back as the tenth century A.D.[9] The influence of its rulers extended far. The kingdom or empire of Bornu had its beginnings probably within two hundred years of the opening of the Mohammedan era. During these centuries the Christian West had remained ignorant, rude, and barbarous, while Saracenic culture passed on the torch of civilization to future ages. The kingdom of Bornu drew its inspiration from Egypt and North Africa. The degree of civilization achieved by its early chiefs would appear to compare favorably with that of European monarchs of that day. It was probably during the twelfth century that a settled capital was founded at Nnjimi (Sima) near Mao, in Kanem, east of Lake Chad. From thence a redoubtable warrior, Mai Dunama Dabalemi (1221–1259), extended the Bornu empire up to Kauwar and Tibesti in the north, and to the regions southwest of Lake Chad.

At the close of the period, rendered illustrious for Bornu by Dunama Dabalemi, there occurred the sack of Bagdad by the Mongols under Hulagu Khan. This event caused an increased number of itinerant Arab divines to go west and enter Egypt and Africa, taking with them the teaching of the various Tarikas of Islam which had arisen in Irak.[10]

Though the royal line was continuous from the beginning (A.D. 750 to 800) till it was superseded by the Kanembu Kuburi about 1810, there were fundamental differences between the Bornu (Kanem) kingdom as it existed at the time of the death of Dunama Dabalemi in the thirteenth century and the revived Bornu kingdom which was established about 1470. The earlier kingdom was a rule established by camel-men over the tribes extending from Lake Chad east to Borku and Wadai. These monarchs conquered the Teda, or Tebu, races which lay to the north of them and solidified their position by marrying into the Tebu royal clan.

Athwart the direct road to the East from Kanem now lay the Fung dynasty of Senaar on the Blue Nile and the Christian Dongola kingdom. One tradition survives of a time when the Meks of Senaar, possibly a remnant of the Meroitic kingdom, were connected with the early Bornu Mais of Wadai.

Within a hundred years of the date of the conquest of Constantinople by the Turks, Idris Alooma had as mercenaries Turkish musketeers. The keeping open of all routes from the Mediterranean and Egypt was at least one service of the kingdom.[11]

Southwest of Lake Chad in 1520 was the sultanate of Bagirmi, which was annexed by the French in 1896. In the eastern Sudan, Darfur and Kordofan arose to power in the sixteenth and seventeenth century. Kordofan was allied with Napoleon in the Egyptian campaign.

In the nineteenth century the central power of eastern Sudan was Rabah. At one time Rabah conquered Bornu and brought a considerable part of North Africa under his control, overthrowing Bagirmi, Bornu, and other states around Lake Chad. He was the son of a Negro woman and was finally conquered and killed by the French in 1900.

Since the fifth century the capital of Nubia had been at old Dongola, where Silko, King of the Beja, had embraced Christianity in 450. As the Mohammedans pressed up the Nile valley, the Nubians held them back for two centuries. For a period of six hundred years they were compelled to pay tribute to the Mohammedans; then were annexed to Egypt in 1275 but became independent in 1403. In the fourteenth and fifteenth centuries fighting went on between the Nubians and Arabians, but the Christian kingdom of Nubia finally fell to Islam in the sixteenth century.

Farther south, the Fung pushed up out of the Sudan and made their capital at the junction of the White and Blue Nile. When Selim invaded Egypt in 1617, the Fung became Mohammedan and arranged to divide Ethiopia between them and the Arabs. They ruled from the Third Cataract to Senaar during the sixteenth, seventeenth, and eighteenth centuries. Eventually they conquered the Shilluk and later the Abyssinians. The state of Darfur reached great proportions in the early seventeenth century.

Meantime the Portuguese had reached Abyssinia and opened it again to the knowledge of Europeans. Abyssinia had reached a high degree of culture before that, but at the time of the arrival of the Portuguese had fallen into a number of petty states. The Fung now tried to annex northern Ethiopia but were driven back with slaughter by the new ruler of Egypt. Mehemet Ali sent his son to conquer them. The son was killed in 1822 just as he had founded Khartoum. His father wreaked a terrible vengeance on the Sudanese for this death and then in 1839 began to plan to take part in the ivory-slave trade which now was reaching up from East Africa.

This trade and turmoil reduced the Sudan to a state of ruin and misery in the nineteenth century. Thereupon Mohammed Ahmad, the Mahdi, revolted in 1881 and, aided by the Dinka, another Negro tribe, drove both the Egyptians and English out of the Sudan for sixteen years. The Mahdi was a black Kushite. He escaped capture and in 1883 saved Kordofan, where he massacred the English army led by Hicks Pasha in southern Equatoria. In 1885 the Mahdi captured Khartoum and killed Chinese Gordon. He died the next year, and his successor attacked Abyssinia and killed the Emperor John.

In Abyssinia, Menelik of Shoa became ruler and resisted the efforts of Italy to reduce his country to vassalage, overthrowing the Italians at the battle of Adua in 1896. The British Empire in Africa was now threatened by two black men, one in Abyssinia and one in the Sudan, and when Menelik and the French made alliance, the English army started immediately, captured Khartoum in 1898, killing twenty-seven thousand natives, and defeated the successor of the Mahdi.

Through this development in Egypt and in the Sudan there had gone on in the thirteenth, fourteenth, and fifteenth centuries a significant interchange of culture between the East and the West through Africa. Greek scientists made pilgrimages to Egypt and Assyria and carried home the lore of yellow and black sages. As the Greek-Roman culture declined, the Arabs seized intellectual leadership and developed it in Africa, marching to western Asia and southern Europe. With the Crusades came a new period of intercourse between Negroid Africa and other areas of civilization.

Constantine the African (1020–1087) may or may not have had some Negro blood. He was born in Carthage where all races were represented. He became one of the important medical writers of the Middle Ages and started the translation from Latin to Arabic. His work began the end of the Dark Ages in Europe, and the dawn of scholasticism and his imperfect efforts marked the flow of Greek culture into Europe through Africa.

Whether or not Constantine himself was Negroid, many Negroes shared in later phases of this same cultural intercourse.

Because of this, by the thirteenth century the European world looked upon the black world with romantic respect. As early as the fifth century the legend of Saint Moor occurs: the legend of a saint of the Roman Catholic Church who was a black man and was reputed to have been a prince in Egypt. In the tenth century Otto of the Holy Roman Empire chose Saint Mauritius as the patron saint of Germany, and from 1000 to 1500 his statues and his worship were dominant in central Europe. Walter von der Vogelweide sang of knightly virtues regardless of skin color:

Many a Moor is rich in virtues within:
Behold their white hearts, if someone turns them round.

In the epic *Parsifal*, Wolfram von Eschenbach in the thirteenth century portrayed a white man and a black man as brothers. A European knight comes to the country of Zassamank, whose Queen Belakane and people were described as *"noch schwarzer waren als die Nacht"* (even blacker than the night). He falls in love with the queen, courts and marries her, because her noble and pure character seems to him quite equal to that of a Christian. Later, however, disturbed by the difference in their religions, he abandons her, and back in his own country of Valois he wins the Queen of Valois in a tournament and becomes king. Yet always he cherishes a deep feeling of love for, and sense of wrong toward, his abandoned black wife. After his death, his son Parsifal becomes the great knight who leads the search for the Holy Grail. But meantime the deserted black queen has given birth to a son, and this son is miraculously black and white ("*ein sohnlein das zweifarbig war*") and therefore named Feirefiz, or "colored man" ("*bunte sohn*"). Later Parsifal meets this brother, and not knowing him, joins battle with

him in the hardest fight he ever had. In the duel his sword breaks and he would
have been killed had it not been for the generous mercy of his colored foe.
Finally they recognize each other as half-brothers and Feirefiz proves as faithful
as any Christian. Led by his love for a white European woman, he agrees to
baptism and then carries Christianity to the East.

This story of the crossing of the paths of Parsifal and Feirefiz is more than a side
issue to the main story of the Holy Grail. It points toward the bridging of the gaps
between creeds and races and is of great significance in revealing the thought of
enlightened and civilized society in Europe in the thirteenth century.[12] Throughout
the Middle Ages, in German and in Latin Europe, statues of the "Black Virgin
Mary" and portraits of Negro saints of the Church were widely exhibited. The
stained glass of the Cathedral at Chartres especially illustrates this.

Shakespeare, writing to entertain England in the late sixteenth and early seventeenth centuries portrayed a black man not only as a courageous soldier, but
also a great gentleman who sued successfully for the hand of the daughter of a
senator of the richest Italian state; and in *The Merchant of Venice*, too, a black
suitor for a white princess is portrayed as natural and equal.

In Shakespeare's *Othello*[13] there are ten allusions to his race and color: to his
thick lips (Act I, Scene II, line 66); to his "sooty bosom" (Act I, Scene II, line 70);
when Emilia calls him "black" (Act V, Scene II, line 130); when the duke alludes
to him as "black" (Act I, Scene III, lines 288–89); and especially when Othello
alludes to himself, "black as mine own face" (Act III, Scene III, lines 286–87), and
says, "haply for I am black" (Act III, Scene III, line 263). There are any number of
other allusions to the contrast of color that first startled Desdemona (Act III,
Scene III, lines 229, 230; Act I, Scene III, line 98); and in Desdemona's defense of
a black woman (Act II, Scene II, lines 132–34). Yet with all this Shakespeare did
not hesitate to allude to Othello as descended from kings (Act I, Scene II, lines
21–22), and all Othello's companions agree as to his nobility of character: "a worthy governor," "brave Othello," "noble" and "true of mind," "great of heart,"
and especially Iago's tribute:

> The Moor, howbeit that I endure him not,
> Is of a constant, loving, noble nature,
> And I dare think he'll prove to Desdemona
> A most dear husband. (Act II, Scene I, lines 278–82)

Despite this there are critics who have almost had hysterics in seeking to
deny that Shakespeare meant to paint a Negro as a noble warrior and successful suitor of a beautiful white woman.

When Italian painters and others began to paint the legend of the three kings
who visited the cradle of Christ, it seemed logical that one of the three princes,
who represent the three great peoples of earth, should be a black Negroid of
Africa as the other two represented yellow Asia and white Europe.

In the same fourteenth century we see growing in the Sudan the expansion of
imperialism in black Africa. The movement of Islam up the Nile continued from
the middle of the thirteenth to the beginning of the nineteenth centuries. As a

result, the Bantu tribes, which probably had originally moved north from the Great Lakes toward the Mediterranean, began a countermovement perhaps long before the eleventh century. They moved toward the West Coast and the kingdom of the Congo, which dominated the valley and forests of the great Congo system; they pressed upon the Great Lakes, threatening the Negroids and mulattoes on the East Coast; and they fell upon the civilization of the Monomotapa centering at Zimbabwe. They overthrew and changed the culture while at the same time continuing it. They marched on in a series of stops and forays until they reached South Africa at the beginning of the nineteenth century.

In the west came greater disaster to black Africa. The city-state coast culture, withdrawing from the Sudanese imperialism, met expanding Europe; and that Europe, beginning with trade in gold and pepper, turned to a trade in human flesh on the greatest scale the world has ever seen. The gain from American black labor together with the loot of India changed the face of world industry. Built on a miraculous union of science and technique, the capitalistic system was founded on African slavery and degradation. The very name of the Songhay was forgotten, and Europe ruled the world.

This thousand years of history might have been different if the Christian Church had retained its hold upon Asia and Africa instead of expelling these countries and turning to the Nordic barbarians. In Northern Africa, the Nile valley, and Ethiopia, in Syria and the Middle East, the Catholic Church had wide range and power during the early Middle Ages. Through the greed of the Eastern Roman Empire, and because of endless controversy and disputes like that of Arianism, all these churches were lost to the Roman hierarchy. Thus when Islam came to the valley of the Nile it came to defend Egyptian Christians and was welcomed by them, instead of meeting opposition from the organized Christian Church. When, on the other hand, Christianity met black folk in the African slave and red men in America, it regarded them as lost heathens to be exterminated or enslaved. Thus the Church upheld the slave trade and its consequences.

Was it possible that so fine a flowering of culture as that of the Sudan should have had no influence on the renaissance of culture in Europe? There was but scant indigenous culture in Arabia. The rise of civilization among Arabs, as among all peoples, took place where they were fired by contact with Mongoloids at Bagdad, Negroids in the valley of the Nile; and in Spain after the Arabs had passed slowly and in comparatively small groups through Africa and augmented their numbers with black and brown Negroids and mixed Berbers. So much so that Europe for five centuries described Islamic culture in Spain as a civilization of colored people, "Moors"—Blackamoors and Tawny Moors; and the whole discussion of human skin color and its social implications in the Middle Ages assumed that Moors and Negroes were identical.

"Adolphe Bloch has given the following precise description of the present race of the Moors and the manner in which black and white amalgamated over long centuries to form it. He says: 'The race which gave birth to the Moroccans can be no other than the African Negroes because the same black type with features more or less Caucasian is found all the way to Senegal upon the right bank of the river without counting that it has been recognized in various parts of the

Sahara . . . and from there come black Moors who still have thick lips as a result of Negro descent and not from intermixture.

" 'As to the white, bronze, or dark Moors, they are no other than the near relations of black Moors with whom they form the varieties of the same race; and as one can also see among the Europeans, blonds, brunets, and chestnuts in the midst of the same population, so one may see Moroccans of every color in the same agglomeration without its being a question of their being real mulattoes.' "[14]

These Moorish sea-rovers sailed along the coasts of Scotland for centuries. David McRitchie has told of them: "Allan McRuari, the black-skinned Hebridean pirate of the fifteenth century, is one notable instance of these black invaders." George Hardy said: "The Moors profited by their maritime situation to create a powerful fleet and to undertake against the Christian countries of the Mediterranean a savage struggle. From their ports left armed ships manned by men of proved bravery and maintained by communal societies. These 'corsairs' descended unexpectedly upon the coasts or isles of the Mediterranean, and they captured and sold as slaves the sailors and the passengers. A veritable terror reigned in the Mediterranean. . . . They ravaged the coasts of Portugal, Spain, Southern France—and even went as far as Britain."[15]

Draper, writing of the eleventh century, speaks of the vastly superior social and artistic development of the swarthy Moors, who, he says, might well have looked "with supercilious contempt on the dwellings of the rulers of Germany, France, and England, which were scarce better than stables—chimneyless, windowless, and with a hole in the roof for the smoke to escape like the wigwams of certain Indians."[16]

Lately some recognition of the part that the Mohammedan East and Asia played in the European Renaissance has been made; but significant silence and indisposition to investigate has been shown in the case of the black Sudan. Centers of culture and learning are known to have existed there long before they arose in France, Germany, or England. But if they are recognized at all, it is assumed that the leaders were "Arab" or "Berber." In literature alone, and there sparingly, have single black men been mentioned; but is it reasonable to suppose that in Cairo and Seville, in the Universities of Sankoré and Timbuktu, black brains did not function? It is unreasonable only to those who accept and spread the American slave theory of the eternal inferiority of Negroes.

Remember that Europe did not raise herself out of the semi-barbarism of the Dark Age and bring back the culture of Greece and Rome. After Greece had floundered in petty feuds and Rome had fallen in senile decay, Byzantium, through Constantinople, handed Greek culture back to Asia and Africa, whence it came. At Bagdad and Alexandria and Cairo it flamed anew under Islam. It was not "Arabian"; the nomad Arabs carried culture but seldom originated it. From the Euphrates and the Nile the renewed civilization moved into North Africa, into Moorish Spain, and into black Africa. Nothing that ever touched Africa could evade the fertilization of Negroid culture and Negroid blood. Black universities sent black scholars to learn and lecture to the Mediterranean world. Black historians, like Abderrahman Es-Sadi, wrote the "Bible of the

Sudan"—Tarikes-Sudan; and the Tarikh-el-Fettach. From this Africa a new cultural impulse entered Europe and became the Renaissance.

Was it possible or inherently probable that black Africa had no creative part in
all this? That none of the science and literature came from black brains? That the
Europe which praised and lauded black folk of that day, did it in mere curiosity
or charity? Or is it more probable that the cultural contributions of many
Negroids have been forgotten or unrecognized because their color seemed unimportant, or was unknown or forgotten; and because to modern Europe, black civilization has been a contradiction in terms? Renaissance Europe, bounding
forward on new cultural conquests, flowered in art, science, and literature; then
traded with the world and discovered endless profit in stealing and selling
human beings and in the scientific enslavement of the major portion of mankind,
until in the twentieth century came suicide and collapse, analogous to, but on a
vaster scale than, the Peloponnesian War.

A determined legend can successfully contradict fact; Australian and New
Zealand soldiers coming to Egypt in 1919 were astonished to find that Egyptians
were "Niggers"; that is, not "white" as they had always been told; troops quar-
tered in Germany by the French in 1919 were reviled by Americans as "Negroes."
No, said the French, they were "white" Algerians! Visitors to North Africa are surprised to find so many Negroes and mulattoes and hasten to explain it as the
result of the modern slave trade. There were Negroes and mulattoes in North
Africa in Egyptian times.

It must be remembered that in ancient and medieval days the color of a man's
skin was usually not stressed or even mentioned unless it had cultural significance; that is, if a group of black folk had a particular cultural pattern, then reference to the skin color of an individual belonging to that group fixed his cultural
status. On the other hand, a man might be black and not belong to a black cultural
group; in that case his skin color would not be mentioned at all. Thus Ra Nesi,
Pharaoh of Egypt, was mentioned as black probably because he was also a member of an Ethiopian clan; while Nofritari, although black, was called Egyptian. In
North Africa a follower of Mohammed in 800, as in 1800, was a Mohammedan, no
matter what his color; but a member of a Sudanese tribal clan was referred to as
"black," because of his political and religious affiliations. So in East Africa, the
powerful Tipoo-Tib is always called an "Arab," when his pictures clearly show
him to be what Americans would denominate a "full-blooded" Negro.

Moreover, "black" is a relative expression; no human skin is absolutely black,
and any so-called black skin can be called "dark." Thus many persons of Negro
lineage appear in history simply as brunets or without reference at all to color. In
African history particularly, tens of thousands of persons have thus been assigned
to the "white" race, partly because their descent was not known and partly
because color did not matter in the twelfth century as it did in the nineteenth.

A work by Al-Jahiz, a writer, whom Christopher Dawson calls the greatest
Arab scholar and stylist of the nineteenth century, is a book entitled *Kitab al
Sudan wa'l-Bidan*, or *The Superiority of the Black Race over the White*. "White" here
does not mean the fair whites, but dark-skinned whites and mulattoes. The fair
white is called "red man." Jahiz included the East Indians among the blacks.

If when the civilization of the Sudan turned eastward it had been inspired by the best culture of Asia and Europe, what might not have happened? But Europe at that hour regarded both continents as enemies of the "City of God" and was also moving rapidly toward a conception of economic mastery of the world beginning with conquest and loot, marching thence to human slavery on an unprecedented scale, and ending in capitalistic exploitation not simply of the working class in Europe but especially of the dark workers of Asia and Africa. All this ended in colonial imperialism. In this direction, then, there was after the Battle of Tenkadibou no hope for a welcoming hand in work, faith, or self-development in culture from Europe. Civilization in the Sudan died of strangulation by slavery and the European determination to master the world, no matter what the cost in degradation and pain.

NOTES

1. Frobenius, *op. cit.*, p. 56.
2. *The Negro,* pp. 50, 51.
3. Rogers, *op. cit.*, Vol. I, pp. 151–52.
4. W. D. Cooley, *The Negroland of the Arabs Examined and Explained* (London: Arrowsmith, 1841), p. 62.
5. Reade, *op. cit.*, p. 30.
6. Ibn Batuta, *op. cit.*, pp. 321–22, 328, 329, 330.
7. Cooley, *op. cit.*, p. viii.
8. Leo Africanus, *History and Description of Africa*, tr. by John Pory (printed for the Hakluyt Society, London, 1896), Vol. III, pp. 824, 825.
9. H. R. Palmer, *Mai Idris of Bornu* (Lagos: Government Publication, 1926), preface.
10. *Ibid.*, p. 2.
11. *Ibid.*, p. 5.
12. *Cf. Phylon*, Vol. II, pp. 375–76.
13. Hudson Shakespeare, edited by E. C. and A. K. Black (New York: Ginn and Company, 1926).
14. Rogers, *op. cit.*, Vol. I, p. 112.
15. George Hardy, *Les Grands Etapes d l'Histoire du Maroc* (Paris, 1921), pp. 50–54.
16. J. W. Draper, *A History of the Intellectual Development of Europe* (London: Bell, Daldy, 1864), Vol. II, pp. 26, 29.

CHAPTER XI

---◆---

Andromeda

Of the future of the darker races and their relation to the white peoples.

In Greek mythology Andromeda was the black daughter of Cepheus, King of Ethiopia and of Cassiopeia,

> The starr'd Ethiop Queen that strove
> To set her beauty's praise
> Above the sea nymphs and their powers offended.

It is said that Poseidon, angry at this black woman's affront to the Nereids, threatened to flood the land and send a sea monster. The Egyptian oracle of Ammon foretold that only the sacrifice of Andromeda to the monster could stay destruction. Thus Andromeda was chained and exposed on a headland facing the sea; Perseus, forefather of the Asiatic Persians of Iran, returning from the slaying of Gorgon, freed Andromeda and married her. After her death she reigned among the stars, her arms extended and chained, together with Cassiopeia and Perseus; and anyone may see them shining upon a beautiful night.

It might be asked what has this or any fairy tale to do with a world stricken, starving, and half-insane; or with the relations of Africa to Europe and America? Very little perhaps; and yet we must remember that this folk tale was part of the culture complex of the Mediterranean area where there was no color bar and no name for race; and where, at least in theory, the world was a fight between civilization and barbarism. Perhaps then in some way this legend may guide us in the present and the future. What in truth is going to be the future of black folk? Are they going to die out gradually, with only traces of their blood to remind the world of their former existence? Are they going to be permanently segregated from the world in Africa or elsewhere, leaving the white world free of its fear and repulsion? Or in some slow or fast intermingling of peoples will all colors of mankind merge into some indistinguishable unity? None of these solutions seems practicable or imminent for many a long day. And, after all, none would really solve the basic problem of the relations of peoples; for even if extremes of human differences vanish, there will always remain differences, and around them the problems of human living-together.

Facing then the present problem, may we not frankly ask: Does the world need Africa? What has Africa to offer Europe, Asia, and America? Does Africa need the world? Certainly in the past the world has needed and used the Negro race: in Egypt and Ethiopia, and even in Asia; in the first building of the Christian Church and in the encouragement and transmission of thought and science from the East to the West that is known as the Renaissance; and especially in the sixteenth, seventeenth, eighteenth, and nineteenth centuries, the Negro race has been the foundation upon which the capitalist system has been reared, the Industrial Revolution carried through, and imperial colonialism established.

If we confine ourselves to America we cannot forget that America was built on Africa. From being a mere stopping place between Europe and Asia or a chance treasure house of gold, America became through African labor the center of the sugar empire and the cotton kingdom and an integral part of that world industry and trade which caused the Industrial Revolution and the reign of capitalism.

Through the nineteenth century America, on the strength of its black labor as well as white, grew in wealth and importance. It became the greatest experiment in modern democracy, seeking to embrace eventually not simply the white but the black worker. Today not only is the Negro an important part of the world of labor and art in all the Americas, but beyond this the trade of America is built in large degree upon the products raised by Africans and their children the world over.

But beyond America and in the main states of the modern world the cold economic fact is that Africa, its labor and products, are of prime importance. Of the typical products of Africa, cotton, one of the oldest there, is still valuable, and cotton cloth was exported from Africa long before it was woven in England. Sisal, hemp, and other fiber plants and flax are indigenous to Africa. The vast demand for vegetable oil has resulted in the oil industry, especially in West Africa. Palm oil is used for margarine, soap, lubrication, "olive oil," and for other industrial purposes. Thus the oil palm of West Africa is a valuable product and supplies palm kernels which are exported from the whole West Coast. The ground nut and cocoa-nut also produce oils. The coconut palm is found all over the continent north of the Tropic of Capricorn and also south of the date-palm line.

The shea-nut tree grows where the oil palm does not, and its fat is used for food, soap-making, and butter. The cocoa industry of West Africa now supplies two-thirds of the cocoa of the world. Kola nuts are also exported. In the Mediterranean area practically all grains cultivated in Europe can be grown. Coffee is native to Africa and is named after the province of Kaffa, Abyssinia. It grows also in Liberia. The greater part of tropical Africa produces some kind of rubber. Nearly all the cloves are gotten from Zanzibar and Pemba. Fruits are grown and exported from nearly every part of Africa, from the bananas and mangoes in the tropics to the wine grapes of the north and south. The date palm flourishes throughout North Africa. Large areas of the continent are suitable for cattle and sheep raising, although flies and diseases keep them out of other districts.

Gold is widely distributed in Africa and has been worked from prehistoric ages on the West Coast, the Nubian desert, Central and South Africa. A third of the world's supply of gold in the world today is mined on the Witwatersrand. Diamonds are found in three districts of South Africa and in the Belgian Congo. They are of immense value. There are coal-bearing areas in South Africa. Iron has been worked from an early age, and on the Gold Coast, manganese is being developed.

There are four great copper-producing areas, principally in Rhodesia and the Belgian Congo, and also in the Northern Transvaal. Lead, graphite, and zinc are widely distributed. Phosphates occur in the North. Mineral oil has been discovered in Egypt near the Red Sea. Soda is largely an African product. Maize is cultivated in many regions. Tobacco is a crop of South Africa. Sugar is grown in Egypt, Mozambique, and Natal. And there is much valuable timber all over the continent.

Besides supplying these materials Africa is one of the largest reservoirs of human labor, not only of common labor, but of semi-skilled and increasing numbers of skilled laborers. For the most part these laborers are unorganized and without political power, and consequently they form the cheapest labor available, save in Asia.

On account of this wealth of labor and material, not only in the past but between the two world wars, capital has poured into Africa. In addition to primary sources of wealth—mining, agriculture, timber—industrialization has begun, and in the postwar period larger and larger investments of the accumulated profits of industry will seek new investments in this industrial paradise, where there are few laws to limit labor, even of women or children, and where profits are lightly taxed.

It has been argued with regard to this matter of profit in colonial regions that the profit has not been large and therefore is not the main object of colonial enterprise. This is especially the carefully worked out thesis of Lord Hailey's "African Survey." The survey follows an old pattern of British imperialism. A colonial official with the facts of the situation under his control writes a history of the condition and past of his region. It is usually done judiciously, and with much historical research, but it is, and in the nature of the case, has to be, a special plea for the defense of imperialism. And it omits consistently the point of view of the native and any body of fact which weighs against European aggression. Sometimes, as in Claridge's *History of Ashanti*, frank criticism of Great Britain creeps in; but for the most part, as in the works by Johnston, Lugard, and others the story is heavily weighted on the side of the imperialists.

It is of especial importance that the assertion of huge profits from cheap and half-slave labor and low price of materials should be answered. Consequently, Lord Hailey's co-workers point out that the "average" rate of profit from investment in Africa during the last century has amounted to little more than 4 per cent. Why is it, one asks on reading this, that profits are always reckoned as a percentage of some fixed sum while wages and salaries are counted in bulk?

It is, of course, as all men know, because the rate of income depends entirely upon the capital sum fixed as its base, and the fixing of the estimated amount of this capital sum is practically always in the hands and the control of the investors. Practically, then, the investors can fix their rate of profit at any sum simply by estimating at their own figure the amount of capital invested.

What is "investment" and how can we measure it? If ten dollars' worth of poisonous synthetic gin is exported to Africa, as it has been by the tens of thousands of gallons, and if there it buys labor and materials, which, when processed, are worth a hundred dollars, what is the value of the investment on which the rate of profit is based? If in the days of Cecil Rhodes lands stolen from the natives were mined with cheap half-slave labor and brought gold and diamonds worth a million dollars to London, at what figure should this mine be "capitalized"? At the figure paid for its acquisition and cost of carrying on, or the figure the shares sold for in the stock market? In the great centers of capital investment, the legal right to determine the value of capital is today to some extent limited, but it was not limited in the wild gambling which accompanied the development of gold and diamond mining in South Africa, nor in the returns to trade in West Africa during the seventeenth, eighteenth, and nineteenth centuries. No matter, then, how vast a profit is made in Africa, and that it has been vast there cannot be the slightest doubt; it can be always made to look modest by watering the actual investment or putting a high estimate on good will. The only reason back of colonial imperialism is a rate of profit which the spread of democracy and trade unions has curtailed in Europe and North America.

The actual value of capital goods at the time of their investment in Africa, as compared with the realized value of the labor and material taken from Africa by investors and other claimants, legal and illegal, would if known, without shadow of doubt prove the enormous theft which Europe has perpetrated on peoples deliberately made helpless before greed and aggression. In the face of fact, statements like that of Lord Hailey as to the meager profits of African exploitation must be reinterpreted.

For these reasons there is ferment in Africa today to which the world must pay more and more attention. Only yesterday a general strike in Nigeria affected nearly forty thousand workers. But this hardly makes headlines in the news, and few people who read daily about Argentina realize that Nigeria is twice as populous.

The effort to make peace in the world today finds one of its stumbling blocks in Italy's former African colonies—Eritrea, Libya, and Somaliland. Two of these are claimed by Ethiopia, whose conquest was one cause of World War II, and whose reconstruction is attracting capital from America. Native congresses in South and East Africa recently appealed to the world for the application of the Atlantic Charter to them. Their voices fell on silent cables, but they were strong enough and passionate in logic. At the recent Trades Union meeting in Paris black African unions were for the first time in history represented by a dozen delegates, telling the world that black labor is labor. Egypt is straining at British control, and the Pan-Arab League is demanding Libya. In Kenya has arisen the problem of forced labor, and all over Africa, the plight of returning black soldiers who fought in Asia and the South Seas. Political change looms in Rhodesia and Southwest Africa, while the Belgian Congo simmers in uneasy consciousness of the anomaly of being fourteen times the size of Belgium itself with none of that democracy for which Belgium fought. Africa is quiet today, but may not be tomorrow.

Perhaps one of the most striking protests against conditions that has come out of Africa is that of the National Congress of British West Africa which met in 1920. As a statement of democratic aims it deserves wider circulation than it has had. I venture to quote parts of it.

MEMORANDUM *of the case of the National Congress of British West Africa for a Memorial based upon the Resolutions to be presented to His Majesty the King Emperor in Council through the Right Honourable the Secretary of State for the Colonies, March 1920.*

"In presenting the case for the franchise for the different colonies composing British West Africa, namely, The Gambia, Sierra Leone, the Gold Coast, and Nigeria, it is important to remember that each of these colonies is at present governed under the Crown Colony System. By that is meant that the power of selecting members for the legislative councils is in the Governor of each colony and not dependable upon the will of the people through an elective system.

"For a long time in the history of each of these colonies the anomaly of the nomination of members of the legislative council by the Governors and not by the people electing their own representatives has struck the inhabitants of each community, and now and again representations have been made with a view to remedying the disability.

"Up to the beginning of the present year (1920), there had been no improvement in the situation, with the result that in March 1920 a Conference of Africans of British West Africa was held at Accra, the Capital of the Gold Coast Colony, at which were present the representatives of each of the four colonies composing British West Africa. . . . A reference to the programme of the subjects discussed will show the various topics of importance that came under the consideration of the Congress. Before the rise of the Conference it resolved itself into the National Congress of British West Africa as a permanent official body for the purpose of representing constitutionally British West African need, political and otherwise. At each of the sessions an opportunity was given for the full discussion of the particular subjects under consideration, and upon the same being fully debated, resolutions arising out of the discussions were passed. . . . It will be noticed that the first resolutions deal with legislative (including municipal) reforms and the granting of the franchise and administrative reforms with particular reference to equal rights and opportunities. . . .

"The first submission with respect to this particular resolution is that in the demand for the franchise by the people of British West Africa it is not to be supposed that they are asking to be allowed to copy a foreign institution. On the contrary, it is important to notice that the principle of electing representatives to local councils and bodies is inherent in all the systems of British West Africa. According to African institutions, every member of a community belongs to a given family with its duly accredited head, who represents that family in the village council, naturally composed of the heads of the several families. Similarly, in a district council the different representatives of each village or town would be appointed by the different villages and towns, and so with the Provincial Council until, by the same process, we arrive at the Supreme Council, namely, the State Council, presided over by the Paramount Chief.

"Again, according to the African System no Headman, Chief, or Paramount Ruler has any inherent right to exercise jurisdiction unless he is duly elected by the people to so represent them. This, coupled with the facts in the preceding paragraph stated, makes the African system essentially a democratic one, and the appointment to political office depends entirely upon the election and the will of the people.

"From the foregoing it is obvious that a system by which the Governor of a Crown Colony nominates whom he thinks proper to represent the people is considered by them as a great anomaly and constitutes a grievance and a disability which they now request should be remedied. Hence the constitutional agitation in the past, as in the present, for a change in the constitution of British West Africa so as to enable the people in the future to elect their own representatives to the Legislative Councils of the different colonies.

"It will be observed in paragraph 2 of the resolutions under consideration that it is not proposed to disturb the Executive Council as at present composed. As regards the Legislative Council, however, a radical change is desired so that one-half of its members shall be nominated by the Crown and the other half elected by the people to deal with legislation generally. A further radical reform is the institution of a House of Assembly, composed of the members of the Legislative Council together with six other financial representatives elected by the people, who shall have the power of imposing taxes and discussing freely and without reserve the items on the Annual Estimates of revenue and expenditure prepared by the Governor in the Executive Council and of approving them. The unofficial elective reform herein proposed includes both European and African representation.

"Before leaving the point under consideration, attention may be drawn to what is stated in *Gold Coast Native Institutions*[1] on page 164:

> Legislation to be effectual, must be with the Chiefs in a representative legislative assembly. Any important measure affecting the people must be passed with the consent and the direct co-operation of the Chiefs themselves.

If the policy of the Government had been based upon this principle there would be no need today for this work. What the country requires most urgently today is a National Assembly wherein all sections of the community will be adequately represented. That is the fundamental element of progress, the reform at which all right-thinking men must directly aim."[2] This was written more than seventeen years ago; and as has been explained above, by the African system of representation even the Chiefs are the mere representatives of the people in a democratic system.

Britain after delay yielded to this demand in characteristic fashion: it gave Negroes partial elective representation in the "Legislative Councils," but the councils still "advised" the governor, who retained large power of legislation. British industry sat directly on the Council and in England continued to name West African governors and dictate colonial policies.

In the first chapter I have told of the Pan-African Congress which met in Paris after World War I. Similar efforts of Africans and peoples of African descent to unite in mutual exchange of culture and co-operation for social betterment have been made since the idea was established in 1919.

We went to work in 1921 to assemble a more authentic Pan-African Congress and movement. We corresponded with Negroes in all parts of Africa and in others parts of the world and finally arranged for a congress to meet in London, Brussels, and Paris in August and September. Of the one hundred and thirteen delegates to this Congress, forty-one were from Africa, thirty-five from the United States, twenty-four represented Negroes living in Europe, and seven were from the West Indies. They came for the most part, but not in all cases, as individuals and more seldom as the representatives of organizations or groups.

The Pan-African movement thus began to represent a growth and development; but it immediately ran into difficulties. First of all, there was the natural reaction to war and the determination on the part of certain elements in England, Belgium, and elsewhere, to recoup their war losses by intensified colonial exploitation. They were suspicious of native movements of any sort.

Then, too, there came simultaneously another movement, stemming from the West Indies. This was a peoples' movement rather than a movement of the intellectuals. It was led by Marcus Garvey and it represented a poorly conceived but intensely earnest determination to unite the Negroes of the world, especially in commercial enterprise. It used all of the nationalist and racial paraphernalia of popular agitation, and its strength lay in its backing by the masses of West Indians and by increasing numbers of American Negroes. Its weakness lay in its demagogic leadership, poor finance, intemperate propaganda, and the natural apprehension it aroused among the colonial powers.

The London meetings of the Congress of 1921 were preceded by a conference with the International Department of the English Labor party, where the question of the relation of white and colored labor was discussed. Beatrice Webb, Leonard Woolf, Mr. Gillies, Norman Leyes, and others were present. Otlet and La Fontaine, the Belgian leaders of internationalism, welcomed the Congress warmly to Belgium, but strong opposition was encountered. The movement was confounded by the press and others as a part of, if not the real "Garvey Movement." The Brussels *Neptune* wrote June 14:

> Announcement has been made . . . of a Pan-African Congress organized at the instigation of the National Association for the Advancement of Colored People of New York. It is interesting to note that this association is directed by personages who it is said in the United States have received remuneration from Moscow (Bolsheviks). The association has already organized its propaganda in the lower Congo, and we must not be astonished if some day it causes grave difficulties in the Negro village of Kinshasa composed of all the ne'er-do-wells of the various tribes of the Colony aside from some hundreds of laborers.

Nevertheless, meetings of interest and enthusiasm were held. The Congress assembled in the marvelous Palais Mondial. There were many more white than colored people, and it was not long before we realized that their interest was deeper, more immediately significant than that of the white people we had found elsewhere. Many of Belgium's economic and material interests center in Africa in the Belgian Congo. Any interference with the natives might result in an interference with the sources from which so many Belgian capitalists draw their prosperity.

Resolutions passed without dissent at the meeting in London contained a statement concerning Belgium, criticizing her colonial regime, although giving her credit for plans of reform for the future. This aroused bitter opposition in Brussels, and an attempt was made to substitute an innocuous statement concerning good will and investigation, which Diagne of France, as the presiding officer, declared adopted in the face of a clear majority in opposition.

At the Paris meeting the original London resolutions, with some minor corrections, were adopted. They were in part:

To the World: The absolute equality of races, physical, political and social is the founding stone of world and human advancement. No one denies great differences of gift, capacity and attainment among individuals of all races, but the voice of Science, Religion, and practical Politics is one in denying the God-appointed existence of super-races or of races naturally and inevitably and eternally inferior.

That in the vast range of time, one group should in its industrial technique, or social organization, or spiritual vision, lag a few hundred years behind another, or forge fitfully ahead, or come to differ decidedly in thought, deed, and ideal, is proof of the essential richness and variety of human nature, rather than proof of the co-existence of demigods and apes in human form. The doctrine of racial equality does not interfere with individual liberty; rather it fulfills it. And of all the various criteria of which masses of men have in the past been prejudged and classified, that of the color of the skin and texture of the hair, is surely the most adventitious and idiotic. . . .

The beginning of wisdom in interracial contact is the establishment of political institutions among suppressed peoples. The habit of democracy must be made to encircle the earth. Despite the attempts to prove that the practice is the secret and divine gift of the few, no habit is more natural or more widely spread among primitive people, or more easily capable of development among masses. Local self-government with a minimum of help and oversight can be established tomorrow in Asia, in Africa, America, and the isles of the sea. It will in many instances need general control and guidance, but it will fail only when that guidance seeks ignorantly and consciously its own selfish ends and not the people's liberty and good.

Surely in the twentieth century of the Prince of Peace, in the millennium of Mohammed, and in the mightiest Age of Human Reason, there can be found in the civilized world enough of altruism, learning, and benevolence to develop native institutions, whose one aim is not profit and power for the few. . . .

What then do those demand who see these evils of the color line and racial discrimination, and who believe in the divine right of suppressed and backward people to learn and aspire and be free? The Negro race through their thinking intelligentsia demand:

I. The recognition of civilized men as civilized despite their race or color.
II. Local self-government for backward groups, deliberately rising as experience and knowledge grow to complete self-government under the limitation of a self-governed world.
III. Education in self-knowledge, in scientific truth, and in industrial technique, undivorced from the art of beauty.
IV. Freedom in their own religion and social customs and with the right to be different and nonconformist.
V. Co-operation with the rest of the world in government, industry, and art on the bases of Justice, Freedom, and Peace.
VI. The return to Negroes of their land and its natural fruits and defense against the unrestrained greed of invested capital.
VII. The establishment under the League of Nations of an international institution for study of the Negro problems.
VIII. The establishment of an international section of the Labor Bureau of the League of Nations, charged with the protection of native labor. . . .

In some such words and thoughts as these we seek to express our will and ideal, and the end of our untiring effort. To our aid we call all men of the earth who love justice and mercy. Out of the depths we have cried unto the deaf and dumb masters of the world. Out of the depths we cry to our own sleeping souls. The answer is written in the stars.

The whole press of Europe took notice of these meetings and more especially of the ideas behind the meeting. Gradually they began to distinguish between the Pan-African Movement and the Garvey agitation. They praised and criticized. Sir Harry Johnston wrote: "This is the *weakness* of all the otherwise grand efforts of the Coloured People in the United States to pass on their own elevation and education and political significance to the Coloured Peoples of Africa: they know so *little about real* Africa."

Even *Punch* gibed good-naturedly: " 'A PAN-AFRICAN MANIFESTO' 'NO ETERNALLY INFERIOR RACES' (headlines in *The Times*) No, but in the opinion of our coloured brothers, some infernally superior ones!" [3]

The Second Pan-African Congress sent me with a committee to interview the officials of the League of Nations in Geneva. I talked with Rappard who headed the Mandates Commission; I saw the first meeting of the Assembly, and I had an interesting interview with Albert Thomas, head of the International Labor Office. Working with Bellegarde of Haiti, a member of the Assembly, we brought the status of Africa to the attention of the League. The League published our petition as an official document saying in part:

The Second Pan-African Congress wishes to suggest that the spirit of the world moves toward self-government as the ultimate aim of all men and nations and that consequently the mandated areas, being peopled as they are so largely by black folk, have a right to ask that a man of Negro descent, properly fitted in character and training, be appointed a member of the Mandates Commission so soon as a vacancy occurs.

The Second Pan-African Congress desires most earnestly and emphatically to ask the good offices and careful attention of the League of Nations to the condition of civilized persons of Negro descent throughout the world. Consciously and subconsciously there is in the world today a widespread and growing feeling that it is permissible to treat civilized men as uncivilized if they are colored and more especially of Negro descent. The result of this attitude and many consequent laws, customs, and conventions, is that a bitter feeling of resentment, personal insult and despair, is widespread in the world among those very persons whose rise is the hope of the Negro race.

We are fully aware that the League of Nations has little, if any, direct power to adjust these matters, but it has the vast moral power of public world opinion and of a body conceived to promote Peace and Justice among men. For this reason we ask and urge that the League of Nations take a firm stand on the absolute equality of races and that it suggest to the Colonial Powers connected with the League of Nations to form an International Institute for the study of the Negro problem, and for the evolution and protection of the Negro race.

We sought to have these meetings result in a permanent organization. A secretariat was set up in Paris and functioned for a couple of years, but was not successful. The Third Pan-African Congress was called for 1923, but the Paris secretary postponed it. We persevered and finally without proper notice or preparation met in London and Lisbon late in the year. The London session was small. It was addressed by Harold Laski and Lord Olivier and attended by H. G. Wells; Ramsay MacDonald was kept from attending only by the pending election, but wrote: "Anything I can do to advance the cause of your people on your recommendation, I shall always do gladly."

The meeting of an adjourned session of this Congress in Lisbon the same year was more successful. Eleven countries were represented there, including Portuguese Africa. The Liga Africana was in charge. "The great association of Portuguese Negroes with headquarters at Lisbon, which is called the Liga Africana, is an actual federation of all the indigenous associations scattered throughout the five provinces of Portuguese Africa and represents several million individuals. . . . This Liga Africana which functions at Lisbon, in the very heart of Portugal so to speak, has a commission from all the other native organizations and knows how to express to the government in no ambiguous terms but in dignified manner all that should be said to avoid injustice or to bring about the repeal of harsh laws. That is why the Liga Africana of Lisbon is the director of the Portuguese African movement; but only in the good sense of the word, without making any appeal to violence and without leaving constitutional limits."[4]

Two former colonial ministers spoke, and the following demands were made for Africans:

1. A voice in their own government.
2. The right of access to the land and its resources.
3. Trial by juries of their peers under established forms of law.

4. Free elementary education for all; broad training in modern industrial techniques; and higher training of selected talent.
5. The development of Africa for the benefit of Africans, and not merely for the
profit of Europeans.
6. The abolition of the slave trade and of the liquor traffic.
7. World disarmament and the abolition of war; but failing this, and as long as
white folk bear arms against black folk, the right of blacks to bear arms in
their own defense.
8. The organization of commerce and industry so as to make the main objects
of capital and labor the welfare of the many rather than the enriching of the
few. . . .

In fine, we ask in all the world, that black folk be treated as men. We can see no
other road to Peace and Progress. What more paradoxical figure today fronts the
world than the official head of a great South African state striving blindly to build
Peace and Good Will in Europe by standing on the necks and hearts of millions of
black Africans?

So far, the Pan-African idea was still American rather than African, but it was
growing and it expressed a real demand for examination of the African situation
and a plan of treatment, from the native African point of view. With the object of
moving the center of this agitation nearer African centers of population, I planned
a Fourth Pan-African Congress in the West Indies in 1925. My idea was to charter
a ship and sail down the Caribbean, stopping for meetings in Jamaica, Haiti,
Cuba, and the French islands. But here I reckoned without my steamship lines. At
first the French Line replied that they could "easily manage the trip"; but eventually no accommodations could be found on any line except at the prohibitive
price of fifty thousand dollars. I suspect that colonial powers spiked this plan.

Two years later, in 1927, American Negro women revived the Congress idea,
and a Fourth Pan-African Congress was held in New York. Thirteen countries
were represented, but direct African participation lagged. There were two hundred and eight delegates from twenty-two American states and ten foreign
countries. Africa was sparsely represented by representatives from the Gold
Coast, Sierra Leone, Liberia, and Nigeria. Chief Amoah III of the Gold Coast,
and anthropologists like Herskovits, then of Columbia, Mensching of Germany,
and John Vandercook were on the program. The resolutions stressed six points:

Negroes everywhere need:

1. A voice in their own government.
2. Native rights to the land and its natural resources.
3. Modern education for all children.
4. The development of Africa for the Africans and not merely for the profit of
Europeans.
5. The reorganization of commerce and industry so as to make the main object of
capital and labor the welfare of the many rather than the enriching of the few.
6. The treatment of civilized men as civilized despite difference of birth, race,
or color.

The Pan-African Movement had lost ground since 1921. In 1929 to remedy this we made a desperate effort to hold a Fifth Pan-African Congress on the continent of Africa itself; we selected Tunis because of its accessibility. Elaborate preparations were begun. It looked as though at last the movement was going to be geographically African. But two insuperable difficulties intervened: first, the French government very politely but firmly informed us that the Congress could take place at Marseilles or any French city, but not in Africa; and second, there came the Great Depression.

The Pan-African idea died apparently until twenty years afterward, in the midst of World War II, when it leaped to life again in an astonishing manner. At the Trade Union Conference in London in 1944 to plan for world organization of labor, representatives from black labor appeared from the Gold Coast, Libya, British Guiana, Ethiopia, and Sierra Leone. Among these, aided by colored persons resident in London, Lancashire, Liverpool, and Manchester, there came a spontaneous call for the assembling of another Pan-African Congress in 1945 when the World Federation of Trade Unions would hold their meeting in Paris.

After consultation and correspondence with trade union, co-operative, and other progressive organizations in the West Indies, West Africa, South and East Africa, a formal invitation for the conference was issued. Most of these bodies not only approved and endorsed the agenda, but pledged themselves to send delegates. In cases where either the time was too short or the difficulties of transport too great to be overcome at such short notice, the organizations gave mandates to the natives of the territories concerned who were traveling to Paris to attend the World Trade Union Conference.

The Fifth Pan-African Congress met October 15 to 21 in Manchester, England, with some two hundred delegates representing East and South Africa and the West Indies. Its significance lay in the fact that it took a step toward a broader movement and a real effort of the peoples of Africa and the descendants of Africa the world over to start a great march toward democracy for black folk.

Singularly enough, there is another "Pan-African" movement. I thought of it as I sat at the San Francisco Conference and heard Jan Smuts plead for an article on "human rights" in the preamble of the Charter of the United Nations. It was an astonishing paradox. The "Pan-African" movement which he represents is a union of the white minority in Kenya, Rhodesia, and the Union of South Africa, to rule the African continent in the interest of investors and exploiters. This plan has been incubating since 1921, but has been discouraged by the British Colonial Office. Smuts is now pushing it again, and the white legislatures in Africa have asked for it. The San Francisco trusteeship left a door open for this sort of thing. Against this upsurges the movement of black union delegates working in co-operation with the labor delegates of Russia, Great Britain, and the United States in order to build a new world which includes black Africa. We may yet live to see Pan-Africa as a real movement.

This Fifth Pan-African Congress placed great hope on the British Labour movement and its sudden induction as the government of the British Empire.

But the Congress had put before it a curious example of how organized labor may handle colonial problems. There came before us literally a Man of Sorrows: black, with a deeply-lined face. Gershon Ashie-Nikoi was in desperate earnest. He shouted repeatedly: "We must be free! We will be free!" He said that he represented three hundred thousand cocoa farmers on the Gold Coast and Nigeria; that he and his committee had come to lay a petition before the new Labor Secretary of State and Colonies. He had been refused audience because Mr. Hall declared that the committee was not "official"; which meant that it was not appointed in accordance with the procedure of the colonial governments, and was not composed of the representatives which these governments had officially chosen.

The committee secured a hearing before the Colonial Section of the Fabian Society, which acts as a sort of Brain Trust to advise the Labour government on colonial affairs. Among them were many people of importance: Mr. Creech-Jones, the Under-secretary of State for the Colonies, Miss Rita Hinden, Lord Farringdon, the Secretary of the Aborigines Protection Society, and others. They listened indifferently. The representatives of the farmers therefore brought their case to the Pan-African Congress and laid it before us. The committee had been sent to London at the expense of the farmers, and had established a permanent office in Arundel Street. They were prepared for a long, hard fight, and the Pan-African Congress pledged help.

It will repay us to glance briefly at this tale of the cocoa crop as illustrating the methods of modern colonial exploitation and its results even under a liberal administration. The world consumption of cocoa has increased from 77,000 tons in 1895 to 700,000 tons at present. Formerly three-fourths of the cocoa was raised in South America. Now two-thirds is raised in West Africa.

This development of a new industry has an interesting history. A black laborer, Tetteh Quarsie, in 1879 brought cocoa beans from Spanish Africa and distributed them among his friends on the Gold Coast, British West Africa. In 1891, eighty pounds of cocoa were raised by West African farmers. By 1936 this crop on the Gold Coast alone had been increased to 250,000 tons. It was purely an indigenous enterprise of black peasant farmers. The deeply laid plan to transfer the raising of cocoa from Spanish Africa to plantations in British West Africa, developed by the Cadbury-instituted "boycott," went astray, and the black peasants took over the job. On their own little farms, averaging about two and one-half acres, they increased crops and made cocoa and chocolate in wide demand throughout the civilized world. Their fathers in Ashanti and Benin had fought Britain for centuries to retain ownership of this land.

For cocoa and chocolate today consumers pay annually at least $500,000,000. Out of each dollar, of this less than three cents goes to the cocoa farmer; and this is another instance of the squeezing of agriculture by trade and manufacture.

Since the cocoa in West Africa is not raised on plantations as it is in the West Indies and South America, the problem of the traders and manufacturers is to make profit by beating down the sale price and by manipulation of the world market. For this reason the price to cocoa farmers has varied from $44 per ton during the depression, to $188 per ton during the time of scarcity in 1927, and about $60 a ton today.

Ostensibly for correcting this price fluctuation, but really for controlling the price, the British buyers on the Gold Coast have for many years tried to come into agreement so as to make one price and one bid for all the cocoa offered. There are thirteen main buyers: the British Unilevers, Cadbury and Fry, buying for themselves and the Lyons' Teahouses; and others.

Finally in 1937 these firms came to a buying agreement. The cocoa farmers desperately resisted. They staged a boycott for eight months, reducing the sale of cocoa from 250,000 tons to 50,000 tons. The buyers resisted. They applied pressure on the Colonial Office in London, and without showing it the text of the "buying agreement," induced it to advise the natives that the proposal was for their benefit and to accept it. The colonial governor, also without sight of the agreement, immediately followed this directive from London and strongly "advised" acquiescence by the natives. The natives still refused. Mr. Cadbury then went to the Gold Coast and talked to the chiefs and farmers. They demanded to see a copy of the agreement. He "regretted" that he had not brought a copy with him. Finally the British government capitulated and sent a Royal Commission to the Coast, under Mr. Nowell. This Commission secured a copy of the agreement, but made public only a part. After careful investigation, they recommended that the buying agreement be terminated and that co-operative enterprise be instituted with representation of the African farmers.

Before this plan could be implemented however, the war broke out and the Government proposed to take charge of the cocoa crop, set prices, and sell it for the farmers. They promised to bear any losses and to distribute any profit among the farmers. This was satisfactory to the farmers, although they protested at the low price per ton which the government set in order to guard itself against loss.

The African colonial governments are virtually ruled by investors in England. Investors not only dictate the choice of governors, but these governors have the sole right of legislation under the Colonial Office in London. They are "advised" by councils on which business interests are directly represented. Recently local natives have been elected to such councils; but even so the real power still rests in the hands of the governor.

Government conduct of industry in West Africa, is therefore conduct by London investors. The whole economy of the colony is rigged by outside business interests. Instead of a tax on imports to encourage local effort, the Gold Coast, for instance, claps an *export* duty on cocoa of $3.75 a ton; and during the war it added a surtax of $4.58, making a total tax of $8.43 on a ton of cocoa, for which the cocoa farmer has at times during this war received as little as $37 a ton; and on the average not more than $52 from 1939 to 1943. At the same time, English exporters of goods to Africa need pay no import tax. As a result the cost of imported goods skyrocketed during the war, so that cotton print which sold before the war for $2.50 rose to $18, Khaki from $.60 to $3.20, and sheet iron from $1.00 to $20. "The result of this situation is that today many of the farmers have been completely impoverished and paralyzed economically." (Speech of Ashie-Nikoi.)

However, the whole picture changed in the minds of the Negro farmers when the Labour party came to power and took over the Colonial Office. Perhaps they were overoptimistic, but they were certainly justified in some degree by the results of government operation during World War II. Instead of the antici-pated losses, the government in five years of operation, netted the neat profit of $25,000,000. Indeed, if they had previously built proper storage facilities on the Gold Coast, instead of compelling farmers to sell and rush the crop immediately to Europe, regardless of prices or conditions of the market; and if they had ever encouraged simple processing operations, which would have saved freight and increased local employment; if such policies had been followed, much cocoa could have been saved from spoiling, and some 150,000 tons need not have been burned. The net profit might have been doubled.

The Labour party came to power and, to the indignation of the black cocoa farmers, proposed to put *all* West African produce under control of a board sitting in England with representation of the manufacturers of cocoa and other materials and with no representation of the farmers! In addition, instead of returning the profits of the cocoa pool to the farmers as promised, the government now proposed to use it "for their benefit," including the hiring of a number of English "experts" at high salaries to protect the cocoa trees from disease. The farmers protested bitterly and demanded:

1. That since the war is over, the recommendations of the Nowell Commission be implemented, and that the Imperial Government now make good the promises made to the African farmers.
2. That the price of $160 per ton should be paid farmers, and should be set for the 1945–1946 season.
3. That the profits from cocoa control since 1939, amounting as it probably will to$25,000,000, be turned over to the farmers' own existing organizations as capital for the establishment of co-operative agricultural banks in British West Africa.
4. That the operations of the West African Produce Control Board should cease, and a new system of centralized marketing should be installed, and effective co-operation, under the control of the farmers' own organizations, be established.
5. That the present quota allocation of the crop to special buyers be abolished, and that the farmers be free to market their crop collectively to their own accredited agencies.
6. That the present restrictions of exports and imports be removed in order to allow the West African farmers to trade with the United Kingdom and other countries through their own agencies.
7. That an International Council on cocoa should be planned, in order to adopt a comprehensive approach to all problems of cocoa as an important world commodity.
8. That the Ordinances of British West Africa with regard to cooperation be changed so as to correspond to practices in the United Kingdom.

And the farmers concluded:

> This delegation of Gold Coast and Nigerian farmers are of the opinion that there are enough men and women of good will in the Imperial Government of Britain who might bring economic justice to bear on these pressing problems, and thus might prevent the occurrence of a tragic economic upheaval, the consequences of which, unfortunately, might affect the peaceful life of innocent people in all parts of the world and not only in West Africa and Britain.

If this is not statesmanship, which eventually must be listened to, I am greatly mistaken. It seems to me to point a path toward the emancipation of the world's colonial populations and the beginning of democracy among the majority of the people of the world, for which we have fought two devastating world wars, without yet seeing the light.

The cocoa situation in West Africa is only one example of what colonial imperialism means to the people involved. Turning from this to our own country, we may ask what is America, and what duty and opportunity has it toward Africa and the peoples of African descent who live within her borders? It is a great working nation, vast, marvelously organized, and rich. We grow and mine materials; we process and manufacture them; we trade them, we transport them, we buy and sell them. Bound up with this, there is not only the planning for this work, but also the hard digging, lifting, and cleaning, and the services of parents, and friends, professional men and servants. With all this we produce goods and homes, buildings and roads, light and heat, tools and machines, and all manner of transport from railways and automobiles to airplanes.

Of course, the basic question here is; for whom is all this work done? How are the goods and services divided among consumers? Here we realize that all the facts are not known in America, just as they are partially unknown in other parts of the world. The distribution of wealth and of human services is a more or less closely guarded secret. We have some general ideas and they are disconcerting: we know that the lowest and hardest work and the work least honored is, despite its necessity, the lowest paid. We know that men do not get rich according to ability or according to the degree in which they serve the public. There is something, of course, of recognition of talent, but it is confined to certain sorts of talent and it is not sufficient to keep down dissatisfaction. The demand of the twentieth century in America, just as the demand of the eighteenth and nineteenth centuries in Europe, is that the distribution of wealth be more logical and ethical.

Men have tried to avoid action to achieve this by arguing that the distribution of goods and services is a matter of "natural" law. We know better than that today; we know, especially in America, that planning of work does go on on wide scale and that it involves personal decisions and is based today on autocratic will and not on democratic methods. Managers and groups have power to plan industry and divide its results: groups carrying on organized industry, like General Motors and General Electric and the British Unilevers—these groups own machines, materials, and inventions which enable them to reap large profits by marvelous and striking organization. Imports and exports depend upon the decisions of captains of industry. Monopoly of natural resources and the ownership of land play a tremendous part. Economic rent that comes with time and with growth of population, city sites, the shores of the ocean, the places suited for business and pleasure, all is controlled and distributed by individual or group decision. We know that the control of credit, the foreseeing of need for materials and machines, and supplying capital to those who can use it most profitably, is in itself a field of tremendous planning and prophecy. We know that the government must come in and help this planning where individual initiative lacks power, and that the field of government in industry is growing and must grow.

What now are the results of this planning and why do these results make Americans dissatisfied? We still have poverty, not nearly as much as many other parts of the world, but most Americans do not receive an income large enough to allow them to live in health and decency. This leads not only to envy but to cheating and stealing, to the kind of competitive struggles which begin as strikes and end as riots. It leads to widespread loss of belief in hard work and increased reliance on chance, so that gambling on horse races is today one of our greatest businesses. All this encourages or compels the postponing of marriage and limiting of children.

Poverty makes for ignorance; not simply illiteracy which is still serious among us, but for inexperience, the neglect of the lessons of history, reliance on selfish prejudices and conventions. Poverty leads to disease; it lets us spend more for war than for the perfectly possible extirpation of tuberculosis, the lessening of cancer, and the physical welfare of children. Poverty, ignorance, and disease are back of most of our crime, and to this is added a curious lack of ethical guidance. Churches tend to teach dogma rather than what is right and wrong; and the funny strips exalt craftiness and laugh at suffering.

In contrast to all this comes the reign of luxury, conspicuous expenditure, the flaunting of diamonds and furs; the demand for great estates and servants, while round about is sickness, starvation, and insanity. We grow used to luxury and display that we know is built upon wealth and work stolen from suffering mankind. We demand profit for investment even at the expense of public welfare. Thus the great business organizations of the United States struck and drove a hard bargain in blood and pain to increase profits during World War II; America invests in colonies—British, Dutch, and French; and colonies are slums used to make a profit from materials and cheap labor. We continually set before us the successful rich man as more typical of what America means than the student or the philanthropist or the unselfish man of small income and simple tastes.

It is this kind of thing which makes for our continued spiritual slavery. We demand Freedom; but thousands upon thousands are toiling discontentedly at work which they hate, when more careful and thoughtful planning could make work much more agreeable by a more efficient distribution according to ability and taste. We curb thought and discussion because we are afraid that those who are powerful and comfortable under present conditions may be disturbed in their present control of the world. Our news is distorted and our newspapers prostituted by those who own and use them for profit and propaganda. Our "free press" is a series of tight little principalities which channel public opinion with prejudiced headlines and screened news.

Our training for careers and opening of opportunity for the working masses has been hailed as the greatest in history. There can be no doubt but that more individuals have had opportunity to rise from repression and obscurity in America than in Europe. But even here we have not done anywhere near what we might, and today in many respects are regressing toward race and class discrimination and special privileges for the rich. Only the Jews among us, as a class, carefully select and support talent and genius among the young; the Negroes are following this example as far as their resources and knowledge allow. It is for this very reason that jealousy of the gifted Jew and ambitious Negro is closing doors of opportunity in their faces. This led to the massacre of Jews in Germany.

In America the only path to preferment and promotion left open and beckoning, is that which industry thinks will make profit. The opening of other paths is left to the rare chance that genius in literature or art be coupled with "push," which means the boldness and crudity for self-advertising from which delicate souls shrink.

When by chance or benevolence a boy "makes good," we grant him a profession. If he studies law he can gain a large salary when he becomes a tool by which great corporations evade those laws which try to curb monopoly and distribute wealth more equitably. Large numbers of such lawyers become lawmakers, and they enact laws which can be circumvented. Others are raised to the bench, where they are above law and highly honored. They in many cases protect wealth and monopoly and "make examples" of the poor. The greatest work of Franklin Roosevelt was to start cleansing the Supreme Court of the accumulated refuse of reaction to economic democracy. Living men may yet see a Supreme Court with the guts and common decency to throw out the window the whole body of legal color-caste in the South and elsewhere as both unconstitutional and uncivilized. At the other end of the scale our labor unions are so monopolizing skills by limited apprenticeship and secret ritual that much "industrial" training is a farce.

Science is becoming increasingly not the work of free universities but the property of organizations for private profit and directed to their objects. Education both in school and out is encouraging that economic illiteracy which keeps the mass of American people from knowing and inquiring just how work is done. To the support of all this comes the theater and the movies and other forms of arts, serving the idea that private profit rather than social welfare is the end and aim of man.

Is there any wonder that the result is widespread Fear? We are afraid of unemployment and loss of work; we are suspicious of other men, other races, and other nations; not because we are the poorest and most wretched, but just because here in America we have tasted the possibility of comfort and happiness. Perhaps all this is best shown by certain paradoxes in our daily life, thought, and action. We Americans boast and strut when we have every cause to be meek and humble. We seek happiness and escape through drunkenness and night clubs. We couple our religion with hate, saying, "God so loved the world," and boasting how much we hate our enemies; we turn the other cheek to make bombs. We want peace and make war. We want truth and curb research. We produce our own wealth and steal it from others.

We Americans have invented an apt phrase to enrich the English language—"So what!" It expresses a singular complex: a great statesman comes from Britain and tells us that he wants a world of free states and democracy—and admits in the same breath that his Britain admits nine-tenths of the subjects to neither freedom nor democracy. So what? We see standing before the United Nations at San Francisco a prime minister elected by two million whites asking for recognition of "humanity"—and in the same voice tells the world that anyone who regards the eight million natives of South Africa as human in the same sense as white folk is "mad, quite mad." We have a Secretary of State who arraigns Russia for lack of democracy while he represents South Carolina, where the majority of the people have never had a chance to vote. So what?

But perhaps our subtlest and most complete contradiction and paradox comes in our attitude toward servants. We know that personal services between mother and child, friend and relative, is the highest form of human effort; but we treat that same personal service when it is done for pay as the lowest form of work, paid least and subject to special forms of personal insult.

What can we do about all this? It is not a matter of law, it is a matter of the human heart. We know what must be done; industry must be carried on not primarily for private profit but for public welfare. We must progressively approach the time when no person shall have cake while any person is deprived of bread. We must increase production and income by the use of the great natural powers which science has placed in our hands: electricity which is being kept from the masses by organized effort in the valley of the Missouri and in the valley of the St. Lawrence, just as once monopoly fought it in vain in the valley of the Tennessee and still fights it at Boulder Dam. We know that automobiles could be built to last ten years at little greater cost than those which last two years, if the object was transportation and not gain. We must have schools that teach truth, despite what some people are afraid to learn. We must use new inventions like the radio for real information rather than for quack advertising, and the cinema for instruction as well as entertainment. We must have a press that is free and not monopolized by business and hate. We must have socialized medicine, following the great example being set today by Britain and going far beyond it as we ought to.

This increase of production for public welfare can only be brought about by careful intelligent planning and thorough democratic methods. The workers of the world must have voice not only on conditions of work but also as to what kinds of goods shall be produced and what methods of production used. Industry ruled by monarchs and oligarchies cannot continue in a democratic world.

Moreover, this increased production must be more equitably and justly distributed among the workers and among all citizens. Distribution of wealth and services by plan, emphasizing ability and deserts, and especially the public weal; and guarding mankind from ignorance and disease must be a primary object of civilization. "To each according to need, from each according to ability." Here again this can be accomplished only by widespread and intelligent democracy. It cannot continue to be a matter of personal wish and whim and of monopolized power; it must be the result of intelligent experience, public opinion working according to enacted law.

Democracy is not privilege—it is opportunity. Just as far as any part of a nation or of the world is excluded from a share in democratic power and self-expression, just so far the world will always be in danger of war and collapse. If this nation could not exist half slave and half free, then the world in which this nation plays a larger and larger part also cannot be half slave and half free, but must recognize world democracy.

How can we accomplish this? We can do it by releasing black Andromeda, and by that act release ourselves. We can rise above the insult of the color line in denying work to able people and in helping hold colonies in thrall; and we can invoke in a real democracy a reservoir of all human ability and dream and with free vote of intelligent men.

The sin of capitalism is secrecy: the deliberate concealing of the character, methods, and result of efforts to satisfy human wants. When men choose and understand their work and see its results and can sell their toil in open market to those who want and use it, there is opportunity for ethical judgment, public justice, and commonweal. But when the nature of work, its methods and results are hidden behind legal barriers so that a man knows neither what he is doing nor what the results of his toil will be, or who will enjoy it, or why nor whence nor how his income is made, nor at whose hurt or weal; then the opportunity for human degradation is limited only by the evil possibilities of the lowest of men; murder and theft may ensue with no chance to fix the guilt. Not mass production but mass concealment is the sin of the capitalistic system. This is the meaning of African slavery and this is the virus it poured into the veins of modern culture and fatally poisoned it. Once all the facts of the industrial process are known, then if a man eats, he should work; and if he does not work he should not eat, unless the free, intelligent judgment of his fellows declares that his existence at public expense is for the public weal. This and this alone is Democracy.

Who are we who call ourselves intelligent, and yet in dire dearth of air and light leave millions of acres of the roofs of New York and a thousand other cities to a black and dirty desert of chimneys and ugliness? The horror which today stops the hearts of men at the mere thought of atomic energy is knowledge of the secrecy which today conceals its use and bids fair to veil its inhuman force tomorrow in the hands of the most ruthless of mankind. The iron curtain was not invented by Russia; it hung between Europe and Africa half a thousand years. When the producer is so separated from the consumer in time and space that a mutual knowledge and understanding is impossible, then to regard the industrial process as "individual enterprise" or the result as "private initiative" is stupid. It is a social process, and if not socially controlled sinks to anarchy with every possible crime of irresponsible greed. Such was the African slave trade, and such is the capitalistic system it brought to full flower. Men made cotton cloth and sold sugar; but between the two they stole, killed, and raped human beings, forced them to toil for a bare subsistence, made rum and synthetic gin, herded white labor into unsanitary factories, bought the results of their work under threat of hunger which forced down their wage, and sold the sugar at monopoly prices to consumers who must pay or go without. A process of incredible ingenuity for supplying human wants became in its realization a series of brutal crimes.

There are people, and wise people, who have said that this can never be accomplished under the present organization of the world for business, industry, and profit; that in order to accomplish this we must establish stern dictatorship of a few who hold to this idea of the commonweal. This is the theory of Communism. There are many who dislike the idea; there are some who fear and hate it for obvious reasons. But to these there is one clear answer: accomplish the end which every honest human being must desire by means other than Communism, and Communism need not be feared. On the other hand, if a world of ultimate democracy, reaching across the color line and abolishing race discrimination, can only be accomplished by the method laid down by Karl Marx, then that method deserves to be triumphant no matter what we think or do.

Here in America we must learn to be proud of the things of which we are ashamed, and ashamed of things of which we are proud. America should be proud of the fact that she is a nation with increasing democracy composed of the most unlikely peoples and groups on earth; that out of criminals, paupers, and slaves she has built this land of promise. We should be ashamed that despite this known historical fact, we are trying to build up class and race differences and refusing to carry out the democratic methods which we profess, because we deal with people too stupid, diseased, and criminal to make our own democracy work.

America has need to remember that out of Asia and Africa, past and present, help can come for this land: Asia has produced a Gandhi who does not strut or wear Savile Row clothes; who will not kill—and whom average Americans regard as a fool. But he is not. Africa has provided in the past group ownership of land, family cohesion, and a curious combination of beautiful art and useful industry. We have helped the world to despoil this land, enslave its people, decry its ability, and distort its history. For three centuries we have led in the attempt to degrade Africa in the eyes of men. We owe it to Africa and ourselves to release Andromeda and place her free and beautiful among the stars of the sky.

If we refuse to do this; if we stubbornly cling to our race prejudices, what of the future of this civilization? The continuity of a social group, the continuity of a civilization is at best doubtful and precarious. Most of the civilizations of the world have lasted less than three centuries, save Egypt. Even Egypt is only an apparent exception since, being for centuries without effective rivals, it did not actually collapse; but it changed so radically from age to age as to become almost a new land and culture. So too India and China lasted longer in name than in real cultural continuity. The broader the basis of a culture, the wider and freer its conception, the better chance it has for the survival of its best elements.

This is the basic hope of world democracy. No culture whose greatest effort must go to suppress some of the strongest contributions of mankind can have left in itself strength for survival. War which typifies suppression and death can never support a lasting culture. Peace and tolerance is the only path to eternal progress. Europe can never survive without Asia and Africa as free and interrelated civilizations in one world.

"I believe it is specifically the mission of African civilization to restore ethical principles to world civilization. Unless this attempt is made all civilization must come to an end. The African by virtue of his detachment, his direct vision, and his innate kindness, is qualified to bring humanitarianism to the technical and materialistic concepts of the Western World." [5]

Few people realize what Africa and her children have done to win the World Wars. In the first, the Senegalese saved France at the first onslaught of the Germans; black soldiers of Africa conquered the German colonies; American Negroes rushed the critical supplies to Europe which turned the tide of victory.

In World War II thousands of Africans fought in Europe, Burma, India, and Africa; they formed a large part of Montgomery's Eighth Army in the decisive North African campaign; an American Negro physician contrived the banks of blood plasma which saved tens of thousands of lives; Negroes built thousands of miles of strategic road under direct enemy fire; Negroes handled three-fourths of the ammunition in the European Theatre of Operations and fired much of it. Negro fighting troops took part in the invasion of Normandy, in the invasion of Italy, and as flight squadrons and hospital corps. In America eight Negro scientists were engaged in the research on the atomic bomb.

The stars of dark Andromeda belong up there in the great heaven that hangs above this tortured world. Despite the crude and cruel motives behind her shame and exposure, her degradation and enchaining, the fire and freedom of black Africa, with the uncurbed might of her consort Asia, are indispensable to the fertilizing of the universal soil of mankind, which Europe alone never would nor could give this aching earth.

NOTES

1. Written by Caseley Hayford, a prominent Negro barrister of the Gold Coast.
2. Quoted from the official text of the Memorandum as published in Lagos, 1920, pp. 1–3.
3. September 7, 1921.
4. Statement to the Congress made by Deputy Megalhaes.
5. Armattoe, *op. cit.*, pp. 18, 19.

The Message

Reader of dead words who would live deeds, this is the flowering of my logic: I dream of a world of infinite and invaluable variety; not in the laws of gravity or atomic weights, but in human variety in height and weight, color and skin, hair and nose and lip. But more especially and far above and beyond this, in a realm of true freedom: in thought and dream, fantasy and imagination; in gift, aptitude, and genius—all possible manner of difference, topped with freedom of soul to do and be, and freedom of thought to give to a world and build into it, all wealth of inborn individuality. Each effort to stop this freedom of being is a blow at democracy—that real democracy which is reservoir and opportunity and the fight against which is murdering civilization and promising a day when neither

> . . . star nor sun shall waken,
>   Nor any change of light:
> Nor sound of waters shaken
>   Nor any sound or sight;
> Nor wintry leaves nor vernal,
> Nor days nor things diurnal;
> Only the sleep eternal
>   In an eternal night.[1]

There can be no perfect democracy curtailed by color, race, or poverty. But with all we accomplish all, even Peace.

This is this book of mine and yours.

NOTES

1. Swinburne, "The Garden of Proserpine."

Writings on Africa
1955–1961

The New Africa

In 1965, there are 37 independent countries in Africa, all but four of which obtained independence in the past decade. The 13 marked with an asterisk * still have a colonial status, as overseas territories or mandates.

The Giant Stirs

A series of ten articles in the National Guardian *(New York), February 14 to April 10, 1955.*

1. AMERICAN NEGROES AND AFRICA

One of the curious results of current fear and hysteria is the breaking of ties between Africa and American Negroes. When we think of the hell which Irish Americans have given Ireland, and how Scandinavia, Italy, Germany, Poland and China have been aided by their emigrants in the United States, it is tragic that American Negroes today are not only doing little to help Africa in its hour of supreme need, but have no way of really knowing what is happening in Africa.

When the Cotton Kingdom of the 19th century built on black slavery led to a campaign in church and society to discount Africa, its culture and history, American Negroes shrank from any ties with Africa and accepted in part the color line. By the 20th century, however, knowledge of Africa and its history spread in Negroes' schools and literature. Negro churches helped Africa, African students appeared here and movements looking toward closer ties with Africa spread. From the First World War to 1945 the Pan-African movement held international conferences to unite the Negro race in mutual aid, information and planning.

A Council on African Affairs was formed in 1939 under the leadership of Paul Robeson, returning from his first visit to Africa. It soon had a membership of 2,000 whites and blacks. It collected a library and some specimens of African art; entertained visiting Africans and students, raised relief funds for starving Negroes in South Africa, issued a monthly bulletin and arranged lectures.

Then in 1949, without hearing or chance for defense, the Council was listed on the Attorney-General's "subversive" list. It remained under attack and most of its support faded away.

In the industrial world the significance of Africa increased. Today out of Africa come 95 per cent of the world's diamonds; 80 per cent of the cobalt; 60 per cent of the gold; 75 per cent of the sisal hemp; 70 per cent of the palm oil; 70 per cent of the cocoa; 35 per cent of the phosphates; 30 per cent of the chrome and manganese; 20 per cent of the copper; 15 per cent of the coffee; an increasing part of the uranium and radium, and large amounts of tin, iron and spices.

Naturally, American investment in Africa has increased: in the first half of
the century it rose from $500 million to $1,500 million; South Africa asked us in
1949 for a loan of $50 million, eventually got nearly twice as much. The Morgan,
Rockefeller and Ford interests have been investing in South Africa; General
Motors, Firestone, General Electric have followed suit. General Lucius Clay,
who headed the "Freedom Crusade" among us, once also headed a mining
company in South Africa which netted $9 million profit in three years.

In 1950 the U.S. Consul General to South Africa said: "This country has a greater
future than almost any young country in the world." The vice president of the
largest U.S. railway equipment manufacturers said South Africa had unlimited
potentiality for development: "I can see it going ahead with great speed for it is so
rich in so many kinds of raw materials. The South Africans are a great people."

The result of exploitation of Africa in the first half of the 20th century was
revolt in the second half, from Tunis to the Cape of Good Hope. There has been
demand for independence in Egypt and for autonomy in the Sudan; bloody
rebellion goes on in Kenya; unrest and threats exist in Uganda; Ethiopia has
regained independence and recovery of her sea coast; West Africa revolted in
1948 and today approaches dominion status in the British Empire for there are
as many blacks in the Gold Coast and Nigeria as there are whites in England.
Both France and Portugal are slowly admitting a black intelligentsia to full civil
rights, while even the Belgian Congo which restrained Negro education will
open a Negro university.

But in the Union of South Africa a white nation has determined on race subordination as a policy, and 2,600,000 whites are attempting to rule and exploit
ten million blacks and colored. The Rhodesias are attempting to follow this policy in part. The looming struggle is of vast portent.

Meantime this current story gets small space in the Afro-American press with
its 150 weekly newspapers circulating among two million readers. Four of the
leading papers have from 100,000 to 300,000 readers each and are in the realm
of big business, subject to the control of finance capital in advertising, allotment
of newsprint and political influence. Political party funds are often available to
swell income during elections, and their main support comes from readers who
must not offend the Department of Justice and the FBI or they will lose their
jobs. Meantime since the Second World War, 15 million American Negroes have
sent less than $10,000 to help the struggles of 200,000,000 Africans.

On the other hand the Negro press discusses race relations in the United
States, reports news of the Negro group and personal items. Its chief demand
for 150 years has been political, civil and social equality with white Americans.

Here they are advancing rapidly, and today it is clear that they have a chance
to trade wide breaks in the American color line for acquiescence in American
and West European control of the world's colored peoples. This is shown by the
pressure on them to keep silence on Africa and Asia and on white working-class
movements, and in return to accept more power to vote; abolition of separation
in education; dropping of "jim-crow" units in our military forces and gradual
disappearance of the Negro ghetto in work and housing. To this is added much
long-delayed recognition of Negro ability and desert.

It is fair to admit that most American Negroes, even those of intelligence and courage, do not yet fully realize that they are being bribed to trade equal status in the United States for the slavery of the majority of men. When this is clear, especially to black youth, the race must be aroused to thought and action and will see that the price asked for their cooperation is far higher than need be paid, since race and color equality is bound to come in any event.

2. ETHIOPIA: STATE SOCIALISM UNDER AN EMPEROR

The Order of the Garter, "the most distinguished and exclusive of the nine British orders of Knighthood," has just been bestowed on the Emperor of Ethiopia. Since the founding of the Order in 1344, only one other colored man has been so honored and that was the Emperor of Japan who won the Russo-Japanese war.

Ethiopia is a nation of 20 million people of mixed Negro and Semitic stock. In ancient days the Greeks called both sides of the Red Sea, "Ethiopia, the Land of the Burnt Faces." On the African side, from the Great Lakes to the First Cataract of the Nile, was the Motherland of Egypt. Eventually it was beset by Asiatics and retired to its mountains, where as Abyssinia it formed a Negro-Semitic state and, as Gibbon puts it, "slept a thousand years, forgetful of the world and of the world forgotten."

It is a land of great mountains rising to 15,000 feet, with beetling crags and deep valleys, split by enormous abysses and ravines, with step-like terraces and cliffs falling sheer from snows to burning desert and jungle. When the British seized Egypt to secure the Suez Canal they occupied the Sudan, which was the Arab name for "Land of the Blacks"; they had designs on Ethiopia, but hesitated to follow up their victory over the Emperor Theodore. When the Sudan revolted, the British egged on Italy to annex the highlands of Ethiopia.

Italy tried this but was soundly beaten by Menelek at Adowa on March 2, 1906, a national holiday which the Emperor just celebrated. The allies promised Italy to give her Ethiopia after the First World War, but failed to do so. Italy, affronted, attacked Ethiopia in 1935. The League of Nations failed to restrain her and Britain and France refused Ethiopia arms. Italy annexed Ethiopia, with Churchill's approval. The Emperor, Haile Selassie, took refuge in England.

In 1941 the Emperor returned and joined Britain to drive out the Italians. Britain was disposed at first to treat Ethiopia as a dependency and allow Italy to retain Eritrea with its harbors. But the Emperor was adamant and finally secured Eritrea despite Britain's deliberate destruction in Massawa and demand for $2.5 million indemnity.

The Emperor now faced the task of rehabilitation in the midst of a distracted and widely hostile world. He has done a shrewd and so far successful job. His plan is to pit the capitalistic nations against each other. It's a dangerous game but it has had much success. First, the Ethiopians have a pretty nearly self-supporting economy. They raise most of their own food and are not poverty-stricken.

The Dutch have opened a sugar plantation and refining mill, able to supply the country and soon to export. The army is being trained by a Belgian mission;

the Swedes are training the airforce; the British have trained the police; roads are being built extending those built by the Italians for conquest.

The feudal rulers are being replaced by appointed governors. The land is rich and plentiful. There is no race nor color prejudice, and inter-marriage is encouraged. Cereals, coffee, oil seeds and cattle form the main wealth of production. The youth are eager for education; schools are increasing but are not yet sufficient. There is a University College at Addis Ababa leading to the Bachelor's degree, and a large number of church schools teaching the 3 R's, which have existed for centuries. The Soviet Union maintains an information bureau, library and reading room, and a free cinema which is always crowded.

The retiring Indian minister recently referred to the unprecedented upsurge of human spirit that we see in Asia and Africa since India achieved her independence. Anybody who agitates for human rights, freedom of speech, freedom of profession and such other freedoms is dubbed a Communist. This allegation of Communism is another aspect taken up by the power politics in the world.

Ethiopia then is a state socialism under an Emperor with almost absolute power. He is a conscientious man. But what will follow his rule? A capitalist private profit regime or an increasingly democratic socialism; or some form of Communism?

3. THE SUDAN: THREE CRITICAL YEARS AHEAD

The Sudan, which means in Arabic the "Land of the Blacks," is today divided into two parts: French Africa to the west, with a population three-fourths that of Spain, occupying a territory nearly as large as that of the United States; and to the east the Anglo-Egyptian Sudan, with nine million people on a million square miles. To this second part of the Sudan belong historically Ethiopia and Somaliland.

World interest has lately been centered on the Anglo-Egyptian Sudan elections of last November and December. Here, by peculiar maneuvers, a new African nation was born under black control, and the tie between the Sudan and Egypt strained to tenuous proportions; and that between the Sudan and the British Empire perhaps reduced to recognition of dominion status for a black nation.

When, after the Second World War, Egypt secured its independence of Britain, dispute arose over the status of the Anglo-Egyptian Sudan. Egypt claimed it as part of her ancient territory, and Great Britain was in actual governmental control. However, the black Sudan demanded the right to decide, and both Egypt and Britain conceded that right. Britain believed that her status in the Sudan and her close alliance with the black intelligentsia trained at Gordon College would insure her long and pretty complete control. Egypt was sure that the desire of the Sudanese to get rid of white colonialism would throw the Sudanese into the hands of Egypt.

But there were flaws in the reasoning of each: the Sudanese under the Mahdi and the Khalifa had once driven the English out of the Sudan and kept them out from 1881 to 1898. The Sudanese on the one hand, and the Egyptians and French on the other, would have killed the British Cape-to-Cairo plan. This induced the

British to threaten the French and overthrow the Sudanese in 1898. But the hatred remained and the leader of the anti-British party in the late election was a descendant of the Mahdi.

On the other hand, a color line had arisen in modern Egypt which the Sudanese had long resented. In the first thousand years of the Christian era Arabs and Sudanese ruled, mingled and fought in the Nile valley. Black sultans like Mustansir ruled and mulatto poets like Antar sang. Finally in modern days Mohammed Ali, an Albanian, conquered the Sudan in 1820 and turned it into a slave-hunting reserve. When Britain secured control of the Nile valley the color line was strengthened in Egypt and all official positions were filled by Asiatics or Englishmen. The recent rise of Naguib, a mulatto, broke the color line, but even the pro-Egyptian party in the Sudan never forgot the race discrimination.

There came in the Sudan a merger of parties; the anti-British Mahdi Party–called the Umma–came to be opposed by the pro-Egyptian Nationalist Unity Party, which annexed the new Socialist Republican Party representing socialists and trade unions. This consolidation was helped by the pressure of orthodox Mohammedanism on followers of the old Mahdi rift. But those who saw in this the triumph of Britain or the triumph of Egypt were in for disappointment. The Nationalist Unity Party swept the elections, with over half the lower-house seats and two-thirds of the senators.

The new prime minister, Ismail el Azhari, is a black man and has taken an independent line. He has made a courtesy call on the British prime minister in Downing Street. At the same time he is proceeding rapidly with displacement of the 1,163 British officials in the Sudan. In the army now only 30 British officers remain among 140; in the police there are only eight Britishers, and in the civil service only 20 white men as compared with 140 before.

The new black administration insists on Naguib's promises. They have refused to leave the backward tribes of the southern provinces to the control of the British government rule, and in 1956 the Sudan administration will decide on the degree of alliance with Egypt and Britain, if any.

This poses numerous difficult problems: can the Sudan successfully govern itself and, if so, what will be the trend of this government? Will it substitute private profit of a black intelligentsia for foreign exploitation, or will it follow socialism? One scheme is most encouraging. Fenner Brockway, British Labour MP, writes in September 1953: "Outside Russia, the Gezira scheme is the largest nationalized land undertaking in the world. A million acres have been converted into profitable cotton and grain growing soil." It is an enterprise begun by government and private companies but now cooperatively run by the tenant farmers, under government supervision.

Watch the Sudan for the next three years. There is religious fanaticism, capitalist reaction, trade union activity, socialism and fear of communism. It will be a fierce fight but, as one black Sudanese said: "Imperialism was dealt a backbreaking blow. A new nation arises which has been suppressed for half a century."

Look at the map of Africa: the Anglo-Egyptian Sudan encloses three-fourths of the valley of the Nile. It borders on independent Ethiopia; on the south are the Great Lakes, with Kenya, Uganda and Tanganyika; to the southwest is the

Belgian Congo; to the west is the vast stretch of French Africa. Freedom and independence in the Sudan depend on the ability of the black leaders to build a self-supporting economy.

If this comes through trade unions and cooperative agriculture, what will this not mean for central Africa? But also for Britain this is Cape to Cairo and London to Calcutta; it will be worth a price.

4. THE BLACK UNION OF FRENCH AFRICA

French Africa is a third larger than the continental United States and has 50 million inhabitants. It began with Algeria in 1830, which long counted as nothing. Then Bismarck handed over Tunis to placate the French after Sudan and in defiance of Italy's deep desire to have the site of ancient Carthage. Mussolini long made this his appeal for empires; he would shout at the end of a speech: "Et Tunisia?" The thousands would yell back: "A nos!"

The partition of Africa after the Berlin Congress of 1878 started France on her imperial path to ape the British. Her explorers swept over North Africa, seizing everything between the Nile and the Atlantic, except the British West Coast and Spanish Africa in the northwest. Madagascar on the southeast was thrown in later.

At first France planned to seize the Nile valley, and with Menelik of Ethiopia nearly accomplished this. But she was blocked by Kitchener at Fashoda and, declining war, turned to consolidating her African empire. North of the Atlas mountains, in Algeria and Tunis, she built a little France with a small resident group of Frenchmen, with plenty of cheap labor from the hills and well-paying crops.

The dark natives, Mohammedan "berbers" with ancient Negroid strains, and the Italians rebelled, and for 50 years have seethed from sullen hate to open revolt. Today in Tunis comes a fierce demand for autonomy, opposed by resident Frenchmen born in Tunis and ruling ten times their number through their political and economic influence. They are set to retain control of the police and foreign affairs while Tunisia is determined to have autonomy in or outside France.

Algeria is cut in two. On the coast the French are securely ensconced on the rich land, with fine houses and cheap servants and laborers. This is an integral part of France. Below the mountains are the mass of poor and sick peasants of the same stock as in Tunisia, beginning to writhe in poverty and revulsion. They furnish "bandits" for Tunisian unrest.

Below the Atlas mountains lies the Sudan, Land of the Blacks, omitting the eastern part in the Nile Valley. These "islands of the West" lie between the desert, the sea and the valley of the Congo. These dark folk have been the site of civilizations and states rivaling Europe—the Ghana, the Mellestine, the Songhay, Haussa and Bornu Kanem; they fell beneath attack from the North, the slave trade to the west, and religious wars from south and east, until in the 19th century European imperialism seized them and they went mainly to France. They have suffered fierce and cruel exploitation, war and neglect. The novel *Batouala*, which won the Goncourt prize, tells of the exploitation; and the late black governor, Eboué, made all effort to help.

Up in northwest Africa lies Morocco, land of the Moors, a nation of mulattoes of Arabian descent (the tawny Moors and Black-a-Moors), from whom came the conquest of Spain and the splendid Moorish civilization. Here, after fantastic history involving expulsion from Spain and infiltration into the Sudan, came the revolt of the Riffs and the interference of France to take Morocco from Spain. She got it, and now wonders what she will or can do with it. The vast island of Madagascar on the southeast, with Negroid Malays, has rebelled and struggled and now pants in sullen unrest.

All this territory France has tried to unite in a French union with France as senior partner. In French law the people of French West Africa and French Equatorial Africa are guaranteed "freedom of religion, press, speech and assembly." A recent labor code guarantees labor union freedom, the right to strike, collective bargaining, paid vacations and the 40-hour week.

But all this means little to illiterate and poverty-stricken millions. Less than a sixth of the children of school age are in school. In French West Africa a few get standard training and some receive training of a high professional excellence.

There is political activity through chiefs in government pay and by popular assemblies. There are Sudanese deputies in the French parliament and a million registered voters in black French Africa among 21 million people. Thus in the "French Union" the blacks of French Africa have recognized status, but the Union has never really functioned.

The secret of French power here is her refusal to draw a color line. A Negro of ability can get recognition and preferment. He can, if he has the money, attend school in France. He can exploit his fellow Negroes as completely and cruelly as any white man if he has capital. Thus the black mass is drained of its natural leadership; the authority and ancient social customs of the tribe are replaced by Paris ideals and the black mass festers. Exceptions to this routine have appeared but social leadership is sorely needed.

The French Union is a fine paper scheme but that inner government of France, its closely knit group of rich industrial monopolists, holds it like a vise and keeps France the center of international cartels and the apex of world capitalism in close conjunction with America. This explains the rise and fall of Mendes-France.

Black French Africa fronts Europe and borders the Anglo-Egyptian Sudan and the Belgian Congo. When it arises, as arise it will, it may form a black bloc which will dominate North Africa.

5. UGANDA—AND THE PRISONER OF OXFORD

Uganda is the size of England and Scotland, with five and one-half million black Africans, 34,000 East Indians and 3,000 Europeans. It is rich in minerals which Canadian and U.S. capital are exploiting. Trade and commerce are monopolized by Europeans and Indians, while 90 per cent of the blacks are farmers raising cotton and coffee as cash crops. Their average income is $25 a year.

In November 1953, His Highness Edward William Walugembe Mutesa II—29-year-old King of Buganda, the largest kingdom in Uganda, and 37th king of his dynasty—was seized in his native country, forced on a plane and flown to

London by Lyttelton, British Colonial Secretary. The young king is a fellow-student at Oxford University of Lyttelton's son. He is held prisoner in England and denied his throne. His subjects are in revolt.

What was his crime? It is a long story. Uganda is part of the great Kitwara empire, one of the best organized African states in the Middle Ages. It declined with the Bantu migration southward and divided, leaving Uganda as its largest remnant. For 500 years Uganda lived as a settled, well-organized kingdom under a line of monarchs. Then it was attacked by religion: Arab Mohammedans from the south representing slave traders; English explorers from the east, reflecting the conquest of India and bringing Protestant missionaries; and finally Catholics from Austria and France.

The rugged pagan, Mutesa I, refused conversion; his son, Mwanga, tried to drive foreign religions out of his realm. When he killed an English bishop who insisted on entering Uganda, a war of religions began until a British commercial company sent in troops, encouraged by the government so as to keep out the Germans. Christians fought Mohammedans and then turned on each other until in 1899 the king was captured and exiled and Uganda became a British protectorate.

By forced treaty the King of Buganda was recognized by the British so long as he remained "loyal." He ruled with a legislature and ministers, but over him was a British governor who must consent to all legislation and who could make some laws all by himself. Uganda began to awake, to demand more democratic government. A Uganda National Congress appeared in 1951, demanding universal suffrage, a constituent assembly and free education for all Uganda.

About this time the Uganda Development Company was formed in England to mine copper in Uganda, with a capital of $18 million; also a smelting mill and textile works were planned with foreign capital; and the Colonial Secretary (this same Lyttelton) promised the whites of Kenya that federation of Uganda with neighboring African territories would insure white control of land and cheap black labor. To such schemes the London *Times* declared that the action of the Buganda legislature in demanding political control was a "great embarrassment." When the young king supported his legislature and demanded more effective government in the hands of Africans, he was judged disloyal, kidnapped and deposed.

Uganda flamed; the legislature refused to elect a new king and demanded the return of Mutesa II. Uganda was put under martial law. A Buganda delegation in London seeking the return of their king said in painfully plain English:

"Africans are not opposed to economic, industrial, commercial and political development. On the contrary, this is welcomed. But they would rather forego all the benefits of these developments if they bring in their wake political and economic domination by outsiders.

"The economic development of Central Africa is not to be bought by a federal constitution imposed on the African inhabitants. Therefore, while welcoming economic expansion in Uganda, Africans are anxious to ensure that the forces of expansion do not overwhelm the Africans so that they will wake up one day to find that they are dominated by powerful factors over which they have no control."

The British are hesitating. In January of this year they ended the "state of emergency" in Uganda imposed in November 1953, and allowed three suppressed papers to be published again. But they still hold Mutesa in England and the legislature still pledges "never to elect a new Kabaka while Mutesa still lives."

The Uganda National Congress has also presented a 20-page memorandum to the Royal Commission on East Africa. It points to the intense and growing national awareness of the peoples of Africa, exhorting the Commission to recognize the necessity of encouraging this development if progress is to be peaceful and stressing that no solutions, however economically sound, can succeed unless supported by the people.

The memorandum holds that political considerations preclude the success of economic solutions for East Africa as a whole, because the settler creed of "white leadership" conflicts with the "paramountcy of native interests" declared as British Colonial Policy in 1923 and cherished by the people of Uganda. It expresses the determination of the people to avoid development by foreign capitalists until Africans have a real share in controlling the government.

6. BRITISH WEST AFRICA: 35,000,000 FREE?

The most extraordinary development in present-day Africa is the approaching independence of 35 million Negroes of British West Africa along what once was called the "slave coast."

The Gold Coast is the size of England with four and one-half million Negroes, 4,000 British and 1,500 Asiatics. It is composed of the Ashanti people who fought off England in six wars; the Fanti people who in 1868 formed a liberal constitution for an autonomous state and had their leaders thrown in jail by the British. Britain has tried to force seven different constitutions on this colony in the last hundred years, each yielding a little more to self-rule.

Nigeria's 30 million people descend from the great state-building nations of the Sudan in the Middle Ages: the Hanassa, Yoruba, Fulani and Ibo. Here lies the mouth of the great Niger River coming down from the centers of Negro culture in the 15th century. On the coast, cities like Lagos, Benin and Port Harcourt developed modern culture, pushed by the profits of the slave trade. Here political organizations began in 1923 under the grandson of the first black West African bishop, Crowther. It was essentially a bourgeois capitalist movement, but it was soon displaced by younger men, and in 1938 Nnandi Azikiwe began to preach a reborn Africa. This developed into the celebrated Nigerian Youth Movement.

In these two colonies, the Gold Coast and Nigeria, West Coast culture in trade and art flourished in the medieval and modern world, and here the American slave trade entered. In both these colonies the British, failing of complete conquest, long tried to rule by indirect use of subsidized chiefs. The British and other Europeans made huge profits from cheap labor in palm oil, ground nuts and metals.

Then from Spanish Africa, a native worker introduced the cocoa tree on the Gold Coast, and it became the greatest cocoa-raising center in the world. The British, Dutch and Americans tried to monopolize the profit on cocoa by a buyers' monopoly. The Negroes replied with a boycott which was so successful and left so many British laborers unemployed that a commission was sent out which strongly condemned the buyers' tactics.

The Second World War came, and the government took charge of cocoa buying. The British, who made profits of nearly $70 million, reneged on their promise to divide them with the producers and allotted only a small part to the Gold Coast. The result was open rebellion in 1948, during which black troops on the Coast refused to serve. The British fleet was ordered from Gibraltar, and looting and rioting over high prices of imported goods ensued. Negotiations between the British and the Gold Coast Negroes followed.

In Nigeria the Youth Movement led to a London Conference and to a general strike of railroad and public workers' unions in 1945. A new constitution followed in 1947, and another one followed the strike of the coal miners and a national upsurge in 1949. There arose a demand for self-government by 1956.

On the Gold Coast after the uprising in 1948, several of the black leaders, including Kwame Nkrumah, were imprisoned and charged with "communism." But in 1951 Nkrumah was released and became leader of the new state. He was the son of a goldsmith, educated in the colony, then in America and at the London School of Economics. As the leader of the "Convention People's Party," and although still haggling over technicalities, there seems to be no doubt but that he will be recognized as Prime Minister.

In Nigeria matters are more complicated because the British tried to set the more primitive tribes of the interior against the educated city groups on the coast. But this has not been successful, and Nigeria is only a step behind the Gold Coast in its readiness for recognition as an independent dominion.

Naturally the opposition to this development is strong, particularly in South Africa and in the new Central African Federation of the Rhodesias, allied with Kenya die-hards. It has been rumored that at the last moment the white dominion of South Africa will try to veto the admission of black African states in the British Commonwealth. The African leaders have said that in this case they will fight before they will yield.

The other attack is more complicated and subtle. West Africa will need capital. Particularly there is the matter of developing the water power of the great Volta River. There is a further question of regulation of the mines in both colonies. Capital is being offered from Britain and the United States, but on conditions. The black leaders, especially on the Gold Coast, are moving carefully so as to avoid the smear of "communism." But the *West African Pilot*, published in Lagos, Nigeria, has recently said:

"We know no more about Communism than what its American and British detractors have pushed across us as propaganda. But judging from what we see and experience from day to day, we feel that all this talk of the so-called 'free world' and 'Iron Curtain' is a camouflage to fool and bamboozle colonial peoples. It is part and parcel of power politics into which we refuse to be drawn until we are free to choose which ideology suits us best.

"For the time being, we shall judge every nation strictly on the merits of the attitude of that nation towards our national aspirations. We have every cause to be grateful to the Communists for their active interest in the fate of colonial peoples and for their constant denunciation of the evils of imperialism. It is then left to the so-called 'free' nations to convince us that they are more concerned about our welfare than the Communists, and in this regard we believe more in action than in mere words."

7. THE BELGIAN CONGO: COPPER CAULDRON

The great Congo River, third longest in the world, curls around the center of Africa where in the past extraordinary human development in handicraft and political organization has taken place. A kingdom of Congo had existed for centuries when the Portuguese arrived in the 15th century. They induced the Mfumu or king to accept Christianity, and his son was educated in Portugal. One of his successors traveled in Europe in 1600. In intricate political organization and weaving of velvets, satins and damasks the Congolese became noted.

Then came centuries of invasion from west and northeast, and finally this valley fell into the claws of Leopold II of Belgium, with Stanley as his press agent. The two inveigled the Congress of Berlin to let Leopold hold the Congo as a sort of great Christian enterprise where "Peace and Religion" would march hand in hand.

The result in theft and sheer cruelty astounded even Europe, more especially as both France and Germany, and Britain hiding behind Portugal, stood ready to show Belgium how and were at the time content with cutting off the coastline. But the Belgian state took over, staggering under this colony 14 times the size of Belgium itself and with many more inhabitants.

Belgium was at that time under socialist leadership, but that did not curb colonial imperialism. First Belgium confiscated all native rights to land ownership. Then they subsidized all chiefs and put labor under vast corporations in which Britain and America invested. They curbed education to elementary instruction under Catholics, with a few exceptions. They gave the natives training in skills of a higher grade than in South Africa or the Rhodesias, but kept wages low and did not give enough education to permit training even for physicians; and for a long time they refused to let Negroes enter Belgian higher schools at home.

Then came demands in Brussels at the Second Pan-African Congress. Immediately black students who were not too radical began to be received in Belgian schools. An official report says in 1954: "In 1947 a school for administrative and commercial training was opened. In the same year the Centre Universitaire Congolais Lovanium was organized with the intention to group the existing schools together and lay the foundations for an institute of higher education."

Meantime the Belgian Congo had become a center of vast investment and profit. The colony raised palm oil and palm nuts, cotton, coffee, rubber, cocoa and ivory. It became one of the greatest copper-producing countries in the world. Also gold, tin, cobalt and silver were exported. It became the largest producer of industrial diamonds, and nearly 60 per cent of the world supply of uranium ore was produced and now goes chiefly to the United States.

There has arisen bitter strife in the copper mines, with the natives organizing a union and seeking higher wages. There is one Negro newspaper representing the intelligentsia but influenced or actually subsidized by the Belgian masters. Perhaps more than in any other African colony the Belgians are making desperate efforts to see that no organized opposition to their ownership of the Congo develops among educated Negroes. Colored West Indian clerks have long been hired, and propaganda against Negro organization is carefully spread. Indeed, as the Council on African Affairs says:

"The Belgian delegate will support his contention by citing the fact that in 1953 the Belgian Chamber of Representatives approved a revision of Article I, Paragraph 4 of the Belgian Constitution to make it clear that Belgium and the Congo together form a single sovereign state.

"Belgian officials have for some time been exasperated by what they regard as the over-zealous concern of the UN for the welfare of the Congolese. The British and French have, of course, also squirmed when their colonial policies were under review, but the Belgian representative, M. Pierre Ryckmans, has been particularly perverse in rejecting any and all UN efforts toward the political and social advancement of colonial peoples, sometimes casting the lone negative vote on such issues. That is why we say—do not be surprised if Belgium employs the above-mentioned technical excuse to try to end, once and for all, UN 'meddling' with the Congo."

The present Belgian Minister of Colonies puts the matter as follows: "On a political and administrative plane, it is necessary to create the psychological conditions for harmonious co-existence and peaceful collaboration between natives and whites. With the birth of a true native middleclass—with interests common to those of the whites—these conditions tend to become closer and closer."

So save in the copper-mine unions, rebellion in the Congo has not yet developed. It is still possible, and if black French Africa bordering on the Congo for 1,600 miles goes socialist, as it may; and if Uganda, Kenya and Tanganyika to the east continue to surge with protest as they do now, the Belgian Congo may yet join the ideology of Black West Africa.

8. KENYA: THE WAR THAT CAN'T BE WON

I saw Jomo Kenyatta in 1945 at the Fifth Pan-African Congress in Manchester, England. He was a big man, yellow in color, intelligent. Today he is in jail convicted of planning the rebellion in Kenya against British oppression. Whether or not he actually planned this rebellion, I do not know; but never in modern history was a nation more justified in revolution than the five million black people of Kenya.

Kenya is a fertile island set in a desert sea. Kenya mountain rises from its northeastern corner, exactly on the Equator, covered with eternal snow. Of the 225,000 square miles in Kenya over half is desert. Of the rest, 3,000 white settlers own 16,700 square miles of the most fertile land and 5,250,000 Africans occupy, without ownership rights, 52,000 square miles of the poorest.

This land originally belonged to cattle-herding tribes without permanent settlements. English missionaries, inspired by Livingstone's appeal, first entered followed by explorers seeking the source of the Nile. Then came the colonial imperialists, England seeking to outrun the Germans. Finally England seized the territory, confiscated all the land and sold it to whites at two cents an acre in baronies of 10 to 100 thousand acres.

Of the good land held by whites, only six per cent is under cultivation. On the native reserves the density of inhabitants per square mile is 674, and half this land is unsuitable for cultivation. Driven from their land, the Africans began to enter the towns, where many thousands of them lived without shelter in conditions of near-starvation. Laborers and servants are paid an average of $5.18 a month, clerks and artisans from $11 to $42.

In the legislature the 29,000 whites have 14 elected representatives; the 90,000 Asiatics have six, and the 24,000 Arabs one elected and one appointed; the 5,251,120 Negroes have no elected representatives but the Governor nominates six to speak for them. The natives pay three different kinds of direct taxes, and indirect taxes are placed on their necessities instead of on luxuries. They have been in the past subjected continually to forced labor, legal and illegal; the successors of the missionaries, including Anglican bishops, once insisted that the settlers should have the right to force the natives to work.

In the last 25 years the policy of England has vacillated. Commission after commission has made proposals, but the basic situation has not been changed. Of the Negro children seven to 11 years old, a third are in school, and Kenya spends about $6 a year on their education. The black folk of Kenya made every effort to obtain relief. They built and ran thousands of schools of their own. They made close contact with the British Labour Party but got nothing from them. They organized the Kenya African Union and held a conference attended by delegates from all Kenya. They declared in 1947:

"That the political objective of the Africans of Kenya must be self-government by Africans for Africans, the rights of all racial minorities being safeguarded.

"That more land must be made available both in the Crown Lands and in the highlands for settlement by Africans.

"That free compulsory education for Africans, as is given to the children of other races, is overdue.

"That the deplorable wages, housing and other conditions of African laborers must be substantially improved and that the principle of equal pay for equal work be recognized."

The Union grew to 10,000 members. Patriotic songs were written and seven weekly newspapers established. Two representatives were sent to England to plead with the British people, but no substantial relief came. As a resident white said: "We are going to stay here for the good of Africa, and as long as we stay we rule!"

At last in 1952 open rebellion flared in Kenya with secret organization, murder and arson. As to just how far this went, how many were killed and how the economy was disrupted, there has been no official report; but clearly the whites were frightened. A state of "emergency" was declared on October 20, 1952. By June 1954, $22,500,000 had been spent to suppress the rebellion and the fight is now costing $2,800,000 a month.

The Royal Air Force has dropped 220 tons of bombs in nine months. British troops and police have killed 130 Africans for every European killed in the Kenya war, without counting the number of Africans killed by RAF bombs. The Kenya African Union has been suppressed and its leaders jailed. Jomo Kenyatta said when sentenced to seven years in jail:

"What we shall continue to object to is discrimination in the government of this country, and we shall not accept that, in jail or out of it . . . What we have done and shall continue to do is to demand rights for the African people as human beings."

As D. N. Pritt, the great British lawyer, says: "A cruel and brutal war has been raging for nearly two and a half years to hold the Africans in subjection and maintain the settlers as masters of the best land in the country. This war cannot be won by the British in a military sense. If it could be, it would still leave unresolved, and indeed untouched, every agrarian, economic and national grievance, and would thus inevitably lead to a new war in the near future."

9. SLAVERY IN THE UNION OF SOUTH AFRICA

It seems almost unbelievable that in the middle of the 20th century the Union of South Africa is widely recognized as a civilized nation. Its history began with the settlement of the Dutch at the Cape of Good Hope in the 17th century, followed by the British who made this an outpost of Empire. Both of them met the advance guard of a great African peoples' migration which had probably been continuous for a thousand years.

The march of the Bantu southward was caused by the state building of the Sudanese Negroes, which started the fight between Christians and Mohammedans in the Nile Valley and between Mohammedans and earlier cultures in northwest Africa. Marching in waves, with long interruptions, retreats and settlements, the Bantu advance guard reached South Africa's great plateau almost simultaneously with the Dutch and British.

There ensued a series of wars, skirmishes and attempts at accommodations between British and Dutch, Dutch and Bantu, British and Bantu. The Dutch at first had mingled with the natives and produced a mulatto population, some of which were incorporated with the Dutch and some of which survive as the so-called colored people of South Africa.

The Dutch and the British tried at first to lay out respective areas of domination and almost succeeded, when all was thrown into confusion by discovery of the world's greatest gold and diamond hoard. Cecil Rhodes started to monopolize for England the wealth of this land and to open the way from the Cape to Cairo. The Dutch not only fought the English in one of the bitterest wars in modern history, but entered into death struggle with the blacks.

General Smuts tried to accomplish the subjection of the Negro with some finesse and regard to civilized opinion, but his successors, Malan and Strydom, were white provincials still marked with 18th century barbarism. They have started out upon a program which is simply impossible. In an economy which calls for larger and larger numbers of black workers who must be thrown more and more in competition with white skilled labor in and out of Africa, they are trying to segregate the workers by race and color, to limit their education and cultural contacts, and to turn them into something as near slavery as modern conditions of industry will permit.

This would be difficult under ordinary circumstances, but today the blacks themselves are under leadership. Their intelligentsia is small but determined and unusually unselfish, with no development of an exploiting bourgeoisie.

Indian labor was introduced, and attempts were made to pit these two groups against each other; but determined effort by Gandhi and later leaders has welded them into a fairly solid whole. Missionary and native effort have furnished some secondary schools, and a public school system gives some inadequate elementary training. The African National Congress and the South African Indian Congress are united to fight racialism. Their efforts have been called "communistic," since in that way the white masters will get the greatest sympathy from the United States and Britain.

In 1937 the United States imported $6.5 million worth of goods from the Union of South Africa. In 1951 this had increased to nearly $100 million. "The public investment of United States money in Africa now runs more than a half-billion dollars," said the Chicago *Daily News* recently, "and the private investments may be as much or more." Every great American corporation has invested funds in South Africa. The U.S. government has loaned it $100 million, and promises more.

The so-called "free democracies" of the West are allowing and encouraging an incredible denial of democracy among South African blacks, who have no representation in the legislature but can send two white people to talk for them. Repeatedly the two who have been elected have been refused seats because of alleged "communism."

The Union of South Africa has also seized Southwest Africa, in defiance of the United Nations, and made every effort to silence the sole voice raised in their behalf by Michael Scott.

The 11 million disfranchised, degraded and exploited brown and black people of the Union of South Africa under the slave rule of two and a half million whites have sent this appeal to the world, which every periodical in the United States, white and black, Republican and Democrat, secular and religious, has ignored:

"WE CALL THE PEOPLE OF SOUTH AFRICA, BLACK AND WHITE—LET US SPEAK TOGETHER OF FREEDOM:

"WE CALL THE MINERS OF COAL, GOLD AND DIAMONDS.

"Let us speak of the dark shafts, and the cold compounds far from our families.

"Let us speak of heavy labor and long hours, and of men sent home to die.

"Let us speak of rich masters and poor wages.

"LET US SPEAK OF FREEDOM.

"WE CALL THE WORKERS OF FARMS AND FORESTS.

"Let us speak of the rich foods we grow, and the laws that keep us poor.

"Let us speak of harsh treatment and of children and women forced to work.

"Let us speak of private prisons, and beatings, and of passes.

"LET US SPEAK OF FREEDOM.

"WE CALL THE WORKERS OF FACTORIES AND SHOPS.

"Let us speak of the good things we make, and the bad conditions of our work.

"Let us speak of the many passes and the few jobs.

"Let us speak of foremen and of transport and of trade unions; of holidays and of houses.

"LET US SPEAK OF FREEDOM."

And what are we Americans, black and white, doing?
Nothing but building a chapel where illiterate Congressmen may pray.

10. DECLARATION OF INDEPENDENCE NEAR?

The British Queen Mother has recently been to South Africa to remind the world how great Cecil Rhodes was. He had elements of greatness, but more than most men he started the modern world toward lying, stealing and killing as a path of modern progress. He lied Oom Paul Kruger to his death, he stole the world's greatest horde of gold and diamonds and he murdered thousands of deceived Matabele in order to establish Anglo-Saxon rulership of the world.

Africa gave tuberculous Rhodes back his health and made him a millionaire at 21. He rushed to Oxford, listened to Ruskin and hurried back to force South Africa out of the grasp of the Boers and lead British domination from the Cape to Cairo. He sowed the wind, reaped the whirlwind: white supremacy, colonial imperialism, world war.

The decline of the British Empire has set in. Canada is practically American. British rule of India, Burma and Ceylon is gone; control of China has dwindled to Hong Kong; Malaya is slipping, rule of Indonesia through Holland has disappeared, and the West Indies are wriggling loose. Africa alone remains and Africa is rising from its long sleep. West Africa will be free or fighting in the next decade. Kenya is bathed in blood. South Africa is daring the world in barbaric reaction and Central Africa is doggedly pursuing the path to certain doom.

The Central African Federation was established by Great Britain in 1953 over the protest of the natives. It includes Northern Rhodesia, Southern Rhodesia and Nyassaland, larger in area than France, Spain, Portugal, Belgium and the Netherlands. It has six and a half million black Africans with no political rights and insecure land tenure, and over these 200,000 white Europeans propose to exercise complete domination.

There is of course "representation" of the blacks by hand-picked stooges, and the natives have indefinite rights to the soil. But this dominion is a vast investment into which British capital is putting $210,000,000 for railroads and power to use cheap labor and land free to whites for copper, cobalt, gold, cotton, tea, rubber and tobacco.

Out of two million black children of school age only 500,000 are in indifferent primary schools. Moreover, the United States is going to have a hand in this exploitation. Secretary of Commerce Sinclair Weeks commends the "marked progress in development of its economic resources" by the Union of South Africa, and commends our increasing South African trade which has risen from $16 million in 1939 to $105 million in 1952.

William H. Ball, personal representative of President Eisenhower, spoke at the Rhodes centenary and gave clear notice that the British were not to regard this Federation as their own private affair. He said the United States desired to preserve the right of equal commercial treatment and to participate commercially and financially in the development. He said that of course the United States was sympathetic to national aspirations, but it was no part of the American policy "to give indiscriminate and uncritical support to nationalist movements." He added: "Our concern, as it is the concern of the administering powers, is that no part of Africa falls under Soviet domination or influence. It is one of our major objectives to see that the peoples of Africa remain wedded to Western ideals."

These "Western ideals" are historically slavery, caste, poverty, ignorance and disease.

Effort is made to make the world think that the African interest is being attended to. A Rhodesian University without color discrimination will be established, to which of course no Negro can receive education enough to gain entrance. On the other hand the Negroes are not asleep. This spring the Federation is having serious trouble in its copper and tobacco industries; 40,000 African workers are striking in the copper belt, second largest copper-producing area in the world.

Despite a surface prosperity with a tremendous building boom, the New York *Times* correspondent Salisbury, visiting the capital, revealed the Federation to be on a precarious economic footing. The Federation was conceived of as a compromise on Negro-white relations, avoiding the extremism of South Africa. But it is an economic unity supported by copper mining, tobacco and cheap labor.

Southern Rhodesia is quite independent, but Northern Rhodesia and Nyassaland are under the British Colonial Office, which spells a small difference in action. The strike in the copper mines is being made by a union of 20,000 members. They are demanding $1.50 a day, a 400 per cent increase over what they are getting now.

In adjacent Tanganyika (not a part of the Federation), there are seven million Negroes in a land nearly as large as France and Spain, where sisal, coffee, diamonds and gold are produced. It is adjacent to British Somaliland with 500,000 people. Here, when the representative of the UN Trusteeship Council visited last November, he received a petition from the workers protesting discrimination in the wages and housing, lack of social services and continued disfranchisement.

In Tanganyika after the war the British tried to herd the inhabitants on to plantations run by the greatest monopoly in the world on land seized from the natives. The scheme failed so completely that Britain now does not even mention it.

One cannot talk of Central Africa and Tanganyika without remembering what has been said of Kenya and Uganda and the Sudan, to the north, and Portuguese Africa to the southeast and southwest.

In Angola and Mozambique, with their 10 million Negroes, is the labor reservoir for the Rhodesias and South Africa, and a nominal recognition of native, mulatto and Portuguese equality, together with an actual exploitation on the lowest scale. A virtual slave trade supplies the need of Rhodesian and South African exploiters.

The end of this disgrace to modern civilization may not be in sight but it is in hearing. At the time that Asia and Africa meet in Indonesia there may come the following declaration of independence from black Africa:

The Peoples of Africa, black and white, brown and yellow, have a right to Freedom and Self-Government, to Food and Shelter, Education and Health.

We hereby warn the world that no longer can Africa be regarded as pawn, slave or property of Europeans, Americans or any other people.

Africa is for the Africans: its Land and Labor; its natural wealth and resources; its mountains, lakes and rivers; its cultures and its Soul.

Hereafter it will no longer be ruled by Might nor be Power; by invading armies nor police, but by the Spirit of all its Gods and the Wisdom of its Prophets.

Men of all races are welcome to Africa if they obey its law, seek its interests and love their neighbors as themselves, doing unto others as they would that others should do to them. But the white bigots of South Africa and Kenya; the exploiters of the Rhodesias, the Congo, West, North and Southwest and Southeast Africa, are solemnly warned that they cannot win. Their doom is sealed. We will be free; we will govern ourselves for our best good. Our wealth and labor belong to us and not to thieves at home nor abroad. Black Africa welcomes the world as equals; as masters never; we will fight this forever and curse the blaspheming Boers and the heathen liars from Hell.

Let the white world keep its missionaries at home to teach the Golden Rule to its corporate thieves. Damn the God of Slavery, Exploitation and War. Peace on Earth; no more war. The earth of Africa is for its people. Its Wealth is for the poor and not for the rich. All Hail Africa.

Ghana and Pan-Africanism

1. THE SAGA OF NKRUMAH

(National Guardian, July 30, 1956)

Kwame Nkrumah was a black boy of Accra, a peasant and not of chieftain rank. He went to the mission school and then to work. He saw the looting of the United Africa Company when, during the depression, this vast monopoly was starving people of the Gold Coast to death. Britain summoned her warships from Gibraltar and alerted her black troops of the West Coast and for the first time these troops refused to budge. England paused. Here was trouble in sight.

Young Nkrumah went to America and to England. He went to Moscow. He was in Paris when the trade unions met after World War II. He helped call the Fifth Pan-African Congress in England in 1945. There I first saw him and Kenyatta of Kenya and Johnson of Sierra Leone. Nkrumah was shabby, kindly, but earnest, and he and others called for justice in the cocoa market and freedom for the Gold Coast. I did not then dream that Nkrumah had the stamina and patience for this task.

That cocoa story was a fairy tale. Spaniards raised cocoa in Fernando Po with slaves; Britain and Holland processed it into chocolate and sold it in New York. Then the Quaker Cadburys of England had a scheme. They induced the world to boycott Spanish slavery so as to bring the cocoa crop to British West African plantations. But Tettie Quarsie balked them. He was a little black cocoa laborer on the island of Principe. He smuggled cocoa plants to the Gold Coast. Soon more cocoa was growing on the Gold Coast than in all the rest of the world and it was growing on little one-acre Negro farms and not on British-owned plantations.

The buyers from London, Amsterdam and New York thus could not control production, but they combined to control buying and bid so low that the growers struck. The cocoa market was thrown into confusion and, with war looming, England was forced to take over all cocoa buying. They offered the farmers the same low price but promised to refund any profit. They made $5,000,000 profit and then reneged on their promise. The Gold Coast seethed and the Fifth Pan-African Congress complained. Nkrumah returned to the Gold Coast determined on independence. He laid out a plan for home rule on socialist lines and the government threw him in jail as a "communist." But the uproar was so great that they had to release him. Quietly and effectively he went into organization.

He worked not from the Chiefs down; not from the black British-educated intelligentia over, but from the working masses up. He lived, ate and slept with them. He traveled among them all over the land; he talked and pled in proud Ashanti, in Togoland, in the dark, crowded cities of the Coast. In the ensuing election his Convention People's Party won a clear majority.

Nkrumah then told Britain in effect that either it would grant independence to the Gold Coast or the Coast would take it. South Africa threatened, but Britain was reasonable. If Nkrumah could secure a steady democratic majority; if Nkrumah could secure the home talent to rule; if Nkrumah could insure the economic stability of the Gold Coast—in such unlikely case the Gold Coast would be recognized as an independent dominion of the British Commonwealth.

Nkrumah took over the sale of cocoa as a government monopoly. He planned an electric power dam on the Volta River with British and foreign capital, but so fenced it in by government supervision that its "free enterprise" was under strict social control. Slowly but surely Nkrumah spread education, and secured educated black civil servants to man the ship of state. In the 1954 election he increased his popular majority. The British began to yield. Some of their best officials on the Gold Coast cooperated whole-heartedly with Nkrumah.

But the Colonial Office in England played its last hand. It sowed seeds of internal dissent; it encouraged tribalism and provincialism; especially among the Ashanti whom the British had conquered in the 19th century after six wars. Now Ashanti chiefs were encouraged to resent the domination of a peasant from the coast. They demanded autonomy for Ashanti and the "Federation" of the many provinces of the Gold Coast, with its total population of only five million.

Nkrumah called for a conference and a British Commission appeared. The Ashanti refused to take part. One of the black Oxford-educated leaders, married to the daughter of Sir Stafford Cripps, leaped to the aid of the dissidents. But cool Nkrumah gave rein to the commission, compromised and kept power in the hands of the central government while recognizing the right of provincial debate and suggestion.

Togoland voted to stand by Nkrumah. Then Nkrumah offered to appeal to the people in a final election. After that he demanded independence with or without British consent. Moreover, he insisted that the new nation be called "Ghana" after that black nation which flourished in Africa one thousand years ago before white slave drivers named the shores of Guinea, "Gold" and "Slave" and "Grain."

Last week Nkrumah increased his majority in a nation-wide election: he secured 71 Legislative Assembly delegates out of a total of 104. I cabled him my congratulations.

2. A FUTURE FOR PAN-AFRICA: FREEDOM, PEACE, SOCIALISM

(National Guardian, March 11, 1957)

On March 6, 1957, the Gold Coast, British colony on the West Coast of Africa, will become a Dominion of the British Commonwealth, ranking with Canada,

Australia and the Union of South Africa. This former center of the slave trade to America will assume the name of Ghana, an ancient Negro kingdom of northwest Africa which, between the 5th and 15th centuries, included much of the present territory of the Gold Coast.

Ghana will occupy an area about as large as the United Kingdom, with 4,125,000 inhabitants, nearly all of whom are black Africans. Within its borders will lie the ancient kingdom of the Ashanti, which fought six wars against England and, despite insult and humiliation, never surrendered the golden stool of its sovereignty. Ghana will be independent and self-governing and the inauguration of this state will be witnessed by officials from many of the world's leading nations, including the Vice President of the United States.

I have just sent the Prime Minister, Dr. Kwame Nkrumah, the following greetings:

I have your kind invitation of January 22, 1957. In behalf of myself and of my wife, Shirley Graham, I thank you for it and want to say how great was our desire to accept it. But since the U.S. government refused to issue us passports, we must with deep regret inform you of our inability to accept. I have recently also, and for the same reason, been compelled to my sorrow to decline a trip to China for lectures and participation in the celebration of the 250th anniversary of the birth of Benjamin Franklin.

However, because of the fact that I am now entering the 90th year of my life, and because of my acquaintanceship with you during the last 12 years, which cover the years of your imprisonment, vindication and political triumph, I trust you will allow me a few words of advice for the future of Ghana and Africa.

I venture the more readily to do this because, 40 years ago at the end of the First World War, I tried to establish some means of cooperation between the peoples of African descent throughout the world. Since then five Pan-African Congresses have met and, at the last one in England in 1945, I had the pleasure of meeting you.

Today, when Ghana arises from the dead and faces this modern world, it must no longer be merely a part of the British Commonwealth or a representative of the world of West Europe, Canada and the United States. Ghana must on the contrary be the representative of Africa, and not only that, but of Black Africa below the Sahara desert. As such, her first duty should be to come into close acquaintanceship and cooperation with her fellow areas of British West Africa and Liberia; with the great areas of black folk in French West and Equatorial Africa; with the Sudan, Ethiopia, and Somaliland; with Uganda, Kenya and Tanganyika; with the Belgian Congo and all Portuguese Africa; with the Rhodesias and Bechuanaland; with Southwest Africa, the Union of South Africa and Madagascar; and with all other parts of Africa and with peoples who want to cooperate. All the former barriers of language, culture, religion and political control should bow before the essential unity of race and descent, the common suffering of slavery and the slave trade and the modern color bar.

Ignoring the old sources of division and lack of knowledge of and sympathy for each other, Ghana should lead a movement of black men for Pan-Africanism, including periodic conferences and personal contacts of black men from the Sahara to the Indian Ocean. With a program of peace and with no thought of force, political control or underground subversion, a new series of Pan-African Congresses should be held; they should include delegates from all groups and especially from the African congresses which already exist in many parts of Africa and which got their inspiration in most cases from the first Pan-African Congress in Paris in 1919.

The new series of Pan-African Congresses would seek common aims of progress for Black Africa, including types of political control, economic cooperation, cultural development, universal education and freedom from religious dogma and dictation.

The consequent Pan-Africa, working together through its independent units, should seek to develop a new African economy and cultural center standing between Europe and Asia, taking from and contributing to both. It should stress peace and join no military alliance and refuse to fight for settling European quarrels. It should avoid subjection to and ownership by foreign capitalists who seek to get rich on African labor and raw material, and should try to build a socialism founded on old African communal life; rejecting on the one hand the exaggerated private initiative of the West, and seeking to ally itself with the social program of the progressive nations; with British and Scandinavian socialism, with the progress toward the welfare state of India, Germany, France and the United States; and with the Communist states like the Soviet Union and China, in peaceful cooperation and without presuming to dictate as to how socialism must or can be attained at particular times and places.

Pan-African socialism seeks the welfare state in Black Africa. It will refuse to be exploited by people of other continents for their own benefit and not for the benefit of the peoples of Africa. It will no longer consent to permitting the African majority of any African country to be governed against its will by a minority of invaders who claim racial superiority or the right to get rich at African expense. It will seek not only to raise but to process its raw material and to trade it freely with all the world on just and equal terms and prices.

Pan-Africa will seek to preserve its own past history, and write the present account, erasing from literature the lies and distortions about black folk which have disgraced the last centuries of European and American literature; above all, the new Pan-Africa will seek the education of all its youth on the broadest possible basis without religious dogma and in all hospitable lands as well as in Africa and for the end of making Africans not simply profitable workers for industry nor stoolpigeons for propaganda, but for making them modern, intelligent, responsible men of vision and character.

I pray you, my dear Mr. Nkrumah, to use all your power to put a Pan-Africa along these lines into working order at the earliest possible date. Seek to save the great cultural past of the Ashanti and Fanti peoples, not by inner division but by outer cultural and economic expansion toward the outmost bounds of the great African peoples, so that they may be free to live, grow and expand; and to teach mankind what non-violence and courtesy, literature and art, music and dancing, can do for this greedy, selfish and war-stricken world.

I hereby put into your hands, Mr. Prime Minister, my empty but still significant title of "President of the Pan-African Congress," to be bestowed on my duly-elected successor who will preside over a Pan-African Congress due, I trust, to meet soon and for the first time on African soil, at the call of the independent state of Ghana.

3 THE PRIME MINISTER OF GHANA[1]

(Mainstream, New York, May 1957)

When one remembers the contempt and insult which for four hundred years white civilization, in literature, church and school has visited on people with black skins, not to mention slavery, caste and lynching, it is extraordinary to read the calm story of a man who lived through some of the worst features of this disgraceful era, and now heads a state with the nations of the world paying homage.

Ghana is not a large nation, just as England was never outstanding for size. But the nine million folk of Ghana have an economic significance, a cultural unity and a *joie de vivre* which makes it remarkable. It has experienced oppression since that British scoundrel, John Hawkins ranged its coast in the ship "Jesus" and stole slaves which secured him knighthood from Queen Elizabeth; to the day, when after six wars ranging over 90 years, England not only conquered the great state of Ashanti but humiliated the king by demanding that he kiss the white governor's feet. When in 1871, the Fanti, who had helped Britain against the Ashanti, drew up a constitution for self-government under the British, their leaders were thrown into jail.

After this history comes Nkrumah. He is from a humble family. He was educated in missionary schools and at the government college at Achimota where he studied under Kwegyir Aggrey, a West African educated in the United States. This determined Nkrumah to seek an education in America. Through letters of introduction from a Negro leader who, following the First Pan-African Congress had called a similar congress in Nigeria, Nkrumah entered Lincoln University, a Negro college near Philadelphia. He stayed ten years in America and learned what it means to be black in the "land of the free." He had very little money and on vacations tried to find work. He sold fish in Harlem, but could make no profit. He got a job in a soap factory and learned that black folk in America usually get the hard and dirty jobs:

"It turned out to be by far the filthiest and most unsavory job that I ever had. All the rotting entrails and lumps of fat of animals were dumped by lorries into a yard. Armed with a fork I had to load as much as I could of this reeking and utterly repulsive cargo into a wheelbarrow and then transport it, load after load, to the processing plant. As the days went by, instead of being steadily toughened, I had the greatest difficulty in trying not to vomit the whole time."

Nkrumah tried waiting on table and dish-washing; he slept outdoors and in parks; he got cheap food in Father Divine's restaurants. Once in Baltimore he asked a white waiter for a drink of water. The waiter pointed to a spittoon.

By work outside his studies and desperate application he was graduated from Lincoln University in 1939 and voted the "most interesting" of his classmates. He wanted to study journalism at Columbia but he had no money and as usual the "missionaries" tried to force him into the ministry. He studied at the Lincoln School of Theology but also took courses at the University of Pennsylvania, 50 miles away; so that in 1942 he became Bachelor of Theology at Lincoln and Master of Science in Education at the University of Pennsylvania. The next year he received his Master of Arts in Philosophy at Pennsylvania and lacked only a thesis to secure his doctorate. During this study he became interested in the future of West Africa and formulated many of the plans which he is now carrying out. He met and talked with African fellow students and did some teaching and lecturing.

For support he took a job in a ship building yard in Chester: "I worked in all weathers from twelve midnight until eight the following morning. It froze so hard on several occasions that my hands almost stuck to the steel and although I put on all the clothes that I possessed, I was chilled to the marrow. At 8 A.M. I used to return to my lodgings, have breakfast, sleep for a few hours and then begin research for the writing of my thesis." Naturally there came an attack of pneumonia. After recovery, in May 1945, Nkrumah left New York for London.

In October of that year I saw Kwame Nkrumah for the first time in Manchester, England, where we were holding the Fifth Pan-African Congress. There were some 200 delegates and he was one of a number of young West Africans many of whom had just attended a trade union meeting in Paris. I did not really get acquainted with Kwame. He was busy with organization work, a bit shabby and not talkative. He was in earnest and intelligent and I never forgot him. We had a mutual friend in George Padmore who had sparked this meeting.

Nkrumah stayed in London two years as Secretary of the West African National Secretariat and to edit a magazine. He tried to organize the colored workers and kept in touch with leaders of the Labor Party. He attended meetings of the Communist Party. But he lost faith in British Labor and in any attempt to lead Africa from Europe. In November 1947, Nkrumah left Liverpool for the Gold Coast after being held up by the authorities because of his political activities while in Britain.

Nkrumah arrived on the West Coast when the long advertised system of "indirect rule" of British officials through African chiefs was beginning to break up. The chiefs had become paid agents of Britain and after the two world wars the people of the Gold Coast were beginning to repudiate the chiefs and to demand self-rule. They felt on the one hand the weakness of poverty, ignorance and disease and on the other, their strength as producers of cocoa and other products which were making white Europe rich. The black folk, however, were divided by age-old tribal jealousies and disputes over the power of chiefs, many of whom traced their aristocratic descent back hundreds of years.

Nkrumah went over the heads of the chiefs and under the authority of British overlords and appealed to the mass of people who never before had had effective leadership. The United Gold Coast Convention was organized as a group of non-partisan leaders. But Nkrumah soon decided that a regular political alignment was needed and he organized the Convention People's Party, a group demanding immediate self-government. He declared himself a socialist and repeats this statement in this book. His plan of organization as stated in "The Circle," reprinted as an appendix, forecasts the creation of a "revolutionary vanguard for the struggle of West African unity and national independence." The Convention People's Party was organized in every hamlet all over the Gold Coast. Social bodies interested in all kinds of welfare work were integrated, a central office opened, newspapers were started and mass meetings held.

Then came an incident which Nkrumah had hoped to avoid but which British officials must have prayed for: ex-service men called a boycott on high prices and the police shot at a peaceful demonstration. The whole town of Accra was soon rioting, with looting of stores and assault of Europeans. The police immediately arrested Nkrumah and his associates although they were not the instigators of the riot and would have strongly advised against it. The uprising was in fact spontaneous and quite beyond control. But it was just the excuse which the government needed. They found on Nkrumah his "Circle" for socialization of the country and they faced him with his London activities. He was accused of being a "Communist" and kept in jail for eight weeks. Many of his associates deserted him. He was finally tried and sentenced to three years imprisonment. In jail he was treated as a criminal, confined with 11 persons in one cell, with a bucket in one corner as a latrine. The food was poor and scanty. They were deprived of writing material and newspapers.

But outside, Nkrumah's party stood firm. After he had been 15 months in jail, the election was held and Nkrumah, as candidate for parliamentary leader received 22, 780 votes out of 23,122 cast. He was released and carried on the shoulders of a vast crowd to party headquarters. He now became Leader of Government Business in Parliament and began reform. He worked on the civil service and began to integrate Negro officials. He reorganized the selling of cocoa by the government and the cutting out of diseased cocoa trees. He began to look into foreign investment and industrial expansion.

It was a hard job; there was opposition from the British officeholders, from Negro leaders and from cocoa farmers, especially from those who defended the traditional authority of the chiefs. Nkrumah pressed Britain to set a definite date for Ghana independence; the British tried to sidetrack and sabotage the demand. At last they asked for a new election before the terms of the Parliament then sitting had ended. They were assured by malcontents that Nkrumah would be overwhelmingly defeated. Nkrumah, contrary to expectations, assented to the test. His party won 72 of the 104 members of Parliament. Nkrumah became Prime Minister and on March 6th Ghana became an independent nation.

What next? A small new nation of nine millions is usually of little significance in the modern world save as the loot of empires. But Ghana is exceptional. It supplies the world with most of its cocoa and chocolate. In the last decade it has raised an average of 228,000 tons of cocoa annually on 300,000 peasant-owned farms. Each year Ghana raises three millions tons of food. The fight on animal diseases has brought herds of cattle and sheep. It has 8,000 square miles in valuable hardwoods under government control; it catches 20,000 tons of fish a year and plans to motorize its fishing crafts. It has vast deposits of bauxite, the raw material of aluminum; it has gold, manganese and diamonds. It has a rapidly growing system of popular education and a native college, and it has a leader of integrity, courage and ideas, who knows the modern world.

Nkrumah is faced by three pressing problems: First, the unity of Ghana, with integration of the chiefs and northern Moslems into the social body of the nation; with development of socialism rather than of a bourgeois democracy with exploited workers, and with private profit. This will be no easy task, but Nkrumah is experienced and fully aware of the difficulties. He has seen private capitalism in Europe and America.

Second, Nkrumah must industrialize Ghana so that it will not remain the exploited victim of foreign investors. Already he faces long-established mining companies who have made vast profits on low rents and wages and inadequate taxation; if such corporations were exterminated forthwith as they deserve to be, where would Ghana get the new capital to mine bauxite and manufacture aluminum? Where would she get the funds for power development of the Volta river? One reason that the inauguration of Ghana attracted the cormorants of private capital from all the world was this chance for tremendous profit, provided the rulers of Ghana will play the game as it is being played in the Middle East. Nkrumah has been non-committal, but reasonable. He is not scaring private investment away; neither is he inviting it with promise of unlimited profit. If he can get capital on reasonable terms he will welcome and protect it. Already he is curbing the greed of the mines and the cocoa crop has been socialized in sales, transport and care of growing trees. Industrialization under government control has begun in small industries like soap, matches, cigarettes and timber sawing. Suppose Ghana should begin to process its cocoa?

Third and beyond all these weighty matters, Nkrumah proposes to attack frankly and head-on the whole question of the status and treatment of black Africans in modern civilization. He proposes to continue the program of Pan-Africa which began in 1919 on the initiative of American Negroes. For this Ghana occupies a strategic position. Liberia was surrounded by Britain and France who systematically choked it and invited Germany in, while America stood aside until it saw a chance of unusual exploitation of land and labor. Ghana is surrounded by 23 million French Africans who are beginning to demand autonomy; not far away is Nigeria, a British colony of 32 million blacks who are already started toward independence. Across the Sahara is the Sudan, once dominated by Britain and Egypt but now free with nine million black folk seated at the head waters of the Nile. East of the Sudan is the long independent Kingdom of Ethiopia with 20 million blacks and mulattoes. Below it is Kenya seething with hate and hurt toward Britain; and Uganda starting toward independence. Here dwell 11 million blacks. Further on is Somaliland to be free from Italy in 1960 and, below, Tanganyika, a mandate set for freedom in the near future; the vast Congo which has just voiced an extraordinary demand for government partnership with Belgium. Then come Portuguese Africa, Bechuanaland, the Rhodesias, Nyassaland and South Africa.

Nkrumah proposes, as one of his first acts of state to invite the rulers of all these lands in addition to Egypt and North Africa to meet and consider the conditions and future of Africa. He says in the last chapter of his book, independence will not be confined to Ghana:

"From now on it must be Pan-African nationalism, and the ideology of African political consciousness and African political emancipation must spread throughout the whole continent, into every nook and corner of it. I have never regarded the struggle for the Independence of the Gold Coast as an isolated objective but always as a part of the general world historical pattern. The African in every territory of this vast continent has been awakened and the struggle for freedom will go on. It is our duty as the vanguard force to offer what assistance we can to those now engaged in the battle that we ourselves have fought and won. Our task is not done and our own safety is not assured until the last vestiges of colonialism have been swept from Africa."

NOTES

1. A review of *Ghana: The Autobiography of Kwame Nkrumah* (Nelson, New York, 1957).

The Future of Africa

ADDRESS TO THE ALL-AFRICAN PEOPLE'S CONFERENCE, ACCRA

Approaching 91 years of age at the time, and in ill health, Dr. Du Bois was advised by his doctors against making the journey to Accra in Africa's hottest season. In his place, the Address was read by his wife, Mrs. Shirley Graham Du Bois. The text is from the *National Guardian*, December 22, 1958.

Fellow Africans: About 1735, my great-great grandfather was kidnapped on this coast of West Africa and taken by the Dutch to the colony of New York in America, where he was sold in slavery. About the same time a French Huguenot, Jacques Du Bois, migrated from France to America and his great-grandson, born in the West Indies and with Negro blood, married the great-great granddaughter of my black ancestor. I am the son of this couple, born in 1868, hence my French name and my African loyalty.

As a boy I knew little of Africa save legends and some music in my family. The books which we studied in the public school had almost no information about Africa, save of Egypt, which we were told was not Negroid. I heard of few great men of Negro blood, but I built up in my mind a dream of what Negroes would do in the future even though they had no past.

Then happened a series of events: In the last decade of the 19th century, I studied two years in Europe, and often heard Africa mentioned with respect. Then, as a teacher in America, I had a few African students. Later at Atlanta University a visiting professor, Franz Boaz, addressed the students and told them of the history of the Black Sudan. I was utterly amazed and began to study Africa for myself. I attended the Paris Exposition in 1900, and met with West Indians in London in a Pan-African Conference. This movement died, but in 1911 I attended a Races Congress in London which tried to bring together

195

representatives from all races of the world. I met distinguished Africans and was thrilled. However, World War killed this movement.

We held a small meeting in 1919 in Paris. After peace was declared, in 1921, we called a much larger Pan-African Congress in London, Paris and Brussels. The 200 delegates at this congress aroused the fury of the colonial powers and all our efforts for third, fourth and fifth congresses were only partially successful because of their opposition. We tried in vain to convene a congress in Africa itself.

The great depression of the 'thirties then stopped our efforts for 15 years. Finally in 1945 black trade union delegates to the Paris meeting of trade unions called for another Pan-African Congress. This George Padmore organized and, at his request, I came from America to attend the meeting at Manchester, England. Here I met Kwame Nkrumah, Jomo Kenyatta, Johnson of Liberia and a dozen other young leaders.

The program of Pan-Africa as I have outlined it was not a plan of action, but of periodical conferences and free discussion. And this was a necessary preliminary to any future plan of united or separate action. However, in the resolutions adopted by the successive Congresses were many statements urging united action, particularly in the matter of race discrimination. Also, there were other men and movements urging specific work.

World financial depression interfered with all these efforts and suspended the Pan-African Congresses until the meeting in Manchester in 1945. Then, it was reborn and this meeting now in Accra is the sixth effort to bring this great movement before the world and to translate its experience into action.

My only role in this meeting is one of advice from one who has lived long, who has studied Africa and has seen the modern world.

In this great crisis of the world's history, when standing on the highest peaks of human accomplishment we look forward to Peace and backward to War, when we look up to Heaven and down to Hell, let us mince no words. We face triumph or tragedy without alternative.

Africa, ancient Africa, has been called by the world and has lifted up her hands! Africa has no choice between private capitalism and socialism. The whole world, including capitalist countries, is moving toward socialism, inevitably, inexorably. You can choose between blocs of military alliance, you can choose between groups of political union; you cannot choose between socialism and private capitalism because private capitalism is doomed!

But what is socialism? It is a disciplined economy and political organization to which the first duty of a citizen is to serve the state; and the state is not a selected aristocracy, or a group of self-seeking oligarchs who have seized wealth and power. No! The mass of workers with hand and brain are the ones whose collective destiny is the chief object of all effort.

Gradually, every state is coming to this concept of its aim. The great Communist states like the Soviet Union and China have surrendered completely to this idea. The Scandinavian states have yielded partially; Britain has yielded in some respects, France in part, and even the United States adopted the New Deal which was largely socialism; though today further American socialism is held at bay by

60 great groups of corporations who control individual capitalists and the trade union leaders.

On the other hand, the African tribe, whence all of you sprung, was communistic in its very beginnings. No tribesman was free. All were servants of the tribe of whom the chief was father and voice.

When now, with a certain suddenness, Africa is whirled by the bitter struggle of dying private capitalism into the last great battleground of its death throes, you are being tempted to adopt at least a passing private capitalism as a step to some partial socialism. This would be a grave mistake.

For 400 years Europe and North America have built their civilization and comfort on theft of colored labor and the land and materials which rightfully belong to these colonial peoples.

The dominant exploiting nations are willing to yield more to the demands of the mass of men than were their fathers. But their yielding takes the form of sharing the loot—not of stopping the looting. It takes the form of stopping socialism by force and not of surrendering the fatal mistakes of private capitalism. Either capital belongs to all or power is denied all.

Here then, my Brothers, you face your great decision: Will you for temporary advantage—for automobiles, refrigerators and Paris gowns—spend your income in paying interest on borrowed funds; or will you sacrifice your present comfort and the chance to shine before your neighbors, in order to educate your children, develop such industry as best serves the great mass of people and make your country strong in ability, self-support and self-defense? Such union of effort for strength calls for sacrifice and self-denial, while the capital offered you at high price by the colonial powers like France, Britain, Holland, Belgium and the United States, will prolong fatal colonial imperialism, from which you have suffered slavery, serfdom and colonialism.

You are not helpless. You are the buyers and to continue existence as sellers of capital, these great nations, former owners of the world, must sell or face bankruptcy. You are not compelled to buy all they offer now. You can wait. You can starve a while longer rather than sell your great heritage for a mess of Western capitalist pottage. You can not only beat down the price of capital as offered by the united and monopolized Western private capitalists, but at last today you can compare their offers with those of socialist countries like the Soviet Union and China, which with infinite sacrifice and pouring out of blood and tears, are at last able to offer weak nations needed capital on better terms than the West.

The supply which socialist nations can at present spare is small as compared with that of the bloated monopolies of the West, but it is large and rapidly growing. Its acceptance involves no bonds which a free Africa may not safely assume. It certainly does not involve slavery and colonial control which the West has demanded and still demands. Today she offers a compromise, but one of which you must beware:

She offers to let some of your smarter and less scrupulous leaders become fellow capitalists with the white exploiters if in turn they induce the nation's masses to pay the awful costs. This happened in the West Indies and in South America. This may yet happen in the Middle East and Eastern Asia. Strive

against it with every fibre of your bodies and souls. A body of local private capitalists, even if they are black, can never free Africa; they will simply sell it into
new slavery to old masters overseas.

As I have said, this is a call for sacrifice. Great Goethe sang, "*Entbehren sollst
du, sollst entbehren*" — "Thou shalt forego, shalt do without." If Africa unites, it
will be because each part, each nation, each tribe gives up a part of its heritage
for the good of the whole. That is what union means; that is what Pan-Africa
means: When the child is born into the tribe the price of his growing up is giving a part of his freedom to the tribe. This he soon learns or dies. When the tribe
becomes a union of tribes, the individual tribe surrenders some part of its freedom to the paramount tribe.

When the nation arises, the constituent tribes, clans and groups must each
yield power and some freedom to the demands of the nation or the nation dies
before it is born. Your local tribal, much-loved languages must yield to the few
world tongues which serve the largest number of people and promote understanding and world literature.

This is the great dilemma which faces Africans today, faces one and all: Give
up individual rights for the needs of Mother Africa; give up tribal independence for the needs of the nation.

Forget nothing, but set everything in its rightful place; the glory of the six
Ashanti wars against Britain; the wisdom of the Fanti Confederation; the
growth of Nigeria; the song of the Songhay and Hausa; the rebellion of the
Mahdi and the hands of Ethiopia; the greatness of the Basuto and the fighting of
Chaka; the revenge of Mutessi, and many other happenings and men; but above
all—Africa, Mother of Men.

Your nearest friends and neighbors are the colored people of China and India,
the rest of Asia, the Middle East and the sea isles, once close bound to the heart of
Africa and now long severed by the greed of Europe. Your bond is not mere color
of skin but the deeper experience of wage slavery and contempt. So too, your
bond with the white world is closest to those who support and defend China and
help India and not those who exploit the Middle East and South America.

Awake, awake, put on thy strength, O Zion! Reject the weakness of missionaries who teach neither love nor brotherhood, but chiefly the virtues of private
profit from capital, stolen from your land and labor. Africa, awake! Put on the
beautiful robes of Pan-African socialism.

You have nothing to lose but your chains! You have a continent to regain! You
have freedom and human dignity to attain!

China and Africa

On February 23, his 91st birthday, Dr. Du Bois was in Peking, where his birthday was celebrated at a public dinner. On the same day he spoke to more than 1,000 students and faculty at Peking University. The text is from *New World Review*, New York, April 1959.

By courtesy of the government of the 680 million people of the Chinese Republic, I am permitted on my 91st birthday to speak to the people of China and Africa and through them to the world. Hail, then, and farewell, dwelling places of the yellow and black races. Hail humankind!

I speak with no authority, no assumption of age or rank; I hold no position, I have no wealth. One thing alone I own and that is my own soul. Ownership of that I have even while in my own country for near a century I have been nothing but a "nigger." On this basis and this alone I dare speak, I dare advise.

China after long centuries has arisen to her feet and leapt forward. Africa arise, and stand straight, speak and think! Act! Turn from the West and your slavery and humiliation for the last 500 years and face the rising sun. Behold a people, the most populous nation on this ancient earth which has burst its shackles, not by boasting and strutting, not by lying about its history and its conquests, but by patience and long-suffering, by hard, backbreaking labor and with bowed head and blind struggle, moved up and on toward the crimson sky.

She aims to "make men holy; to make men free." But what men? Not simply the rich, but not excluding the rich; not simply the learned, but led by knowledge to the end that no man shall be poor, nor sick, nor ignorant; that the humblest worker as well as the sons of emperors shall be fed and taught and healed and that there emerge on earth a single unified people, free, well and educated.

You have been told, my Africa, in Africa and all your children's children overseas, you have been told, and the telling so beaten into you by rods and whips that you believe it yourselves, that this is impossible; that mankind can only rise by walking on men, by cheating them and killing them; that only on a doormat of the despised and dying, the dead and rotten, can a British aristocracy, a French cultural elite or an American millionaire be nurtured and grown. This is a lie. It is an ancient lie spread by church and state, spread by priest and historian, and

199

believed in by fools and cowards, as well as by the downtrodden and the children of despair.

Speak, China, and tell your truth to Africa and the world. What people have been despised as you have? Who more than you have been rejected of men? Recall when lordly Britishers threw the rickshaw money on the ground to avoid touching a filthy hand. Forget not the time when in Shanghai no "Chinaman" dared set foot in a park which he paid for. Tell this to Africa, for today Africa stands on new feet, with new eyesight, with new brains and asks: Where am I and why?

The Western sirens answer, Britain wheedles, France cajoles; while America, my America, where my ancestors and descendants for eight generations have lived and toiled, America loudest of all, yells and promises freedom, if only Africa allows American investment. Beware Africa, America bargains for your soul. America would have you believe that they freed your grandchildren; that Afro-Americans are full American citizens, treated like equals, paid fair wages as workers, promoted for desert and free to learn and earn and travel across the world.

This is not true. Some are near freedom, some approach equality with whites, some have achieved education; but the price for this has too often been slavery of mind, distortion of truth and oppression of our own people. Of 18 million Afro-Americans, 12 million are still second-class citizens of the United States, serfs in farming, low-paid laborers in industry, and repressed members of labor unions. Most American Negroes do not vote. Even the rising six million are liable to insult and discrimination at any time.

But this, Africa, relates to your descendants, not to you. Once I thought of you Africans as children, whom we educated Afro-Americans would lead to liberty. I was wrong. We could not even lead ourselves, much less you. Today I see you rising under your own leadership, guided by your own brains.

Africa does not ask alms from China nor from the Soviet Union nor from France, Britain, nor the United States. It asks friendship and sympathy and no nation better than China can offer this to the Dark Continent. Let it be given freely and generously. Let Chinese visit Africa, send their scientists there and their artists and writers. Let Africa send its students to China and its seekers after knowledge. It will not find on earth a richer goal, a more promising mine of information.

On the other hand, watch the West. The new British West Indian Federation is not a form of democratic progress but a cunning attempt to reduce these islands to the control of British and American investors. Haiti is dying under rich Haitian investors who with American money are enslaving the peasantry. Cuba is showing what the West Indies, Central and South America are suffering under American big business.

The American worker himself does not always realize this. He has high wages and many comforts. Rather than lose these, he keeps in office by his vote the servants of industrial exploitation so long as they maintain his wage. His labor leaders represent exploitation and not the fight against the exploitation of labor by private capital. These two sets of exploiters fall out only when one demands too large a share of the loot. This China knows. This Africa must learn. This the American Negro has failed so far to learn.

I am frightened by the so-called friends who are flocking to Africa; Negro Americans trying to make money from your toil, white Americans who seek by investment at high interest to bind you in serfdom to business as the Near East is bound and as South America is struggling with. For this, America is tempting your leaders, bribing your young scholars and arming your soldiers. What shall you do?

First, understand! Realize that the great mass of mankind is freeing itself from wage slavery, while private capital in Britain, France and now in America, is still trying to maintain civilization and comfort for a few on the toil, disease and ignorance of the mass of men. Understand this, and understanding comes from direct knowledge. You know America and France and Britain to your sorrow. Now know the Soviet Union and its allied nations, but particularly know China.

China is flesh of your flesh and blood of your blood. China is colored and knows to what a colored skin in this modern world subjects its owner. But China knows more, much more than this: she knows what to do about it. She can take the insults of the United States and still hold her head high. She can make her own machines or go without machines, when America refuses to sell her American manufactures even though this throws her workers out of jobs and hurts American industry. China does not need American nor British missionaries to teach her religion and scare her with tales of hell. China has been in hell too long, not to believe in a heaven of her own making. This she is doing.

Come to China, Africa, and look around. Invite Africa to come, China, and see what you can teach just by pointing. Yonder old woman is working on the street. But she is happy. She has no fear. Her children are in school and a good school. If she is ill, there is a hospital where she is cared for free of charge. She has a vacation with pay each year. She can die and be buried without taxing her family to make some undertaker rich.

Africa can answer: but some of this we have done; our tribes undertake public service like this. Very well, let your tribes continue and expand this work. What Africa must realize is what China knows: that it is worse than stupid to allow a people's education to be under the control of those who seek not the progress of the people but their use as means of making themselves rich and powerful. It is wrong for the University of London to control the University of Ghana. It is wrong for the Catholic Church to direct the education of the black Congolese. It was wrong for Protestant churches supported by British and American wealth to control higher education in China. The Soviet Union is surpassing the world in popular and higher education, because from the beginning it started its own complete educational system.

The essence of the revolution in the Soviet Union and China and in all the "iron curtain" nations, is not the violence that accompanied the change—no more than starvation at Valley Forge was the essence of the American revolution against Britain. The real revolution is the acceptance on the part of the nation of the fact that hereafter the main object of the nation is the welfare of the mass of the people and not of a lucky few.

Government is for the people's progress and not for the comfort of the aristocracy. The object of industry is the welfare of the workers and not the wealth of the owners. The object of civilization is the cultural progress of the mass of workers and not merely of an intellectual elite. And in return for all this, communist lands believe that the cultivation of the mass of people will discover more talent and genius to serve the state than any closed aristocracy ever furnished. This belief the current history of the Soviet Union and China is proving true each day. Therefore don't let the West invest when you can avoid it. Don't buy capital from Britain, France and the United States if you can get it on reasonable terms from the Soviet Union and China. This is not politics; it is common sense. It is learning from experience. It is trusting your friends and watching your enemies.

Refuse to be cajoled or to change your way of life so as to make a few of your fellows rich at the expense of a mass of workers growing poor and sick and remaining without schools so that a few black men can have automobiles.

Africa, here is a real danger which you must avoid or return to the slavery from which you are emerging. All I ask from you is the courage to know; to look about you and see what is happening in this old and tired world; to realize the extent and depth of its rebirth and the promise which glows on yonder hills.

Visit the Soviet Union and visit China. Let your youth learn the Russian and Chinese languages. Stand together in this new world and let the old world perish in its greed or be born again in new hope and promise. Listen to the Hebrew prophet of communism:

Ho! every one that thirsteth; come ye to the waters; come, buy and eat, without money and without price!

Again, China and Africa, hail and farewell!

The Belgian Congo

1. THE WORLD MUST SOON AWAKE TO BAR WAR IN CONGO

(National Guardian, September 26, 1960)

Congo was a tragic miscalculation. Little Belgium had inherited El Durado. Hundreds of millions of dollars poured into this land annually from a great territory 40 times its size. In this empire was one of the world's greatest deposits of copper to carry electric power over sea and land; elephant tusks to furnish piano keys for lovely music, palm oil, fruit, rare woods, fibers and lately uranium for bombs to raise hell.

Nobody knows how vast a horde of wealth Congo has poured into Belgium, Europe and North America in the last century, for this is a secret of individual initiative in the capitalist world of Nordic supremacy. But all men including Pope and Protestant hierarchy and learned colleges know how many cheap laborers were slaves of white Europe to make Belgians clean, comfortable and learned and leaders of civilization. Once the atrocities of the Congo aroused the world and the Belgian folk took Congo out of the private purse of Leopold to rule themselves.

I remember talking to the first Belgian Socialist premier in the 'twenties, and his firm promise to institute reform and stop cutting off the hands of lagging black workers. I remembered the legends of the King of Congo whom the Portuguese met in the 15th century and whose royal son was educated in Lisbon. I had read as a boy Stanley's flamboyant and lying proclamation of the great new Christian Kingdom of Congo which civilization was about to rear in the Dark Continent, to lead the natives to God.

Centuries passed: The 16th with its great flowering of imperial black Africa south of the Sahara; the 17th, with the duel of Fetish and Moslem, and the Long March of Bantu from Niger to Zambesi; the 18th century and the British trade in slaves from Africa to America; and the 19th century when Europe stole the world and built its culture on the degradation of Asia and Africa.

Out of this wretched past was naturally born this century of war and destruction, with the West stubbornly determined to restore its domination of mankind, and with the East—in Europe, Asia and Africa—increasingly set on freedom and

203

independence. Belgium, despite its baptism in war and rapine, because it lay in the crossing paths of greedy empires, made peace with all, and came to understanding with the wheeling buzzards of the West.

If you want to make money invest in the Congo enterprises: profitable, respectable private enterprise, paying high and regular dividends, and no questions asked. Moreover the natives were happy; their tribal rule was intact and their chiefs happy so long as the black slaves toiled for their white masters, and the wealth rolled into Europe.

When in 1921 I held a session of the Pan-African Congress in Brussels, and one young Congolese, Panda, ventured to join us in criticism of Belgian rule, the Belgian press raged: "Bolsheviks," spies and revolutionists they called us; the natives were content and the Holy Catholic Church was giving them enough education for their good; not too much, not enough to make them unhappy and demanding more than their few brains could use.

Congo had no such unhappy intelligentsia as the British had nursed in West Africa and the French in Senegal. Even if Belgium did not have enough trained Congolese to educate as physicians, at least Black Congo did not want to vote. So Belgium crowed even as late as the World Exposition of 1958.

And then in 1960 the bubble burst and black Congo demanded not only a share in government but independence. It was inconceivable. It was unbelievable. Even when my wife, Shirley Graham, who read my message to the Sixth Pan-African Congress, meeting as the All-African Conference in Accra in 1958, told me of Lumumba there demanding independence for Congo, I thought he was an unthinking fanatic.

But I pride myself on ability to learn; on seeing what appears before my eyes. Yesterday, I was paying farewell to the President of Ghana, just as he was taking leave of Lumumba, Prime Minister of Congo, who was on his way home from a meeting of the Security Council which had ordered Belgium out of Congo because it dare not do otherwise. After Lumumba flew home in a Russian jet plane, President Nkrumah and I talked for a few moments.

We knew that the trials of Congo had not ended but just begun. The luxury-loving West, which was parading and yachting, gambling and horse-racing, dressing and dancing and keeping darkies out of highly paid unions, was not going to give up Congo millions without a desperate struggle even if it involved world war. Ghana, the Soviet Union and China must furnish capital and technical skill to keep the great wheels of Congo enterprise running; but running not for profit of white skilled labor and the idle rich, but for the starving, sick and ignorant Africans.

From me the President asked but one service: the starting again of the *Encyclopedia Africana* which I tried desperately to begin back in 1900. We must unite Africa, he said, and know its history and culture. Against all dreams of an independent black Congo stand arrayed today forces of terrible strength: the organized business enterprise of the Western world; incorporated monopoly, with secret concealed, anonymous personalities, ruled by dictators, amenable to no laws of morality whose only object is gain of wealth, at any cost of life, liberty or of human happiness.

This faceless, conscienceless power is today armed to the teeth and spending for force and violence more money than for anything else on earth and hiring all the ability and genius of the world which is for sale, for the murder, rape, destruction and degradation of man, which big business wants accomplished; and hiding this from common knowledge by every device available to man.

Ranged therefore against free and independent Congo is the Oppenheimer gold and diamond trust, the Lever Brothers world monopolies under its legion of names; the oil trusts, Standard, Shell and others, the French, Swiss and West German cartels, and that part of the Christian church and Moslem religion which is dependent on the charity of the rich.

But the truth is winning; socialism is spreading, communism is becoming more and more possible to increasing millions:

"Fear not, O little flock the foe,
That madly seeks thine overthrow
Fear not its rage and Power!"

Finally down toward Land's End, on the Cape of Evil Omen, are some three million whites in the Union of South Africa, the Rhodesias and Southwest Africa, who are determined to rule 20 or more million blacks as slaves and servants. They say this brazenly and openly in the face of the world and none do anything, save black Africa. And here the next world war will begin unless the world wakes up and wakes soon.

2. A LOGICAL PROGRAM FOR A FREE CONGO

(National Guardian, May 15,1961)

The Congo is a mighty valley which is—without its artificial political boundaries—half the size of the United States outside Alaska. It is rich in known and undeveloped resources: copper, gold, silver, industrial diamonds, uranium and many other metals. It has vast forests of hardwoods, and palms of all sorts. Its elephants furnish ivory, its people grow fruits, fibers and vegetable oils. There is unbounded water power from nearly 3,000 miles of the vast and curving Congo and its tributaries.

For this wealth and for the cheap labor of its 15,000,000 of peoples, the Western world today is staging one of its greatest and most ruthless battles. Corporate industry today is making a last and desperate stand to control Africa. It is not merely little Belgium or Tshombe of Katanga; it is the organized wealth of North America, the British Commonwealth, France, West Germany, Switzerland and Italy. The West still believes that it can buy the world with money, own it and live on it in ease and luxury. To this end, the citizens of the United States alone are spending $50,000,000,000 a year and more.

Because of the increased and world-wide use of electricity which demands copper for transmission, because of the use of ivory in modern art and industry and because of the increasing use of atomic energy, the Congo has become a center of African development, and the reason for the desperate determination of America and Western Europe to control this part of Africa.

The Congo valley is not, as currently painted, a nest of howling savages with a few half-educated leaders filled with crazy and impossible ambitions. The history of this territory today is confused, disjointed and deliberately misinterpreted. But history there is, and it must be studied and understood.

All this story cannot yet be united into one continuous and scientifically provable history, but there are parts of it well known and of great fascination. The culture of the Bushongo, who were part of the Ba-Luba family, is noteworthy. The Luba-lunda people founded Katanga and other states, and in the 16th century came the larger and more ambitious realm of the Mwata Yanvo.

The last of the 14 rulers of this line was feudal lord of about 300 chiefs, who paid him tribute in ivory, skins, corn, cloth and salt. This included about 100,000 square miles and 2,000,000 or more inhabitants. The use of the loom in Africa reached the coast after its use inland had become general. Velvets, brocades, satins, taffetas and damasks were imported to Congo by those great traders, the Bateke.

During the last 20 centuries the Congo saw a series of cultural developments which rose, spread and fell before the oncoming Bantu of the north, or the western rush of the Zeng of Zanzibar, and, perhaps, because of the northern march of the empire of the Monomotapa. There arose the manufacture of brocades and velvets, iron-making spread, and work in copper and bronze. The art of West Africa spread through parts of the Valley and the extraordinary political organization of the Bushongo—with its organization of government with representatives of arts and crafts, where every chief represented not only a territory but an industry.

Then, with the imperial expansion of the Sudan southward and the westward growth of Atlantis came the thousand-year march of the Bantu from the Sahara to the Cape. Across all this struck the slave trade, from Africa to America, for 100 fatal years; and on that rose the Industrial Revolution. Europe seized Africa; France in the north; Britain in the east and south; and Germany, at long last forcing herself into east, south and west Africa; and, finally, Leopold of Belgium, slipping craftily in between the rivalries of France, Britain and Germany, helped by an American explorer, Henry M. Stanley, organized the so-called Congo Free State. The great powers allowed him to proceed, though curbing his boundaries, each planning eventual seizure.

But Leopold was crafty. He called religion and trade to his aid and flamboyantly announced a great development of the African peoples. The Congo Free State, however, instead of becoming a center of civilization and religion, sank to such cruelty and exploitation that the world screamed in protest. Leopold was forced to surrender control of the Congo to the State of Belgium.

Once I talked with Vandervelde, a Socialist Minister of Belgium, concerning the future of the Congo. He planned much and tried hard, but the industry which Leopold had begun in the Congo was now in the hands of great corporations owned by Britain, France, Germany, Switzerland and the United States. Despite Socialist plans, they seized the land, exploited the labor and began to make huge profit from ivory, copper, diamonds and uranium.

They planned to avoid the mistakes of France and Britain in developing a class of educated natives who might aspire to share rule with the colonial power.

On the other hand, they tried to appease the native. They left much home rule in the hands of recognized tribal chiefs paid by the State. They gave skilled work and wages larger than customary to an increasing group of workers. They allowed the Catholic Church and a few Protestant sects to give primary education to numbers of children. But they kept the natives from attending Belgian higher schools or establishing such schools in the Congo.

For a time this seemed an ideal plan. Peace reigned and profits soared. In the end the plan failed and somewhat suddenly. Instead of Negro ambition being confined and drained off slowly into an intelligentsia such as both France and Britain had produced, the Congolese movement swelled within almost silently and then suddenly burst into a demand for complete independence—a demand led by young men like Patrice Lumumba. The demand was so unexpected that the Belgians were at first at a loss as to how to meet it.

Then they turned swiftly. They planned a small introduction of higher learning to supply the Congolese with the professional help which they so desperately needed, physicians, dentists, social workers, and even lawyers. On the industrial side they encouraged a Congolese bourgeoisie, skilled workers, and even managers, who would be paid enough to join the Belgians in exploiting the masses. Thus arose Kasavubu and Tshombe.

Notwithstanding their efforts the Belgians could not win the battle. A young man, Patrice Lumumba, led a movement for a Congo State completely independent of Belgium. He had a fair education although never allowed to attend an institution of higher learning. But he was honest and sincere and had an increasing following. The Belgians first attacked him as all colonial powers attack native leaders. He was accused of dishonesty in his position in the Post Office. He was sent to jail, just as all colonials have been like Nehru, Gandhi, Nkrumah and Macauley. Later he was even accused of debauchery and drug taking.

These were all lies, just as other Western tales about Soviet women and Chinese workers. My wife has seen and heard and talked with Lumumba. I have seen him. He was a clean and frank young man, nervous, excitable, but no criminal, no drunkard. The Belgians saw that they could not keep him from gaining a majority of the new Congolese parliament and so they maneuvered to have Kasavubu, a man whom they could control, made president, with Lumumba's consent, so long as Lumumba was Prime Minister. By all rules of modern politics the executive power of the country lay in Lumumba's hands while the majority of parliament supported him. But Kasavubu, after being made an officer in the Belgian army, usurped power and dismissed Lumumba without a parliamentary vote.

In addition to this, a further and more desperate effort was resorted to. Katanga, in southeast Congo, bordering the Rhodesias and Portuguese Angola, was rising to fantastic prosperity through the mining and sale of copper. The profits to Europeans and North America in 1960 were the largest in the history of the Congo. The need of this colonial foundation to support Western industry was greater than ever; and it was not difficult to bribe a black man to throw in his efforts with the Belgians and their allies.

Tshombe was the son of a bourgeois Congolese. In the All-African Congress held in Accra in 1958 he had pledged himself to work for African independence.

But, on the other hand, he had seen what European industry and wealth could mean. The Belgians had flattered him and pushed him forward, and he conceived that the independence of Katanga from the rest of the Congo would mean the rise of black men like himself. He therefore led a movement of secession to take the prosperous and industrial Katanga out of the new, black, independent state. This was just what Western Europe and North America wanted: fragmentation of this vast center of cheap labor and valuable material.

But this plan could not be realized so long as Lumumba held a majority in parliament. The conspirators did not dare to reassemble parliament and they silently agreed upon a bloody and revolting deed which curiously illustrates the difference between what we call "backward" and "modern" civilization. To Congolese of the Tshombe type, evil is done away with by a direct, decisive blow. The West does the same thing but pauses in the execution, so as to avoid or postpone criticism. They use hypocrisy and deceit. The West was going to displace Lumumba, but by imprisonment or deportation or "accident," simply by denying him protection. Tshombe, or his men, on the other hand, murdered him in cold blood. The West then hastened to cash in on the new Madagascar which had just slipped out of colonial hell. They got together a hurried meeting. But the world shuddered at murder and hesitated. The Belgian ministry fell. The British Commonwealth split. The United States gagged.

Here, then, we stand today, and the chief object of our periodicals and literary writers, of our industrial leaders and great corporations, is to make America believe that African freedom depends upon the transforming of the Congo Republic into a series of small, antagonistic states whose chief function is to furnish profits for Western capitalism.

A logical program for an independent Congo State is clear. Let the people of the Congo recede from catering almost solely to the wants of the Western world and begin working for their own simple needs. Let them decrease the amount of copper mined and of uranium exported. The copper will not spoil if it lies longer in the ground. The present need for atomic energy does not call for continued Congo effort.

The people of the Congo should till the soil, raise the food they need, the fiber they wear and material for their homes. To do this effectively they need education, especially in agriculture. A wide and desperate effort to educate the people of the Congo should be started. They must learn to read, write and count; and also they must have nurses, physicians and dentists, and above all, teachers, but not flunkies screened by the FBI.

Much of this education they can do for themselves; help can be obtained from neighboring African states, and the money which the West is furnishing for investment and bombs could be loaned the Congo for schools. Ancient African barter can be restored in the marketplace; simple industry for local needs can be established with modern methods. Trade with their African neighbors can increase and also such European trade as the Congo needs, and not solely for Western profit. In this way a united people could become self-supporting, intelligent and healthy, and take their place among the nations of the world.

Nigeria

1. NIGERIA BECOMES PART OF THE MODERN WORLD

(*National Guardian, January 16, 1961*)

I have just spent two weeks in Nigeria. I hesitate to record even briefly the tremendous impression which this land made on me because my stay was so short and because the meaning of this nation is so momentous to the modern world. Nigeria, as large as France and Italy combined, with as many people as England, is a portion of the Middle Ages set suddenly into the last half of our century. It brings in Benin and Ife, an art form which already has transformed modern art and a technique of casting bronze and copper which has amazed historians of technology. It flatly contradicts modern history as received today and makes morals and religion in Europe and America largely hypocrisy.

The black people of Nigeria stride into this modern world with no dream that their color is a disgraceful insignia of inferiority. I sat, November 12, in the dining room of an air-conditioned modern hotel in Lagos, when suddenly the black waiters stood at attention; there arose the whistling cry "Zeek!" by which for 25 years Nigeria has hailed Nnamdi Azikiwe as he agitated for independence; out of a private dining room at the far end strode a six-foot black man robed in flowing white and crowned in embroidered velvet. He was the Governor-elect of this nation; he had left his dinner guest, the retiring British Governor, to come greet me and my wife to Nigeria.

Why was this man being made the first black Governor of a British colony? Because Britain in a last subtle move had decided to yield to Nigeria's irresistible demand for independence by granting to a Nigerian the formerly powerful office of Governor-general, now shorn of its power to make laws and dictate policy, but still robed in the tinsel of pomp and circumstance. One hundred thousand people witnessed this inauguration. I had traveled 6,000 miles at Azikiwe's invitation to be sure that socialism would be represented on this occasion. For this the Governor-elect greeted me. And I had come to learn just how powerless the new Governor would be. I knew that already Britain had been disappointed in failing to keep Northern Nigeria out of federation with the south and how Moral Rearmament, financed by big business, had been working on Azikiwe.

America was discovered and Guinea and India invaded by Europe in the same decade and then there began a phantasmagoria which for 300 years transformed the modern world. A British Protestant Christian, William Howitt (*Colonization and Christianity,* London, 1838), recorded the truth:

"The barbarities and desperate outrages of the so-called Christian race, throughout every region of the world, and upon every people that they have been able to subdue, are not to be paralleled by those of any other race, however fierce, however untaught, and however reckless of mercy and of shame, in any age of the earth."

Out of this tragic past the Nigerians of today march, largely ignorant of the significance of what has happened to them. They have never been conquered by Europeans, but, through bribery and deception, were so manipulated by the British Empire as to regard the British mainly as benefactors.

Nigerians through the lore of their fathers look back on a mighty past. They remember the empire of the Songhay where in the early 16th century the black Mohammed Askia ruled an empire as large as all Europe; and as the Arab chronicle says: "There reigned everywhere great plenty and absolute peace!" Their University of Sankoré was a world center of learning among the peoples of the Mediterranean.

What happened? European traders came to barter with a trading people in spices and gold. Domestic slaves furnished labor and gradually became themselves material for labor exported to Spain and Portugal long decimated by war. Then in America came a wider demand for labor promising fabulous wealth. Britain, starting with white indentured servants, seized and dominated a vast and profitable black slave trade. Africa lost a hundred million souls from the middle of the 16th to the middle of the 19th centuries. Slave raids became tribal wars, and slave labor changed the face of commerce and industry in Europe. Industrial Revolution built a new world based on wealth in private hands. Whence came this wealth?

Karl Marx tells us: "The discovery of gold and silver in America, the extirpation, enslavement and entombment in mines of the aboriginal population, the beginning of the conquest and looting of the East Indies, the turning of Africa into a warren for the commercial hunting of black-skins, signalised the rosy dawn of the era of capitalist production . . .

"*Tantae molis erat,* to establish the 'eternal laws of Nature' of the capitalist mode of production, to complete the process of separation between laborers and conditions of labor, to transform at one pole the social means of production and subsistence into capital, at the opposite pole, the mass of the population into wage-laborers, into 'free laboring poor,' that artificial product of modern society. If money, according to Augier, 'comes into the world with a congenital blood-stain on one cheek,' capital comes dripping from head to foot, from every pore, with blood and dirt." (*Capital,* Vol. 1, Kerr edition, pp. 823–34).

But the Nigerians knew little of the wider meaning of this. They only felt the impact of black invaders from the East like the Haussa and later the Fulani; and the push of the Ibos and Yoruba from western Atlantis. War raged among these African peoples, wars which changed their folkways and art; which built their economy on far-off slavery and tempted missionaries from Europe to uplift their morals, bring them primary schools, but often interfere ignorantly with their folkways. Traders like Goldie and his Niger company sailed up the Niger and gradually turned the face of Nigeria from the Mediterranean to the slave-trading Atlantic. The coast of the Gulf of Guinea was annexed by force and by treaties with chiefs which made them pensioners of England and by bribery expanded the empire.

Thus arose modern Nigeria, untouched by color caste, proud and masterful but living in an unknown world. The vast territory, which stretched north and west from the island of Lagos, became loosely unified under British administrators and was called Nigeria after the fabulous river, which for 2,500 miles flowing north, east and south puzzled and misled the world, until it poured into the Atlantic through a hundred mouths forming a delta twice the size of the state of New Jersey. A freebooter, Frederick Lugard, after fighting in China and India and killing Christians and Moslems in Uganda, was recognized by the British government as an "empire builder" and raised to the peerage. By skillful bribery called "indirect rule" he annexed all Nigeria to the British Empire.

A black man who later became Bishop Crowther helped explore the Niger in 1841. But the coasts of the Gulf of Guinea became restless under this pressure of Europe. The Slave Coast, the Grain Coast, the Gold Coast agitated for greater voice in government. Crowther's grandson, Herbert Macauley, agitated for voice in government and was jailed in 1928. Young Nnamdi Azikiwe, educated in the United States, founded the *West African Pilot* in 1937, followed by a string of other protesting papers. Before World War I, the British ruled all Northern Nigeria by a Governor-general and the rest of Nigeria through a council on which the Governor had a majority composed of officials and merchants. The West African Congress, inspired by and following the First Pan-African Congress, secured some elected members to this council.

There followed the participation of Nigerians in World War II by which the Allies drove Germany out of Africa and then came the rise of trade unions. These unions met with the world unions in Paris in 1945, struggled for and won their right to speak for themselves, and joined in calling the Fifth Pan-African Congress that year in England.

The agitation of Azikiwe and others in Nigeria increased until the wiser Britishers advised yielding, but the die-hards tried to hold Northern Nigeria from joining the South. They failed. Northern Nigeria joined the Federation and with the Governor-generalship stripped of power, Azikiwe was nominated to the place, after escaping a charge of misusing funds in organizing his bank. It was hoped his good will had been secured and could be made certain by a privy councilorship and a possible knighthood later.

There came disquieting difficulties. I do not know all the facts, but these seem true. Using British social contacts with the proud Sultans and Emirs of Northern Nigeria it had been planned that the son of the Sultan of Sokoto would be educated at Oxford and become leader of Northern Nigeria. However, the Sultan could not stomach the idea of his son being educated at a Christian college. He therefore substituted a young Nigerian of lower rank, Abubakar Tafawa Balewa, a teacher trained at the University of London. Knighted by the Queen, he became Prime Minister of a Federated Nigeria and the most powerful official in the nation. But curiously, Balewa is a friend of Azikiwe and working amicably with him. He is no socialist in the modern sense, but he is not frightened of communism, because he knows the ancient communal African family and state. Azikiwe also is no communist, but I have talked socialism with him and found him most interested.

Power of directing legislation and proposing policy lies in the hands of the Prime Minister of Nigeria; the Prime Minister of the Federation, and the three Prime Ministers of Northern, Eastern and Western Nigeria. But these must all consult the Governor. He cannot force their decisions, but he is by far the most popular man in Nigeria and his word is influential.

2. WHAT FUTURE FOR NIGERIA?

(National Guardian, January 23, 1961)

Nigeria is a rich land. By this the West means that it has an abundance of cheap labor; immense areas of rich land and forests; and stores of coal, oil, lead, tin, zinc and other metals. It can produce palm oil, raise cocoa and fruit, and has vast potential water power. If developed by Western capital and technique as colonies have been, Nigeria could be a vast source of wealth and power to the world.

When, on the other hand, Nigerians call their country rich, they mean that there can be raised in this land enough to feed, clothe and shelter the people, and surplus to sell abroad for machinery and skills and comforts. In the past, Nigerians have by their folkways in family and clan life avoided extreme poverty and hunger; settled the problem of women so as to support widows, taken care of orphans and avoid prostitution; they have fought disease and crime and been on the whole a contented people. But contact with the modern world has shown them the possibility of greater happiness. They see the necessity of education in modern knowledge, the possibilities of more comfort in living, better fighting of disease, larger production of goods with less work and a broader life. How can this be attained?

The British teach that if Nigerians accept their leadership and advice, all will be well, but the Nigerians, looking back on the past, are beginning to realize the slave trade, the cheating in commerce and exploiting in work. They remind the British that only agitation, punished often by jail, has forced the British to yield the blacks a voice in government. They are glad to make the transfer of authority from white to black in peace and harmony but are determined to be watchful in the future. They are, however, not disposed to question the usual investment procedure of business and individual initiative and are willing that a Nigerian bourgeoisie should share profit arising from foreign exploiting of land and labor.

Americans, on the other hand, announced at the summer meeting of NATO a plan to drive both Britain and France from Africa and to put American capital in full charge. They would be willing to associate American Negro capitalists with them and such Nigerian businessmen as are willing to let white Americans lead. This NATO meeting was considerably upset when an American Negro present dissented from their plans.

Facing these plans are two kinds of thinking. There is a trend toward socialism, not dominant but strong and Azikiwe is in sympathy with this. It believes in raising capital as much as possible at home, and in borrowing from communist countries rather than from Britain or the United States. It does not welcome American Negroes unless they are thoroughly African in sympathy and suspicious of the West.

There is, however, a third force which must be watched: that is the ancient faith in communal family and clan. This method of protecting the masses is distinctly socialist. In the past no member of the tribe need go hungry while any had food. Widows married the dead man's brother. Orphans were adopted in the family. Capital was raised by the tribe and profits belonged to the tribe. Land could not be sold and all had land to use. Trade was carried on by small distributors, chiefly women, in vast markets where the consumer came in direct contact with producer.

These old folkways and this economic organization have changed by the breaking up of families, by some rise of mass industry and the growth of cities. A new and pushing bourgeoisie is gaining power and foreigners with capital are widely in evidence. British, Swiss and Lebanese corporations do large business and in America lately there are 12 organizations which profess great interest in Africa or knowledge of it. They are called variously "American Committee on Africa," "African Studies Association," "African Defense Aid," etc. They are mainly financed by the government or by big business.

These organizations and other persons almost without exception dub any return to African communalism as "communism" and sternly warn Africans against it. This does not please men like Azikiwe or the Federal Prime Minister. While Britain advises Nigeria to advance by installing private capitalism and individual initiative, a growing number of educated Nigerians are beginning to ask if their country cannot step directly from communalism to socialism and avoid the catastrophe of modern private capitalism. The investors and the native bourgeois are still in the lead but the race is not to the swift.

This puts a hard strain on Northern Nigeria. Here is the stronghold of hereditary power, restrained by ancient custom and the domination of women and now pushed by the demands of democracy. The chiefs are yielding by accepting election as local councilors, but the House of Chiefs is still of great influence and the Sultans and Emirs will long rank as more than ordinary citizens. They are yielding in hospitals and schools but how far will they yield in trade and industry? It was an inspiration to see the University College at Ibadan and the new University at Enugu, built by the joint effort of Nigerian and British but now turned over to black administration.

Lagos and lower Nigeria were always centers of town life. I rode through Ibadan, a city of a million inhabitants. There the bourgeois merchant and civil servant are powerful but so also is the consumers' market. At Onitsha I saw one of the largest markets in Africa, selling cotton and velvet, dishes and tools, food and drink and all manner of materials stretched over acres, dominated by women and seething with activity.

We paid our respects before to the Asantahene in Kumasi, and now to the Obi of Onitsha in Nigeria, a mild man of dignity and education before whom thousands still prostrate themselves. We rode by the throngs at the palace of the Aleko of Abeokuta. Such kings have reigned longer than any European dynasty and they feel it. But they despise the rule of the mob and the assumption of the tinker and the shopkeeper. Here they draw close to British aristocracy and British aristocracy cultivates them almost obsequiously. At the State Ball of the new black Governor, British ladies (and not barmaids) sat with and danced in the arms of robed and crowned black Emirs. How will democracy fare in this fight?

On the other hand where lie the interests of the Western world?

There are in the world today at least 25 giant corporations which are international empires and interlocked centers of vast wealth and power. British Unilever alone has a billion dollars in capital and a new annual income of more than a quarter of a billion and trade in every corner of the Western and colonial worlds. These corporations control armies, navies and nuclear weapons, screen news and direct public opinion, and make the laws which curb or let them. They rule Western Europe and all America. They have lost most of Asia but they are now set to dominate Africa. Nigeria has its own 40,000,000 and is tied by blood and custom to at least 60,000,000 other blacks in the Sudan, Uganda, Kenya and other regions.

If Western capital can put into world industry and commerce this cheap black labor working on rare raw materials, it can by modern methods leave in the hands of capitalists as profit incalculable power to control mankind. On the other hand, if this profit can be kept in the hands of the workers, socialism can triumph tomorrow in a world devoid of poverty, ignorance and unnecessary disease.

American Negroes and Africa's Rise to Freedom

(National Guardian, February 13, 1961)

In the United States in 1960 there were some 17,000,000 persons of African descent. In the 18th century they had regarded Africa as their home to which they would eventually return when free. They named their institutions "African" and started migration to Africa as early as 1815. But the American Negroes were soon sadly disillusioned: first their immigrants to Liberia found that Africans did not regard them as Africans; and then it became clear by 1830 that colonization schemes were a device to rid America of free Africans so as to fasten slavery more firmly to support the cotton kingdom.

Negroes therefore slowly turned to a new ideal: to strive for equality as American citizens, determined that when Africa needed them they would be equipped to lead them into civilization. Meantime, however, American Negroes learned from their environment to think less and less of their fatherland and its folk. They learned little of its history or its present conditions. They began to despise the colored races along with white Americans and to acquiesce in color prejudice.

From 1825 to 1860 the American Negro went through hell. He yelled in desperation as the slave power tried to make the whole union a slave nation and then to extend its power over the West Indies; he became the backbone of the Abolition movement; he led thousands of fugitives to freedom; he died with John Brown and made the North victorious in the Civil War. For a few years he led democracy in the South until a new and powerful capitalism disfranchised him by 1876.

Meantime a great change was sweeping the earth. Socialism was spreading; first in theory and experiment for a half century and then at last in 1917 in Russia where a communist state was founded. The world was startled and frightened. The United States joined 16 other nations to prevent this experiment which all wise men said would fail miserably in a short time. But it did not fail. It defended its right to try a new life, and staggering on slowly but surely began to prove to all who would look that communism could exist and prosper.

What effect did this have on American Negroes? By this time their leaders had become patriotic Americans, imitating white Americans almost without criticism. If Americans said that communism had failed, then it had failed. And this of course Americans did say and repeat. Big business declared communism a crime and communists and socialists criminals. Some Americans and some Negroes did not believe this; but they lost employment or went to jail.

Meantime, many thoughtful white Americans, fearing the advance of socialism and communism not only in Europe but in America under the "New Deal," conceived a new tack. They said the American color line cannot be held in the face of communism. It is quite possible that we can help beat communism if in America we begin to loosen if not break the color line.

The movement started and culminated in a Supreme Court decision which was a body blow to color discrimination, and certainly if enforced would take the wind out of the sails of critics of American democracy.

To the Negroes the government said, it will be a fine thing now if you tell foreigners that our Negro problem is settled; and in such case we can help with your expenses of travel. A remarkable number of Negroes of education and standing found themselves able to travel and testify that American Negroes now had no complaints.

Then came three disturbing facts: (1) The Soviet Union was forging ahead in education and science and it drew no color line. (2) Outside the Soviet Union, in England, France and all West Europe, especially Scandinavia, socialism was spreading: state housing, state ownership of railroads, telegraphs and telephones, subways, buses and other public facilities; social medicine, higher education, old age care, insurance and many other sorts of relief; even in the United States, the New Deal was socialism no matter what it was called. (3) The former slave South had no intention of obeying the Supreme Court. To the Bourbon South it was said: don't worry, the law will not be enforced for a decade if not a century. Most Negroes still cannot vote, their schools are poor and the black workers are exploited, diseased and at the bottom of the economic pile. Trade unions north as well as south still discriminate against black labor. But finally a new and astonishing event was the sudden rise of Africa.

My own study had for a long time turned toward Africa. I planned a series of charts in 1900 for the Paris Exposition, which gained a Grand Prize. I attended a Pan-African conference in London and was made secretary of the meeting and drafted its resolutions.

In 1911 the Ethical Culture Societies of the world called a races congress in London and made Felix Adler and me secretaries for America. In 1915 I published my first book on African history and there was much interest and discussion. In 1919 I planned a Pan-African Congress, but got little support. Blaise Diagne of Senegal, whose volunteers had saved France from the first onslaught of the Germans in World War I, induced Clemenceau to allow the Congress despite the opposition of the United States and Britain. It was a small meeting, but it aroused a West African Congress the next year which was the beginning of independence for Ghana and Nigeria.

In 1921 I called a second Pan-African Congress to meet in London, Paris and Brussels. This proved a large and influential meeting, with delegates from the whole Negro world. The wide publicity it gained led to the organization of congresses in many parts of Africa by the natives. Our attempt to form a permanent organization located in Paris was betrayed but I succeeded in assembling a small meeting in London and Lisbon in 1923. I tried a fourth congress in Tunis but France forbade it. At last in 1927 I called the Fourth Pan-African Congress in New York. It was fairly well attended by American Negroes but by few Africans. Then the Second World War approached and the work was interrupted.

Meanwhile methods changed and ideas expanded. Africans themselves began to demand more voice in colonial government and the Second World War had made their cooperation so necessary to Europe that at the end actual and unexpected freedom for African colonies was in sight.

Moreover there miraculously appeared Africans able to take charge of these governments. American Negroes of former generations had always calculated that when Africa was ready for freedom, American Negroes would be ready to lead them. But the event was quite opposite. The African leaders proved to be Africans, some indeed educated in the United States, but most of them trained in Europe and in Africa itself. American Negroes for the most part showed neither the education nor the aptitude for the magnificent opportunity which was suddenly offered. Indeed, it now seems that Africans may have to show American Negroes the way to freedom.

The rise of Africa in the last 15 years has astonished the world. Even the most doubting of American Negroes have suddenly become aware of Africa and its possibilities and particularly of the relation of Africa to the American Negro. The first reaction was typically American. Since 1910 American Negroes had been fighting for equal opportunity in the United States. Indeed, Negroes soon faced a curious paradox.

Now equality began to be offered; but in return for equality, Negroes must join American business in its domination of African cheap labor and free raw materials. The educated and well-to-do Negroes would have a better chance to make money if they would testify that Negroes were not discriminated against and join in American red-baiting.

American Negroes began to appear in Africa, seeking chances to make money and testifying to Negro progress. In many cases their expenses were paid by the State Department. Meantime Negro American colleges ceased to teach socialism and the Negro masses believed with the white masses that communism is a crime and all socialists conspirators.

Africans know better. They have not yet all made up their minds what side to take in the power contest between East and West but they recognize the accomplishments of the Soviet Union and the rise of China.

Meantime American Negroes in their segregated schools and with lack of leadership have no idea of this world trend. The effort to give them equality has been overemphasized and some of our best scholars and civil servants have been bribed by the State Department to testify abroad and especially in Africa to the success of capitalism in making the American Negro free. Yet it was British capitalism which made the African slave trade the greatest commercial venture in the world; and it was American slavery that raised capitalism to its domination in the 19th century and gave birth to the Sugar Empire and the Cotton Kingdom. It was new capitalism which nullified Abolition and keeps us in serfdom.

The Africans know this. They have in many cases lived in America. They have in other cases been educated in the Soviet Union and even in China. They will make up their own minds on communism and not listen solely to American lies. The latest voice to reach them is from Cuba.

Would it not be wise for American Negroes themselves to read a few books and do a little thinking for themselves? It is not that I would persuade Negroes to become communists, capitalists or holy rollers; but whatever belief they reach, let it for God's sake be a matter of reason and not of ignorance, fear, and selling their souls to the devil.

Index

Colonies and Peace
COLOR AND DEMOCRACY

◆

W. E. B. Du Bois

Series Editor, Henry Louis Gates, Jr.

Introduction by Gerald Horne

OXFORD
UNIVERSITY PRESS

Contents

Introduction

Gerald Horne, University of Houston

What is striking about W. E. B. Du Bois's remarkable book *Color and Democracy: Colonies and Peace* (1945) is the capaciousness and prescience of his vision. Published as World War II was grinding to a bloody end, the book shows that Du Bois was consumed with the idea that colonialism—which he saw as a major reason for the conflict—would survive and thus set the basis for future wars. In this sense *Color and Democracy* is an extended version of what may be Du Bois's most insightful essay, "The African Roots of the War," published in the *Atlantic Monthly* in 1915, which posited that the world war then unfolding was driven by competition among the major European powers for colonial possessions, notably in Africa. Indeed, Du Bois's stern focus on colonialism was a critical element in his disagreements with both Booker T. Washington and members of the NAACP board; his conflict with the NAACP board led to his 1934 resignation from this group that he had helped to found.

But even before these insightful interventions, as early as 1884 when he delivered his high school graduation speech on the abolitionist Wendell Phillips, Du Bois indicated an awareness of the inviolate link between color and democracy; that is, so long as the color bar obtained at home and abroad, any talk of democracy was fatuous. Yet strikingly, Du Bois—unlike any other black intellectual writing today—did not just engage Africa and black America, though this was admittedly his primary focus. He also recognized that the fate of both was influenced decisively by global currents and that these perforce included Asia—the planet's most populous continent.

When he returned to the NAACP in 1944 for his second tour of duty, there was considerably less resistance to Du Bois's capacious vision, not least since global currents had intruded so decisively on the United States. The nation had been plunged into yet another war, and this time the United States found itself sharing a trench with the Soviet Union as they confronted their common foes in Berlin, Rome, and Tokyo. In such a hothouse environment, progressive sentiments bloomed. For example, the membership of the NAACP itself during the war skyrocketed from 40,000 to 400,000—a figure that it has hardly reached since.[1] The leading colonial powers—Great Britain and France—were compelled to give at least lip service to anticolonialism in such high-minded declarations as the

Atlantic Charter and the Four Freedoms. The budding radical who was to become Du Bois's second wife—Shirley Graham—had joined the staff of the NAACP and played a pivotal role in the rise of the organization's fortunes.[2]

The heightened engagement with global affairs, which was driven by the war and manifested itself in increased focus on colonialism, was widespread. The March on Washington movement of the leading African American trade union leader, A. Philip Randolph, demanded "representation for the colored and minority racial groups in all missions, political and technical, which will be sent to the peace conference."[3] The epochal "Declaration of Negro Voters," issued in late 1943 and ratified by leading trade unionists, sorority and fraternity leaders, and the left-leaning National Negro Congress, as well as the NAACP, stated bluntly, "we are concerned that this war bring to an end imperialism and colonial exploitation. We believe that political and economic democracy must displace the present system of exploitation in Africa, the West Indies, India and other colonial areas."[4] Months later, in the spring of 1944, Paul Robeson's Council on African Affairs foreshadowed the theme of Du Bois's *Color and Democracy*, emphasizing that a precondition for global stability was the abolition of the antidemocracy that was colonialism and that was visited upon millions of those who did not happen to be "white." It was in such an atmosphere that Du Bois decided to write *Color and Democracy*, which he completed in a matter of months.

Though *Color and Democracy* was written hurriedly, it would be a mistake to see the ideas represented in it as ill-digested. Throughout the war Du Bois had been engaged with the question of the fate of colonialism—whether it would survive this titanic conflict and, if not, what was to follow.[5] A central task of the new post that he assumed in 1944 was precisely to coordinate the global efforts of the NAACP, particularly in the fraught realm of anticolonialism. At the none-too-tender age of seventy-six, he announced that the single most profound issue facing humanity was the abolition of colonialism, the essence of antidemocracy: "This is the problem to which I propose to devote the remaining years of my life," he announced portentously.[6] Thus the book at hand is a direct product of Du Bois's final mission.

What is remarkable about Du Bois's handiwork is his capaciousness. Central to his argument is Japan and the inability of the United States and leading European powers to accept this Asian nation on the basis of "racial equality." Failure to do so at the League of Nations, Du Bois argues, set the stage for Tokyo's styling itself as the "champion of the colored races," which thereby turned the white supremacy of London in particular—the bedrock of its control of its colonies—into a profound liability.[7] The leading powers chose to incorporate China as the sole representative of the "colored" on the powerful Security Council of the United Nations, a maneuver designed, Du Bois suggests, to deflect attention from Tokyo's powerful clarion call. Despite China's inclusion, Du Bois continued to insist that the Security Council was "practically … under the control of white Europe and America." It was "because of Japan rather than of China herself," he says, that the most populous nation on earth was "being pushed forward in theory as the representative of Asiatic peoples and as promise of Western sincerity toward the yellow race."

Today, India, South Africa, and Brazil—the nation with the largest number of people of African origin outside of the continent itself—are clamoring to be included as permanent members on the Security Council, as the world's majority continues to argue that a lack of democracy continues to mar this potent body.

Though the colonized—particularly of Asia and Africa—were a primary concern of his, Du Bois was also attentive to the plight of minorities languishing within the boundaries of the leading powers. Special attention here was placed on one of the primary ethno-religious minorities of Europe: "The greatest tragedy of this war," said Du Bois, "has been the treatment of the Jewish minority in Germany. Nothing like this has happened before in modern civilization." This, intoned Du Bois, was a "calamity almost beyond comprehension."

Naturally, in declaiming on this potent matter of the "little nations within nations," he did not neglect his homeland. It was "left to the greatest modern democracy, the United States," he wrote, "to defend human slavery and caste, and even defeat democratic government in its own boundaries, ostensibly because of an inferior race, but really in order to make profits out of cheap labor, both black and white." As Du Bois saw it, racism was used to create a caste of cheap dark-skinned labor that simultaneously dragged down wage levels for all compelled to sell their labor, not least white labor.

Once more, this was a phenomenon with both economic and political consequences, he suggested. The deprivation of voting rights of African Americans inflated the power of states of the former slaveholding South, because it propelled the election and reelection of Jim Crow advocates who leaned sharply to the right. Jim Crow, Du Bois stressed, "forces the United States to abdicate its natural leadership of democracy in the world and to acquiesce in a domination of organized wealth which exceeds anything elsewhere in the world."

As Du Bois saw it, colonialism and its handmaiden white supremacy were about not just political but also economic domination. Colonies were lucrative sources of raw materials, but they were also closed markets for the dumping of products from the colonizing power. Such unjust enrichment, he argued, inexorably attracted the jealous attention of other powers—in this case Japan and Germany—whose elites felt that they had been deprived of their place in the sun. Therefore they sought aggressively to seize the colonies for their own benefit. As Du Bois saw it, there was a further economic benefit to colonial elites: the cheap labor of the colonies attracted investors from the colonizing power, and thus the interests of labor in the colonies were whipsawed against those in the colonizing power, to the detriment of both. Colonialism, Du Bois writes, "is a part of the battle between capital and labor in the modern economy."

Du Bois also saw a link between, for example, the oppression of Africans and the oppression of African Americans. "So long as the colonial system persists and expands," Du Bois contended, "theories of race inferiority will help to continue it. Right here lies the great danger of the future." Furthermore, this sinkhole of racism was a breeding ground for bloody revolts: "no matter how degraded people become, it is impossible to keep them down on a large scale and forever. Rebellion will certainly ensue." Du Bois would have been surprised neither by the waves of racially tinged urban unrest that rocked the

United States in the 1960s and thereafter nor by what has befallen France in the early twenty-first century,[8] nor would he have been surprised by the anticolonial revolts that shook South Africa, which, too, had racial overtones.[9]

Of course, prescience and capaciousness were not the sole hallmarks of Du Bois's vision. His call for a "Mandates Commission," a global body to administer the colonies—as opposed to self-determination and independence for these vast lands—may strike some as overly cautious. Others may feel that his paeans of praise to Washington's wartime ally, the Soviet Union, are misguided at best. Still, given the earth-shattering, dizzying, and precedent-shattering consequence of the war that he was analyzing as it was unfolding, Du Bois's ability to strike notes that continue to resonate is nothing less than remarkable.

Today colonialism is viewed unpleasantly in the colonized lands, though a discernible trend is detectable in the land of the colonizer to view this era nostalgically. The former viewpoint is resonant in Africa and Asia particularly, as the planet's majority continues to wrestle with the legacy of poverty and disease bequeathed by colonialism. Yet Du Bois's prescient words and his capacious vision still ring true as we continue to tally and assess the devastating legacy of colonialism and its accompanist, Jim Crow and apartheid.

NOTES

1. Gerald Horne, *Black and Red: W. E. B. Du Bois and the Afro-American Response to the Cold War, 1944–1963* (Albany: State University of New York Press, 1986), passim.
2. Gerald Horne, *Race Woman: The Lives of Shirley Graham Du Bois* (New York: New York University Press, 2000).
3. Herbert Aptheker, editor, *A Documentary History of the Negro People in the United States*, vol. 3 (Secaucus, N.J.: Citadel Press, 1973), p. 421. Like all scholars of Du Bois, I am indebted to the work of his friend and comrade Aptheker, particularly Aptheker's insightful introduction to this very text. See W. E. B. Du Bois, *Color and Democracy: Colonies and Peace*, with an introduction by Herbert Aptheker (Millwood, N.Y.: Kraus-Thomson, 1975), pp. 5–18.
4. *The Crisis*, January 1944, pp. 16–17.
5. W. E. B. Du Bois, "The Realities in Africa: European Profit or Negro Development," *Foreign Affairs* 21 (July 1943): 721–732; W. E. B. Du Bois, "Prospect of a World without Race Conflict," *American Journal of Sociology* 49 (March 1944): 450–456.
6. *Amsterdam News*, August 19, 1944.
7. Gerald Horne, *Race War: White Supremacy and the Japanese Attack on the British Empire* (New York: New York University Press, 2004).
8. See, for instance, Gerald Horne, *Fire This Time: The Watts Uprising and the 1960s* (Charlottesville: University Press of Virginia, 1995).
9. See, for instance, Gerald Horne, *From the Barrel of a Gun: The United States and the War against Zimbabwe, 1965–1980* (Chapel Hill: University of North Carolina Press, 2001).

Preface

The present war has made it clear that we can no longer regard Western Europe and North America as the world for which civilization exists; nor can we look upon European culture as the norm for all peoples. Henceforth the majority of the inhabitants of earth, who happen for the most part to be colored, must be regarded as having the right and the capacity to share in human progress and to become copartners in that democracy which alone can ensure peace among men, by the abolition of poverty, the education of the masses, protection from disease, and the scientific treatment of crime.

From these premises I have written this book, to examine our current efforts to ensure peace through the united action of men of goodwill. I have sought to say that insofar as such efforts leave practically untouched the present imperial ownership of disfranchised colonies, and in this and other ways proceed as if the majority of men can be regarded mainly as sources of profit for Europe and North America, in just so far we are planning not peace but war, not democracy but the continued oligarchical control of civilization by the white race.

I am aware that such a thesis needs to be backed by a far wider collection of facts, scientifically arranged, than are at present available. But I am convinced from long study and wide travel that the truth of what I say is fairly well attested, and at least the dangers which I seek to point out are sufficiently evident to call for action.

W. E. Burghardt Du Bois

New York, January 1, 1945.

COLOR AND DEMOCRACY

CHAPTER I

◆

Dumbarton Oaks

The efforts to inaugurate a Federation of Mankind, which culminated in the conference at Dumbarton Oaks in 1944, sought to ensure peace and restore civilization; but left a danger and a recurring cause of war in the failure to emphasize the rights of colonial peoples.

In 1921, I sat in the Palace of Justice in Brussels, Belgium, with Paul Otlet, who has often been called the Father of the League of Nations. He and his friend Senator La Fontaine were helping me convene a Pan-African Congress to meet successively in London, Paris, and Brussels. In their long efforts to bring civilized nations into unified action and thought, they agreed with me in looking upon the question of imperialism and colonies as a central subject for these efforts.

In 1944, after the rise and fall of the League of Nations, there met at Dumbarton Oaks a conference with the same objects in mind: to bring mankind into unified effort for cultural progress. This conference was made vivid and imperative by realization of the awful catastrophe of a Second World War.

Dumbarton Oaks is an estate granted by the Crown of England to Ninian Beall in 1702. The mansion was built a century later just as South Carolina, fearing Federal legislation, opened her harbor to a flood of new African slaves. Thus this property dates from the day of that curious combination of Negro slavery and British imperialism when America was a colony of Britain and conceived of as primarily a matter of income and investment for British merchants and aristocrats. This proud estate lived to see the fire of war and a nation born out of the chaos of the colonial theory of the eighteenth century. It saw swift and impressive progress and bitter civil strife and emancipation of slaves in the nineteenth century, and finally in the twentieth century it witnessed the fall of modern civilization into two world wars so widespread, bitter, and costly that the whole question of the future of mankind suddenly became critical.

Perhaps again today some brooding residue of colonial problems intertwined with problems of race and color, into which Dumbarton Oaks was born, lingered at this conference held to seek the rebuilding of a stricken world. There sat at the table of Dumbarton Oaks, fears, jealousies, and hopes: fears of renewed German aggression and Asiatic revolt; fears of postwar poverty and despair; jealousies of national rights and imperial power; and hopes for eventual peace and progress. There emerged a tentative plan for world government designed especially to curb aggression, but also to preserve imperial power and even extend and fortify it.

The first and guiding ideal of this conference was to stop war by organization of the most powerful nations on earth against aggression; so that at the head of the organization designed to ensure peace for progress in the future world was placed a Security Council, and security was the keynote.

We, however, who are filled with conflicting hope and doubt must ask ourselves how far a peace resting on force will ensure the defense and rebirth of civilization, and what the real relation can be between military power on the one hand and wealth, contentment, and progress on the other. Ultimate and lasting peace will rest on consent and agreement, not on armies.

There are those of us who see in the rifts of race many and multiplying causes of war, and therefore scan the proposals made at Dumbarton Oaks with misgiving. Such persons, of course, are aware that this conference was called primarily to solve not problems of race but problems of peace, and it had to get the consent of nations with varying histories and ideals. And yet they know that if war has been and may be the result of race hate, and of colonial might based on racial repulsions as well as on greed for wealth and power, we must beware how far we build the new world upon military force and ignore such known and existent causes of war.

Perhaps first we may seek enlightenment by arranging the proposals made at Dumbarton Oaks in accordance with conventional lines of race and color, which we know fit with curious historical sequence into colonial problems.

We find here proposed a government of the world in which 800,000,000 white and yellow peoples will rule mankind through a Security Council. By agreement between the world's greatest powers, this Council will be an executive body implemented by treaty with military power sufficient to enforce its decisions.

At first sight, this Security Council reassures the thoughtful because it is not simply a white European organization. Yet on second thought, that assurance is not so strong. While the Security Council in theory is bi-racial, we cannot forget that over half of the peoples included are represented by China and that the status of China in the postwar world is uncertain. In the latter part of the nineteenth century China was at the point of being definitely divided into a group of European colonies. Spheres of influence almost colonial in conception had been laid out by Great Britain, Russia, France, Germany, and very nearly by the United States. The series of events which held up the consummation of this plan accompanied the rise of Japan: her war with China, which placed her beside the European aggressors; later her defeat of Russia, which made her an imperial partner and so recognized by England; and finally after the First World War her grudging recognition as a leading world state.

But the world and Western civilization were not willing to receive Japan in complete partnership with recognition of the racial equality of yellow peoples. The result of this, in the kaleidoscopic changes between the First World War and the Second, was that Japan after demanding racial equality in the League of

Nations, and being rather peremptorily denied even theoretical confirmation by Great Britain and the United States, gradually turned and began to work toward the hegemony of Asia. It was no longer a question of partnership with the West, but one of the domination of the major part of mankind by an Asiatic imperialism. When this imperialism made common cause with dictatorship in Germany and Italy, world war was inevitable.

Thereafter China became a symbol in the West of a power which might dominate Asia but would do so in collaboration with Europe and the United States and indeed under their guidance, if not actually under their power. The plan was all the more plausible because China could look only to Europe and the United States for rehabilitation after her long and almost hopeless struggle against Japan in the midst of her own internal revolution, which in itself needed every ounce of her energy.

China has therefore been built up in current comment and at Dumbarton Oaks as one of the great powers, with a permanent seat in the Security Council. Yet as a matter of fact this ancient and magnificent civilization, which has again and again set goals for human culture, is today staggering and uncertain and can look for rapid rebirth only if she has the goodwill, the economic support, and the social co-operation of the United States and Western Europe.

It is significant that in the conference of Dumbarton Oaks three powers consulted for six weeks, while China was called in only for the last six days. The proposals as we have them were agreed upon by Great Britain, Russia, and the United States. Afterward the Chinese delegation was called in to a sort of review. It is not at all clear as to just why this procedure was followed.

It would rather seem that at Dumbarton Oaks China was deliberately confronted with a fait accompli. Even if this was so, it was probably, but unfortunately, done with China's full consent. She presented finally to the United Nations her own plan for the government of the world. The Chinese stressed a commission to administer internationalized territory and to introduce measures for the protection and welfare of the colonial peoples. All this they wished to invest in an International Social Welfare Office relating to all peoples.

Finally and significantly, China presented again (in perhaps somewhat altered form, since the text has never been revealed) a proposed international declaration on racial equality. The United Nations were suave, and doubtless to a degree sympathetic. They agreed in principle that the proposals of China were important, but they suggested that action upon them be postponed to a later date and to other organs of discussion and recommendation; in particular, the racial-equality proposal was suppressed.

The Security Council, therefore, which is the executive center of the proposed new world organization, will practically be under the control of white Europe and America; while the yellow peoples will be recognized as having the right to share in this partnership, their effective assertion of this right will depend upon the long and difficult path which the reorganization of China and the rebuilding of her culture will surely demand.

Six hundred and fifty million persons, predominantly white folk but not entirely, will function under the Dumbarton Oaks proposals in a General Assembly together with 800,000,000 in the larger nations. Effort—and well-meaning effort—has been made to emphasize the role of the General Assembly; but that role in reality depends upon the course of human history in the next generation, because, save in two particulars, the General Assembly is an organization without power, which may discuss situations and give them publicity, but has no right of action save as its discussions and recommendations are consented to by the various nations of the world; and there would seem to be no possible way of compelling any nation to consent to these proposals if it did not care to, unless its refusal to consent was an immediate threat of world war.

In two respects the General Assembly has power. First, it nominates six of the eleven members of the Security Council. If that Council reaches a decision in any matters by unanimity, the nominees of the Assembly or any one of them voting as national units, can stop such unanimous action. In whatever matter the Council reaches a decision by majority vote, the nominated states hold the majority. In the second place, the power of the budget is in the hands of the Assembly.

There is another power of the proposed General Assembly which has been stressed, and that is the appointment of an Economic and Social Council. This is composed of eighteen members appointed by the General Assembly, and to this Council questions relating to social welfare, cultural progress, and human rights may be referred. This may include such matters as aviation and radio, labor and education, food and agriculture, currency, finance, and economic co-operation, public health, and also "human rights"—the vastest field imaginable for co-operation of human agencies for the welfare of the world.

Many of these matters will be fundamental for the future of the world. The question of the future of colonies and the treatment of colonial peoples, which has been in the past a fruitful cause of dissension and war, comes under the purview of this committee. Questions relating to the unfree peoples, to the minorities, and to the depressed social classes also fall to its survey.

But the committee has no power of action. It has the right of discussion and of recommendation to the Security Council and to the various states of the world; but its power of investigation of actual facts and conditions is limited on the one hand by the Security Council, and on the other hand by the national states. If world opinion sets strongly in certain directions, doubtless the influence of the General Assembly through the Economic and Social Council may accomplish much. On the other hand, all too often its proposals and complaints may simply beat the air in vain.

We must also remember that the so-called free states represented in the Assembly are not in all cases really free. In some cases, like those of Canada, Australia, and the Union of South Africa, they are parts and closely integrated parts of the British Empire. And the various states of Soviet Russia have similar chance to sit in the Assembly as free nations. In addition to this, there are many nations of the world who because of their debts to the great industrial empires, and because of intricate industrial and commercial relations, in many cases cannot speak or act with freedom or independence.

There will be at least 750,000,000 colored and black folk inhabiting colonies owned by white nations, who will have no rights that the white people of the world are bound to respect. Revolt on their part can be put down by military force; they will have no right of appeal to the Council or the Assembly; they will have no standing before the International Court of Justice. Any dispute concerning their status is put beyond the jurisdiction of either the Council or the Assembly, unless it threatens world war.

Here, to my mind, lies the broadest ground for criticism of the Dumbarton Oaks proposals. There is no need here to discuss the advantages or the disadvantages of modern imperialism, or to attempt to assess the gain or the loss to peoples arising from their subordination to the great nations. That the colonial system has involved in the past much that was horrible and inhuman must be admitted. That vast numbers of backward peoples have made notable cultural advance under the colonial regime is equally true. Despite this, if the world believes in democracy, and is fighting a war of incredible cost to establish democracy as a way of life, it is both intolerable in ethics and dangerous in statecraft to allow, for instance, 8,000,000 Belgians to represent 10,000,000 Congolese in the new internation without giving these black folk any voice even to complain. It is equally unfair that 9,000,000 Dutchmen should be the sole arbiters and spokesmen for 67,000,000 brown men of the South Seas. It cannot be reconciled with any philosophy of democracy that 50,000,000 white folk of the British Empire should be able to make the destiny of 450,000,000 yellow, brown, and black people a matter solely of their own internal decision. Or again, inside that same empire it is astonishing to see among the leading "free nations" battling for "democracy" the Union of South Africa, where 2,000,000 white folk, not only in international affairs but openly in their established government, hold 8,000,000 black natives in a subordination unequaled elsewhere in the world.

This is not for a moment to deny the techniques and the elementary schools Belgium has given the black Congo; or the fact that The Netherlands has perhaps the most liberal colonial program of any modern empire; or that Great Britain gave the African freedom and education after slave trade and slavery. But it is equally true that the advance of colonial peoples has been hesitant and slow, and retarded unnecessarily because of the denial of democratic method to the natives, and because their treatment and government have had, and still have, objects and methods incompatible with their best interests and highest progress.

The substantial and permanent advance of a group cannot be allowed to depend on the philanthropy of a master if the desires and initiative of its members are given no freedom, no democratic expression; and if, on the other hand, the will of the master is swayed by strong motives of selfish aggrandizement and gain.

How often this selfish interest has prevailed in the past is too well known to require reminder. But today the temptation is stronger rather than weaker. With Holland reeling under murder, theft, and destruction, can the world expect unselfish surrender by the present Dutch generation of the profit of rich colonies capable of helping to restore her losses? Is it likely that after her crucifixion Belgium will be satisfied with less profit from the Congo and greater expenditure there for education, health, and social service? With Great Britain straining every nerve to satisfy the demands of her own laboring classes, is it likely that she will of her own initiative, or even with pressure from her own Labor party, extend these reforms to India, coupled with the autonomy necessary for Indian initiative and self-government?

No. The united effort of world opinion should now be brought earnestly to bear on the nations owning colonies, to make them realize that, great as the immediate sacrifice may be, it is the only way. To set up now an internation with near half of mankind disfranchised and socially enslaved is to court disaster. In the past, and the recent past, we know how the lure of profit from rich, unlettered, and helpless countries has tempted great and civilized nations and plunged them into bloody rivalry. We know what part colonial aggression has played in this present world disaster. We know how colonies give power, wealth, and prestige, employment, monopoly, and privilege. We know that capital investment can earn more in Africa, Asia, and the South Seas because there it suffers few of the restrictions of civilized life; that the foreign investor in these lands is himself the prime ruler and seat of power, and without local democratic control he has but to appease public opinion at home, which is not only ignorant of the local facts, but perhaps all too willing to remain ignorant so long as dividends continue.

If this situation is not frankly faced and steps toward remedy are not attempted, we shall seek in vain to find peace and security; we shall leave the door wide-open for renewed international strife to secure colonies, and eventually and inevitably for colonial revolt.

To these objections the persons making the proposals at Dumbarton Oaks may well answer: What besides public opinion have we to depend upon for the reclamation of mankind after the present disaster? What power could possibly be evoked and put into the hands of an executive which would ensure social justice? None, they would answer. And we have to agree with them, save in one respect: The experience of the First World War put into the hands of the League of Nations a power of action beyond that of military compulsion. A recognized cause of that war was the status of colonies; the demand of Germany for a new allocation of colonial territory, for a "place in the sun," was one of the main reasons that brought on the war. It was because of this that the League of Nations, in depriving a conquered Germany of her territories, established a Mandates Commission. This Mandates Commission was designed as a body with supervisory power established by the common consent of the Allies. The former German and Turkish territories in Africa and the Pacific and in the Near East were placed under the League of Nations, with certain principles of administration, Article 22.

1. To those colonies and territories which as a consequence of the late war have ceased to be under the sovereignty of the States which formerly governed them and which are inhabited by peoples not yet able to stand by themselves under the strenuous conditions of the modern world, there should be applied the principle that the well-being and development of such peoples form a sacred trust of civilization and that securities for the performance of this trust should be embodied in this Covenant.
2. The best method of giving practical effect to this principle is that the tutelage of such peoples should be intrusted to advanced nations who, by reason of their resources, their experience or their geographical position, can best undertake this responsibility, and who are willing to accept it, and that this tutelage should be exercised by them as Mandatories on behalf of the League.

3. The character of the mandate must differ according to the stage of the development of the people, the geographical situation of the territory, its economic conditions and other similar circumstances.
4. Certain communities formerly belonging to the Turkish Empire have reached a stage of development where their existence as independent nations can be provisionally recognized subject to the rendering of administrative advice and assistance by a Mandatory until such time as they are able to stand alone. The wishes of these communities must be a principal consideration in the selection of the Mandatory.
5. Other peoples, especially those of Central Africa, are at such a stage that the Mandatory must be responsible for the administration of the territory under conditions which will guarantee freedom of conscience and religion, subject only to the maintenance of public order and morals, the prohibition of abuses such as the slave trade, the arms traffic and the liquor traffic, and the prevention of the establishment of fortifications or military and naval bases and of military training of the natives for other than police purposes and the defense of territory, and will also secure equal opportunities for the trade and commerce of other Members of the League.
6. There are territories, such as South-West Africa and certain of the South Pacific Islands, which, owing to the sparseness of their population or their small size, or their remoteness from the centres of civilization, or their geographical contiguity to the territory of the Mandatory, and other circumstances, can be best administered under the laws of the Mandatory as integral portions of its territory, subject to the safeguards above mentioned in the interests of the indigenous population.
7. In every case of mandate, the Mandatory shall render to the Council an annual report in reference to the territory committed to its charge.
8. The degree of authority, control or administration to be exercised by the Mandatory shall, if not previously agreed upon by the Members of the League, be explicitly defined in each case by the Council.
9. A permanent Commission shall be constituted to receive and examine the annual reports of the Mandatories and to advise the Council on all matters relating to the observance of the mandates.

This was new international law, which the United Nations are ignoring today. The proposals at Dumbarton Oaks say nothing about the mandates or the Mandates Commission. Apparently the colonies taken from Germany are to become integral parts of present empires. This would seem to be not only a dangerous infraction of the new international law which the League of Nations established, but a deliberate throwing-away of a chance to come to grips with the colonial problems. It also ignores the possibility of arranging easily for control of new internationalized territory, such as the Rhineland.

Realism is here calling for awakened action. Evidently the weak point in this Dumbarton outline for a government of men is the fact that under this proposal something between one-fourth and one-half the inhabitants of the world will have no part in it—no power of democratic control and scarcely an organized right of petition. Most efforts at reform and social uplift will depend upon the free states and the empires, acting individually, and they will be asked to act at a time when, because of the loss and disruption of war, they will be least inclined to face philanthropic enterprise of any sort.

It has been explained by the various persons and official commentators that the outline of the Dumbarton Oaks proposals is not yet complete. There has been a tendency to admonish critics not to rock the boat in these difficult times. First we want peace and security; then we will have a chance to pursue political rebuilding and social uplift. Many organizations that in the early stages of the discussion of postwar difficulties had stressed problems of colonies in the matter of human rights are today hesitating.

I summed the matter up at a conference in Washington when Mr. Stettinius called together ninety-six social organizations to study the proposals at Dumbarton Oaks: "As I have gone through the published proposals at Dumbarton Oaks, I am depressed to realize with what consistency the matter of colonies has been passed over. In Chapter one, paragraph three, the emphasis is on the fact that this is a union of nations, not of races, groups, or organizations of men not recognized as nations; in Chapter two, paragraph one, peace-loving 'States' alone may join the Union; in Chapter six, apparently an aggrieved party must be a state in order to complain or to appear before the Council; similarly in Chapter seven, no colonies as such can appeal for hearing before the International Court of Justice. Elaborate effort is made to protect 'States' from aggression, but I find no provisions in Chapter seven even to consider the aggression of a nation against its own colonial peoples, while apparently international military force can be called in to suppress revolt. Indeed paragraph seven of that chapter seems to say definitely that colonial disputes lie entirely beyond the jurisdiction of this proposed government of men. The Economic and Social Council set up in this chapter can recommend and consider complaints and situations; but there is no direct power to investigate conditions. The Council is appointed by eighteen states, with no colonial participation indicated. In other words, this proposal, as I read it, virtually says to 750,000,000 human beings, if not to a majority of mankind, that the only way to human equality is the philanthropy of masters who have historical and strong interest in preserving their present power and income."

It is not today fashionable to quote the poet of the Victorian Age:

Till the war-drum throbb'd no longer, and the battle-flags were furled.
In the Parliament of man, the Federation of the world.

Dumbarton Oaks is the latest of a long and desperate line of human endeavor seeking some modicum of unity in the government of mankind to displace the horror of the planned murder which is war. The Double Crown of Egypt, the Achaean League, the Empire of Rome and the Holy Roman Empire, the Holy Alliance and the League of Nations, all listened to that high and striving chord of human unity above the discord of hate, hurt, and pain—like the thrilling melody of Lohengrin's swan above his disaster:

CHAPTER II

◆

The Disfranchised Colonies

Colonies and the colonial system make the colonial peoples in a sense
the slums of the world, disfranchised and held in poverty and disease.

Colonies are the slums of the world. They are today the places of greatest
concentration of poverty, disease, and ignorance of what the human mind has
come to know. They are centers of helplessness, of discouragement of initiative,
of forced labor, and of legal suppression of all activities or thoughts which the
master country fears or dislikes.

They resemble in some ways the municipal slums of the nineteenth century
in culture lands. In those days men thought of slums as inevitable, as being
caused in a sense by the wretched people who inhabited them, as yielding to no
remedial action in any conceivable time. If abolished, the dregs of humanity
would re-create them. Then we were jerked back to our senses by the realization
that slums were investments where housing, sanitation, education, and spiritual freedom were lacking, and where for this reason the profits of the landlords, the merchants, and the exploiters were enormous.

To most people this characterization of colonies will seem overdrawn, and of
course in one major respect colonies differ radically from slums. Municipal slums
are mainly festering sores drawing their substance from the surrounding city
and sharing the blood and the culture of that city. Colonies, on the other hand,
are for the most part quite separate in race and culture from the peoples who
control them. Their culture is often ancient and historically fine and valuable,
spoiled too often by misfortune and conquest and misunderstanding. This
sense of separation, therefore, makes colonies usually an integral entity beyond
the sympathy and the comprehension of the ruling world. But in both city and
colony, labor is forced by poverty, and crime is largely disease.

What, then, are colonies? Leaving analogies, in this case none too good, we
look to facts, and find them also elusive. It is difficult to define a colony precisely.
There are the dry bones of statistics; but the essential facts are neither well measured nor logically articulated. After all, an imperial power is not interested primarily in censuses, health surveys, or historical research. Consequently we know
only approximately, and with wide margins of error, the colonial population, the

number of the sick and the dead, and just what happened before the colony was conquered.

For the most part, today the colonial peoples are colored of skin; this was not true of colonies in other days, but it is mainly true today. And to most minds, this is of fatal significance; coupled with Negro slavery, Chinese coolies, and doctrines of race inferiority, it proves to most white folk the logic of the modern colonial system: Colonies are filled with peoples who never were abreast with civilization and never can be.

This rationalization is very satisfactory to empire-builders and investors, but it does not satisfy science today, no matter how much it did yesterday. Skin color is a matter of climate, and colonies today are mainly in the hot, moist tropics and semitropics. Naturally, here skins are colored. But historically these lands also were seats of ancient cultures among normal men. Here human civilization began, in Africa, Asia, and Central America. What has happened to these folk across the ages? They have been conquered, enslaved, oppressed, and exploited by stronger invaders. But was this invading force invariably stronger in body, keener in mind, and higher in culture? Not necessarily, but always stronger in offensive technique, even though often lower in culture and only average in mind.

Offensive technique drew the conquerors down upon the conquered, because the conquered had the fertile lands, the needed materials, the arts of processing goods for human needs. With the conquerors concentrating time and thought on these aspects of culture, usually the conquered could not oppose the barbarians with muscle, clubs, spears, gunpowder, and capital. In time, the invaders actually surpassed, and far surpassed, the weaker peoples in wealth, technique, and variety of culture patterns, and made them slaves to industry and servants to white men's ease.

But what of the future? Have the present masters of the world such an eternal lien on civilization as to ensure unending control? By no means; their very absorption in war and wealth has so weakened their moral fiber that the end of their rule is in sight. Also, the day of the colonial conquered peoples dawns, obscurely but surely.

Today, then, the colonial areas lie inert or sullenly resentful or seething with hate and unrest. With unlimited possibilities, they have but scraps of understanding of modern accumulations of knowledge; but they are pressing toward education with bitter determination. The conquerors, on the other hand, are giving them only the passing attention which preoccupation with problems of wealth and power at home leaves for colonial "problems."

What, then, do modern colonies look like, feel like? It is difficult to draw any universal picture. Superficial impressions are common: black boys diving for pennies; human horses hitched to rickshaws; menial service in plethora for a wage near nothing; absolute rule over slaves, even to life and death; fawning, crawling obeisance; high salaries, palaces, and luxury coupled with abject, nauseating, diseased poverty—this in a vague, imperfect way paints the present colonial world.

It is not nearly so easy as it would appear to fill in this outline and make it precise and scientific. Empires do not want nosy busybodies snooping into their territories and business. Visitors to colonies are, to be sure, allowed and even encouraged; but their tours are arranged, officials guide them in space and in thought, and they see usually what the colonial power wants them to see and little more. Dangerous "radicals" are rigorously excluded. My own visits to colonies have been rare and unsatisfactory. Several times I have tried in vain to visit South Africa. No visas were obtainable. I have been in British and French West Africa and in Jamaica.

In Sierra Leone I landed at Freetown in 1923. I was passed through the customs without difficulty, as my papers were in order. Then for some reason the authorities became suspicious. With scant courtesy, I was summoned peremptorily down to headquarters, to a room off the common jail, with pictures of escaped criminals decorating the walls. What did I want in Sierra Leone? I handed in my passport, showing that I was United States Minister Plenipotentiary to Liberia, stopping simply to visit on my way home. The commissioner unbent and dismissed me. That afternoon I was invited to a tea party at the governor's mansion! What would have happened to me if I had not had a diplomatic passport, or if I had been merely a colored man seeking to study a British colony?

The same year I visited Senegal and Conakry. I was received with great courtesy, but into the ruling caste; I had no contact with the mass of the colonial people. I lodged with the American consul; the French consul had me at dinner and the English consul at tea in his palatial mansion. But little did I see or learn of the millions of Negroes who formed the overwhelming mass of the colonial population.

In 1915, I visited Jamaica. I landed at Kingston and then, being tired and on vacation, did the unconventional thing of walking across the island to Mantego Bay. I immediately became an object of suspicion. It was wartime. I was in a sense, albeit unconsciously, intruding into Jamaica's backyard. I had proper visas, but I was not following the beaten path of the tourist. I was soon warned by a furtive black man that the police were on my track. My only recourse was to look up a long-time friend, principal of the local school. He ostentatiously drove me downtown, seated with him high in his surrey behind prancing horses. Thus was I properly introduced and vouched for. The point is that in all these cases one saw the possibility of arbitrary power without appeal and of a race and class situation unknown in free countries.

In the main, colonial peoples are living abnormally, save those of the untouched or inert mass of natives. Where the whites form a small ruling group, they are most abnormal and are not, as is assumed, replicas of the home group. They consist chiefly of representatives of commercial concerns whose first object is to make money for themselves and the corporations they represent. They are in the main hard-boiled, often ruthless businessmen, unrestrained by the inhibitions of home in either law or custom. Next come the colonial officials, either identical with the commercial men or more or less under their domination, especially through home influence. Colonials and businessmen clash, but business usually wins. Sometimes philanthropic career officials get the upper hand; but they are in danger of being replaced or losing promotion. The official class—heads, assistants, clerks, wives, and children—are apt to be arrogant, raised above their natural position and feeling their brief authority; they lord it over despised natives and demand swift and exemplary punishment for any affront to their dignity. The courts presided over by whites are usually even-handed in native quarrels, but through fear are strict, harsh, and even cruel in cases between natives and whites. White prestige must be maintained at any cost. There is usually a considerable group of white derelicts, hangers-on, sadistic representatives of the "superior race," banished to colonies by relatives who are ashamed to keep them at home.

This whole group of whites forms a caste apart, lives in segregated, salubrious, and protected areas, seldom speaks the vernacular or knows the masses except officially. Their regular income from colonial services is liberal according to home standards and often fantastic according to the standard of living in colonies. Conceive of an income of $10,000 a year for a colonial governor over people whose average income is $25 a year! The officials get frequent vacations with pay, and are pensioned after comparatively short service. The pensions are paid for life by colonial taxation, and the pensioners are regarded as experts on colonial matters the rest of their lives.

Where the white resident contingent is relatively large, as in South Africa and Kenya, the caste conditions are aggravated and the whites become the colony while the natives are ignored and neglected except as low-paid labor largely without rights that the colonists need respect.

Below this group of white overlords are the millions of natives. Their normal and traditional life has been more or less disrupted and changed in work, property, family life, recreation, health habits, food, religion, and other cultural matters. Their initiative, education, freedom of action, have been interfered with to a greater or less extent. Authority has been almost entirely withdrawn from their control and the white man's word is law in most cases. Their native standards of life have been destroyed and the new standards cannot be met by a poverty that is the worst in the world. The mass of natives sink into careless, inert, or sullen indifference, making their contact with whites as rare as possible, and incurring repeated punishment for laziness and infraction of arbitrary or inexplicable rules.

Up from these rise two groups: the toadies or "white folks niggers," who use flattery and talebearing to curry favor; and the resentful, bitter, and ambitious who seek by opposition or education to achieve the emancipation of their land and people. The educated and the half-educated, in particular, are the object of attack and dislike by the whites and are endlessly slandered in all testimony given visitors and scientists.

The missionaries form another class. They have been of all sorts of persons: unworldly visionaries, former pastors out of a job, social workers with and without social science, theologians, crackpots, and humanitarians. Their vocation is so unconventional that it is almost without standards of training or set norms of effort. Yet missionaries have spent tens of millions of dollars and influenced hundreds of millions of men with results that literally vary from heaven to hell. Missionaries represent the oldest invasion of whites, and incur at first the enmity of business and the friendship of natives. Colonial officials, on pressure from home, compromise differences, and the keener natives thereupon come to suspect missionary motives and the native toadies rush to get converted and cash in on benefits. The total result varies tremendously according to the pressure of these elements.

Despite a vast literature on colonial peoples, there is today no sound scientific basis for comprehensive study. What we have are reports of officials who set out to make a case for the imperial power in control; reports of missionaries, of all degrees of reliability and object; reports of travelers swayed by every conceivable motive and fitted or unfitted for testimony by widely varying education, ideals, and reliability. When science tries to study colonial systems in Africa and Asia, it meets all sorts of hindrances and incomplete statements of fact. In few cases is there testimony from the colonial peoples themselves, or impartial scientific surveys conducted by persons free of compulsion from imperial control and dictation.

The studies we have of colonial peoples and conditions are therefore unsatisfactory. Even the great *African Survey* edited by Lord Hailey is mainly based on the testimony and the figures of colonial officials; that is, of men who represent the colonial organization, who are appointed on recommendation of persons whose fortunes are tied up with colonial profits, and who are naturally desirous of making the best-possible picture of colonial conditions. This does not mean that there is in this report, or in many others, deliberate and conscious deception; but there is the desire to make a case for the vested interests of a large and powerful part of the world's property-owners.

Other studies are made by visitors and outsiders who can get at the facts only as the government officials give them opportunity. Many opportunities have been afforded such students in the past, but the opportunities fall far short of what complete and scientific knowledge demands. Moreover, such visitors arrive more or less unconsciously biased by their previous education and contacts, which lead them to regard the natives as on the whole a low order of humanity, and especially to distrust more or less completely the efforts of educated and aspiring Natives. The native elite, when through education and contact they get opportunity to study and tell of conditions, often, and naturally, defeat their own cause before a prejudiced audience by their bitterness and frustration and their inability to speak with recognized authority.

Thus, unfortunately, it is not possible to present or refer to any complete and documented body of knowledge which can give an undisputed picture of colonies today. This does not mean that we have no knowledge of colonial conditions; on the contrary, we have a vast amount of testimony and study; but practically every word of it can be and is disputed by interested parties, so that the truth can be reached only by the laborious interpretation of careful students. Nearly every assertion of students of colonial peoples is disputed today by colonial officials, many travelers, and a host of theorists. Despite this, greater unanimity of opinion is growing, but it is far from complete.

If, for instance, we complain of the conquest of harmless, isolated, and independent groups by great powers, it is answered that this is manifest destiny; that the leaders of world civilization must control and guide the backward peoples for the good of all. Otherwise these peoples relapse into revolting barbarism. If under this control colonial peoples are unhappy, it is answered that they are happier than they were formerly without control; and that they make greater progress when guided than when left alone.

If slavery and forced labor are complained of, the answer is that the natives are congenitally lazy and must be made to work for the good of mankind. Indeed, if they were not enslaved by Europeans, they would enslave each other. Low wages are justified by the fact that these peoples are simple, with low standards of living, while their industrialization is a boon to the world, and the world's welfare is paramount. Lack of broad educational plans is justified by their cost. Can England be asked to undertake the education of British Africa when she has not yet fully planned the education of British children at home? Moreover, why educate these simple folk into unhappiness and discontent? If they are trained at all, it should be to produce wealth for the benefit of themselves in part and of the empire in general. The seizing of the land and dividing it is looked upon not only as a policy which puts unused acreage into remunerative use, but also as one that compels folk to work who otherwise would sing and dance and sit in the sun. And in general, is it not clear from the testimony of history that the mass of colonial peoples can progress only under the guidance of the civilized white people, and is not the welfare of the whites in reality the welfare of the world?

Practically every one of these assertions has a certain validity and truth, and at the same time is just false and misleading enough to give an entirely unfair picture of the colonial world. The recent advance of anthropology, psychology, and other social sciences is beginning to show this, and beginning to prove on how false a premise these assertions are based and how fatal a body of folklore has been built upon it. These beliefs have been influenced by propaganda, by caricature, and by ignorance of the human soul. Today these attitudes must be challenged, and without trying to approach anything like completeness of scientific statement we may allude here to certain general matters concerning colonial peoples the truth of which cannot be disputed.

These are the figures for colonies taken from the *Statesman's Yearbook* and the *World Almanac* for 1944:

BRITISH EMPIRE

(Colonial domain, excluding white self-ruling Dominions, but including colonies of those Dominions and including mandates and condominiums)

	COLONIAL POPULATION	AREA IN SQUARE MILES
Asia		
Ceylon	5,300,000	25,000
Hong Kong	1,071,000	32,000
India	389,000,000	1,580,000
Burma	14,600,000	192,000
Malaya	1,485,000	1,300
Federated Malay States	2,200,000	7,900
Unfederated Malay States	737,000	7,000
New Guinea	50,000	93,000
Borneo	270,000	29,000
	414,713,000	1,967,200

	COLONIAL POPULATION	AREA IN SQUARE MILES
Africa		
Kenya	3,690,000	224,000
Uganda	3,890,000	94,000
Zanzibar	250,000	1,000
Mauritius	408,000	720
Nyasaland	1,680,000	37,000
Somaliland	500,000	68,000
Basutoland	562,000	12,000
Bechuanaland	260,000	275,000
Swaziland	156,000	6,705
Southern Rhodesia	1,448,000	150,000
Northern Rhodesia	1,380,000	290,000
Nigeria	21,000,000	372,000
Gambia	14,000	69
Gold Coast	3,960,000	92,000
Sierra Leone Colony	121,000	2,500
Sierra Leone Protectorate	1,670,000	27,000
Sudan	6,590,000	967,000
Tanganyika	5,000,000	360,000
Southwest Africa	343,000	317,000
Union of South Africa (native, colored, Asiatic)	7,586,000	300,000?
	60,508,000	3,595,994
West Indies and South America		
Bermuda	33,000	19
Guiana	361,000	89,000
Honduras	62,000	8,800
Bahamas	19,000	4,000
Barbados	156,000	166
Jamaica	1,237,000	4,000
Leeward Islands	98,000	422
Trinidad	522,000	2,000
Granada	90,000	133
St. Vincent	48,000	150
St. Lucia	73,000	233
	2,699,000	108,923
Pacific Ocean		
Pacific Islands	108,000	12,000
Papua	337,000	2,750
	445,000	14,750
Near East		
Cyprus	389,000	3,500
Palestine Mandate	1,600,000	27,000
	1,989,000	30,500
Total	480,354,000	5,717,367

THE UNITED STATES OF AMERICA

	COLONIAL POPULATION	AREA IN SQUARE MILES
Alaska	72,000	586,000
Hawaii	423,000	6,400
Puerto Rico	1,869,000	3,400
Virgin Islands	22,000	133
Philippines	17,000,000	115,000
Samoa	10,000	76
	19,396,000	711,009

BELGIUM

Belgian Congo	10,386,000	900,000

CHINA

Tibet	1,500,000	463,000
Mongolia	850,000	1,875,000
	2,350,000	2,338,000

FRANCE

Asia		
French India	323,000	196
French Indo-China	24,000,000	286,000
Syria and Lebanon	3,630,000	58,000
	27,953,000	344,196
Africa		
Algeria	7,200,000	840,000
Tunis	2,600,000	48,000
French Equatorial Africa	3,425,000	959,000
Madagascar	3,800,000	241,000
French West Africa	15,000,000	1,800,000
Togo	780,000	33,700
Cameroons	2,500,000	166,000
	35,305,000	4,087,700
West Indies and South America		
Guadeloupe	304,000	688
Guiana	31,000	35,000
Martinique	246,000	385,000
	581,000	420,688
Total	63,839,000	4,852,584

ITALY

Libya	888,000	679,000
Eritrea	600,000	15,700
Somaliland	1,000,000	194,000
	2,488,000	888,700

JAPAN

Manchukuo	39,000,000	500,000
Korea	22,800,000	85,000
Formosa	5,800,000	14,000
	67,600,000	599,000

THE NETHERLANDS

Surinam	187,000	54,000
Curaçao	114,000	400
Netherlands Indies	67,000,000	735,000
	67,301,000	789,400

PORTUGAL

10,800,000	800,000

SPAIN

1,100,000	135,000

In the compilation above, the self-governing colonies of the British Empire have been omitted, except that in the case of the Union of South Africa the native population and the population of the mandate have been included as colonial. Summarizing these figures, we have this table:

COLONIAL REGIONS

	Colonial Population	Area in Square Miles
British Empire	480,354,000	5,717,367
United States	19,396,000	711,009
Belgium	10,386,000	900,000
China	2,350,000	2,338,000
France	63,839,000	4,852,584
Italy	2,488,000	888,700
Japan	67,600,000	599,000
Netherlands	67,301,000	789,400
Portugal	10,800,000	800,000
Spain	1,100,000	135,000
	725,614,000	17,731,060

Thus we see that there live in colonies today more than one-third of the world's inhabitants, occupying more than one-third of the land space of the globe.

In Africa today the best estimates count 148,000,000 Natives, 4,000,000 whites, and 1,500,000 Asiatics, making something over 150,000,000 persons occupying 11,000,000 square miles of territory. This includes many territories, such as Egypt, Ethiopia, and Liberia, which are quasi-colonies rather than colonies. It includes

French North Africa, partially absorbed into France and partially protectorates. It includes self-governing colonies, such as Southern Rhodesia and the Union of South Africa.

The situation in Asia is even more complicated. There is the vast realm of China with at least 400,000,000 human beings, one-fifth of the total population of the world, and occupying 4,250,000 square miles. We may regard China as an independent country or as a quasi-colony of Europe and Japan. As an independent country, China controls, outside of the main province, Tibet, Mongolia, and Sinkiang, with 2,500,000 inhabitants.

Then there comes the British Empire in Asia. Besides the Dominions of Australia and New Zealand, here is a population (in Borneo, Ceylon, Hong Kong, India, Burma, Malaya, and Palestine) of 415,000,000, occupying 1,950,000 square miles of land. Before the present war, in Asia France governed 28,000,000 persons, occupying 344,000 square miles. The Netherlands ruled in Asia over 67,000,000 natives, occupying 599,000 square miles. To all this may be added the colonies in the West Indies, where Britain governs over 2,500,000 persons, and France and The Netherlands 1,000,000.

It seems queer to be able to omit Spain from any treatment of colonial powers. Time was when the Spanish Empire was the most grandiose of modern governments. The sixteenth century saw Spain lord of most of Europe and nearly all the Americas, with claims in Asia. The wealth of the empire was fabulous, and changed the financial organization of the modern world. Envious of this Spanish wealth, in the seventeenth century England, France, and Holland, by war, theft, and treaty, seized Spanish trade and colonies. In the eighteenth century England gained control of the lucrative Spanish slave trade, and in the nineteenth century colonial revolution, aided by Haiti, deprived Spain of her South American colonies. Finally, in the twentieth century civil war in Spain began world war in Europe. Today 26,000,000 Spaniards control 1,000,000 colonials, most of whom are in Morocco. As does no other empire, Spain illustrates the interaction between European labor and colonial slavery, between democracy and oligarchy. Today the valiant ancient heart of Spain lies near death, overrun with the lice of grandees, land hogs, and piteous ignorant masses. Only the beautiful limbs are alive and twitching with the dream of *La Hispanidad*.

The policies which the mother countries have adopted toward these colonies vary tremendously. There are deep racial tensions which made the Belgians fear the appointment of the Negro Eboué as Governor-General of French Equatorial Africa. There is the Union of South Africa, where 2,000,000 Europeans segregate and disfranchise 8,000,000 Africans and 200,000 Indians, and which has carried racial cleavage to an extent only paralleled by Hitler's attitude toward the Jews.

French policy has swung from concessions to forty exploiting companies to the enfranchisement of some of the Negroes of Senegal. The Belgian policy grew, after King Leopold, toward careful organization for industrial profit, with limited education for the natives. Labor policies varied from forced labor, which is practical slavery, to the beginnings of modern labor legislation.

Concerted attempt has been made recently to remove the discussion of India from the colonial category by calling it a dependency—just as other colonies are called protectorates or included in "spheres of influence." Change of name makes no essential change in fact. The history of India in the modern world is a disgrace to civilization. Granting the complication of problems exhibited there, we have a series of facts which cannot be denied. Nearly every Indian leader since 1920 has spent long years in jail and been permanently injured in health by imprisonment. Lajpat Rai, C. R. Das, Motilal Nehru, Gandhi and his wife, Mrs. Sarojini Naidu, and Dr. Syed Mahmud are among those jailed and injured in health, not to mention Jawaharlal Nehru, now in prison for the ninth time, having spent fourteen years there in all. There is no possible defense for such a system of oppression by a great modern country.

The opinion of Ambassador William Phillips, grandson of the great abolitionist Wendell Phillips, gives ample testimony to this. Mr. Phillips is a conservative and not a radical. He went to India as the personal representative of the President of the United States. His conclusions in May 14, 1944, were as follows:

> At present, the Indian people are at war only in a legal sense, as for various reasons the British Government declared India in the conflict without the formality of consulting Indian leaders or even the Indian legislature. Indians feel they have no voice in the government and therefore no responsibility in the conduct of the war. They feel that they have nothing to fight for, as they are convinced that the professed war aims of the United Nations do not apply to them. The British Prime Minister, in fact, has stated that the provisions of the Atlantic Charter are not applicable to India, and it is not unnatural therefore that Indian leaders are beginning to wonder whether the Charter is only for the benefit of white races. The present Indian army is purely mercenary and only that part of it which is drawn from the martial races has been tried in actual warfare; and these martial soldiers represent only 33 per cent of the army. General Stilwell has expressed his concern over the situation and in particular in regard to the poor morale of the Indian officers.
>
> The attitude of the general public towards the war is even worse. Lassitude and indifference and bitterness have increased as a result of the famine conditions, the growing high cost of living and continued political deadlock.
>
> While India is broken politically into various parties and groups, all have one object in common—eventual freedom and independence from British domination.
>
> There would seem to be only one remedy of this highly unsatisfactory situation in which we are unfortunately but nevertheless seriously involved, and that is to change the attitude of the people of India towards the war, make them feel that we want them to assume responsibilities to the United Nations and are prepared to give them facilities for doing so and that the voice of India will play an important part in the reconstruction of the world.[1]

As in India, so in other colonies there is little to prove that colonial policy aims at inducting the colonial peoples into self-government and independence. Britain has pursued this policy only in the case of colonies settled mainly by Englishmen and other white peoples. In distinctly colored colonies, little advance in this direction has been made for decades. In India, an Englishman says that in the states where political control is shared between the British and the Indians, and in a land where the average annual income of a family is $25 a year, 80 per cent of the revenue is still demanded by the Imperial Government. With the 20 per cent left, the Indian Congress cannot work miracles for a people bled white to supply the 80 per cent. Yet if it does not work miracles, it is to be judged as incapable.

Also, in these states the final word on every law is still to be that of the Imperial Government. And in these states, the army is still entirely in the control of the Imperial Government. The Imperial Government remains as totalitarian as ever, since its power to enforce its will is almost absolute. Recently it has been announced that Burma will be granted greater freedom after the war. If 50,000,000 in Burma, why not 350,000,000 in India? Or is Britain less sure of Burma, and Burma less remunerative? Or is the cooperation of the Burmese essential to the recovery of Singapore?

Black West Africa remembers when the government of Queen Victoria promised independence and self-rule to the African Crown colonies. One hundred years later, ten British Crown colonies in Africa were still ruled through governors and legislative councils. The governor is appointed by the Colonial Office in England, where the Natives of the colony have no voice and little influence. The legislative councils are nominated by the governors and advise him; but the governor need not follow their advice, and himself makes and enforces the laws and interprets them through judges whom he appoints.

Much has been made of the fact that in some of these colonies there are elected members in the legislative council; but these elected members form usually a minority, and even when they form a majority, they can only advise, not legislate or enforce. In the ten colonies mentioned there are altogether 169 members of legislative councils, of which 131 are ex-officio or nominated members. Of elected members there are only 41 in five colonies, and of these, 24 are whites elected in Kenya and Northern Rhodesia; in several other colonies there are no elected members at all. Moreover, in all these councils, industry is represented directly by delegates from the industrial corporations working in the colony, and these corporations, centered in England, exercise there large and decisive power upon Parliament and the Colonial Office.

Much has been made in England of the policy of "Indirect Rule," which has been advertised as a school of self-government for the natives. This is not necessarily so. Indirect Rule is a method of leaving as wide opportunity to local government, according to ancient native cultural patterns, as is compatible with imperial aims. In this way it would, to be sure, be quite possible to guide the native state gradually toward larger and larger control of its political and social life and toward independence. In no region of indirect control has there been any indication of continuous progress to these ends. Under strong and benevolent governors like Guggenheim on the West Coast and Cameron on the East, there has been considerable progress. But in no case has this progress been allowed to interfere with the controlling interests of industry and foreign investment. Britain gave no political protection to the Natives of South Africa when they were incorporated into the new Union, and but little in the Rhodesias. In the remaining protectorates, and in Kenya, she has repeatedly retreated before landlords and investors.

In the West Indies continued agitation during the last fifty years is beginning to show results. Jamaica, after being deprived of effective representative government since 1855, has today a new constitution; but its democratic possibilities are under limitation and control backed by the governor's irresponsible veto, and right of independent legislation. Other English colonies are even less fortunate.

The French colonial system has always in theory contemplated the eventual incorporation of Africans into the French state. This has not had much practical effect. In 1936, there were less than 100,000 black French citizens in all Africa. There are four African Natives on the administrative council which advises the Governor-General of French Equatorial Africa. In the other French colonies a few Africans are members of these councils. In Senegal alone do the Africans have a decisive place in government, and some 80,000 vote. In that colony, three-fourths of the members of the colonial council are Africans. On the other hand, the mass of Africans in French colonies have little voice in government, although the new colonial policy as laid down by De Gaulle and Eboué looks toward distinct improvement in this respect.

Portugal for years made her colonial policy subservient to the South African demand for labor in the mines. At the same time, in theory she granted political freedom and privilege to the Natives without discrimination. Finally, in 1938, colonial status was recognized, with stronger legislation and the colonies bound more closely to the Portuguese home government; but in practice the theory has as yet hardly worked. There is, however, a minimum of race discrimination in Portuguese colonies, and racial admixture goes on.

Belgium has no colonial policy designed to elevate the political status of the native population. She has trained the natives for industry, but not for independent life. As an industrial policy she has paid attention to their health and to village economy, and the great industrial organizations have many paternalistic policies. Large corporations like the British Lever Brothers, the Huileries du Congo Belge, and the Sucrière Congolaise have few restrictions upon their control which cannot be arranged to their advantage; the economic development is still largely a matter of compulsion. The Belgians have never made a statement concerning the ultimate end of their colonial policy.

In Asia, under The Netherlands the peoples of Indonesia have been given some advisory part in government, although native demands for greater freedom have been ruthlessly suppressed. There is no persecution of half-castes, as in British India, and intermarriage is legal. More effective partnership is forecast between the colonies and the mother country, without discrimination as to race or nationality. But this is a postwar plan, and much depends on how far the poverty and destruction in Holland will allow political freedom and industrial planning for the Natives to proceed in East Asia at the expense of Dutch investors.

Under governmental policies like this, colonies are being developed and industrialized, and to many this seems the logical solution to the colonial question. But is it? For whose benefit do industry and commerce invade Asia and Africa? For the benefit of the colonial power, or for the benefit of the Natives? This can be judged, certainly in part, by the wages paid native labor. These wages are low, varying from 25 to 75 cents a day; they are low even when they come into direct competition with European and American labor. They constitute the main cause of poverty in colonies. When the native economy is broken up, land sequestered, and tribal communism destroyed, the only recourse of the Native is to this poverty wage.

In the American colony of Puerto Rico, Diffie says that

> all available land is being taken by the sugar barons. The oriental coolie laborer is obliged to spend 90 per cent of what he makes on food and the European laborer 80 per cent; while the native Puerto Rican is obliged to spend 94 per cent, leaving only 6 per cent for all the other essentials. . . .
>
> More than 40,000 women and children are working under sweat shop conditions, working on embroidery, at a wage which fluctuates between 15 and 25 cents a day. . . . To earn two dollars a week not less than sixty hours' work every six days is necessary. In 1889 (at the time the United States took possession) 17 per cent of the male population was unemployed. Bonds issued by the Puerto Rican Government (that is by the United States Government in Puerto Rico) amounted in 1930 to approximately $50,000,000. These bonds are held in the United States, and American investors realize an annual income of more than $2,500,000 a year therefrom. The interest is paid by the Puerto Ricans, who also pay the enormous salaries given to Americans. The absentee owners in the United States evade the greater part of the taxation which supplies this money, leaving it to the starving to pay.[2]

Sugar is almost entirely absentee-controlled. Tobacco is 95 per cent absentee-controlled; banks, 60 per cent; railroads, 60 per cent; public utilities, 50 per cent; and steamship lines, approximately 100 per cent. So that the dollars which on paper appear to give Puerto Rico a favorable trade balance are dollars which are never seen in Puerto Rico, but are given by the banks to the absentee holders of shares in industry.

The pay of African native laborers is often as low as 1 shilling a day; seldom, even in skilled labor, does the wage reach 2 or 3 shillings. Moreover, since labor thus remunerated does not attract laborers, contract and forced labor still exist widely in Africa, not only as a legacy of slavery and the slave trade but as a policy of twentieth-century industry.

War has increased labor conscription. At the end of March 1943, 16,000 Africans were conscripted in Kenya for forced labor by private employers. In Nigeria, 14,000 out of 70,000 workers in the tin mines were conscripted; and in Tanganyika the number of conscripts varied from 5,000 to 18,000.

Efforts by native workers to improve their condition through unionization have naturally been frowned on. They have led to the imprisonment of workers in West Africa, to strikes in the copper mines of Central Africa, to riots in the Caribbean area, and to the successful attempt in Southern Rhodesia and the Union of South Africa to protect union white labor and outlaw native unions. The report of the Institute of Intellectual Co-operation in 1939 said,

> With some notable exceptions, the importance of labour policy in colonial administration has only begun to receive more than grudging recognition by colonial ministries and local governments during the last two decades. Even now, as recent events have brought only too clearly to notice, labour problems are sometimes disregarded until they lead to open troubles. As long as labour was docile and plentiful, the tendency in many colonial areas was to leave in operation that policy of

laissez faire which had been largely abandoned in industrial relations in the home countries.[3]

The labor policies of Africa have disrupted the home life of the Natives, and the tribal organization. In some sections from 32 per cent to 55 per cent of the men have to leave home periodically in mass migrations to the mining areas and other centers of work in order to raise the poll taxes laid upon them.

The colonies, then, are poor. They know poverty such as has long disappeared from civilized areas. There are statistics which show that between 1800 and 1825 there were famines in India in which 1,000,000 persons were starved to death. The British Parliament took charge of India in 1813, and between 1875 and 1900 there were famines in which 15,000,000 Indians were starved to death. A thousand million Asiatics receive a real wage of less than $1 a week.

This poverty has been increased by the extraordinary stealing of colonial land. Just as in the later Middle Ages in Europe seizure of the land forced the peasants into wage labor at low rates, so in Africa and elsewhere there is systematic effort to deprive the native of his land. In the Union of South Africa, the Europeans, forming only 20 per cent of the population, and of these only one-third living on farms, control 87 per cent of the land; the natives, forming 80 per cent of the population, have less than 13 per cent of the land. This situation exists even after long and repeated effort to better native land conditions.

In Southern Rhodesia, 60,000 Europeans have 47,000,000 acres of the best land, leaving 21,000,000 acres as reserves for 1,500,000 natives, and of these 17,000,000 acres may be given to whites. In Kenya less than 2,000 Europeans hold 4,500,000 acres of the best farm land in the country, which was practically given to them, and only 11 per cent of this is under cultivation. The native reserves are so crowded that in some places there is a density of 145 and even 283 persons per square mile.

Under these circumstances, native contribution toward social services is almost impossible. Recently the British Government allocated £5,000,000 annually for ten years as permissible expenditure for social services in the colonies—in agriculture, education, health, and housing. Some actual appropriations have been made. But it must be remembered that private investments in these colonies at that time reached a total of £250,000,000, in addition to £120,000,000 in public investment. The Natives would need increased ownership of capital, which their poverty cannot now afford, and increased political power of taxation of foreign industry, which they do not have, to begin anything like adequate social service among themselves.

The result is that little is done for the development of possible democracy through education. It is ostentatiously pointed out that democracy is impossible in Africa, Asia, and many parts of the Caribbean because the people are too ignorant. This ignorance cannot be corrected by education because education is too costly. The possibility of paying for education and other social services is precluded by land sequestration and low wages. Here you have the perfect logical circle.

On the other hand, some education has been furnished, principally by the missionaries. The missionaries were not trained in modern business; they were economically illiterate; they were the easy prey of industry and commerce, who used them to open the way for forced labor and land theft. But from the time of the Protestant Reformation through the era of political reform in England and revolution in France, the missionaries did believe in education, and they carried that belief to Africa and Asia. They started schools; and industry, although it tried, was unsuccessful in closing them. The Foreign Missions Conference of North America declares that in Africa it is estimated today that 85 per cent of the educational load is still carried by Christian missions, the government controlled by invested capital furnishing less than 15 per cent.

The compromise reached was approached by means of agreement as to what kind of education should be given and who should meet the cost. The governments for the most part do not spend on education today as much as they raise from native poverty by taxation. Education in Africa and higher training in Asia are supported largely by charitable dole, and the education given is often limited to elementary and technical education, as in the Belgian Congo, which deprives the native of modern leadership in teaching and medical and social development, but is building a middle class of skilled workers. Only one child in twelve is today receiving primary school training. In some colonies education is emphasizing class differences by giving special training only to chiefs' sons and thus erecting a social aristocracy; in other areas, effort is being made to confine native education to vernacular tongues, which will keep the natives from knowledge of modern literature and modern cultural patterns. The result of this is a sudden interest of industry in the preservation of native culture, which imperial policy has done everything to ruin for three centuries.

In one respect, much has been done for the natives of the colonies, and that is in health and sanitation; but this is primarily a matter of self-defense in order to preserve the life and health of the resident whites. The latter not only seize the healthy regions of Freetown and Kenya and the hills of India for residence, but provide careful study of tropical diseases and tropical medicine and some medical practitioners. But here again they face the paradox: If there is to be a sufficient number of physicians and nurses in colonies, a native professional class must be trained. To train such a class means education, and careful education, for a large number of natives. This is not available and the results of education are feared. We have therefore in the Union of South Africa and in the Belgian Congo only limited training for Negroes as physicians and nurses, because facilities are not provided and are being only partially planned.

As a result of all these reasons and movements between 1913 and 1939, rudimentary education was extended in the colonies; primary instruction was almost universal in the American Philippine Islands, and was general in Malaya, Burma, and the Netherlands East Indies. In the Caribbean area, primary education has become widespread, and in American dependencies compulsory. Yet with all this, as the 1944 conclusions of the International Labor Office say of the school reports:

> Only limited inferences can be drawn from them, since they represent mainly the nominal enrolment of children at elementary schools. The quality of the education varied widely. There were often neither the trained teachers nor the schools to

provide for, still less to extend, the total numbers enrolled. In Puerto Rico, to cite one example, buildings and teachers only sufficed for one half of the child population, and a classroom with one book for every two pupils was considered fortunate. Progress had been accomplished, substantial in the number of children touched by school training, but ignorance and frustration were wide spread, for the schooling, such as it was, had little relation to the lives of the people.[4]

Perhaps the greatest disaster that the colonial system has brought to primitive peoples is the ruthless and ignorant destruction of their cultural patterns. Family life has been disrupted, women have been violated, children corrupted and freed of control, political organization overthrown, property ownership and control overridden, and the whole of the primitive life caricatured and made mock of. Only in recent days have scientists called to the attention of the world the values of primitive culture—the fact that in many respects these ways of living have solved social difficulties better than civilized lands have been able to do.

Something has been rescued of African art, of Asiatic religion; but so long as colonial exploitation is looked upon as a necessity despite all its cost, just so long the development of human progress in colonial areas will be frustrated and misled. Today especially, when we face the problem of war, we have to remember that war has not brought peace to the colonies. As Anna Graves writes: "Colonialism has been the cause of still more deaths than have wars in their active phases in Europe and North America."[5] Marcel Sauvage says: "French Equatorial Africa had at the beginning of the century twenty million inhabitants. She had only eight million in 1920–31. . . . Today [1934] after a mortality due to an increase in the great colonial maladies, to a murderous extension of roads and railroads, to a badly understood exploitation, to famines, to lack of care, to emigrations . . . A.E.F. possesses no more than three millions, scarcely three millions, scattered over a territory five times the extent of France."[6] In Kenya during the First World War, fourteen thousand natives were enrolled as fighters and one hundred and fifty thousand as porters and stevedores. Of these black men, 1,743 were killed and 44,875 died of disease—a total loss of 46,618, which is greater than any loss through tribal wars for generations. The relatives of most of these dead men have never been traced and there was in 1924 a balance of pay and wages due them unclaimed, amounting to $775,000.[7]

What is the reason for this? We may look first at colonial history. The earliest colonists were merchants and adventurers who went out from the mother city for trade and adventure; who became little centers of cultural dissemination, associated with native populations, until at last states grew which dominated the native populations with migrant masters and yet interfered little with these peoples, save to tax them and to require some submission to general laws. This culminated in the Roman Empire, and when that vast government of men fell apart, individual nations arose the world over, independent and coming in contact with each other only through trade and travel, with little or no foreign conquest.

The trade with India and the discovery of America changed this. India and early America furnished wealth which was brutally stolen by foreign peoples, and native power to resist was so reduced that vast regions became colonies. This new wealth was invested in the degradation of black labor through the African slave trade, in order to raise new crops in world-wide demand—tobacco, sugar, and cotton. New machines and techniques to process these materials made the Industrial Revolution. A new colonial era dawned upon the world. The people in the colonies sifted themselves into three sorts: the representatives of the mother country settled there for the most part temporarily for the one purpose of gain; other persons from the mother country fleeing to the colony as fugitives seeking intellectual and economic freedom; others stolen and transported to the colonies as slaves and indentured servants.

The fugitives and the indentured servants were despised and discriminated against, but the height of legal discrimination fell upon the Negro and other colored slaves. Then came the great era of investment, when the reason for the colony was not settlement but foreign profit, and during which the institution of slavery was rebuilt and revivified in the modern world.

All this was quickly rationalized. It is the habit of men, and must be if they remain rational beings, to find reasons, and comforting reasons, for lines of action which they adopt from varying motives. First of all, religion rationalized slavery as a method of saving souls, but this bade fair to interfere with profit and investment and soon was changed by the new science to a doctrine of natural human inferiority on the part of the majority of mankind, making them forever inferior and subservient to the ruling nations of the world.

The doctrine of the "White Man's Burden" appeared. The motive behind this burden-bearing was income: first wealth, such as gold, silver, and jewels; then profit from the crops raised by slaves; then markets wherein goods processed at home from these crops could be sold for new materials; then lands and native labor in which capital could be invested for larger profit than at home.

Much has been said, for instance, of the fact that colonies do not pay the mother country, in the sense that usually the direct payments of the mother country to the colony exceeds the money returns of the colony to the country which owns it. This is true today, although in the sixteenth century it was not true. In the fifteenth and sixteenth centuries, the object of colonial territory was the direct returns in gold, silver, jewels, and luxuries. Why, then, does the mother country today not only wish to retain the colonies but also is willing to fight expensive wars for such retention and for increasing the colonial area? The answer to this question has often been that raw material in colonial regions is of such value that countries must control it in order to retain their "place in the sun." This was true in the eighteenth century, when cotton, sugar, tobacco, were the monopolies of empires owning colonies which raised these materials. But here again this was once true but is not universally true today. It has been shown recently that only 3 per cent of the more valuable raw materials of the world are in colonial areas. Still empires want colonies.

The answer to all this seeming paradox is the fact that colonies are today areas for the investment of capital in which the investor can make a rate of profit far beyond that which comes to him from domestic ventures. Profit in home industry is being increasingly limited by organized labor; by the demand for higher wages and shorter hours; by limitation of the labor of children and women; and by other devices for diverting the profit of the investor and property-owner to the income of the wage-earner. Much accumulated wealth lies idle at home.

On the other hand, in colonial regions not only is there opportunity for investment, but the investor is part of the government or has large influence with the government, and can secure labor at the lowest wage and for the longest hours; he can evade taxation and profit-limiting legislation. American investors in Puerto Rico during recent years have received dividends of 6 to 100 per cent on their investments. Not only that, but the investor can often put upon the shoulders of taxpayers at home in the name of "Empire" colonial payments and improvements, especially in long-term investments such as roads and harbors, which will increase his profit.

Many unnoticed facts prove this thesis. The great Lever Brothers organization, which dominates the economic life of West Africa, announces that the net profits of their enterprises there after paying heavy taxes amounted in 1943 to $26,000,000, which was divided between 200,000 stockholders in Europe. This involved the labor of many millions of Africans at less than 50 cents a day. The British Government took over during the war the cocoa-raising industry of 800,000 farms on the Gold Coast, West Africa; and from 1939 to 1943 made a net profit of $1,200,000, while the black farmers fought bankruptcy. The head of the government cocoa-marketing board was John Cadbury, one of the greatest chocolate manufacturers of England. This body fixed prices without competition. This profit may be used for social purposes on the Gold Coast but if it is British industry will be the judge.

Today, when the use of industrial diamonds is necessary to the war effort, it is interesting to know that in 1939 the De Beers organization was buying material due to cheap black labor in the Belgian Congo at 7 cents a carat and selling it for 80 cents. The price has dropped today, but it still stands at monopoly heights.

One of the most powerful cartels in Europe, the Société Générale de Belgique, collaborated with the Germans during the occupation and sold to the United Nations Belgian products, including industrial diamonds, cobalt, and radium, not to mention copper and rubber. The director of the Netherlands East India Rubber Institute is leaving for Australia to organize plans for the rehabilitation of the rubber industry in the liberated parts of the East Indies. He has funds available for the equipment and production of 25 per cent of the rubber resources of the Indies. When Queen Wilhelmina calls for a constitutional assembly after the war with full colonial participation, how far will Dutch investors allow these people to interfere with the profits of investment?

Under the covenant of the Versailles Treaty, the West African Cameroons became "a sacred trust of civilization," the largest part of which was transferred to Britain. The British auctioned fifty German estates, comprising 258,000 acres, to their former German holders, who were the only ones able to bid, and these got back their properties for a fraction of their real value. These estates are worked by Negro labor at the average pay of 1 shilling a day.

War and depression wreaked more havoc on colonial labor than on labor at home. The International Labor Office reports in 1944 that in colonies

the 1919–39 period proved the importance of the external aspects of economic policy. It showed the growing dependence of colonial social progress on world economic conditions, while the transition of colonial life and labour under the influence of the penetrating economic forces was complicated by the uncontrollable changes in these forces.

All was changed by the depression. So long as trade was on the whole expanding, the increasing integration of dependent territories in a world of imperial economy promised increasing financial resources for the development of social services and opportunities to remedy any lack of balance as between educational, public health and other forms of progress. With the collapse of markets from 1929, however, the weakness of the whole colonial situation was betrayed.

It became abundantly clear that a system, whereby the whole country was being wrecked economically through outside influences, could not be permitted to continue without radical modifications and it was also quite evident that the economic basis of society was much too narrow. When the hard-pressed estates in their fight for existence fired many thousands of workers, screwed down wages sometimes to below subsistence level, and repudiated on a large scale agreements with the Indonesian small holders for the lease of land, profiteering unduly from the typical Indonesian reluctance to hold a man to an unfavourable contract; when rice prices on which millions of Indonesian farmers depended, dropped steeply in sympathy with foreign cereals; when a shipping company got into difficulties and railroads failed to meet their obligations; when imports shrank and the regular buyers of our commodities in Europe became restless, because we could no longer afford their industrial products; when Japan, disguised as a blessing, flooded the country with cheap textiles, threatening to annihilate the young local weaving industry; when Government revenues became so meagre that the most essential health, welfare, educational, technical services had to be cut down to below a bare minimum, then there was a sharp reaction of public opinion. And when the play of free enterprise in these years developed into a death struggle for the survival of the fittest, bleeding the community white, while Government, according to the traditions of "laissez faire" had to remain a passive on-looker, there grew a general realisation that the system in its pre–World War I form had had its day and that it was the bounden duty of the Administration to intervene and to take over the supreme control of the country's economy.[8]

The whole economic situation in colonies is but imperfectly known. Professor Frankel estimates that down to the close of 1934, £1,222,000,000 had been invested by foreigners in capital enterprises in Africa south of the Sahara. Forty-three per cent of this went to the Union of South Africa and 55 per cent to British territory. Next to the British territories, the Belgian Congo received £143,000,000 and French Africa £70,000,000, Portuguese territories about £67,000,000.[9]

The diamond mines of South Africa between 1886 and 1934 paid £80,000,000 in dividends on an investment of £20,000,000; but how much of this £20,000,000 represented actual wealth and not stock dividends and speculation will never be known. Frankel believes that average investment in Africa received but moderate returns; but amid speculation, gambling, cheating and force, the expected gain is more potent than occasional loss. Indeed investments in American and English industry have not only averaged less than 4 per cent but even represent a loss. But there is no meaning in the word "average" in this case. What is of importance is that returns on investment in American and English industry have been in a sufficient number of actual cases so steady that they are the basis of our whole industrial organization. This, of course, is true in the colonies, but there is another truth there. The returns of investment which depend upon labor and raw material raised by labor may be very small on paper, because of low wages and prices deliberately kept down; but on the other hand, the processing of this material and its transportation have yielded correspondingly higher returns, although these profits are not credited to colonial investment. Herein lies the secret of the lure of investments in colonies. The actual profit was so high that in the twentieth century, long-term foreign investments by British, French, German, and American capital increased from £4,642,000,000 in 1900 to £7,770,000,000 in 1929; of this, three-fourths was sent to colonial and quasi-colonial territory.

We append one illustration of actual investment:

The 1937 income and expenditures of the Copper Industry in Northern Rhodesia, under European control, read as follows:

INCOME		EXPENDITURES	
Copper exported	£12,000,000	1. Dividends	£5,000,000
		2. Royalties	500,000
		3. Income tax	700,000
		4. Salaries of 1,690 Europeans	800,000
		5. Wages of 17,000 Africans	244,000
		6. Balance (other costs of operation, maintenance, stores, freight, insurance, etc.)	4,756,000

(1) The entire output of copper for the year 1937 in Northern Rhodesia was sold outside the country and it yielded twelve million pounds. (2) Five million pounds of this sum went to share-holders as dividends, and not one of these shareholders was an African—nor was the money spent in or for Matabele. (3) One-half million was paid as royalty, not to the inhabitants of Matabele, but to the British South African Company because of the so-called treaty by which Lewanika, an African King, transferred the ownership of the minerals in this area to the Company. (4) Eight hundred thousand pounds of this money went in payment of the salary of sixteen hundred and ninety Europeans, *approximately five thousand pounds per person;* two hundred and forty-four thousand pounds went to the wages of seventeen thousand Africans, *which approximates fourteen pounds per person.*

In short, it means that of the twelve million pounds accruing from the copper industry of Northern Rhodesia, the inhabitants thereof, the legitimate owners of the land, got only one-quarter of a million pounds, while the balance of four and a half million pounds went to the imperialists.[10]

With this mere sketch of the meaning of colonialism today, let us now pause to see what the imperial setup between the First World War and the Second became.

We note in that period six imperial powers. Naming them in the order of the number of people which they dominated, they were: first, Britain, who has in her colonies (not counting the autonomous regions like Canada, Australia, and New Zealand) 495,000,000 persons ruled by the 50,000,000 in the United Kingdom, including the 2,000,000 whites in the Union of South Africa. Second comes Japan, where before the present war 73,000,000 in Japan proper ruled 80,000,000, including the disputed Chinese territory of Manchukuo. Next France, where 38,000,000 ruled 71,000,000. Then comes The Netherlands, where 9,000,000 ruled 67,000,000. Then the United States of America, where 130,000,000 ruled 19,000,000, including the inhabitants of Alaska and the Philippines. Finally comes Belgium, where 8,500,000 ruled 10,500,000 in the Belgian Congo, and Portugal, where 7,000,000 rule 10,000,000.

Another way of listing these colonials would be to take into account the disproportion between the numbers of the ruling class and of those ruled. This would put the British Empire again first, with each British subject ruling ten colonials. Next would come The Netherlands, where each Dutch citizen rules between eight and nine colonials. In France, a citizen rules something less than two colonials; in Japan and Belgium he rules a little more than one. The United States and Spain are the only imperial powers where the number of colonials ruled is very much smaller than the number of citizens, amounting for the United States to over six rulers to one ruled; and for Spain, twenty-six to one.

Of course mere numbers do not give the whole picture. A much more revealing study would give the extent and kind of land and the value of the materials furnished. Beyond this we need, and have never had, a very careful study of the industrial and financial arrangements of colonial organization: just what has been actually invested and by whom; how the invested wealth has been used in the colony; what has been the rate of profit, and the wages paid; and how far the investment has helped the colony by taxation. By manipulation of investment figures, it has been rather easy in the past to argue that the rate of return for colonial investment has been low and the profit to the colonial peoples high. But such factual studies are absolutely disproved; first, by the astonishing way in which capital investment has poured into the colonies; and second, by the fact that the colonial peoples almost without exception have the lowest standard of living on earth, with the fewest social services for education, health, and other means of social uplift, and almost no chance to participate in government or even to voice their complaints in an orderly manner. In colonies today millions of normal human beings are deliberately held in poverty and ignorance by force and fraud, because of the often conscientious belief on the part of their masters that no other condition is either possible or desirable for colonial peoples.

A century ago the explanation of this whole development was clear, and it was something like this: You had in the world a minority of people who were capable of civilization, who by their inherent gifts and long and difficult trial and experience were the natural rulers of the world. They composed most of the white peoples of the world, although even among those peoples there was a certain proportion of the "lower classes" who were incapable, because of deficiency in natural gifts, of taking effective part in democracy.

On the other hand, the majority of the people of the world, consisting mainly of the brown, yellow, and black races, were naturally so inferior that it was not to be hoped that in any reasonable time, if ever, they would be capable of self-government. This was supposed to be proved by their history, and current scientific investigation seemed to back up historical judgment.

Since the beginning of the twentieth century there has come great change in these judgments. In the first place, we have practically given up the idea that there is any considerable portion of the civilized peoples who cannot by education and by the training of experience be made into effective voters and administrators in democratic governments. Further than this, we are not nearly so sure today as we used to be of the inherent inferiority of the majority of the people of the earth who happen to be colored. We know, of course, that skin color itself has no particular significance, and the other physical characteristics, whatever their significance, are not certain indications of inferiority.

The testimony of history we naturally realize is not decisive. History has been written deliberately to emphasize the accomplishments of certain peoples and to decry or omit the work of other peoples. It is always astonishing for Americans to contrast the history of the Revolutionary War as set down in English and American textbooks.

In addition to that, the testimony of biology and anthropology and of various social studies convinces us more and more that absolute and essential differences between races as self-perpetuating groups are difficult to fix, if not nonexistent. And that consequently we have no way of being certain that education and experience will not do for the backward races of man what it has already begun to do for the depressed classes in civilized states.

But these facts do not affect our actions today, because government and economic organization have already built a tremendous financial structure upon the nineteenth-century conception of race inferiority. This is what the imperialism of our day means.

Not until we face the fact that colonies are a method of investment yielding unusual returns, or expected to do so, will we realize that the colonial system is a part of the battle between capital and labor in the modern economy. This profit has been the foundation of much of modern wealth, luxury, and power; and the envious competition to dominate colonial fields of industrial enterprise led to the First World War and was a prime cause of the Second World War. Its vicious influence was attacked by the legislation which established the Mandates Commission in the League of Nations; but this proved abortive, because that Commission was denied all real power.

Attempted sanctions against Italy at the beginning of the Second World War again failed, because of the sympathy which her colonial ambitions aroused in England, France, and the United States. Then arose another phase of colonial competition: Japan was determined to supplant Europe as the chief exploiter of Asiatic labor and materials. Thus a new and vaster social problem in the guise of world race rivalry in Asiatic investment came into the picture, and remains there threateningly today.

The depressed standards of living in colonial areas, the poverty, disease, and ignorance, are an enduring threat to civilization, backed by the insatiable demand for high profit in commerce and industry. The world wails with Conrad Aiken,

It is a sound of everlasting grief,
The sound of weeping,
The sound of disaster and misery,
The sound of passionate heartbreak at the centre of the world.[11]

After the Second World War we are going to be faced by an attempt to extend and reorganize the colonial system. Britain is going to insist upon her prewar colonial empire, including the mandated German territories and Chinese Hong Kong. Strong interests in the United States are going to ask for colonial outposts in the guise of defense stations throughout the Pacific and in the Caribbean area. France wants her colonies in Asia and her mandates returned; and a newly reformed and reborn Germany is bound to push the question of colonies again to the front.

This finds us today facing an unsettled problem, and a problem far greater than the number of people apparently involved might lead us to think. The colonial organization today is primarily economic. It is a method of carrying on industry and commerce and of distributing wealth. As such, it not only confines colonial people to a low standard of living, and encourages by reason of its high profit to investors a determined and interested belief in the inferiority of certain races, but it also affects the situation of the working classes and the minorities in civilized countries.

When, for instance, during and after this war the working people of Britain, The Netherlands, France, and Belgium, in particular, are going to demand certain costly social improvements from their governments—the prevention of unemployment, a rising standard of living, health insurance, increased education of children—the large cost of these improvements must be met by increased public taxation, falling with greater weight than ever heretofore upon the rich. This means that the temptation to recoup and balance the financial burden of increased taxation by investment in colonies, where social services are at their lowest and standards of living below the requirements of civilization, is going to increase decidedly; and the disposition of parties on the left, liberal parties, and philanthropy to press for colonial improvements will tend to be silenced by the bribe of vastly increased help by government to better conditions. The working people of the civilized world may thus be largely induced to put their political power behind imperialism, and democracy in Europe and America will continue to impede and nullify democracy in Asia and Africa.

In this way the modern world after this war may easily be lulled to sleep and forget that the exclusion of something between one-fourth and one-half of the whole population of the world from participation in democratic government and socialized wealth is a direct threat to the spread of democracy and a certain promise of future war—and of war not simply as justifiable revolt on the part of colonial peoples who are increasing in intelligence and efficiency, but also of recurring wars of envy and greed because of the present inequitable distribution of colonial gain among civilized nations.

Moreover, the continuation of the belief of vested interests in the theory of racial inferiority and their dislike of minorities of any sort will be encouraged by failure to face the problem of the future of colonies—the problem of those hundreds of millions of people on whom the world long has walked with careless and insolent feet.

NOTES

1. Quoted from a MS. letter sent to the officials of the N.A.A.C.P., October, 1944.
2. B. W. and J. W. Diffie, *Puerto Rico,* Vanguard Press, 1931, Chapters 4 and 8.
3. C. W. H. Weaver: *The Problem of Native Labour in Colonial Questions and Peace,* Paris, 1939, p. 220.
4. *Social Policy in Dependent Territories,* 1944, p. 5.
5. Anna Graves is a widely traveled student of social conditions much of whose valuable work is still in manuscript. The quotations from her writings used in this book are from her manuscript material, which she has kindly put at my disposal.
6. M. Sauvage, *Les Secrets de l'Afrique Noire,* Paris, 1937, pp. 20, 21.
7. *Cf.* N. Leys, *Kenya,* London, 1924, p. 287.
8. *Social Policies in Dependent Territories,* 1944, pp. 16, 17.
9. S. H. Frankel, *Capital Investment in Africa,* London, 1938, p. 170.
10. A. A. N. Orizu, *Without Bitterness,* New York, 1944, pp. 191, 193.
11. "Priapus and the Pool," quoted in Alfred Kreymborg, *Lyric America,* new ed., Tudor Publishing Company, 1925, p. 518.

CHAPTER III

◆

The Unfree Peoples

In addition to the some seven hundred and fifty millions of disfranchised colonial peoples there are more than a half-billion persons in nations and groups who are quasi-colonials and in no sense form free and independent states.

From Shanghai in 1936, I went down to the ghost capital of New China. Here on the flat alluvium of the Yangtze Kiang and between the great port of Shanghai dominated by Europe and the sea, New China was building a beautiful city. Some half-dozen of its marble palaces were finished and waiting. Eventually, without the difficulty and pain of ousting the foreigners from Shanghai, this new port would intercept and dominate the commerce between China and the world. But the city was still empty; the palaces were untenanted and the dream has not yet come true.

I was still in Shanghai when the northern Chinese war lords seized Chiang Kai-shek and made him fight Japan. I remember sitting with a group of Chinese leaders at lunch; there was the superintendent of the Chinese schools of the city, editors of leading papers, the president of a university supported by American funds, and various publicists and officials. I said to them tentatively that I could well understand the Chinese attitude toward Japan, its bitterness and determined opposition to the substitution of Asiatic for an European imperialism; but what I could not quite understand was the seemingly placid attitude of the Chinese toward Britain. That very day I had seen a little six-year-old Britisher order two Chinese children to walk in the gutter and they had silently complied. I had seen the race track where until 1912 no Chinese could be admitted; and I knew the shameful history of the determined and unrelenting aggression upon China by the British Empire and other European and American nations, beginning with the Opium War in 1839. China had been browbeaten, cheated, oppressed, and dominated until at the beginning of the twentieth century she was all but a colony or a series of colonies of European masters.

To this the Chinese made no reply. They talked long and informingly; they pointed out the fact that China was regaining her independence; Chinese customs were at last being controlled by the Chinese; Chinese currency had replaced foreign currency; and there were other like developments. They talked long, but they did not really answer my question.

All this reminds us again that there is something unreal in the almost ostentatious way in which China is being built up today as one of the world's great nations, destined to sit with Great Britain, Russia, the United States, and France as co-ruler of the world. This development is devoutly to be wished. The contribution of Chinese culture to the world has been splendid and peculiar. Here is a nation that accomplished peace to a greater degree than any other culture. I walked once in the Summer Palace, in that marvelously beautiful estate with lovely buildings, lakes, and gardens which the Empress Dowager laid out with moneys designed to establish a Chinese navy for defense against Europe. There was something splendid in this gesture of ignoring barbarism and aggression by building a supremely beautiful monument.

In the history of Chinese culture, there has been repeated retrogression and recovery; but there has always remained that fine central core of effective human progress. Given time and opportunity, China will again become great and powerful. For causes that are not far to seek, although perhaps difficult to evaluate, we all know that today China is broken and weak—poor and ignorant, torn by internal dissension and hag-ridden by graft and incompetence. But we know also that it is because of Japan rather than of China herself that she is being pushed forward in theory as the representative of Asiatic peoples and as promise of Western sincerity toward the yellow race. All this, lest the cry of Asia for the Asiatics make peace between East and West impossible.

Under such circumstances the situation is dangerous. The restoration of China can be accomplished most expeditiously only with Western capital and techniques, together with a policy of non-interference; that is, by a new philanthropic, industrial colonialism without imperial control. Especially, the object of the rebuilding of China cannot be mainly private profit for foreign investors. Can we hope for this? Can we hope that the chance for remunerative investment in Chinese cheap labor and rich natural resources will yield to the great object of establishing independence and autonomy in the East and peace on earth?

One fears not. Once fears that China, even though today she may be nominally recognized as among the leading nations, will not be allowed autonomy and will not be able to achieve freedom in our time. Great Britain, France, and the United States will have eyes fixed upon the wealth of China and her possibilities as a subject nation; and thus, like many another people, the Chinese will remain bound by debt, by commercial combines, and by monopoly industry in continued subjection to the great industrial nations of the West.

The phrase "free states" as used in the Dumbarton Oaks proposals is based upon the theory that the United Nations are predominantly democratic, with enjoyment in great degree of the Four Freedoms of President Roosevelt's interpretation of the Atlantic Charter. As a matter of fact, only a few nations of this world are free in this sense. There are many states which will sit in the General Assembly without having independent power.

Consider first the Free Commonwealths (Dominions) of the British Empire: Canada, Australia, New Zealand, and the Union of South Africa. Canada is dependent upon Britain for military and naval defense and for large investments in her land and resources. In Australia we have a group of white people corresponding in number to the inhabitants of the city of New York who dominate a land quite as large as the United States, though poorer in natural resources. They are deliberately holding this as a bastion to keep out the crowded and land-hungry millions of Asia; and to make it a point d'appui for the impact of Western power upon the East. Australia again is guarded not only by the British navy, but also by the American navy. She will sit among the free states of the United Nations, but she will not be free.

One country which has already been referred to stands out as an extraordinary case of paradox and deliberate confusion of thought—the Union of South Africa. Here a group of 2,000,000 whites absolutely dominates the lives and destinies of over 8,000,000 black natives, colored folk and Indians; and yet this country poses as one of the "free nations" fighting for "democracy." In truth, its whole internal economy is dominated by the enormous investment in gold, diamonds, copper, and other raw materials made by the businessmen of Britain and the United States. The integrity of the country has long been guaranteed by the British navy. The Union of South Africa will sit in the council of the United Nations, but its vote and policy will of necessity be dictated from without.

In all these Free Commonwealths, not only is there the domination of the physical force of the imperial army and navy, but the much more effective domination of debt, investment, and commercial monopoly; and also social ties with rewards and distinctions, with the prestige of being a British subject and occupying a position in many respects superior to other persons in the world. Canada, despite her strong economic ties with the United States, is held strongly in leash to Britain by such considerations.

The history of the rise and multiplication of the unfree nations is clear and logical, but seldom considered in proper perspective. The fall of the Roman Empire was the occasion for the rise of small separate countries in Europe. Nationalistic aims led to wars designed to increase the size of these nations and fix their boundaries. But these nationalistic wars soon changed in character and became wars in which the dominant element of each state tried to annex to their states areas and persons whose ownership would be to their advantage.

This was the genesis of imperialism, and at this stage the first modern empire, that of Spain, arose when the peoples and countries annexed were those which furnished gold and silver, jewels, and other materials for the dominant aristocracy of Spain. But the real modern imperialism arose when the state came more and more to be dominated by the owners of capital, who wished to use that capital for owning labor, raising material, and processing that material. It was at this stage that the British, French, American, and other empires arose.

When the Spanish Empire fell, the British Empire first, then the French, and finally the American tried to take her colonies and colonial labor. The Haitian revolt frustrated this by help twice at critical times which enabled Bolívar to make the revolt of South American nations against Spain successful. Out of that revolt there arose a group of nations nominally free, but bound by investment interests and continual danger of political conquest. We must therefore today regard as among those unfree nations such countries as Venezuela, Colombia, Ecuador, Peru, Bolivia, Chile, Uruguay, Paraguay, and the Argentine. These countries were threatened with annexation by Britain and later by France and the United States. Brazil also falls in this class, although her revolt came later and was against Portugal.

Britain and France were ruled out by the Monroe Doctrine, which was first a defensive measure but later became a measure back of which the United States tried to dominate the Caribbean, Central America, and South America. This explains the Mexican War and the repeated filibusters in Central America and the Caribbean by means of which slave power sought to establish a slave empire. Later the United States dominated Panama and browbeat other Central and South American countries, temporarily seized Haiti, took Puerto Rico and, partially, Cuba from Spain, and today has in mind taking over certain of the British West Indies. Political domination changed later to domination through invested capital, a stage in which we are today.

Britain succeeded in seizing parts of Central America and the Caribbean and a bit of South America and then turned to domination through invested capital. Anna Graves writes: "In 1934, I visited the gold mines at Moro Velho, in the state of Minas Gerais, Brazil. They are British owned. They are said to be the deepest mines in the world. The conditions are so appalling and the pay so little that it is said that every miner who does not die because of accident dies sooner or later of tuberculosis. I said to a manager who was showing us around, 'Suppose Brazil should have a Labour Government and minimum wage and maximum hour laws should be passed?' 'Oh,' he interrupted, 'that would not affect us.'"[1]

France seized a few of the Caribbean islands, tried to stem the Haitian revolt and to annex the Mississippi Valley. She made her last bid under the third Napoleon to dominate Mexico.

To turn now to Asia, the idea of making China into a series of colonies like India was given up because of the rise of Japan. China thereupon began to assert herself as a free nation in the early part of the twentieth century, but was hindered by Japan, who conceived the idea of dominating Asia as an imperial master. Consequently the development of nations even partially free in Asia waits on the conclusion of this war.

In Africa there has been similar development. England seized Egypt and South and West Africa, but was repulsed by Abyssinia (later Ethiopia). Thus Abyssinia rose to be one of the partially free nations. But England was beaten back by colonial revolt under the Mahdi in the Sudan, and urged Italy to conquer Abyssinia. Italy failed, but she was encouraged to repeat the effort after the First World War, and her attempt precipitated the Second World War. Ethiopia was hailed as the first of the captive nations to be freed. Then followed an extraordinary conspiracy. The Union of South Africa and Kenya seek to dominate Ethiopia. England seeks to reduce it to a "sphere of influence" by seizing Ethiopia's seaports and getting control of her natural resources. The result is not yet evident, but Ethiopia is certainly not free.

On the African West Coast we have a number of powerful Negro nations; but the total colonization of the coast has been hindered by the persistence of tiny Liberia, so that France and England have had to give way to American commercial interests. Today partially free nations like Nigeria, the Gold Coast, and Sierra Leone are striving for recognition but are still under the colonial status; while in North Africa, Algeria, Tunisia, and Morocco are also semi-free colonies. It is in this way that in the Americas, Asia, and Africa, partially free nations have arisen, some of which come under the designation of free states as understood at Dumbarton Oaks.

On the other hand, within the imperial nations, the status of the colonies has been determined largely by the attitude of the mass of the working people, whereas in Spain, where workers were disfranchised and had little power, colonial labor conditions prevailed even in the mother country. In the British Empire colonialism could be carried through only when it was applied to alien peoples and not to white people, especially those of English descent. The growing home vote vetoed this. In the United States fear of European aggression was back of the Monroe Doctrine, but later the doctrine was continued as the white laborers tried to establish in the United States and under American control outside the United States, colonial labor conditions bordering on slavery. They were following unconsciously the later labor patterns adopted by the Union of South Africa. Today the American Federation of Labor, with its exclusion of Negro members in many of the powerful unions, is still following that pattern, and this is the reason that the AFL will not make common cause with Russian labor. The CIO is trying to recognize depressed labor in the United States and in colonial areas dominated by the United States, as part of the national labor problem. The Labor party in England, while giving theoretical assent to this attitude, has never had the courage to follow it up with action.

Egypt today is still partly under the domination of England and will be so long as her army is under British control and so long as the richest of her provinces, like the Sudan, are under British condominium. "In 1936, there was an Anglo-Egyptian Treaty of Alliance signed in London. According to the terms of the treaty, England was allowed to maintain for twenty years a military force up to 10,000 men and 400 airplanes at the Suez Canal 'till such time as Egypt could build up a force sufficiently powerful to take over such duties.' The British were also allowed to use Alexandria and Port Said as naval bases, and their troops could be moved over Egyptian territory."[2]

Egypt has had a long history of aggression from investing countries, and is perhaps one of the typical examples of European investments being made in such a way and of such kind and by such methods that the country practically loses all political and economic freedom. Much of that debt control still remains in water development and railway ownership.

Along with that we may consider the promises of freedom to certain countries: to the Arabs of the Middle East and to Palestine. One has only to read of the chagrin and despair of Lawrence when a promise of Arabian freedom turned into further experiment in imperialism; or the history of Balfour's promise of a homeland to the Jews. As Freda Kirchwey writes:

Palestine was not the intellectual creation of persons searching, objectively, for a solution of the specific problems of Jewish minorities. It was much more truly an organic outgrowth of that problem. . . . To a western mind, all the old difficulties still obstructed the road, and do today: the political problem of reconciling a Jewish National Home with the political expediencies of British imperial ambitions; the problem of Arab-Jewish relationships, both as part of the political problem and as part of the social-religious complex of the Middle East; the internal Jewish problem, bound up in the divergencies of opinion and of interests in Europe and the West. These are complicated enough to afford the subject matter for endless arguments, to create international controversies and partisan divisions. But they become relatively simple if they are viewed in the light of a warm yet realistic understanding of all the human needs involved.[3]

In the Balkans are 60,000,000 persons in the "free states" of Hungary, Romania, Bulgaria, Yugoslavia, Albania, and Greece. They form in the mass an ignorant, poor, and sick people, over whom already Europe is planning "spheres of influence."

Even greater is the pressure upon negroid nations, a pressure which depends not simply upon investment and prospective investment in Ethiopia, Haiti, Liberia, and the Dominican Republic, but even more than that upon deliberate and persistent propaganda. It has for years been the unquestioned dictum of literature and history that the inferiority of Negroes could be proved by the failure of efforts like those of these countries to establish independent nations. As proof of this, the world has long asserted that the attempts of Liberia, Haiti, and even Ethiopia to be progressive independent nations have utterly failed. Yet this is no proof of inferiority in ability, but only one of weakness before greater and organized force. The proof of this is easily adduced: Liberia for a century has had to fight first the natives for a foothold on the continent and has then been browbeaten and held in leash and coerced by Great Britain and France and now by the United States. For a hundred years Britain, France, and Italy have oppressed and outmaneuvered Ethiopia. The freeing of Ethiopia by British and Ethiopian troops was hailed by Churchill as the beginning of the fall of Fascism; and yet Great Britain today by treaty and military pressure is seeking to deprive Ethiopia of territory, seaport, and independent action. The rise of Haiti has been a splendid triumph of unlettered slaves against the world. History has no parallel of equal accomplishment. Haiti needs today only freedom from unjustly imposed American debt, and from industrial fetters laid upon her agriculture and commerce, to prove again to the world her ability and progress.

Even the freer small nations were unhappy and apprehensive under the League of Nations, and perhaps will be more so under the United Nations. Holland and Belgium are deeply intertwined with the industrial organization of Britain; France was partly subservient to the industry of Germany. All South America is a fief in the feudal organization of the modern organization and power from without, which varies from domination of the tin mines of Bolivia and the petroleum of Venezuela to that of the cattle and coffee of Argentina and Brazil. As Sumner Welles has said recently: "The larger nations must not be permitted to set up spheres of influence 'behind a façade of world organization' and 'ride roughshod over the sovereign liberties of their small neighbors.' Many of the smaller nations," he declared, "were profoundly concerned by some recent developments." He asserted that they had obtained as yet "no satisfactory assurance that as a result of the plans for world organization which were devised at Dumbarton Oaks they are going in fact to obtain the authority and the rights to which they believe themselves legitimately to be entitled."[4]

> One has only to look at a map of the world (not a mercator projection, which distorts relative size, making Greenland look as large as South America, India look tiny and Norway and Sweden monstrous.) One has only to look at a political map of the two hemispheres and cannot help but see who are the great grabbers of others' land and liberty and the great holders of others in chains. And even the pink and green on the world do not tell all, for south China and Egypt and Iraq, and Portugal and still more lands should be pink, too, if *practical* subjugation were recognized as what it really is. What colour should Cuba be?[5]

The situation in the Middle East—the oil of Iran, the subjugation of Syria, the unrest among the Arabs—is a serious threat to the possibility of maintaining peace after this war. As Walter Winchell said to Churchill in a column which was suppressed,

> From Palestine, Syria, Lebanon, Egypt, Iraq and Ethiopia—the list is large— Americans bring back the same story. No Atlantic Charter, no self-determination, pro-English quisling-like governments—effected at the point of British arms. Rightly or wrongly, the American people believe this is the policy of your government—and they are against it. They are determined to fight Hitler to the finish, but they will not see an English reactionary program substituted for a German one.[6]

The situation in Europe is not hopeful: France has survived the persistent lack of sympathy of the United States; the determination of Britain to control governments in Belgium with her vast colonial Congo; Italy with its geographical domination of the Mediterranean, and residual claims in Ethiopia; and in Greece—all this is all too well known. In fact, the nineteenth-century dream of the poets of a world filled with peaceful but independent nations each pursuing its own variety of culture, supremely valuable in their very difference and nonconformity with set patterns, was a dream of real intellectual and political freedom. It had been illustrated in the settlement of Massachusetts and Maryland and even in Oglethorpe's Georgia. It was proclaimed by Toussaint and Dessalines in Haiti; it was even planned in the Balkans and Far Asia. Then gradually it was overwhelmed, and with a dying gasp in 1919 was beaten back by recurrent and mounting waves of imperialism, compelling the world to follow one increasing line of profitable industry, concentrated luxury, and power. The small free nation began to disappear from reality. The one great ideal was empire, and increasing empire. The one sure outcome was war.

If now we are going to re-establish peace on earth and goodwill toward men, we must re-establish the right of small nations really to be free. So long as the chief business of free nations today is to tax and starve their peoples so as to pay their debts to the empire, and so long as these imperial debts do not always represent actual hire of real wealth so much as speculation, legal claims, and threats of aggression, just so long world politics will be bedeviled by hunger and hate.

Beyond the colonies and the free nations which are not free, is the plight of the minorities in the midst of both the great and minor nations. There are the Jews of Europe, the Negroes of the United States, the Indians of the Americas, and many other smaller groups elsewhere. They form often little nations within nations, who are encysted and kept from participation in the full citizenship of their native lands.

The greatest tragedy of this war has been the treatment of the Jewish minority in Germany. Nothing like this has happened before in modern civilization. Out of a total Jewish population of 6,000,000 souls 1,000,000 have migrated from Germany and other parts of Europe; 500,000 have been forcibly deported; over 4,000,000 have died or been deliberately killed. Three hundred thousand Jews survive in poverty and helplessness. Considering the cultural accomplishments of this group of people, the gifts they have made to the civilization of the world, this is a calamity almost beyond comprehension.

The Negroes in the United States, despite a determined and unremitting effort to achieve freedom and citizenship, have not yet escaped the position of a submerged group under a system of legal caste. We are farther in thought than in fact from Whittier's forgotten song of nearly a century ago:

> Oh, goodly and grand is our hunting to see,
> In this "land of the brave and this home of the free."
> Priest, warrior, and statesman, from Georgia to Maine,
> All mounting the saddle, all grasping the rein;
> Right merrily hunting the black man, whose sin
> Is the curl of his hair and the hue of his skin![7]

The Indians of the Americas are for the most part disfranchised, landless, poverty-stricken, and illiterate, and are achieving a degree of freedom only as by the death of individuality they become integrated into the blood and culture of the whites. This is widely approved as the only sensible outcome.

There are other groups and classes, part and parcel of the great nations, who because of their incomes live in a degree of poverty which makes it impossible for them to take any effective part in democratic procedure. This is true to a great degree in Britain, France, and Italy, to a lesser degree in Scandinavia and the United States; but even in the United States, the number of people who live with an income below the limits of proper subsistence constitutes a major part of the nation.

If the social development in these cases led to the gradual integration of mass and class, of minority groups into the dominant culture, bringing with them such cultural gifts and modifications as would enrich and vary that culture into a new national unity; if the colony gradually became the partially autonomous dependency and eventually a free and independent nation—this would be a development satisfactory in the end and calling for patience in the process. But no, the development as we see it is cock-eyed and illogical; the group antagonism leads to friction and tensions in the country, and is usually solved only by the physical elimination of some minorities or the cultural disappearance of any individual patterns which they might contribute. Americanization has never yet meant a synthesis of what Africa, Europe, and Asia had to contribute to the new and vigorous republic of the West; it meant largely the attempt to achieve a dead level of uniformity, intolerant of all variation. The ideal of the poor in America is usually to become rich and ride on the necks of the poorer.

The free nations tend to sink into "spheres of influence" and investment centers, and then often succumb into disfranchised colonies. All this has been rationalized by universal sneering at small nations, at "Balkanization" and helpless Haitis, until the majority of the world's people have become ashamed of themselves. As Harold Vinal says in "Voices":

> But Aegir is no more, Zeus is a dream,
> The valiant, the mighty are fled and lost forever,
> And what are we but sleepers lost in sleep.

Thus in much current literature of the early twentieth century the Latins were inferior and ineffective; the French were "frogs"; the Mexicans and South Americans were "mongrels"; the peoples of Asia and Africa were nothing and of no worth. The hope of the world lay in the union of Britain and the United States to dominate mankind. Yet up from the throats of these peoples—the colonials, the minorities, and the depressed classes—one increasing cry for freedom, democracy, and social progress continually wells.

NOTES

1. Anna Graves, *op. cit.*
2. Orizu, *op. cit.*, p. 31.
3. "Zionism and Democracy," a chapter in the book *Chaim Weizmann*, ed. by Meyer W. Weisgal, Dial Press.
4. Public address, October, 1944, reported in *New York Times*.
5. Anna Graves' MS.
6. Radio broadcast, October, 1944.
7. "The Hunters of Men."

CHAPTER IV

◆

Democracy and Color

The effect which the disfranchisement of colonial peoples and the dependence of free nations on the empires has on the development of democracy in the world.

In this war even more than in the last we face the problem of democracy. How far are we working for a world where the peoples who are ruled are going to have effective voice in their governments? We have stated and reiterated that this democratic method of government is going to be applied in the future as widely as possible. But of course in this program we are compelled to recognize that beyond this logic of democracy looms the fact that most people in the world have not in the past been ruled by democratic methods, and that even in the so-called democracies now fighting for democracy democratic methods have been only partially successful.

The experiment of democracy has proceeded slowly because the mass of people do not have the intelligence, the knowledge, or the experience to enable them to bear the responsibility of rule. This lack of intelligence is not a matter of congenital stupidity or of biological race. Indeed, the rise and development of the so-called lower classes among the leading nations during the last century has been phenomenal. The working people of Britain, France, and the United States have increased markedly in intelligence and in influence upon government. The forward rush of the Russian worker and peasant has been the miracle of our age. Within less than a generation Russian illiteracy has been reduced from 90 per cent to less than 10 per cent, and the industrial and social efficiency of this vast nation has placed it in the front rank of modern states. The Webbs declare: "There is no other fragment of the earth's surface, at all comparable in extent, where anything like this conception of an educational service prevails."[1] No one today doubts that with time and opportunity the descendants of American freedmen and the peoples of Italy, Spain, and the Balkans can equal, if not surpass, the progress of Russia.

The real reason for lack of intelligence and experience among the mass of people is poverty. Poverty and its accompanying problems of ignorance, sickness, and crime remain major problems in every leading country of modern civilization. Unless these problems are sincerely and frankly faced and solutions attempted for their settlement, there can be no satisfactory development of the democratic ideal.

Assuming then, as we logically must, that poverty is the basic problem and the problem chiefly responsible for ignorance, ill-health, and crime, we are confronted by the question: How is it possible in an age when the use of natural forces and technical ingenuity for the conversion of raw material into consumable goods, and the consequent enormous increase in the potency of human services, has reached a degree of efficiency never dreamed of, that poverty has only begun to be abolished?

The possibility of producing wealth in our age has repeatedly been estimated to be great enough to furnish all the peoples of the world with the necessities of life and some of the comforts. Despite this, we have not only the miserable poverty of colonial peoples and the great poverty among most of the smaller nations of the world, but a problem of poverty in the richest and most intelligent countries which leaves the majority of their peoples below the line of healthful existence.

There can be no question that the answer is that most modern countries are in the hands of those who control organized wealth, and that the just and wise distribution of income is hindered by this monopoly. This power is entrenched behind barriers of legal sanction, guarded by the best brains of the country trained as lawyers, appointed to the bench, and elected to the legislature. The retention of this power is influenced tremendously by the propaganda of newspapers and news-gathering agencies, by radio, and by social organization.

The hand of organized wealth guides the education of youth. It not only furnishes the endowment and influences the teaching in great private institutions, but throughout the whole school system it makes any real, frank study of the production and distribution of wealth so difficult that the great danger of our age is economic illiteracy—the fact that professional men, businessmen, and even workers are trained not simply to believe in the present organization of industry as the best possible, but to refuse to let anyone study or question it intensely. We are taught to regard poverty as inevitable.

We produce goods, share them, and allocate services for the well-being of mankind. This is no fixed mechanical process. It is in part a matter of choice and plan. We ought to know accurately the facts of the situation, the amount and distribution of property, the amount and distribution of income, the kind of work that people do and how it is rewarded. If after knowing matters of this sort we decide that present conditions are either inevitable in the nature of things, or on the whole fair and just and need only to be corrected in particulars and in application, then our civilization is safe. But if, on the other hand, such a body of knowledge should discover such injustice, inefficiency, waste, and deliberate oppression as stops and turns awry the chief objects of work and wage, then we must seek such change in our basic industrial system as will avoid disaster. This knowledge at present we do not have in accurate and complete form. It is not fully available and may not be frankly and openly studied. The result is that our whole industrial progress resolves itself continually into blind leadership of the blind.

None of the democracies fighting for democracy today is really democratic. Britain is ruled by concentrated and organized wealth derived not simply from her own labor but from the exploitation of colonies and dependencies. Her government is limited by ideals of hereditary privilege carried out by an aristocracy whose influence is carefully increased by propaganda and social distinctions.

Against this combination of influences, nonetheless the democratic control by the mass of the people has progressively increased during the last century; but even today majority rule in Britain is limited by the suspensory vote of the House of Lords and by a series of cultural patterns and inhibitions. Only overwhelming mass public opinion can overcome these hindrances. Britain, therefore, is at home a democracy not by majority but by a vote which must sometimes approach unanimity to become law; while throughout the British Empire democracy is recognized and implemented only in the white dependencies.

In France the democratic method has had wider scope, but here again it has been limited by the conservatism of the small peasant property-owners and by the path of escape which the French freedom of learning, thought, and art has kept open to the gifted of every class and race.

The recent history of Germany is an extraordinary commentary on the way democracy has fought for expression in a great modern land. Back in the nineteenth century there was a strong drive to increase the income of the ruling classes by expanding Germany into an empire with wide-flung colonies. This was only partially successful, and was succeeded in the twentieth century by the rationalization movement in German economy. Rationalization meant planning. It is full mobilization of all scientific information and techniques, and the utilizing of all possible means for one end. The end sought by these means was a new economic system which foresaw the fall of Manchester economics, and the beginning of a new era to meet the rising pressure of democracy and furnish an object for the State Socialism upon which Germany embarked during the Bismarckian era.

The effort to accomplish this by world war for colonies and commercial empire failed. Then came revolution in Russia and finally the Treaty of Versailles. Germany entered upon another phase of development, which culminated in the Second World War and which in the end will either reorganize modern culture or destroy it.

After the First World War, a series of penetrating government reports and studies by individual students began searching analysis into the economic condition of Germany.[2] These studies brought extraordinary results. Vast inflation had destroyed fixed incomes, investments, savings, property values, pensions, and the like. At the same time it enabled big industry to pay off its debts, scrap its old equipment, and rebuild in preparation for a planned economy in a German industrial world mastery. The opportunity for positive rationalization followed; that is, for the systematic introduction of thoroughly scientific techniques, methods, and equipment covering every aspect of production, distribution, and consumption.

Prosperity based on borrowing followed, raising speculative values and the hopes of middle-class citizens. In 1929, came sudden deflation. The middle class of civil servants and clerks suffered more than industrial leaders or laborers, and was even more racked by fear of being leveled down to workers. The revolution thus threatened found no united program among the workers, who were distracted by contradictory advice from poor leadership.

I knew Germany as a student in the last decade of the nineteenth century and as a visitor in 1928 and 1936. In the Germany I knew before the First World War, the people who counted, the people for whom Germany was primarily administered and arranged, were the nobility, high and low, and the rising capitalists in finance and large industry. The members of the large civil service, including professors and teachers, were in the near background, but they depended for advance and favor on monarchy, nobility, and capital. Defeat in war permanently changed this. The monarchy and the ruling nobility were gone forever.

The Weimar Republic was based on a more democratic foundation: the upper classes of workers, the shopkeepers, and the civil servants, with the still powerful influence of the Junkers and the captains of industry on one side and the rising threat of the proletariat on the other. In big industry, the power of engineers and technicians increased, and they and salaried clerks rose in comparison with the hand laborers.

An extraordinary revolution ensued. It was a class struggle, but there was no unity in the groups on either side. The bourgeois were divided into big landholders, captains of industry, leaders in the Catholic Church, and many of the petty bourgeois. The laborers were even more hopelessly divided into Social-Democrats and Communists and such petty bourgeois as grim necessity forced into the laboring class.

Logically, the next step in this planning was to determine whom the results of planned industry should primarily benefit—who would reap the profit? The logical answer here seemed that of Russian Communism. Industry would be planned for the economic uplift of the mass of workers. This was the specter that scared the industrial owners and leaders of Germany to death and threw the country headlong into the arms of Hitler. Hitler, swinging from the worker as an object of planning to a powerful Germany as a greater object, soon interpreted Germany as representing the industrialists, the Junkers, and Hitler's own compact party. Out of this he welded National Socialism and regimented Germany into a planned economy for the benefit of capital and political oligarchy.

This compact inner group which rose to rulership was composed of former soldiers, unemployed white-collar workers, socialists, capitalists, Jew-baiters, and psychopathic fanatics, united into a most dangerous unity by the boundless energy and single-aimed will of Adolf Hitler. But back of it and conditioning it was the increased democratic consciousness of a new Germany, of a Germany which dreamed of a wide democratic basis for the nation, if not the widest. To this movement Hitler seemed the Messiah. Financed by industry and popular contributions and inflamed by one of the most extraordinary efforts at national propaganda ever attempted, the Nazis drove their compact machine in among the bickerings, hesitations, and deceptions of the other parties, and by murder, mobs, intimidation, lies, and frantic appeals changed a ridiculous handful of fanatics and bullies into one of the greatest of modern political parties.

By the ineptitude of the Junkers, the jealousies of the workers, and the senile betrayal of Hindenburg, the Weimar Republic was sabotaged and a Nazi oligarchy was erected on its ruins. Once Hitler and the Nazis had obtained power, they built an oligarchy, not a democracy. They seized and monopolized a long-neglected weapon of democracy: they began a course of Adult Education on a tremendous scale, helped enormously by recent inventions—the radio, the loud-speaker, the airplane. The older democracies in the world had left popular education as a privilege of freedom, without at first bothering to see whether the masses could afford to buy it with their low wage. The state had eventually been forced to furnish elementary instruction in reading and writing, but went little farther than this, except for the richer few. The education of the masses for the major part of their lives was left to chance or to the will of private profit.

Russia started mass education by propaganda, and Mussolini followed. Hitler took up this technique with a population much more intelligent than the Russian or the Italian, and a population peculiarly susceptible in a critical time to suggestion for methods of maintaining public order, private discipline, authority, employment, the reconstitution of German confidence in Germany, and defense against Germany's enemies. At the same time Hitler's propaganda was aimed at a lower level of the national intelligence than that which dominated prewar German thought.

To accomplish his aim, Hitler did not hesitate to borrow the technique of Russia: dictatorship of one party, with limited membership; special education of youth and children for membership in this party; propaganda for justification; stern repression of counterrevolution; attack on the Church. His oligarchy of a million Nazis succeeded, by arms and a wide spy system, first, by beating all opposition into submission by force, imprisonment, exile, or death; second, by smashing the particularism of the separate German states and concentrating power in the central government; third, by rearming Germany and reasserting sovereignty over the industrial Rhineland.

To obtain the power to do this, Hitler must in his propaganda and acts offer the people an ideal. He could not offer the rule of the workers in a democracy of equal economic opportunity, for this would destroy the private profit of his backers, who were armed with the elaborate planned industry of the German engineers; but he could attract followers by various devices: to the powerful bodies of civil servants and shopkeepers, he appealed by a vicious attack on the Jews, who were their intellectual rivals and commercial competitors. This effort too pleased many of his big-business backers and gave him a new racial slogan; the racial slogan helped to gain the allegiance of labor: he substituted "Germanism" for the class struggle; Germans belonged to the noblest breed on earth—far superior to Jews, Asiatics, or Africans, and also to Latins, "Negroid" French, and Slavs. He proposed to build a new Germany in which all Germans would share; he stressed the solidarity of *Deutschtum,* which included employer and worker; to prove this he formed the Work Front—*Arbeitsfront*—into which he put employer and employee, disbanding the trade-unions and referring all work disputes to compulsory arbitration by his appointees. He ended unemployment by labor in munitions and armament; by a vast program of housing; by building a new network of roads suitable for military use as well as automobiles; by compulsory labor service on military lines; and by wholesale resettlement of workers from city to country and from region to region.

With all this went a continuous fanfare of propaganda, vacation excursions, national guest houses, celebrations; and above all a new army in air and on land and sea, which brought back the dream of the lost glory of German militarism.

No such mighty military and civic displays ever glorified even William II as Hitler staged, and in Hitler's case the pomp and circumstance could be heard and seen by every German in every corner of the land, and it was repeatedly re-enforced by subtle allusions to the fact that the Führer had been a paperhanger.

The middle class, having lost all economic foundations, was easily integrated into the new attitudes offered. The farmers and peasants, on the other hand, were reduced to subjection by catastrophic changes: their old indebtedness had been swept away in the inflation, but their soil was depleted, their methods were obsolete, their tools old-fashioned, and they had to compete with the best agricultural areas of the world. They were at the absolute mercy of the new Nazi state and that state, far from neglecting them, organized them and directed their work and made them an integral part of the whole industrial planning. They became in that way allies not of a radical laboring proletariat, but of the newly organized business and industrial interests under state direction.

On the other hand, the business interests gradually succumbed to the state, because of losses which Germany had endured through war and treaties, inflation and deflation. Something between a third and a half of her prewar capital disappeared. The state became, therefore, the source of new capital and absolute master of industry.

What German technocracy did then was to take advantage of nearly total revolution in Germany to establish the most complete and efficient planned economy that the modern world has seen since the rise of the Industrial Revolution—a planning which must not be ignored nor lost, as Anne Lindbergh sought to say. Then Hitler and his gang hurled themselves into the picture and undertook to divide the profit: more to labor, in wage, enjoyment, and perquisites, than ever before—which explains its desperate loyalty; but by far the most of the profit to his cronies, his industrial backers, and the Junkers, who despised him but had to hold on. But Hitler could not stop here, lest German labor follow Russia. Labor must be diverted by nationalism, pride of race, and hope of world conquest. Poland, Czechoslovakia, Austria, and France fell; Britain sank to her knees, but stubbornly stuck. Russia must therefore be liquidated, so that the full force of Germany could be brought to bear on Britain without threat in the rear. Hence the last throw of the dice—and failure.

The inner significance of this movement is that under these revolutionary ideas, started by the Russian experiment, the state with Germany changed from a political to an economic organization; and within this new economic state the whole fight for democracy, for the power of the individual to determine policies and for the freedom of individual thought and critical opinion, must be fought again, not only in Germany and in Europe, but in the world.

In the dictatorships developed in Russia, Germany, and Italy there was a certain scientific foundation. The social sciences have been remiss in not pointing out a natural realm of dictatorship to which all government must bow; that is, the physical laws governing the constitution of materials, the application of natural force, and the availability of certain techniques in using matter and force, which are all subject to law and cannot be changed by popular vote. Thus the production of goods and to some degree their distribution is not a matter of argument, decision, or majority opinion, but an inexorable system which men must follow under the trained guidance of managers and technicians if they would get the necessary results.

On the other hand, questions as to the kind of goods to be produced and their distribution among nations, classes, and individuals for consumption, and most questions of personal service, as to both recipient and servant, are questions where democratic argument and democratic decision are absolutely necessary to the widest human happiness. It may well be that the real fight which is dividing the world today is the question as to how much of human action must by the laws of science be subject to scientific control; and on the other hand, how large a section of life, above the absolute necessities of health and subsistence, can be reserved as the area of human freedom for individual action, creative thought, and artistic taste.

Meantime, however, the mounting pressure of popular demand for democratic methods must be counted on throughout the world as popular intelligence rises. Its greatest successful opponent today is not Fascism, whose extravagance has brought its own overthrow, but rather imperial colonialism, where the disfranchisement of the mass of people has reduced millions to tyrannical control without any vestige of democracy.

It happens, not for biological or historical reasons, that most of the inhabitants of colonies today have colored skins. This does not make them one group or race or even allied biological groups or races. In fact these colored people vary vastly in physique, history, and cultural experience. The one thing that unites them today in the world's thought is their poverty, ignorance, and disease, which renders them all, in different degrees, unresisting victims of modern capitalistic exploitation. On this foundation the modern "Color Line" has been built, with all its superstitions and pseudo-science. And it is this complex today which more than anything else excuses the suppression of democracy, not only in Asia and Africa, but in Europe and the Americas. Hitler seized on "negroid" characteristics to accuse the French of inferiority. Britain points to miscegenation with colored races to prove democracy impossible in South America. But it is left to the greatest modern democracy, the United States, to defend human slavery and caste, and even defeat democratic government in its own boundaries, ostensibly because of an inferior race, but really in order to make profits out of cheap labor, both black and white.

The attitude of the United States in this development puzzles the observing world of liberalism. Intelligence and high wages in this land are linked with an extraordinary development of the rule of wealth and sympathy with imperial ambition in other lands, as well as steps toward greater American imperialism. Why is this? The answer lies in two parts: first, in a peculiar extension of provincialism which exhibits itself in the composition of the United States Senate and springs from colonial America before the nation had become democratic. The second cause lies in the Negro problem. Both these tie in with empire and the disfranchisement of a majority of the peoples in the world. The following figures, maps, and plans show why American democracy cannot be rational and progressive. Basing our study on the presidential election returns of 1944, we may divide the United States into groups based on historical, conventional, and economic factors. We have the following:

	REPRESENTATIVES ELECTED TO CONGRESS 1944*	TOTAL VOTE	PER REPRESENTATIVE
The New England states			
Connecticut	5 (+1 at large)	825,116	
Massachusetts	14	1,889,753	
New Hampshire	2	215,857	
Vermont	1	123,036	
Maine	3	183,771	
Rhode Island	2	293,481	
	27	3,531,014	130,778
Middle Atlantic states			
New Jersey	14	1,859,425	
New York	45	6,024,597	
Pennsylvania	33	3,712,570	
	92	11,596,592	126,049
The Border states			
Delaware	1	126,440	
Kentucky	9	843,843	
Maryland	6	544,324	
Missouri	13	1,520,412	
Tennessee	10	398,622	
Virginia	9	342,980	
West Virginia	6	718,509	
	54	4,495,130	83,243
Southern former slave states			
Alabama	9	222,338	
Arkansas	7	217,207	
Florida	6	416,353	
Georgia	10	274,374	
Louisiana	8	282,569	
Mississippi	7	152,712	
North Carolina	12	754,658	
Oklahoma	8	684,560	
South Carolina	6	100,862	
Texas	21	1,058,419	
	94	4,164,052	44,298
The Middle West			
Illinois	25 (+1 at large)	3,874,845	
Indiana	11	1,651,216	
Iowa	8	972,759	
Kansas	6	664,192	
Michigan	17	2,163,487	
Minnesota	9	1,109,109	

Nebraska	4	514,926	
Ohio	22 (+1 at large)	2,954,334	
Wisconsin	10	1,162,858	
North Dakota	2	197,594	
South Dakota	2	225,738	
	116	15,491,058	133,543
The Far West			
Arizona	2	128,036	
New Mexico	2	151,888	
California	23	3,007,499	
Idaho	2	205,579	
Montana	2	197,217	
Nevada	1	51,744	
Oregon	4	442,476	
Utah	2	247,681	
Washington	6	803,093	
Wyoming	1	96,102	
Colorado	4	493,862	
	49	5,825,177	118,881
Total	432	45,103,023	104,405

* These figures are based on the *Statistics of the Presidential and Congressional Election of November 7, 1944 . . .* compiled from official sources by William Graf under direction of South Trimble, Clerk of the House of Representatives, corrected to January 16, 1945, United States Government Printing Office, Washington, 1945. The figures are based on the recapitulation of votes cast for United States Representatives, p. 52. The figures for Alaska, Hawaii, and Puerto Rico are omitted. In case of Representatives elected at large, no account is taken of their vote, but the vote is calculated on the total cast by the various districts.

In the late election the composition of the Senate was determined in an extraordinary way: In Mississippi 172,000 voters have the same power in the Senate as 6,000,000 voters in New York. In Delaware 125,000 voters balance 4,000,000 in Illinois, and the same figures apply to Vermont and Pennsylvania. Massachusetts and New Jersey each have about 2,000,000 voters and are balanced by 100,000 voters in Wyoming and 54,000 voters in Nevada. In fact, 28,000,000 voters in New York, New Jersey, Pennsylvania, Illinois, Ohio, California, Indiana, and Michigan will have any wishes that they may care to express on the peace treaty in the Senate absolutely balanced by 1,250,000 voters in Mississippi, South Carolina, Wyoming, Nevada, Delaware, Vermont, Rhode Island, Arizona, and New Mexico. The Middle Atlantic states with 12,000,000 votes sent 6 members to the Senate, while the Southern former slave states with 4,500,000 voters sent 20 Senators.

To this extraordinary situation there is neither rhyme nor reason. It is a survival of eighteenth-century American Tory hatred and fear of democracy, surviving as a fetish, like the German particularism, the abolishment of which was Hitler's one gift to civilization. In certain small states monopoly and industry can by this rotten-borough system turn the state into a medieval fief and usurp the functions of the state in education and road-building. The scandal of our silver policy rests on the composition of the Senate. In the main this situation serves neither democracy nor industry, but makes government a matter of chance rather than one of majority rule, with some analogies to the suspensory veto of the British House of

Lords in the case of senatorial "courtesy." By national tabu, the situation in the Senate must not be discussed; it includes "States Rights" and local government— two contradictory terms. Of course it all adds up to one result: the frustration of popular rule.

This lack of democratic methods not only gives the South four times the political power of the Middle West, but also gives it control of some of the most powerful committees in the Senate.

Naturally, other and different discrepancies based on different reasons appear in the election of Representatives, as the following table and map show:

SECTION	VOTES CAST	REPRESENTATIVES ELECTED	VOTES PER REPRESENTATIVE
South	4,164,052	94	44,298
Border states	4,495,130	54	83,243
Far West	5,825,177	49	118,881
Middle West	15,491,058	116	133,543
New England	3,531,014	27	130,778
Middle states	11,596,592	92	126,049
Total	45,103,023	432	104,405

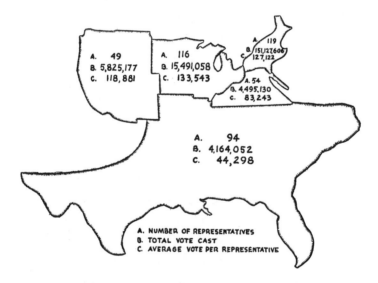

Why is it that 44,000 voters in the former slave states have power equal to 134,000 in the Middle West or 140,000 in the Middle Atlantic states? The first is the part of the United States which, as the President has said, constitutes our major economic problem in its poverty, illiteracy, and disease. It is the national slum area of our country. But its political power is distorted because of the Negro problem. The race problem has been deliberately intermixed with state particularism to thwart democracy. The former slave states, with their illiteracy, sickness, poverty, and crime, not only among the children of freedmen but too largely among the whites, have made it impossible since the Civil War to get an honest and intelligent expression of public opinion from this part of the nation. Consequently a block of 134 electoral votes is quadrennially delivered to one party, in defiance of law and justice.

Not only that, but the democratic process in the whole nation is thus frustrated and crippled. Alone and among modern countries the United States has set up in the twentieth century a legal system of caste among its citizens. This body of law interferes with marriage and the family, with education, health, work, and wealth.

For instance, a report made to the city by Negroes of Atlanta shows this discrimination today:

> Of the 70,894 Atlanta children of school age 26,528 are Negroes; 44,456 are whites. There is one school for every 855 white children but one school for every 2,040 Negro children. We invest in school land and buildings $2,156 for each white pupil but $887 for each Negro pupil. In 1942, we expended for education $108.70 for each white pupil but $37.80 for each Negro pupil. The double session is the black market of public education for Negroes in Atlanta. The white child goes to school 6½ hours a day from nine a.m. until three-thirty p.m. The Negro child goes to school 3½ hours a day from nine a.m. until twelve-thirty p.m. or twelve-thirty p.m. until four p.m. The Negro pupil thus loses at least 2,700 class-hours during the first six years of his elementary school education.
>
> The results are unsupervised leisure hours; ineffective compulsory education laws; irregular attendance, retardation, delinquency; reduced efficiency of overburdened teachers. The Negro pupil lacks: teachers; the teachers have an average of forty pupils in each class compared with twenty in white classes; library facilities, an average of 1.4 books per pupil compared with 6.5 for whites; vocational training facilities; only a few ill-equipped shops at Booker T. Washington High School; kindergarten, no Negro school has one; clerical help, no Negro elementary school has any clerical help.[3]

Such discrimination turns 13,000,000 Americans into second-class citizens, with rights which the rest of the nation need respect only in partial and limited degree. Nothing like this has happened among other civilized peoples except in colonies and in quasi-colonies like the Union of South Africa.

The Negro problem forces the United States to abdicate its natural leadership of democracy in the world and to acquiesce in a domination of organized wealth which exceeds anything elsewhere in the world. It gives rein and legal recognition to race hate, which the Nazis copied in their campaign against the Jews, establishing it on American lines of caste conditions, disfranchisement, mob murder, ridicule, and public disparagement.

The methods of carrying through this discrimination against Negroes are extraordinary. For instance, in the Immigration and Naturalization Service of the United States Department of Justice passengers arriving on aircraft are to be labeled according to "race," and race is determined by the stock from which aliens spring and the language they speak, and to some degree by nationality. But "Negroes" apparently can belong to no nation: "Cuban," for instance, refers to the

Cuban people "but not to Cubans who are Negroes"; "West Indian" refers to the people of the West Indies "except Cubans or Negroes"; "Spanish American" refers to people of Central and South America and of Spanish descent; but "Negro" refers to the "black African whether from Cuba, the West Indies, North or South America, Europe or Africa," and moreover "any alien with admixture of blood of the African (black) should be classified under this heading" ["Negro"].[4]

The awareness of Negroes of their second-rate citizenship can no longer be questioned. There was a time when a number of Negro voices, timid or afraid of personal repression and mob violence, asserted their general agreement with present policies in the United States. This is no longer true, as the recent book *What the Negro Wants*[5] proves. The book had an extraordinary birth. It was asked for by the director of the University of North Carolina Press. When a well-known Negro scholar secured manuscripts representing all shades of Negro opinion, the director of the press was so disturbed and angered by the evident and clear statement of Negroes as to their wishes that he refused to publish the book. When threatened by a lawsuit, he finally published the book, but inserted without the editor's consent a "Publisher's Preface" which was practically a repudiation of everything the authors said.

This man represents a singularly large and dangerous section of American public opinion, not only in the South but throughout the country, which is forced to yield even the dogma of "race inferiority" but still clings to subordination. In the South, according to a survey made by the National Opinion Research Center at the University of Denver, less than one-fifth of the population would give Negro workers an even chance at jobs; and throughout the nation only 42 per cent. Three-fourths of the Southerners would not work beside the Negro at the same job, and throughout the nation only 43 per cent would be willing that a Negro should get a better job than a white man, even though he were better qualified.

The young Negro attitude as voiced by the All Southern Youth Conference is clear, calm and logical:

> We stand prepared to play our rightful part in making available to all Americans the fruits of industry, the benefits of enormous resources, and the application of the democratic tradition—with which blessings our country is so richly endowed.
>
> In this spirit, Negro youth are called to counsel and to action! Negro youth are asked to turn their eyes to an America which can afford:
>
> 1. The unrestricted right of franchise;
> 2. The security of jobs with adequate pay and opportunity for advancement;
> 3. Equal opportunities for our veterans and service men and women;
> 4. An education improved in quality and available to all;
> 5. Recreational, health and housing facilities corresponding to our community needs;
> 6. The strict and impartial enforcement of constitutional liberties;
> 7. A steadily advancing level of culture.[6]

The extent to which the American state is controlled by organized wealth cannot be definitely stated, because scientific study in this direction has been successfully hindered or carelessly neglected; but we do know certain facts. We know that international cartels have kept their organization and their profits even in time of war and across the lines of warring nations. This has been shown in the case of the dye trust and that of synthetic rubber, and in other patented processes. We know that during the First World War and during this war there have been made immense unearned fortunes in capital and accumulated incomes of financial and industrial combinations. The People's Lobby reports

> unearned fortunes in capital and accumulated incomes of industrial and financial combinations would pay at least a sixth of the national debt. . . . The result of concentration of war orders in a few great corporations has been to give 16 non-financial enterprises, 50 per cent more assets than all the corporations the Government owns. The assets of these 16 concerns increased in the four war years from 1939 to 1943 by $5,239,000,000—that is 20.2% or one-fifth. On December 31, 1940, the total assets of the 403 corporations having over $100,000,000 assets, were $153,711,500,000, an increase in one year of $9,506,700,000, or 6.6%. The assets of these corporations amounted to 48%—nearly half of the total assets of the 413,716 corporations reporting. In 1940 these 403 corporations had surplus reserves and surplus and undivided profits of $23,400,200,000. Their net profit was $2,823,500,000 and some of them have doubled their net profit, above taxes, in the war years since 1940.[7]

The extraordinary profits rolled up today by department stores, meat-packing companies, and such firms as the American Tobacco Company do not mean necessarily the addition of actual wealth to the nation. They mean the increased legal rights of certain persons to take from the current income of the nation after the war large percentages of consumable goods and services which consequently cannot be distributed among laborers or go to the common funds of the nation, states, and cities—unless the tax on such profits is increased rather than lowered, as present demands ask.

All the facts and all the implications of figures like these are not sufficient for scientific conclusions; but they certainly indicate that wealth today is centered in the hands of certain powerful corporations, not according to the labor that has been expended, nor the actual capital invested, nor the public service rendered, but rather by chance, power, and intrigue; and that the distribution of this wealth is determined by custom or monarchial or oligarchical decision and not by democratic methods. Nor is public welfare necessarily the object and the method of its expenditure. These conclusions are not the ranting of revolutionists or the envious gossip of persons of small ability. They are the clear conclusions of reasonable men who scan the facts and who ask for more and more scientifically gathered facts in order to be surer of their conclusions.

It is the concentrated power of wealth that is putting the United States side by side with Britain against all the leftward trends in democracy in Europe. Every country that has been conquered by Hitler and is now regaining its freedom is tending toward greater democracy in industry, greater government control of industry, and economic planning for the future. Against this democracy in Belgium, Holland, Italy, Greece, and other countries, the organized political and military might of the United States and Britain is apparently being organized and exercised.

More important than political democracy is industrial democracy; that is, the voice which the actual worker, whether his work be manual or mental, has in the organization and the conduct of industry. The organization of industry is of first importance in the state and determines its political pattern. For a long time in American labor unions the Negro was practically disfranchised. Since the Civil War he has been gradually forcing himself into recognition. The Knights of Labor tried to include him; the AFL for many years usually excluded him, and in some of the large unions, continues to excludes him; the CIO in most unions has from the beginning sought to bring him into membership.

Increasingly in the annual convention of the AFL the discrimination against the Negro is debated. The Machinists and the Boilermakers defend their discriminatory tactics and cling to them. The railway unions are silent, although they exclude the Negro by positive legislation; but most disgusting is the case of unions—like that of the Fireman's Union recently adjudicated before the Supreme Court, which had been given by law the sole right to represent Negro labor in negotiation with employers, and yet excludes Negroes from membership and is using its power to eliminate him entirely from the vocation.

It only increases the paradox when we remember that organized labor in the United States and Europe has seldom actively opposed imperialism or championed democracy among colonial peoples, even when this slave labor was in direct competition with their own. The Social-Democratic party of prewar Germany once openly declared that the wages and working-conditions which it asked for white labor did not include any such demand for yellow labor.

One writer says of colonial labor:

> If it is said that the raw materials which these lands contain should be produced for the benefit of "all humanity," why is it that the people of these colonial lands are not considered? Are they not a part of "all humanity"? The production of raw materials in their lands, the working and developing of these raw materials cannot be done for their benefit, if they are held in subjection. And also the production, working and developing of the raw materials in the lands of the subjugated peoples is not done for the benefit of the majority of the people in the lands of the possessing powers. Ask the people of the "depression areas" of England, Scotland and Wales, and the miners of England, Scotland and Wales how much their well-being is considered. And they are inhabitants of Great Britain which owns as colonies, or controls as semi-colonies, almost one third of the world.[8]

The so-called democracies, Britain, France, and the United States, have become lands where back of a façade of political "freedom" dictatorship helped by imperialism and under the guise of economic anarchy has had a chance to develop to such a colossal degree that it has practically committed suicide. The only remedy for this which is for a moment listened to in the United States is a continuance of this "freedom for industrial enterprise" and "rugged individualism," remedied of its worst excesses and failures by various types of state intervention. Such intervention however must not, to any great extent, interfere with the "freedom" of private profit-making. Britain under war pressure is growing less dogmatic. Pushed by her suffering, she realizes that whenever and however peace comes, the control of industry by the state is going to increase and more and more largely yield to democratic processes.

So long as the colonial system perists and expands, theories of race inferiority will help to continue it. Right here lies the great danger of the future. One of the vast paradoxes of human nature is that no matter how degraded people become, it is impossible to keep them down on a large scale and forever. Rebellion will certainly ensue. If this is true of Europe, it is just as true and just as significant for Asia and Africa. The continents which have withstood the European exploitation of the nineteenth century are for that very reason not going to remain quiescent under a new order—unless that new order has a distinct place for them which allows their progress, development, and self-determination.

There is no reason to believe that the domination of Europe over Asia and Africa would have had any greater chance for ultimate success under the leadership of rationalized industrial Germany than it had under the freebooting, slave-trading Crown-colony economic anarchy of the British Empire. At any rate, the will to revolt on the part of the colored people is immeasurably greater today than yesterday, and the attempt of Britain or Neuropa absolutely to dominate the world without fundamental change in methods and objectives is inconceivable. Edwin Markham's "The Man with the Hoe" is a world figure in colonies as well as in empires:

Down all the caverns of Hell to their last gulf
There is no shape more terrible than this—
More tongued with cries against the world's blind greed—
More filled with signs and portents for the soul—
More packet with danger to the universe.

The present attitude of the United Nations is bound to invite paradox and failure. The new planned economic order in Europe cannot be smashed physically and will not die with German defeat. There is not enough physical power and certainly not enough reason in the attitude of the United States, combined with that of Britain, to accomplish this. If, on the other hand, the United States, seeing the movement of the stars in their courses, realizes that American industry has got to be rationalized and controlled, that profit-making must be made absolutely subordinate to the general will, then it can join with the new order in any economy carried on for the benefit of all the people.

If the United States really wishes to seize leadership in the present world, it will attempt to make the beneficiaries of the new economic order not simply a group, a race, or any form of oligarchy but, taking advantage of its own wealth and intelligence, will try to put democracy in control of the new economy. This will call for vital, gigantic effort; real education for the broadest intelligence and for evoking talent and genius on a scale never before attempted in the world, and putting to shame our present educational camouflage. With that program the sympathy and interest of the majority of the people of the world, particularly of the emerging darker peoples, will make the triumph of American industrial democracy over the oligarchical technocracy of Neuropa inevitable.

Democracy has failed because so many fear it. They believe that wealth and happiness are so limited that a world full of intelligent, healthy, and free people is impossible, if not undesirable. So the world stews in blood, hunger, and shame. The fear is false, yet naught can face it but Faith. Once two great Germans appealed to this faith in brotherhood. With high art in word and melody, they called all men to the magic of life; they summoned them, fire-drunk and reeling through stars of God into the sanctuary of Joy, daughter of Elysium:

Alle menschen—
Seid umschlungen, Millionen!

NOTES

1. Sidney and Beatrice Webb, *Soviet Communism,* 2 vols., Scribner, 1936, Vol. II, p. 891.
2. Cf. R. A. Brady, *The Rationalization Movement in German Industry,* University of California Press, 1933.
3. "A Report of Public School Facilities for Negroes in Atlanta, Georgia," The Atlanta Urban League, 1944.
4. United States Department of Justice, Immigration and Naturalization Service, Form I–466 (see instructions on back).
5. *What the Negro Wants,* ed. by R. W. Logan, University of North Carolina Press, 1944.
6. Manifesto, October, 1944, Birmingham, Ala.
7. Published newspaper reports, October, 1944.
8. Anna Graves, *op. cit.*

CHAPTER V

◆

Peace and Colonies

Is peace possible by force in the hands of the world's great nations so long as these nations, in the main, follow the plan of imperial control of colonial peoples and of others who have no effective voice in government?

We are seeking desperately to save modern civilization from the repetition of two disastrous and world-wide wars. We hope to do this by a union of nations who will collectively organize to stop aggressive action on the part of other nations with selfish programs or programs incompatible with reasonable human progress. For a time it was argued that the main protagonists of the new order thus united were nations which professed and followed the democratic method of government, and that they were fighting against two or three dictatorships where the power of great nations had been concentrated in the hands of a few leaders backed by organized power and determined to dominate the world.

Unfortunately this theoretical pattern, as the last chapter has shown, is not altogether true to fact. As we have pointed out, in the first place the united free nations own colonies with some 750,000,000 inhabitants and occupy perhaps one-third the area of the earth where there is at present no definite plan of spreading democracy and lifting the standards of life out of poverty, ignorance, and sickness. In the next place there are masses of people living within the free nations, and others in nations which are not really free, whose government and social status are dominated by current demands for individual profit in organized industry and commerce.

There is consequently not only the danger of eventual colonial revolt, of class struggle and minority discontent, but the continual danger of that rivalry for the distribution of profit among dominant nations which has already caused two world wars in our time, as well as being a partial cause of endless wars in the past, and a temptation to murder, destruction, and disorder in the future.

The conference at Bretton Woods was called to explore the economic reorganization of the world after the Second World War. It gave its chief attention to the stabilization of currencies and loans for reconstruction; but it gave no attention at all to colonies and investments in colonial cheap labor and raw materials. Yet here, more than elsewhere, lurk the main causes of modern war.

304 + COLOR AND DEMOCRACY

It is impossible, of course, to determine with accuracy the causes of particular wars. Just because war is not rational, there are many threads interwoven to make the fabric of dissension, organized murder, and destruction. But back of the history of the eighteenth century, the nineteenth, and even the seventeenth, we can see how national defense and group self-expression gradually became transformed as the Industrial Revolution was ushered in by the new capitalism and the annexation of territory came more and more to be confined to and aimed at the annexation of certain kinds of territory; that is, of territory inhabited by "lesser" peoples, of territory rich in the possibilities of exploitation.

In the Seven Years' War, which became a world war, some of these new patterns were evident; and in the continuous war between Europe and Asia which resulted in the subjugation of India, the new colonialism was born. In Africa, from the investment imperialism which subdued Egypt and North Africa there was developed the missionary imperialism of the Congo Free State and the Congress of Berlin. Fire and blood swept over Africa in continuous flood from the beginning of the nineteenth century until well into the twentieth. There was increased effort, however, to keep the wars against the natives of Asia and Africa confined to limits where they would not set the peoples of Europe aflame in their relations to each other.

Throughout the Napoleonic Wars this danger was faced and partially averted. It was present in the holocaust of Haiti. It appeared in the War of 1812, it smoldered in the troubles of the Near East. It came near setting fire to the world in the Boer War and in the incidents of Khartum and Fashoda. But on the whole, European diplomacy succeeded until 1914 in keeping most European nations from each other's throats in armed rivalry for the proceeds of investment in Africa and Asia. Then it failed, and the world fell.

As Alvin Johnson says in the *Encyclopaedia of the Social Sciences:*

> In the second half of the nineteenth century the development of high capitalism with its dependence on foreign supplies of raw materials and on foreign markets gave new value, in the eyes of statesmen, to colonial dominion. Colonies could be handled as closed trading areas, if necessary. Hence a new imperialism, which resulted in the swift partition of Africa, the extension of British and French dominion in the Indo-Chinese peninsula, extensive schemes for the partition of China and a disposition on the part of the stronger powers to wrest colonial dominions from the weaker ones. Among the results of this imperialistic movement were the Sino-Japanese and the Russo-Japanese War, the Boer War and the Spanish American War. The Fashoda incident came near involving France and England in war, as the Morocco dispute came near involving Germany in war with England and France.[1]

Today as we try in anticipation to rebuild the world, the propositions of Dumbarton Oaks center their efforts upon stopping war by force and at the same time leaving untouched, save by vague implication, the causes of war, especially those causes which lurk in rivalry for power and prestige, race dominance, and income arising from the ownership of men, land, and materials. So long as colonial imperialism exists there can be neither peace on earth nor goodwill toward men.

If we confine ourselves to the nineteenth and twentieth centuries, when colonial imperialism became a dominant world force, we have the following wars which seem to have been mainly wars between imperial powers for colonies; wars for "spheres of influence"; wars against countries or groups to reduce them to colonial status and to annex their territory and labor; wars against subordinate and unintegrated groups at home, such as the American Indians in the United States; revolts in the colonies and strife between elements and parties in colonies and quasi-colonies caused by outside pressure. Many persons naturally will dissent from cataloguing several of these wars as colonial or caused by the strife for colonies. Strict interpretation might reduce the list, but with the greatest logical reduction we nevertheless have a formidable array of wars which took place in an era dominated largely by organized pacifism but, as the event proved, pacifism designed "for white people only."

WARS FROM 1792 TO 1939

DATE	COUNTRIES INVOLVED	
1792–1815	War in Europe, America, and Africa	A*
1810–22	Spain *vs.* South America	E
1816–18	Britain *vs.* India	C
1817–18	United States *vs.* American Indians	D
1821–22	France *vs.* Haiti	E
1824–25	Britain *vs.* Burma	C
1832–33	United States *vs.* American Indians	D
1832–33	Turkey *vs.* Egypt	E
1835–42	United States *vs.* American Indians	D
1836	Mexico *vs.* Texas	C
1839–42	Britain *vs.* India	C
1840–42	Britain *vs.* China	B
1844	France *vs.* Morocco	C
1844–49	Santo Domingo *vs.* Haiti	F
1845–46	Britain *vs.* India	C
1846–48	United States *vs.* Mexico	C
1848–49	Britain *vs.* India	C
1849–61	United States *vs.* American Indians	D
1850–64	Revolt in China	F
1851	Spain *vs.* Cuba	E
1851–64	War between Russians and Circassians	E
1851–53	British *vs.* Kaffirs	E
1851–56	United States *vs.* American Indians	D
1852–53	Turkey *vs.* Montenegro	E
1855–57	United States filibuster in Central America	C
1855–58	United States *vs.* American Indians	D
1856–57	Britain *vs.* Persia	B
1856–60	Britain and France *vs.* China	B
1857–58	Britain *vs.* India	C
1859–60	Spain *vs.* Morocco	C

* A.Rivalry for colonies. B. Spheres of influence. C. Colonial conquest. D. Internal-group conquest. E. Colonial revolt. F. Strife within colonies.

Date	Countries Involved	
1862	French *vs.* Annam and Cochinchina	C
1862–63	United States *vs.* Sioux Indians	D
1862–67	France *vs.* Mexico	B
1862–90	United States *vs.* American Indians	D
1863–69	United States *vs.* Cheyenne Indians	D
1865–70	Argentina and Brazil *vs.* Paraguay	F
1866	Turkey *vs.* Crete	E
1867–68	Britain *vs.* Abyssinia	B
1868–78	Spain *vs.* Cuba	E
1871	United States and France *vs.* Korea	B
1872–73	United States *vs.* Modoc Indians	D
1873–74	Britain *vs.* Ashanti	C
1875	Turkey *vs.* Bosnia, etc.	C
1876	American Indians *vs.* the United States	D
1877	Nez Percé Indians *vs.* the United States	D
1878–81	Britain *vs.* Afghans	C
1879	Britain *vs.* Zulus	E
1880–81	Britain *vs.* Boers	E
1881	France *vs.* Tunis	C
1882	Britain *vs.* Egypt	C
1882–86	United States *vs.* Apache Indians	D
1883	Revolt in Crete	E
1883–85	Revolt in Sudan	E
1883–95	France *vs.* Madagascar	C
1884	Revolt in Egypt	E
1884–85	France *vs.* Indo-China	C
1885	Russia *vs.* Afghans	B
1887–95	Italy *vs.* Abyssinia	B
1889	Revolt in Hawaii	E
1889–93	Germany *vs.* Southwest Africa	C
1890–91	United States *vs.* Sioux Indians	D
1890	Revolt in Syria	E
1890	War in Central America	F
1890–92	France *vs.* Dahomey	C
1891	Revolt in India	E
1892	Revolt in Morocco	E
1893	Revolution in Hawaii	F
1893	France *vs.* Siam	C
1893–94	Britain *vs.* Matabele	E
1894	Portugal *vs.* Kaffirs	E
1894–95	Japan *vs.* China	B
1895	Jameson Raid	C
1895–96	Armenian Massacres	D
1896	Revolt in the Philippines	E
1896	Matabele Revolt	E
1896–97	Turkish-Greek War and revolt in Crete	E
1897	Britain *vs.* Nigeria	E
1897	Britain *vs.* India	E
1898	Britain *vs.* Sudan	E
1898	Revolt in Cuba	E
1898	Spanish-American War	C
1899–1901	Filipino Insurrection	E
1899–1902	Britain *vs.* Boers	C

Date	Countries Involved	
1900	Boxer Revolt in China	F
1902	Britain *vs.* Revolts in Africa	E
1903	Revolt in Panama	E
1904	Britain *vs.* Tibet	B
1904	Revolt of Herreros	E
1904–05	Russo-Japanese War	A
1906	Revolt in the Philippines	E
1906	Dutch *vs.* Malays	C
1907	Japan *vs.* Korea	C
1907	Revolt in Morocco	E
1907–09	Revolt in Persia	F
1908	Italy *vs.* Abyssinia	C
1908	Civil War in Morocco	F
1908	Revolt in Portuguese Guinea	E
1908–12	Revolt in Algeria and Morocco	E
1911–12	Italy *vs.* Turkey	A
1912	Balkan War	A
1912	Revolt in Santo Domingo	F
1914–16	United States *vs.* Mexico	B
1914–18	First World War	A
1918–20	Intervention in Russia	A
1919	Revolt in Korea	E
1919	Revolt in Egypt	E
1919	Massacre in India	D
1921	Revolt in Persia	F
1921	Russia *vs.* Bessarabia	E
1921–22	Turkey *vs.* Greece	D
1921–26	Revolt in Morocco	E
1922	Civil conflict in India	F
1925–26	Revolt in Syria	E
1927–28	United States *vs.* Nicaragua	B
1928–29	Revolt in Morocco	E
1929	Britain *vs.* Arabs	B
1929	Revolt in Persia	F
1929	Britain *vs.* India	E
1929	Revolt in Mexico	F
1930	Rebellions in South America	F
1931	Rebellion in Panama	F
1931	Revolts in South America	F
1932	Japan *vs.* China	B
1932	Revolution in Chile	F
1932	Revolt in Cuba	E
1934	Revolt in Spain	D
1934	Italy *vs.* Ethiopia	C
1935	Bolivia *vs.* Paraguay	F
1936	Rebellion in Morocco	E
1936–39	Civil War in Spain	D
1937	Revolt in China	E
1937	Japan *vs.* China	A
1939	Second World War	A

Nationalistic motives are mingled with efforts at colonial imperialism. The motive of investment of private profit was preceded by vast treasure hunts, slave-trading, and labor-kidnapping; suppression of labor revolt in colonies among slaves and indentured servants; pressure for markets; clearing of territory of groups hostile to agriculture and trade—all these incentives to war culminated in the First World War.

The First World War had among its causes some nationalistic urges, but they alone were not potent enough to set the world aflame. This needed the culminating rivalry of great world states, determined to settle once for all dominion over the world's colonial wealth and power. Britain and France had, by pact and understanding, divided the best of Africa, including mortgages on Portuguese and Belgian colonies. Their colonial and commercial strength in Asia was likely to grow. Germany was convinced that her possessions in Africa were far too restricted, in view of her growing technique in manufacture and her expanding capital and commerce. Japan, deeply resentful of her failure to keep close alliance with Britain and full partnership with Europe in Asia, was already planning supremacy over the yellow race and mastery of Asia.

This war, terrible as it was, left the colonial question with only token settlement. Its peace terms sought disarmament among rivals for world power, sought to cripple one rival permanently and put on Germany full blame for making war. It stripped Germany of colonies, and with the pretense of handing these and eventually all colonies over to international and philanthropic control, established a Mandates Commission without power. Here and not in the question of reparations lay the tragedy of Versailles.

Thus there remained, almost untouched, the same temptations to war among the great empires that had existed in 1914. Feeling herself cheated in this settlement because the explicit promises of the Treaty of London were not fulfilled, Italy, first in the Balkans and then in Africa, reopened the war, which after futile negotiation and appeasement became the Second World War in 1939.

When we come finally to the consideration of the present world-wide war, we must remember that one of its causes was our failure to implement the magnificent promise of the Mandates Commission; we failed to come to grips with the colonial problem, and the Second World War found the colonial question unsettled and was precipitated by the determination of Italy to enter upon an enlarged imperial career in Africa.

In like manner Japan, still smarting under European race prejudice and open contempt, hastened war by attacking and dismembering China as a beginning of her determination to supplant Europe and the United States as the colonial exploiter of Asia.

Thus in the Second World War there arose not simply the rivalry of European powers for imperial domination, but above and beyond this there looms the shadow of world conflict based on race and color, on the new determination of Japan to exploit Asia for herself, since Europe and the United States had excluded her from partnership. A new Asiatic dream of imperialism has arisen, and also a new determination on the part of Europe never to surrender without world-wide struggle the advantages of investment in Asiatic cheap labor, in abundant Asiatic raw materials, and in the prestige of world-wide technical leadership based on these advantages. The long fight between Japan and China, acquiesced in and even encouraged by Europe so long as the result might leave Asia open to European control, now suddenly takes on new complexion and new meaning, when Japan's real aim is clear and feasible. Thus it is evident that imperialism is a twofold cause of war: It encourages war within the colonies themselves and between the powers which possess them.

Within colonies, absolute conquest being costly if not impossible, the empire following age-old wisdom divides to conquer. If there are several races, cultures, and religious faiths in the colony, the empire incites the people of one race against those of another; those of one religion against those of another—for example, the Moslems against the Hindus in India; Arabs and Jews against each other in Palestine; and even, in Uganda, the Catholic Christian converts against the Protestant Christian converts. If there are already struggles between divided groups in the territory conquered, the empire increases the tendency to struggle and incites the differing groups to violence; and if there are no divisions, the colonial power deliberately creates them, for example, the divisions between the Arabs of Syria, Iraq, Palestine, and Trans-Jordan.

This does not mean that Britain or France or Japan in all cases plan such maneuvers, officially or openly. It does mean that the commercial and investment agencies behind imperial government openly demand development for profits; their local agents, however, know their real aims, and these agents, who are not always or usually the highest type of civilized man, are in power, or in control of those who are. If in the end the colony is kept at work, made to pay interest, and turns out materials at low cost, few persons at home are going to ask how this was accomplished; and the men who bring this to pass, no matter at what cost or by what disreputable means, stand to receive wealth and honor. Under this veil, cheating, lying, murder, and rape, force, deception, bribery, and destruction, become methods of achieving imperial power, with few questions asked.

But the forces and the peoples at home do not and cannot escape the moral pollution of such methods in dark Africa, heathen Asia, and the forgotten South Seas. Colonialism divides and confuses many groups of ardent social reformers. Because of colonialism, Socialists have long been unable to be true to their principles. The questions of Egypt and India, Kenya and Palestine, made it impossible for Ramsey MacDonald, Lord Olivier, Sidney Webb and many others to follow out their Socialist principles. Pacifists have been frustrated because of their sympathy with imperial aims. At the time when the peace movement was at its zenith and when every effort was being made to keep Europe from fighting Europeans, pacifists were willing to ignore the fact that the peace of Europe was maintained only by a series of colonial wars which lasted almost continuously from the last half of the nineteenth century to the present, and subdued most of the peoples of the world to partial or complete subserviency to imperial powers.

I remember once attending a meeting at the Hotel Astor of a pacifist organization, presided over by Andrew Carnegie. In the midst of a debate on world peace, the then current strife in the Balkans was mentioned. Mr. Carnegie brushed it aside. He said we were talking about peace among the great nations and not about the hordes of the Balkans. Many of those who call themselves pacifists and who are also citizens of countries possessing colonies, semicolonies, or concessions resent criticism of governments and resent criticism of the "protection" by their governments of investments in these regions, and are irritated at any suggestion that these colonies, semicolonies, or concessions should be surrendered.

At a meeting of the Women's International League for Peace and Freedom in 1931, called especially to discuss the colonial question, the British delegates ruled out all discussion on India because it was a "dependency" and not a colony! A British pacifist Quaker wrote to *Peace News* that the Japanese had been guilty of seizure in China, but that the concessions in Shanghai and other Chinese ports had not been seized, but bought, and were free to all peoples. As Anna Graves writes:

> It is the system of colonialism which is responsible for the blindness of the workers in the possessing countries. The sentiment of pride in possessing others is so instilled into them by the Government through propaganda in the schools and the press, that they think of "these others" as quite "different" from themselves—as not worthy of the rights and the well-being they are struggling to gain for themselves; and even if hardly more than slaves themselves, are proud of owning others. The Labor party in England before the first World War voted for appalling expenditure on armaments, an expenditure which they knew very well would prevent sufficient expenditure on housing, on education, on health, et cetera, and the majority even voted for this extraordinary expenditure avowedly because they were afraid of losing India.[2]

When the Labor party came to partial power under MacDonald, it did less for the colonies than the Conservatives had done. They may be excused in part because they never commanded a majority in the House of Commons. Today they demand freedom for India, but their ministers in government stand by Churchill.

No matter how thoroughly and widely we may in the present war conquer Germany and Japan, we still have the welfare of over 150,000,000 human beings in these countries to face and to satisfy with a program adapted to the best interests of Germans and Japanese as well as other normal human beings. Any refusal to face this problem, to evade the problem of colonies, to forget injustice to minorities, to deny the rising struggle between economic classes, and above all to deal frankly and openly with the question of private profit and government control in industry—this is to make impossible a solution of the problem of world peace.

But imperialism does not stop there; it not only promotes civil war, strife, and jealousy within the colony, but it is, as we have seen, a main cause of struggles between powers to possess colonies. Thus colonialism separates peoples and workers and is perhaps the greatest proof of Tolstoy's dictum: "I say that there is an absolute good and absolute bad; for all that unites humanity is good and beautiful; and all that separates humanity is absolutely bad and ugly."[3] Its essential ugliness is shown in the present war.

In the First World War, each nation frantically gathered all its people for defense—nationals, colonials, white, brown and black; in this war, we are letting whites kill whites by the latest and best weapons rather than let our victory depend on colored folk, or risk their learning either our techniques or their common humanity.

Stephen Crane, who knew imperialist wars, cried, in "War Is Kind":

Is this God?
Where, then, is hell?
Show me some bastard mushroom
Sprung from a pollution of blood.
It is better.

It does not, therefore, seem possible or even probable that a union of nations to keep the world's peace is going to succeed so long as these nations are divided in interest over the control and possession of colonies. If colonial imperialism has caused wars for a century and a half, it can be depended upon to remain as a continual cause of other wars in the century to come.

NOTES

1. Vol. XV, p. 335.
2. Anna Graves, *op. cit.*
3. Quoted by Anna Graves, *op. cit.*

CHAPTER VI

◆

The Riddle of Russia

What are the possibilities of the union between Russia on the one hand and the British Empire and the United States on the other? How far after the war are these two elements so lately in violent opposition going to remain united for the advance of civilization, especially in the face of proposed continued disfranchisement and suppression of half the peoples of the earth?

The paradox of the present war is Russia. While on the one hand Russian Communism as organized under Stalin is helping to rescue the world from the greatest disaster that has ever threatened civilization, on the other hand the partners of Russia in this crusade—Britain, the United States, and China—are opposing and denouncing Communism. This is a dangerous situation, not only ideologically but practically.

Desperate effort is being made by thinkers of our day to explain and reconcile this paradox. In the United States many persons have firmly convinced themselves that Russian Communism is going capitalist; that the already established differences of income level and rewards for quality of work rather than quantity will eventually be supplemented by increased private property and even to some extent by private ownership of capital; that Russia will eventually join in the subjugation of Japan; and that she will continue to refuse to have direct connection with the Communists of China.

Movements which seem to bolster this line of thinking are the effort of Russia to share in the oil of Iran and her official abolition of the Comintern, together with the adoption of a new national hymn, which does not start with the revolutionary line "Arise, ye prisoners of starvation!" The fight of the United Nations against left-wing tendencies in the Balkans, in Italy, in Belgium, and in France shows in another way this line of thought; the upholding of Franco in Spain by Britain and the United States is further proof.

In addition to all this and even more significant, Russia needs capital from Western Europe and the United States. She has been getting large amounts during the present war, she is going to need larger amounts and long-time credits after the war, What bargain will the West drive in furnishing this capital, and how far and how completely will Russia be able to withstand its demands?

On the other hand, there is no doubt that a large section of the world's thinking and working peoples see in Russia the greatest hope of the future. They regard Russia as the central country to be considered in this reorganization of the world; and this not mainly because Russia has followed Marxian Communism or sought to control religious organization or preached the inevitability of the rise of the common man in modern times. For a century or more the Russion mushik was bracketed with the Negro slave and the Latin peasant as the most stupid and unhopeful of modern men. It was pointed out that the rule of the Czar and the aristocracy was absolutely necessary in a country so dismally ignorant and unprogressive as Russia.

Despite this, in a revolution which after a century of abortive attempts came to culmination in 1917, we have had an extraordinary uplifting of a whole nation; a nation has been taught to read and write, to organize industry, to heal its sickness and suppress its crime; and above all, so to reorganize its industry and internal economy as to make a larger number of Russians comfortable and happy than ever before in their long history; a nation which had in 1913, 859 newspapers with a circulation of 2,700,000 had in 1939, 9,000 newspapers with a circulation of 38,000,000 copies. This is a phase of progress toward democracy of which most people do not think. Democracy is not simply the self-defense of the competent; it is the unloosing of the energies and the capabilities of the depressed. This is what the USSR is accomplishing in its own land. It has withstood the armed onslaught of Europe and America; it has beaten back Nazi Germany and is now co-operating with the United Nations.

The future of the USSR holds two possibilities: the first is that its admission to full partnership with the capital-exporting and technically efficient countries of Western Europe and the United States will make it a party with them in the exploitation not only of working classes in general but especially of working classes in colonial areas. This would bring in Russia as coexploiter and dominant power in Asia, and through Russia, the British Empire would be restored. The second alternative is that the Soviet Union, clinging tenaciously to its program of socialized wealth, will refuse to be beguiled or tempted by either England or America; will refuse to have its armed forces used for the restoration of the British Empire in Asia or for the establishment of a new American empire in the Pacific; will have no part in the exploitation of workers in any of the leading countries or of laboring classes in any colonial area; and after developing capital for its own industries will consent to export it only under conditions which will ensure the ends of social uplift and not those of individual wealth or national power politics.

The first hope is indicated by such strains as the praise of Lady Astor, a snobbish daughter of Virginia slavery, in the British Parliament, after years of doubt:

> Communism in Russia has taught the people to read. . . . A people can't think or reach God until they learn to read. I don't dislike Russian communism. It has changed the European policy of keeping the people poor and ignorant—look at Spain and Italy.[1]

But this and Churchill's astute courting of Stalin merely show that the restoration of the British Empire, even to partial prewar power, is absolutely dependent upon Russia.

The USSR has already established a record which does not presage the use of its vast resources for restoring to Great Britain her lost colonies in Asia or for defending her possessions in Africa. The record of Soviet Russia in the matter of racial tolerance has been extraordinary. From a land noted for its fierce and brutal anti-Semitism and for other racial antagonisms and tensions, it has become today a community of two hundred, more or less, diverse groups of people, speaking different languages, with different heredity and to some extent clashing ideals, bound together in an extraordinary unity of effort and enthusiasm for its ideal. Its science and its system of education lead the world; and especially its attempted abolition of private profit points to the greatest revolution of modern times.

During the last century the world saw in Russia an autocratic and magnificent Czar surrounded by a rich, powerful, and extravagant aristocracy. In many respects this Russia was the social ideal of the beau monde and played its gorgeous part in Vienna, Paris, and London. Then came the Bolshevik Revolution. The Western world, almost with one accord, without waiting for legal sanction in all cases, threw itself upon Russia, made alliance with every Russian aristocrat, pretender, scoundrel, and adventurer, and tried by sheer force to beat the Russian masses back into their place.

While the war for Western Europe ended in 1918, for Russia it continued through nearly ten years of upheaval and disaster. Nevertheless a new state was born, with a new idea of economic organization. The USSR can never forget the well-nigh universal campaign of slander and lying that accompanied its struggle from 1917, almost to the outbreak of the Second World War. After being compelled to fight practically with bare hands in the First World War, and being cheated with glib promises of reform which did not materialize, it was met by every sort of calumny; its people were represented as dying by famine and starvation; its women were pictured as a nation of prostitutes; its industry was shown to be inefficient and its workers stupid and lazy.

The Church Universal viewed Rasputin and his ilk with grave and detached tolerance. But when the Bolsheviks cleansed the cesspool of superstition and greed which underlay Christianity in Russia, and gave the Russian people, for the first time in history, real religious freedom—the right to be atheists, freethinkers, Methodists, or Catholics—then the Church in Western Europe and America shrieked itself black in the face against "godless Russia" and Lenin, "the Antichrist."

Above all, Russia was condemned for murder—not only for the complete wiping out of the degenerate imperial family, but for purging a group of its own revolutionary officials; and one of the leaders in this pharisaical attack was the British, who in 1919 at Amritsar, India, killed 379 persons and wounded 1,200 others in order to keep India in subjection and avoid "being laughed at," as General Dyer explained. Even his mild "punishment" was condemned by a resolution in the House of Lords and £20,000 was raised for him by public subscription in honor of his heroic conduct at Jalianwala Bagh and his enforcement of the order to make Indians crawl on their bellies in crossing the square.

The United States, which was also a leader in anti-Russian propaganda, had lynched 3,047 Negroes in thirty-five years, and in 1917 was still lynching over 50 a year and refusing to take effective legal steps to stop this lawlessness.

Every line of argument was brought to bear to show that the Russian experiment was, in the words of Lathrop Stoddard, "a revolt against civilization." And finally, to complete the paradox, here is Russia today leading the forces of the world in an endeavor to save civilization.

Pushed hastily into altogether unexpected alliance with the capitalist countries of the West, after a generation of their attempts at force and vilification, Russia's full program so far as they are concerned has not been developed. The Soviet Union has not forgotten and could not forget the desperate efforts of France, England, and the United States to stem its revolution, force it back into czarism, and make it pay for the losses of their dispossessed capitalists, who had been for decades reaping enormous profit from exploitation of Russia. It must remember vividly that the present world-wide war could probably have been halted if England and France had made common cause with the USSR before Hitler invaded Poland. It found itself compelled to accept alliance with Hitler because alliance with the now United Nations was almost contemptuously denied it. Then because Hitler treacherously turned back to his original program of Eastern conquest and tried to unite the West against Russia, at the price of German industrial and imperial dominance, Soviet Russia finds itself in partnership with the extremist development of modern capitalism. Will it succumb to their doctrine?

There is absolutely nothing to compel it to do so. It does not even have to renounce its propaganda for Communism in order to win the world to its way of thinking. The Western world has had and still has today every opportunity to show mankind the advantages of privately owned capital, private profit, and "individual" enterprise. The result of their efforts to do so has had both success and disaster. There is still a chance for the capitalist nations to set their houses in order, and to show that neither Socialism nor its extreme, Communism, is necessary for human happiness and progress. If Great Britain and the United States can do this, they do not need to fear Russia, or Communism. All they need to fear is poverty, unemployment, ignorance, race hate, and the combination of these things, which has been modern imperialism.

On the other hand, in the restoration of the world if this war, like the First World War, is followed by widespread economic disaster, by starvation and disease, by continued ignorance and the attempt of certain races and peoples absolutely to dominate and condition others—then any attempt to fight Socialism, Communism, or other leftward movements will be absolutely without result, unless those movements also fail to bring happiness and contentment to mankind.

Seemingly today the peoples of Russia under Communism are more content and more united than any other mass of laborers. A study like the impartial survey of the Sidney Webbs says:

Will this new civilization, with its abandonment of the incentive of profit-making, its extinction of unemployment, its planned production for community consumption, and the consequent liquidation of the landlord and the capitalist, spread to other countries? Our own reply is: "Yes, it will." But how, when, where, with what modifications, and whether through violent revolution or by peaceful penetration, or even by conscious imitation, are questions we cannot answer.[2]

The future may prove that this judgment and appearance are deceptive and that the Russian economic organization will not continue to make this great mass of people homogeneous in ideal, prosperous in work, and willing to sacrifice for their country and their economic system more than any other nation in the world is sacrificing today. In that case, again the world will have no need to fear Communism. Thus in a sense Russia and the future of Russia are absolutely indispensable for a correct interpretation of the Second World War and for any realization of permanent peace.

The situations in China and India, in Burma and Indonesia, in the Near East and the Balkans, impose questions upon Russian diplomacy which will be most difficult to answer. Beyond this ranges the hopes of the labor parties and the left-wing elements in Europe, North America, and South America. Any change in the attitude of the USSR which will lead it to range itself with the former policies of the British Empire and the present aims of organized industry in the United States would spell a complete reversal of its recent past, and can hardly be expected.

If this is true, as the present war moves along its tragic and fatal course there looms a problem of colonies, unfree peoples, and suppressed classes concerning whose treatment there will be no unity of purpose in the United Nations. If we add to this the problem of a Germany with which Russia has always had ties of blood and cultural understanding; and of a Japan which, freed of dictatorship, may become a people demanding the same freedom as the free peoples of the West—in such case the problem of the postwar world will be of increased difficulty.

Whitman puts the world-wide and soul-deep dilemma:

And you O my soul where you stand,
Surrounded, detached, in measureless oceans of space,
Ceaselessly musing, venturing, throwing, seek in the spheres to connect them,
Till the bridge you need be form'd, till the ductile anchor hold,
Till the gossamer thread you fling catch somewhere, O my soul.[3]

Come what may, it is to the glory of God and the exaltation of man that the Soviet Union, first of modern nations, has dared to face front-forward the problem of poverty, and to place on the uncurbed power of concentrated wealth the blame of widespread and piteous penury. It has not lied about poverty. It has not distorted the facts. It has not, like most nations, without effort to solve it, declared the insolubility of the problem of the poor. And above all, it has not falsely placed on the poor the blame of their wretched condition. Even should the Russian experiment fail and Communism be proved unable to cope with the problems of land, property, and income, Russia deserves all credit for having at least faced the problem and for having tried to solve it; and other nations must eventually face and solve the same problem if civilization is going to be preserved.

NOTES

1. Associated Press dispatch, October, 1944.
2. Sidney and Beatrice Webb, *Soviet Communism*, Vol. II, p. 1143.
3. "A Noiseless Patient Spider."

CHAPTER VII

◆

Missions and Mandates

Failure of the United Nations to come immediately to grips with the problem of colonies will invite catastrophe; effective action calls for a new mandates commission implemented by that unselfish devotion to the well-being of mankind which has often, if not always, inspired the missionary crusade.

It is clear that in this world, as manifested by these terrible wars and by the suffering of mankind and the sacrifice of peoples, there is a tremendous available amount of goodwill and desire for the uplift of mankind. This has been shown in the past in all sorts of ways: in China's love of peace, in the charity of the medieval Christian Church, in the missionary crusades of Buddhists, Christians, and Mohammedans; especially in the Christian missions of the eighteenth and nineteenth centuries; in the suppression of slavery and the slave trade; and in the various attempts to alleviate, if not abolish, poverty and to do away with ignorance.

The difficulty in this particular era is that this goodwill must be organized and canalized. It must not aid and abet reaction in social progress, nor be used like the missionary effort in Africa to exploit and subdue peoples in the name of Jesus Christ for the use of profit-making industry. It must, on the contrary, become organized as missions of culture to carry to backward peoples, minority groups, and lower economic classes the cultures and education which they are capable of absorbing and using. It must narrow the frightful and dangerous differences between current custom and the scientific knowledge that there are no races and great groups incapable of the same kind of advance that has been made by the most cultured peoples; and that what is needed is opportunity; that we can have democracy and peace only if the menace of poverty, ignorance, and crime are met by positive and organized human action—Poverty, Ignorance and Crime—these three—but the greatest of these is Poverty.

Poverty can be attacked and abolished by government action and social organization. The way to make this clear to the world is to attack the economic illiteracy, the ignorance of economic facts and developments, now deliberately encouraged in our schools and colleges, in our press and periodicals and in our books. Here is the field for the Great Crusade which will lead to democracy and peace.

The Atlantic Charter brought a new examination of the colonial question. The second point declared that the United Nations "desire to see no territorial changes that do not accord with the freely expressed wishes of the peoples concerned."

The third point was: that "they respect the right of all peoples to choose the form of government under which they will live; and they wish to see sovereign rights and self-government restored to those who have been forcibly deprived of them."

The sixth said: that "after the final destruction of the Nazi tyranny, they hope to see established a peace which will afford to all nations the means of dwelling in safety within their own boundaries, and which will afford assurance that all the men in all the lands may live out their lives in freedom from fear and want."

When, however, the attempt was made to apply these points to colonies and particularly to India, Mr. Churchill limited their application to Europe, while President Roosevelt proclaimed the Four Freedoms:

Freedom of speech and expression
Freedom of every person to worship God in his own way
Freedom from want
Freedom from fear

Since then social thought has forged ahead. British Christians asked that: "Every child, regardless of race or class, should have equal opportunities for education."

The Council for Social Action adopted a charter in June, 1944, which asked in international affairs:

> The closest collaboration among states on all matters of international moment, including especially the problems of trade and migration barriers, the advancement and eventual self-government of colonial peoples, determination of military armament, provisions for relief and rehabilitation of afflicted peoples, assistance in the advancement of handicapped countries, treatment of minorities and of vanquished nations, and settlement of international disputes. . . . As their center, we envisage an international body with wider functions and more fundamental power than the League of Nations.

The Christian Church was aroused, and the Council of Congregational Churches said in June 1944 that "our churches" should support American participation in an international organization including "co-operation for world trade, employment, currency stabilization and equitable access to raw materials; and supervision of the treatment of all subject peoples, that ultimately they may achieve nationhood and autonomy or voluntary full participation in a larger political unit."[1]

The Commission to Study the Organization of Peace especially advocated an elaborate statement of human rights for the protection of minorities and peoples. This Commission said:

> We may be chastened by Wilson's rejection at Paris of the principle of racial equality—a rejection which embittered the Oriental world. The Negro situation in our country and expressions of anti-Semitism, which foster enemy propaganda, are not to be passed over. There is, however, a vast difference between a governmental policy of persecution, as in Germany, and laggard customs which have not yet been broken by a legal policy which forbids them. We cannot postpone international leadership until our own house is completely in order. Nor can we expect nations to agree that their own houses should be brought into order by the direct intervention of international agencies. We have only to consider the difficulties which any such course would encounter in our own or other countries. Through revulsion against Nazi doctrines, we may, however, hope to speed up the process of bringing our own practices in each nation more in conformity with our professed ideals [2]

A formula by H. G. Wells said:

> I believe in the right of every living human being, without distinction of color, race, sex or professed belief or opinion, to liberty, life and subsistence, to complete protection from ill-treatment, equality of opportunity in the pursuit of happiness and an equal voice in the collective government of mankind.[3]

The American Council of the World Alliance representing six international agencies said on November 10, 1944:

> Recognizing that most of the difficulties which have brought about the most serious results in the world during the last half century have arisen from complaints of minorities, we urge that when the final constitution for the United Nations is drafted there shall be appended to it a "bill of rights" for all men in all nations.
>
> To us it seems important for the nations to give greater attention to the needs of people in dependent and backward areas. We urge that the whole scheme of mandated territories and the continuance of colonial systems be brought under close scrutiny and better control by the international organization.[4]

Stephen Duggan writes:

> What will be the probable attitude of the Allies toward colonies and mandates in the case of victory? The mandate system is so distinctly an improvement over the colonial system that many political scientists advocate the extension of its principles to all colonies. They would place the sovereignty over colonies and mandates in the central agency of the New World Order that is to be organized, with the addition of direct power of investigation and sanctions for breach of trust. Would that mean the transfer of the colonies to the new collective organization? To ask the question is to pose the difficulty. To shift the actual administration from the experienced officials now in control would be a most serious risk. To permit the present

holders of colonies to continue in control would not allay the discontent of the Have Not Powers. But if the New World Order would establish agencies that could secure equitable distribution of raw materials and access to markets, the justifiable demand for colonies would be largely removed. If in addition the existing services in colonies would become responsible to the supra-nationals, the discontent of the Have Nots ought at least to be reduced. This may be a counsel of perfection.

According to the Covenant, the mandate system has for its objective "the well-being and development" of the peoples of the mandates. The intent repeatedly expressed at League meetings was unquestionably that the natives be trained in self-government and that the economy of the country be gradually brought under their control. This is a big order. Vested interests in the meantime will have been formed and it is asking a good deal of human nature to request the colonial service to prepare people to displace themselves. Success will depend upon the will really to achieve the aim.[5]

The National Association for the Advancement of Colored People has approached the Department of State with this statement:

As the territory of France, Italy, certain areas in the Balkans, and other lands occupied by peoples generally classified as "white" are recaptured from the enemy by the allied armies, provisions of one kind or another have been made to return control of those lands to the peoples who occupied them prior to the outbreak of World War II; but the National Association for the Advancement of Colored People notes with deep regret that when continental and insular areas of Africa and Asia, occupied by so-called colored colonials, are retaken, control and administration of them are immediately reassumed by the white colonial powers who ruled these areas before. Quite cold-bloodedly, these colonial powers do not even attempt to ascertain what the wishes of the occupants of these lands may be. Quite to the contrary, their wishes are ignored. The National Association for the Advancement of Colored People is well aware of the fact that while the battles for these and other territories occupied by the enemy are being waged, policies as to future control cannot be determined immediately. But those policies must be decided upon and put into effect soon. It is imperative that the Allies now take positive action toward self-determination for colonial peoples as a goal which must be achieved before peace is truly secure.

The Board of Directors of the National Association for the President of Avancement of Colored People therefore petitions the President of the United States to make clear now that the United States Government will not be a party to the perpetuation of colonial exploitation of any nation; that, on the contrary, the United States Government is utterly opposed and will make that opposition clear at the Quebec and all subsequent conferences to any policy which means freedom for white people or any part of the white people of the earth on the one hand, and continued exploitation of colored peoples, on the other. We ask that it be made clear that the United States will not in any fashion, direct or indirect, uphold continued exploitation of India, China, Abyssinia and other African areas, the West Indies, or of any other part of the world. The NAACP Board of Directors further urges again that qualified Negroes be appointed to serve as representatives of the United States Government at conferences in which the United States Government is a participant, which are called to determine war or post-war policies, principles and commitments, to which the United States is a party, dealing with both global and domestic policies.[6]

The State Department answered:

> As you are no doubt aware, there is in the Department of State a deep appreciation of the importance of the problems of dependent peoples referred to in your resolution, and of the need for devising practicable solutions which will represent the greatest tangible advancement that may be possible during and after the war. The appropriate divisions and committees of the Department which are studying the problems of post-war territorial settlements base their views, I may assure you, upon the fundamental principles of equitable and just treatment of all peoples.
>
> I wish to bring particularly to your attention two recent statements of the Secretary of State which bear significantly upon the points raised in your resolution. In his radio address of July 23, 1942, the Secretary stated:
>
> "We have always believed—and we believe today—that all peoples, without distinction of race, color, or religion, who are prepared and willing to accept the responsibilities of liberty, are entitled to its enjoyment. We have always sought— and we seek today—to encourage and aid all who aspire to freedom to establish their right to it by preparing themselves to assume its obligations. We have striven to meet squarely our own responsibility in this respect—in Cuba, in the Philippines, and wherever else it has devolved upon us. It has been our purpose in the past— and will remain our purpose in the future—to use the full measure of our influence to support attainment of freedom by all peoples who, by their acts, show themselves worthy of it and ready for it."
>
> In the memorandum on Bases of the Foreign Policy of the United States, released to the press on March 21, 1944, the Secretary included the following statement with respect to dependent peoples:
>
> "There rests upon the independent nations a responsibility in relation to dependent peoples who aspire to liberty. It should be the duty of nations having political ties with such peoples, of mandatories, of trustees, or of other agencies, as the case may be, to help the aspiring peoples to develop materially and educationally, to prepare themselves for the duties and responsibilities of self-government, and to attain liberty. An excellent example of what can be achieved is afforded in the record of our relationship with the Philippines."
>
> I also appreciate the significance of your suggestion concerning the composition of American delegations to international conferences. It is our aim always to appoint the persons best qualified to represent the United States in the specific field of the Department's responsibilities.[7]

Some of the free nations have spoken, as New Zealand has:

> Advocacy of the principle of trusteeship for all colonial peoples was proposed by Prime Minister Peter Fraser as one result of the Australia-New Zealand conversations. . . .
>
> Recalling the enunciation of principles in the Canberra agreement of last February, Mr. Fraser said the Antipodean dominions felt that as part of a general international organization there should be an international body analogous to the Mandates Commission, but having powers of inspection and publishing reports of its findings.[8]

Anson Phelps Stokes has written the present Secretary of State:

I hope that there may be time for giving some attention to the important problems connected with colonies and other dependencies. I am convinced that until the colonial problems, especially those related to Africa, are constructively and wisely settled, there is not likely to be permanent peace, especially at a time when the darker people of the world are becoming more and more self-conscious, and are eager to play an increasing part in national and international affairs.

In this connection two or three things seem to me of special importance:

(1) That the permanent Commission of Mandates be re-established, or something similar created, and that it be given power not only to receive reports from mandatory powers as in the past, but to make reports on conditions, and in cases of abuse, to take steps to see that they are, if possible, remedied. The mandates plan was a great advance on anything which preceded it, but it did not go far enough.

(2) That the experiment be made in one or two suitable areas of international mandates. Some parts of Africa formerly owned by Italy, or some Japanese islands in the Pacific might well furnish the place for a trial of this plan. The United States should, of course, be prepared to play its part in this and other international responsibilities.

(3) That emphasis be placed in any new charter for mandated areas more definitely than was done in the past on the intention of the international organization to see to it that people in mandated areas are prepared for and given a larger and larger share in determining the policies of their area and more definite assurance that they will be given self-government at the earliest practicable time. . . .

(6) That some arrangements be made by which colored people of the world should have an opportunity to present their views to the Peace Conference or Peace Conferences, and that in keeping with this plan there should be one or more representative Negroes attached in some official capacity to the United States delegation to the Peace Conference immediately following the war.[9]

Sumner Welles, former Under-Secretary of State, has proposed the establishment of an international trusteeship which shall see to it that all dependent peoples and colonies are granted autonomy and are properly prepared for their freedom:

I cannot believe that the United Nations, now banded together to destroy the tyrannies which have attempted to exercise their sway over free men and women throughout the world, will countenance an outcome of their common victory which would merely perpetuate the exploitation and servitude so long imposed upon colonial peoples.

For that reason the establishment by the future international organization of an international trusteeship, which will not only eliminate the inequities of the mandate system of the past, but which will also assure all dependent peoples that they will be accorded autonomy and their independence as soon as they are capable of exercising these rights, must be assured.

Such a trusteeship should have as its supreme objective the preparation of all independent peoples as speedily as possible for the assumption of the responsibilities and the obligations for freedom. The creation of an international trusteeship, holding itself ultimately responsible to public opinion throughout the world, would be one sign that the people's peace, of which we often so complacently speak, can become a reality.[10]

Not only has Winston Churchill definitely refused to consider the matter of international control of colonies but the liberal British Secretary of State for Colonies, Oliver Stanley, apparently is ready to surrender international control of mandated territories and has consequently incurred the protest of several eminent leaders, including John W. Davis, Emory Ross, James T. Shotwell, Sumner Welles, and Quincy Wright. They said in the *New York Times*, February 18, 1945:

"Trusteeship" represented the first and a reasonably successful attempt to put into practice the principle that "the well-being and development of such (dependent) peoples form a sacred trust of civilization." Under the mandates system, national and international machinery was set up to carry out this trust. International colonial experts, for instance, reviewed and criticized the conditions which brought on the rebellion against the French in Syria in 1925, raised serious questions as to Japanese fortifications in the Pacific islands as far back as 1932, and dealt with many hundreds of other matters involving native welfare and the open door for all nations in the development of these territories.

The abandonment of the gains which were inherent in this system might imply a step toward the division of the world into several great power zones of exclusive domination. It would weaken the system of international responsibility for dependent peoples which was actually practiced between the wars. The continuance and development of this principle and its extension to other dependent territories, especially those to be taken from the enemies at the end of this war, would imply just that much more confidence on the part of the United Nations in the success of their new venture.

But little has yet been done. Harried hope is still wringing helpless hands, dripping with the blood of Poland and of Spain. Prayer and masses, fast and death, are impotent. Surely this statement might be made by the United Nations: "It is the opinion of the United Nations that no state has any historic or ethical right to hold a group, colony, or dependency under control against the freely expressed will of its people; and if by reason of poverty, illiteracy, and disease these inhabitants cannot voice their own best interests, it is the bounden duty of the religious conscience, the civilized intelligence, and the industrial economy of the world under international mandate to remove at the earliest moment, such impediments to world democracy and permanent peace."

Lowell sings of Truth:

Those love her best, who to themselves are true,
And what they dare to dream of, dare to do.[11]

The question whose answer balks us is: How, with international control, are we going to get a great philanthropic deed done efficiently and scientifically? With the image of totalitarianism before us, added to our experience of war bureaucracy, we are afraid even of national, much more of international, action. The choosing of proper men to carry on the work, the organization of the work with scientific precision, and above all the ideal, the will to good, back of it—all this seems an almost impossible accomplishment.

It is an extraordinary commentary upon this that at this very time, and for centuries gone by, we have in theory, and in deep and abiding faith, an instrument for just this kind of work among human beings, and that is organized religion—the Christian Church, Catholic and Protestant; the work of Jews, Buddhists, and Mohammedans; even the work of philanthropic and ethical-culture organizations. Why is it that we do not think of these as organs for attacking the problem of colonies at this critical time?

The interesting and startling fact is that we do not think of them. There is a dichotomy between religion and social uplift, the Church and sociology, which leads to deplorable loss of effort and division of thinking. Religion has been an emotional release and escape method for pessimism and despair, coupled with utter doubt, so far as this world is concerned. While science, as social reform, has been the optimistic belief in human uplift, without any compelling reason for accomplishing this for any particular persons, or at any particular time. It is as so often happens: religion without science, science without guiding ideals.

The Church, Catholic and Protestant, has expended tremendous effort in mission work for colonies in Asia and Africa during the last two or more centuries. The one great and unquestionable accomplishment of this effort, as has been noted, has been the beginnings of education. The starting of modern education in Africa, and its maintenance in spite of strong opposition, is due almost entirely to missionary effort. Much, although less, has been done for modern education in Asia and the Near East.

The great criticism of this work is that from the beginning it co-operated, perhaps unconsciously, with industrial exploitation. The missionaries for the most part had training in elementary schools, supplemented by some higher training in literature and ethics, together with technical training in theological dogma. But they knew little or nothing about modern economics, anthropology, and the social sciences, and were guided in this growing realm of thought and action by culture patterns belonging to a different era and differing groups. In the expert hands of an industrial world, organized for precise aims and capable of hiring the best brains of the day, the missionaries easily became in many cases tools of exploitation.

In this world, people who wish to do good and are without careful training and wide experience are easily the victims of politicians and industrial leaders. Eugene Jung, who for a long time held high position in French Indo-China, has said: "It is in fact by the missionaries that one penetrates first into a region and that one gets a foothold in it."[12] Governments use missionaries and other people of this type as smoke screens to hide the truth from the people of the possessing country. They use them as aids in forming prejudices against the culture, the civilization, the religion of the "natives" of the colony.

Even if among these people of kindly intent there should be some who really succeed in doing an appreciable amount of good, the good they do often is not sufficient to compensate for the bad for which the system back of them is responsible. Sleeping sickness and tuberculosis, venereal diseases, and maladies due to undernourishment have all increased by leaps and bounds in the colonies because of the system of colonialism, and in spite of many good and faithful physicians.

Even in the education which the missionaries have fostered, pressure has made them consent to serious limitation. In the Belgian Congo, the Catholics are furnishing some good primary training and the industrialists are teaching skills; but there is almost no secondary or higher training for leadership or even for necessary professions like medicine and teaching.

In other cases of vaster and more tremendous social implication, like the slave trade, slavery, serfdom, and concubinage, religion usually, after a first flare of idealistic opposition, has sunk to a place where it condoned and even defended these evils. Both Catholic and Protestant churches became in the United States ardent defenders of Negro slavery. The Christian Church in America today is almost completely separated along the color line, just as are the army, the navy, the nursing service, and even the blood banks. In many cases where moral opposition is needed, the Church became strangely silent and complacent, and gave the world a right to say with Lenin, "Religion is the opium of the people."

We must add to this that the Church as organized in modern civilized countries has become the special representative of the employing and exploiting classes. It has become mainly a center of wealth and social exclusiveness, and by this very fact, wherever you find a city of large and prosperous churches, such as Atlanta, Georgia, or Dallas, Texas, or Minneapolis, Minnesota, you find cities where the so-called best people, the educated, intelligent, and well-to-do, are critical of democracy, suspicious of the labor movement, bitter against Soviet Russia, and indifferent to the Negro problem, because their economic interests have put them in opposition to forward movements and the teachers and preachers whom they hire have fed them on that kind of prejudice, or maintained significant silence.

Notwithstanding this, it is all too clear today that if we are to have a sufficient motive for the uplift of backward peoples, for the redemption and progress of colonials, such a motive can be found only in the faith and ideals of organized religion; and the great task that is before us is to join this belief and the consequent action with the scientific knowledge and efficient techniques of economic reform.

It would be unfair to myself, and perhaps to others, if I did not frankly say that my attitude toward organized religion is distinctly critical. I cannot believe that any chosen body of people or special organization of mankind has received a direct revelation of ultimate truth which is denied to earnest scientific effort. I admit readily that it would be most satisfactory if instead of occupying a little island of knowledge in the midst of vast stretches of unknown truth, we could with conviction and utter faith plant ourselves on a completely revealed knowledge of the ends and aims of the universe. But no matter how satisfying this would be, it does not therefore follow that it is true, or that those who assert it and believe in it have the right to persecute and condemn those who cannot accept urgent desire, or myth and fairy tale, as valid truth. It may well be that God has revealed ultimate knowledge to babes and sucklings, but that is no reason why I, one who does not believe this miracle, should surrender to infants the guidance of my mind and effort. No light of faith, no matter how kindly and beneficent, can in a world of reason guide human beliefs to truth unless it is continually tested by pragmatic fact.

On the other hand, I must just as frankly acknowledge that the majority of the best and earnest people of this world are today organized in religious groups, and that without the co-operation of the richness of their emotional experience, and the unselfishness of their aims, science stands helpless before crude fact and selfish endeavor. The reason for this religious majority may be inexperience and lack of education; it may be divine grace and human sin. Whatever it is, the fact is unquestionable today.

Is there not, then, a chance to find common ground for a program of human betterment which seeks by means of known and tested knowledge the ideal ends of faith? This would involve on the part of the Church a surrender of dogma to the extent of being willing to work for human salvation this side of eternity, and to admit the possibility of vast betterment here and now—a path the Church has often followed. The Church should in colonies voluntarily adopt a self-denying ordinance: not to stress doctrine or dogma until social uplift in education, health, and economic organization have progressed far enough to enable colonial peoples intelligently and independently to compare the religion offered with their inherited cultures. This would involve on the part of science the admission that what we know is greatly exceeded by what we do not know, and that there may be realms in time and space of infinitely more importance than the problems of this small world. Nevertheless, a realistic program of making this world better *now* ought to combine the efforts of Church and science, of missionary effort and social reform.

Before, and more especially after, the First World War, the conscience of mankind, as well as its political wisdom, faced the situation in colonies. Before 1914, the world had rationalized the situation and kept its uneasy conscience more or less asleep. The old race theory of the nineteenth century was potent. We still envisaged the world as capable of civilization but engulfed and threatened by hordes of folks whose great and permanent progress was unthinkable. Their destiny was to serve, and the burden of the white man was to protect these "lesser breeds without the law" from unnecessary cruelty but at the same time firmly "keep them in their places."

These and a large number of other matters gave Europeans pause when after the First World War the question of the disposal of German colonies came up for discussion. It was then that the world slowly rose to a new conception of human responsibility for colonial conditions. The lone facts, although difficult to substantiate by actual figures, were an indictment against colonial government to which the world had to listen. This indictment was felt, and felt strongly, at the time of the Treaty of Versailles; and in the organization of the League of Nations advantage was taken of the situation of the German colonies to attempt a solution to the whole colonial problem. The German colonies were distributed among France, Britain, and Japan under the control of a Mandates Commission. The Mandates Commission was supposed to see that the people of these colonies were fairly treated, and that something was done for their social uplift and their economic betterment.

But modern industrialism and investment policy were not to be balked of their prey. The statute that governed the Mandates Commission was deliberately limited in such a way that the Commission really had very little power. It could not of its own initiative inquire into or investigate facts in the various colonies; the colonial peoples themselves had no vested right of appeal to the Commission, and as a matter of fact the mandated colony soon became indistinguishable from the other colonies of the countries holding the mandates.

It had been hoped that the opposite would happen, and that the authority of the Mandates Commission would eventually extend not only to the former German colonies, but to all colonies of all nations. This never took place, and the only organ of the League of Nations that substantially helped the colonial situation was the International Labor Office, which succeeded in setting up certain minimum standards of labor usage.

What is needed today is a new Mandates Commission calling upon the United Nations to recognize the fact that the first Mandates Commission established by the statute which organized the League of Nations has a place in international law, and that the United Nations have no right in law or justice to ignore this statute and hand over the former colonies of Germany to France, Britain, the Union of South Africa, or Japan; that a new Mandates Commission should immediately be organized to take charge of the mandated colonies and to go farther, as was suggested in the original Covenant, and lay down new procedures for the treatment of all colonial peoples.

The General Assembly of the United Nations should begin by insisting that there sit in the Assembly not simply representatives of the free nations, but with them representatives of all colonial peoples over whom they claim control. The matter of the number of such colonial delegates can well wait on time and experience. The method of their choice and the fair representation of all angles of opinion can be gradually adjusted as the Economic and Social Council gains power to investigate. But it is absolutely essential that, at the beginning, the voices of all peoples that on earth do dwell be raised fearlessly and openly in the parliament of man, to seek justice, complain of oppression, and demand equality. Difficult as this program will doubtless prove, it will not be nearly so difficult, horrible, and utterly devastating as two world wars in a single generation.

Evidently there is indicated here the necessity of earnest effort to avoid the nondemocratic and race-inferiority philosophy involved. There should be consultation among colonial peoples and their friends as to just what measures ought to be taken. This consultation should look toward asking for the following successive steps:

One, representation of the colonial peoples alongside the master peoples in the Assembly.

Two, the organization of a Mandates Commission under the Economic and Social Council, with definite power to investigate complaints and conditions in colonies and make public their findings and to hear oral petitions.

Three, a clear statement of the intentions of each imperial power to take, gradually but definitely, all measures designed to raise the peoples of colonies to a condition of complete political and economic equality with the peoples of the master nations, and eventually either to incorporate them into the polity of the master nations or to allow them to become independent free peoples.

We all know well exactly why a Mandates Commission with power over former German colonies, and at least the right of investigation and report over all colonies, was not included as a part of the proposals of Dumbarton Oaks. This reason was the opposition of Britain as represented by Winston Churchill. Mr. Churchill stands for that part of Britain which is stubbornly determined to maintain the place of the British Empire as a super state ruling a large part of the world. Back of this determination is the motive of maintaining the power of the British aristocracy privileged by birth and wealth.

But this is not the only Britain. There is a Greater Britain, spiritually descended from those equally determined souls who for a half-century fought the African slave trade and Negro slavery, and their successors who later stood back of the Reform Bill, popular education, and woman suffrage. It is this Greater Britain that is so often betrayed by its European and American friends, and which finds itself without allies in the liberal world and blamed for sins that were never its own. The credit for what it has done is calmly annexed by the privileged classes, and we hear continually of the Britain which fought slavery, as though it were one with the brutal empire-builders who for a century used the abolition of slavery and the suppression of the slave trade as an excuse for stealing the land and the liberty of 100,000,000 Africans. What is true of Britain is true in other ways of many another nation, including our own.

Social science has not yet established a vocabulary and a method of statement which makes it possible to distinguish between these elements of all national life, but it remains true that to fight the Britain of Winston Churchill is giving support, moral and material, to the Britain of Wilberforce, Wesley, Owen, and Colenso. Let imperialism perish—British, German, Japanese, Italian, Spanish—with that of ancient Rome, empire with its aristocratic tinsel and greed, cruel conquest, slavery of souls, and slave trade in human rights. Let Greater Britain grow, leading in the future as in the past; French equality and Yankee push, with British love of liberty, stubborn courage, sportsmanship, and common sense.

There will return one day to all nations another group with which the world must reckon; young, disillusioned, bitter voters, disillusioned because they realize the futility of war as a settlement of human problems, because they saw its glory in mud, pain, and torn flesh. They will return maimed inevitably in body and mind and ripe for extremity in thought and action. Propaganda, as in the last war, may make them reactionary, anti-labor, anti-Negro, anti-Semitic, anti-foreign-born; counterpropaganda may make them food for revolution and violence of every kind. Their guiding and healing is a major problem. But how can it be applied if the democracy, the one tangible ideal for which most of them fought, fails miserably and at home?

Wild is the world and witless, terrible in its beauty and crime. Can one forget sunrise on Lake Baikal, the gray oaks of Nara, the hills of light of Manhattan? Who may not remember the lynching of Mary Brown, the suicides of bankers in 1929, and the cripples crawling out of Guadalcanal, Aachen, and Leyte? Behold the starving children of Europe, Asia, and Africa. Such a world, with all its contradictions, can be saved, can yet be born again; but not out of capital, interest, property, and gold, rather out of dreams and loiterings, out of simple goodness and friendship and love, out of science and missions.

There has been surfeit of creed, dogma, and priestly assumption to bridle the intelligence of men; there has been enough of the aimless arrogance of science used to heal and kill, destroy and build. The day has dawned when above a wounded, tired earth unselfish sacrifice, without sin and hell, may join thorough technique, shorn of ruthless greed, and make a new religion, one with new knowledge, to shout from old hills of heaven:

Go down, Moses!

NOTES

1. Adopted at Grand Rapids, Michigan, June 27, 1944.
2. *Fourth Report* of the Commission to Study the Organization of Peace, Part III, p. 21.
3. Quoted in *Fourth Report* of the Commission to Study the Organization of Peace, May, 1944, p. 20.
4. World Alliance *News Letter*, November, 1944.
5. Institute of International Education, *News Bulletin*, February 1, 1942, p. 5.
6. Resolution, Board of Directors, N.A.A.C.P., September 11, 1944, sent by telegram to President Roosevelt.
7. Reply of Under-Secretary of State Stettinius, October 4, 1944.
8. Associated Press dispatch, *New York Times*, October, 1944.
9. MS. copy of a letter sent to the author.
10. Reported in the *New York Times*, October, 1944.
11. "Tercentenary Ode."
12. Quoted by Anna Graves, *op. cit.*

William Edward Burghardt Du Bois: A Chronology

Compiled by Henry Louis Gates, Jr. and Terri Hume Oliver

1868	Born William Edward Burghardt Du Bois, 23 February, in Great Barrington, Massachusetts—the only child of Alfred Du Bois and Mary Silvina Burghardt. Mother and child move to family farm owned by Othello Burghardt, Mary Silvina's father, in South Egremont Plain.
1872	Othello Burghardt dies 19 September and family moves back to Great Barrington, where Mary Silvina finds work as a domestic servant.
1879	Moves with mother to rooms on Railroad Street. Mother suffers stroke, which partially paralyzes her; she continues to work despite her disability.
1883–1885	Writes occasionally for *Springfield Republican*, the most influential newspaper in the region. Reports on local events for the *New York Globe*, a black weekly, and its successor, the *Freeman*.
1884	Graduates from Great Barrington High School. Works as time-keeper on a construction site.
1885	Mother dies 23 March at age 54. A scholarship is arranged by local Congregational churches so Du Bois can attend Fisk University in Nashville. Enters Fisk with sophomore standing. Contracts typhoid and is seriously ill in October; after recovering, resumes studies and becomes editor of the school newspaper, the *Fisk Herald*.
1886–1887	Teaches at a black school near Alexandria, Tennessee, for two summers. Begins singing with the Mozart Society at Fisk.
1888	Receives BA from Fisk. Enters Harvard College as a junior after receiving a Price-Greenleaf grant.
1890	Awarded second prize in Boylston oratorical competition. Receives BA *cum laude* in philosophy on 25 June. Delivers commencement oration on Jefferson Davis, which receives national press attention. Enters Harvard Graduate School in social science.

1891	Awarded MA in history from Harvard. Begins work on doctorate. Presents paper on the suppression of the African slave trade at meeting of American Historical Association in Washington, D.C.
1892	Awarded a Slater Fund grant to study in Germany at Friedrich Wilhelm University in Berlin.
1893	Grant is extended for an additional year.
1894	Denied doctoral degree at Friedrich Wilhelm University due to residency requirements. Denied further aid from Slater Fund; returns to Great Barrington. Receives teaching chair in classics at Wilberforce University in Xenia, Ohio.
1895	Awarded a PhD in history; he is the first black to receive a PhD from Harvard.
1896	Marries Nina Gomer, a student at Wilberforce. His doctoral thesis, *The Suppression of the African Slave-Trade to United States of America, 1638–1870*, is published as the first volume of Harvard's Historical Monograph Series. Hired by the University of Pennsylvania to conduct a sociological study on the black population of Philadelphia's Seventh Ward.
1897	Joins Alexander Crummell and other black intellectuals to found the American Negro Academy, an association dedicated to black scholarly achievement. Appointed professor of history and economics at Atlanta University. Begins editing a series of sociological studies on black life, the *Atlanta University Studies* (1898–1914). First child, Burghardt Comer Du Bois, is born in Great Barrington on 2 October.
1899	*The Philadelphia Negro* is published by the University of Pennsylvania. Burghardt Gomer Du Bois dies on 24 May in Atlanta and is buried in Great Barrington. Publishes articles in *Atlantic Monthly* and *The Independent*.
1900	In July attends first Pan-African Congress in London and is elected secretary. In an address to the congress, he declares that "the problem of the twentieth century is the problem of the color line." Enters an exhibit at Paris Exposition and wins grand prize for his display on black economic development. Daughter Nina Yolande born 21 October in Great Barrington.
1901	Publishes "The Freedman's Bureau" in *Atlantic Monthly*.
1902	Booker T. Washington offers Du Bois a teaching position at Tuskegee Institute, but Du Bois declines.
1903	*The Souls of Black Folk* is published in April. Publishes the essay "The Talented Tenth" in *The Negro Problem*.
1904	Resigns from Washington's Committee of Twelve for the Advancement of the Negro Race due to ideological differences. Publishes "Credo" in *The Independent*.
1905	Holds the first conference of the Niagara Movement and is named general secretary. Founds and edits *The Moon Illustrated Weekly*.

1906	Second meeting of the Niagara Movement. *The Moon* ceases publication. The Atlanta riots, in which white mobs target blacks, occur in September; Du Bois responds by writing his most famous poem, *A Litany of Atlanta*. After the riots Du Bois's wife and daughter move to Great Barrington.
1907	Niagara Movement in disarray due to debt and dissension. Founds and edits *Horizon*, a monthly paper that folds in 1910.
1908	Fourth conference of Niagara Movement; few attend.
1909	The National Negro Committee, an organization dominated by white liberals, is formed (it will later be renamed the National Association for the Advancement of Colored People [NAACP]); Du Bois joins. The fifth and last Niagara Conference is held. *John Brown*, a biography, is published.
1910	Appointed director of publications and research for the NAACP; becomes the only black member of the board of directors. Moves to New York City to found and edit *The Crisis*, the official publication of the NAACP.
1911	Attends Universal Races Conference in London. Publishes his first novel, *The Quest of the Silver Fleece*. Joins the Socialist Party.
1912	Endorses Woodrow Wilson in *The Crisis*. Resigns from Socialist Party.
1913	Writes and presents *The Star of Ethiopia*, a pageant staged to commemorate the fiftieth anniversary of emancipation.
1914	Supports women's suffrage in *The Crisis*. Supports the Allied effort in World War I despite declaring that imperialist rivalries are a cause of the war.
1915	Booker T. Washington dies on 14 November. *The Negro* is published. Protests D. W. Griffith's racist film *The Birth of a Nation*.
1917	Undergoes kidney operations early in the year. Supports the establishment of separate training camps for black officers as the only way to insure black participation in combat.
1918	In his July editorial for *The Crisis*, he publishes "Close Ranks," urging cooperation with white citizens. The War Department offers Du Bois a commission as a captain in the army in an effort to address racial issues, but the offer is withdrawn after controversy. Goes to Europe in December to evaluate the conditions of black troops for the NAACP.
1919	Organizes the first Pan-African Conference in Paris, and is elected executive secretary. Returns to the U.S. in April and writes the editorial "Returning Soldiers," which the U.S. postmaster Albert Burleson tries to suppress; the issue sells 106,000 copies, the most ever for *The Crisis*.
1920	Founds and edits *The Brownies' Book*, a monthly magazine for children. Publishes *Darkwater: Voices from within the Veil*, a collection of essays.

1921	The second Pan-African Conference is held in London, Brussels, and Paris. Du Bois signs group protest against Henry Ford's support of the anti-Semitic forgery, *Protocols of the Elders of Zion.*
1922	Works for passage of the Dyer Anti-Lynching Bill, which is blocked by Senate.
1923	Writes "Back to Africa," an article attacking Garvey for encouraging racial division. Organizes the third Pan-African Conference in London, Paris, and Lisbon; declines to attend Paris session due to disproval of French assimilationists. Receives the Spingarn Medal from the NAACP. Travels to Liberia to represent the United States at the Liberian presidential inauguration.
1924	Publishes *The Gift of Black Folk: The Negroes in the Making of America.*
1925	Contributes "The Negro Mind Reaches Out" to Alain Locke's *The New Negro: An Interpretation,* one of the most influential works of the Harlem Renaissance.
1926	Founds the Krigwa Players, a Harlem theater group. Travels to the Soviet Union to examine life after the Bolshevik Revolution. Praises Soviet achievements in *The Crisis.*
1927	The fourth and last Pan-African Conference is held in New York City.
1928	Daughter Yolande weds the poet Countee Cullen in Harlem; the marriage ends within a year. Du Bois's novel, *Dark Princess, A Romance,* is published.
1929	*The Crisis* faces financial collapse.
1930	Awarded honorary Doctor of Laws degree from Howard University.
1932	Du Bois's daughter Yolande and her second husband, Arnett Williams, have a daughter, Du Bois Williams.
1933	Losing faith in the possibilities of integration, Du Bois begins to publicly examine his position on segregation. Accepts a one-year visiting professorship at Atlanta University. Relinquishes the editorship of *The Crisis* but retains general control of the magazine.
1934	Writes editorials encouraging voluntary segregation and criticizing the integrationist policies of the NAACP. Resigns as editor of *The Crisis* and from the NAACP. Accepts the chairmanship in sociology at Atlanta University. Named the editor in chief of the *Encyclopedia of the Negro,* which is never completed or published.
1935	Publishes the revolutionary historical study, *Black Reconstruction.*
1936	Spends five months in Germany on a grant to study industrial education. Travels through Poland, the Soviet Union, Manchuria, China, and Japan.
1938	Receives honorary Doctor of Laws degree from Atlanta University and honorary Doctor of Letters degree from Fisk.
1939	*Black Folk, Then and Now,* a revised edition of *The Negro* is published.

1940	Publishes his first autobiography, *Dusk of Dawn*. Founds and edits *Phylon*, a quarterly magazine examining black issues. Awarded honorary Doctorate of Humane Letters at Wilberforce.
1941–1942	Proposes and then coordinates the study of southern blacks for black land-grant colleges.
1943	Organizes the First Conference of Negro Land-Grant Colleges at Atlanta University. Informed by Atlanta University that he must retire by 1944, he attempts to have the policy reversed.
1944	Named first black member of the National Institute of Arts and Letters. Despite his protests, he is retired by Atlanta University. Although hesitant to work with Walter White, he rejoins the NAACP as director of special research and moves back to New York. Publishes the essay "My Evolving Program for Negro Freedom" in Rayford Logan's collection *What the Negro Wants*.
1945	Writes a weekly column for the *Chicago Defender*. Serves as consultant, with Mary McLeod Bethune and Walter White, at the San Francisco conference that drafts the United Nations charter; criticizes the charter for failing to oppose colonialism. In October he presides at the Fifth Pan-African Conference in Manchester, England. Nina Du Bois suffers a stroke, which paralyzes her left side. Publishes the first volume of *Encyclopedia of the Negro: Preparatory Volume* with coauthor Guy B. Johnson. Publishes an anti-imperialist analysis of the postwar era, *Color and Democracy: Colonies and Peace*. Resigns from the American Association of University Professors in protest of conferences held in segregated hotels.
1946	Invites leaders of twenty organizations to New York to draft a petition to the United Nations on behalf of African Americans; the appeal becomes an NAACP project.
1947	Edits and writes the introduction to *An Appeal to the World*, a collection of essays sponsored by the NAACP to enlist international support for the fight against racial discrimination in America. At the United Nations, the appeal is supported by the Soviet Union but opposed by the United States. Publishes *The World and Africa*.
1948	Fired from the NAACP after his memorandum critical of Walter White and the NAACP board of directors appears in the *New York Times*. Supports Henry Wallace, the Progressive Party candidate for president. Takes unpaid position as vice chairman (with Paul Robeson) of the Council of African Affairs, an organization listed as "subversive" by the U.S. attorney general. Begins writing for the *National Guardian*.
1949	Helps sponsor and addresses the Cultural and Scientific Conference for World Peace in New York City. Attends the First World Congress of the Defenders of Peace in Paris. Travels to the All-Union Conference of Peace Proponents in Moscow.
1950	Nina Gomer Du Bois dies in Baltimore in July; she is buried in Great Barrington. Elected chairman of the Peace Information

Center, an organization dedicated to the international peace movement and the banning of nuclear weapons. Organization disbands under pressure from the Department of Justice. Du Bois is nominated by the American Labor Party for U.S. senator from New York. Receives 4 percent of the vote statewide, 15 percent in Harlem.

1951 Secretly marries Shirley Graham, aged 45, a writer, teacher, and civil rights activist, on Valentine's Day. Indicted earlier that month as an "unregistered foreign agent" under the McCormick Act: Du Bois, along with four other officers of the Peace Information Center, is alleged to be agents of foreign interests. He suffers the indignity of being handcuffed, searched, and fingerprinted before being released on bail in Washington, D.C. National lecture tours and a fundraising campaign for his defense expenses raise over $35,000. The five-day trial in Washington ends in acquittal.

1952 Publishes *In Battle for Peace*, an account of the trial. The State Department refuses Du Bois a passport on grounds that his foreign travel is not in the national interest. Later, the State Department demands a statement declaring that he is not a Communist Party member; Du Bois refuses. Advocacy of leftwing political positions widens the distance between Du Bois and the black mainstream.

1953 Prints a eulogy for Stalin in *National Guardian*. Reads 23rd Psalm at the funeral of Julius and Ethel Rosenberg, executed as Soviet spies. Awarded International Peace Prize by the World Peace Council.

1954 Surprised by the Supreme Court decision in *Brown v. Topeka Board of Education*, which outlaws public school segregation, Du Bois declares "I have seen the impossible happen."

1955 Refused a U.S. passport to attend the World Youth Festival in Warsaw, Poland.

1956 Supports Reverend Martin Luther King Jr. during the Montgomery bus boycott. Refused a passport in order to lecture in the People's Republic of China.

1957 Publishes *The Ordeal of Mansart*, the first volume of the *Black Flame*, a trilogy of historical novels chronicling black life from Reconstruction to the mid-twentieth century. A bust of Du Bois is unveiled at the Schomburg Collection of the New York Public Library. Refused a passport to attend independence ceremonies in Ghana. His great-grandson Arthur Edward McFarlane II is born.

1958 A celebration for Du Bois's ninetieth birthday is held at the Roosevelt Hotel in New York City; 2,000 people attend. Begins writing *The Autobiography of W. E. B. Du Bois*, drawing largely from earlier work. A Supreme Court ruling allows Du Bois to obtain a passport. His subsequent world tour includes England, France, Belgium, Holland, Czechoslovakia, East Germany, and the Soviet Union. He receives an honorary doctorate from Humbolt University in East Berlin, known as Friedrich Wilhelm University when Du Bois attended in 1892–1894.

1959 Meets with Nikita Khrushchev. In Beijing, makes broadcast to Africa over Radio Beijing and meets with Mao Zedong and Zhou Enlai. Awarded the International Lenin Prize. Publishes the second volume of the *Black Flame* trilogy, *Mansart Builds a School.*

1960 Participates in the celebration of Ghana's establishment as a republic. Travels to Nigeria for the inauguration of its first African governor-general.

1961 Du Bois's daughter Yolande dies of a heart attack in March. *Worlds of Color*, the final book in the *Black Flame* trilogy, is published. Du Bois accepts the invitation of Kwame Nkrumah to move to Ghana and direct a revival of the *Encyclopedia Africana* project. Before leaving for Africa, Du Bois applies for membership in the Communist Party.

1962 Travels to China. His autobiography is published in the Soviet Union.

1963 Becomes a citizen of Ghana. Turns ninety-five in February. Dies in Accra, Ghana, on 27 August, on the eve of the civil rights march on Washington. W. E. B. Du Bois is buried in a state funeral in Accra on the 29th.

1968 *The Autobiography of W. E. B. Du Bois* is published in the United States.

1992 Honored by the United States Postal Service with a 29-cent commemorative stamp as part of the Black Heritage Series, and again in 1998, with a 32-cent commemorative stamp.

1999 Du Bois's efforts to produce alternately an encyclopedia of the Negro and of Africa and Africans are realized when *Encarta Africana* is published by Microsoft, and *Africana: The Encyclopedia of the African and African American Experience*, edited by Kwame Anthony Appiah and Henry Louis Gates Jr. is published by Basic Civitas Books. In 2005 a second much-expanded edition of *Africana* is published by Oxford University Press.

Selected Bibliography

WORKS OF W.E.B. DU BOIS

The Suppression of the African Slave-Trade to the United States of America, 1638–1870. New York: Longmans, Green, 1896.

Atlanta University Publications on the Study of Negro Problems. Publications of the Atlanta University Conferences, ed. Du Bois (1898–1913).

The Philadelphia Negro: A Social Study. Boston: Ginn and Company, 1899.

The Souls of Black Folk: Essays and Sketches. Chicago: A. C. McClurg, 1911.

John Brown. Philadelphia: George W. Jacobs, 1909.

The Quest of the Silver Fleece: A Novel. Chicago: A. C. McClurg, 1911.

The Negro. New York: Harcourt, Brace, 1928.

Darkwater: Voices from within the Veil. New York: Harcourt, Brace and Howe, 1920.

The Gift of Black Folk: Negroes in the Making of America. Boston: Stratford, 1924.

Dark Princess: A Romance. New York: Harcourt, Brace, 1928.

Africa—Its Place in Modern History. Girard, Kansas: Haldeman-Julius, 1930.

Africa, Its Geography, People, and Products. Girard, Kansas: Haldeman-Julius, 1930.

Black Reconstruction: An Essay toward a History of the Part Which Black Folk Played in the Attempt to Reconstruct Democracy in America, 1860–1880. New York: Harcourt, Brace, 1935.

Black Folk Then and Now: An Essay in the History and Sociology of the Negro Race. New York: Henry Holt, 1939.

Dusk of Dawn: An Essay toward an Autobiography of a Race Concept. New York: Harcourt, Brace, 1940.

Color and Democracy: Colonies and Peace. New York: Harcourt, Brace, 1945.

Du Bois, W. E. B., and Guy B. Johnson. *Encyclopedia of the Negro, Preparatory Volume with Reference Lists and Reports*. New York: Phelps-Stokes Fund, 1946.

The World and Africa: An Inquiry into the Part Which Africa Has Played in World History. New York: Masses & Mainstream, 1947.

I Take My Stand for Peace. New York: Masses & Mainstream, 1951.

The Ordeal of Mansart. New York: Mainstream, 1957.

In Battle for Peace: The Story of My 83rd Birthday. With Comment by Shirley Graham. New York: Masses & Mainstream, 1952.

Fourty-Two Years of the USSR [sic]. Chicago: Baan Books, 1959.

Worlds of Color. New York: Mainstream, 1961.

An ABC of Color: Selections from over a Half Century of the Writings of W. E. B. Du Bois. Berlin: Seven Seas, 1963.

The Autobiography of W. E. B. Du Bois: A Soliloquy on Viewing My Life from the Last Decade of Its First Century, ed. Herbert Aptheker. New York: International Publishers, 1968.

COLLECTIONS

Aptheker, Herbert, ed. *Creative Writings by W. E. B. Du Bois: A Pageant, Poems, Short Stories, and Playlets.* New York: Kraus-Thomson Organization, 1985.

Aptheker, Herbert, ed. *The Complete Published Works of W. E. B. Du Bois.* 35 vols. Millwood, NY: Kraus-Thomson, 1973.

Aptheker, Herbert, ed. *The Correspondence of W. E. B. Du Bois.* 3 vols. Amherst: University of Massachusetts Press, 1973–1978.

Aptheker, Herbert, ed. *Writings by W. E. B. Du Bois in periodicals Edited by Others.* 4 vols. Millwood, NY: Kraus-Thomson, 1982.

Foner, Philip S., ed. *W. E. B. Du Bois Speaks: Speeches and Addresses 1890–1919.* New York: Pathfinder, 1970.

Huggins, Nathan I., ed. *W. E. B. Du Bois: Writings.* New York: Library of America, 1986.

Lewis, David Levering, ed. *W. E. B. Du Bois: A Reader.* New York: Henry Holt, 1985.

Sundquist, Eric J., ed. *The Oxford W. E. B. Du Bois Reader.* New York: Oxford University Press, 1996.

BIBLIOGRAPHIES

Aphtheker, Herbert. *Annotated Bibliography of the Published Writings of W. E. B. Du Bois.* Millwood, NY: Kraus-Thomson, 1973.

McDonnell, Robert W., and Paul C. Partington. *W. E. B. Du Bois: A Bibliography of Writings About Him.* Whittier, CA: Paul C. Partington Book Publisher, 1989.

Partington, Paul C. *W. E. B. Du Bois: A Bibliography of His Published Writings.* Whittier, CA: Paul C. Partington Book Publisher, 1977.

BIOGRAPHIES

Broderick, Francis L. *W. E. B. Du Bois: A Negro Leader in Time of Crisis.* Stanford: Stanford University Press, 1959.

Du Bois, Shirley Graham. *His Day is Marching On: A Memoir of W. E. B. Du Bois.* Philadelphia: Lippincott, 1971.

Lewis, David Levering. *W. E. B. Du Bois: The Fight for Equality and the American Century, 1919–1963.* New York: Henry Holt, 2000.

Marable, Manning. *W. E. B. Du Bois: Black Radical Democrat.* Boston: Twayne, 1986.

Rudwick, Elliot M. *W. E. B. Du Bois: Propagandist of the Negro Protest.* 1960; reprint. New York: Atheneum, 1968.

CRITICAL WORKS

Appiah, Anthony. "The Uncompleted Argument: Du Bois and the Illusion of Race." *Critical Inquiry* 12 (Autumn 1985): 21–37.

Aptheker, Herbert. *The Literary Legacy of W. E. B. Du Bois.* Whit Plains, NY: Kraus International, 1989.

Ashton, Susanna. "Du Bois's 'Horizon': Documenting Movements of the Color Line." *MELUS* 26.4 (2001): 3–23.

Baker, Houston A., Jr. "The Black Man of Culture: W. E. B. Du bois and *The Souls of Black Folk.*" In *Long Black Song.* Charlottesville: University of Virginia Press, 1972.

Balfour, Lawrie. "Representative Women: Slavery, Citizenship, and Feminist Theory in Du Bois's 'Damnation of Women.'" *Hypatia: A Journal of Feminist Philosophy* 20.3 (2005): 127–148.

Bauerlein, Mark. "Booker T. Washington and W. E. B. Du Bois: The Origins of a Bitter Intellectual Battle." *Journal of Blacks in Higher Education* 46 (Winter 2004–2005): 106–114.

Bell, Bernard, Emily Grosholz, and James Stewart, eds. *W. E. B. Du Bois on Race and Culture: Philosophy, Politics, and Poetics.* New York: Routledge, Chapman, and Hall, 1996.

Bhabha, Homi K. "The Black Savant and the *Dark Princess.*" *ESQ: A Journal of the American Renaissance* 50.1–3 (2004): 137–155.

Blight, David W. "W. E. B. Du Bois and the Struggle for American Historical Memory." In *History and Memory in African-American Culture*, ed. Genevieve Fabre and Robert O'Meally. New York: Oxford University Press, 1994.

Bremen, Brian A. "Du Bois, Emerson, and the 'Fate' of Black Folk." *American Literary Realism* 24 (Spring 1992): 80–88.

Bruce, Dickson D., Jr. "W. E. B. Du Bois and the Idea of Double Consciousness." *American Literature: A Journal of Literary History, Criticism, and Bibliography* 64.2 (June 1992): 299–309.

Byerman, Keith. *Seizing the Word: History, Art, and the Self in the Work of W. E. B. Du Bois.* Athens: University of Georgia Press, 1994.

Castronovo, Russ. "Beauty along the Color Line: Lynching, Aesthetics and the *Crisis.*" *PMLA: Publications of the Modern Language Association of America* 36.2 (2006): 1443–1159.

Crouch, Stanley, and Playthell Benjamin. *Reconsidering the Souls of Black Folk: Thoughts on the Groundbreaking Classic Work of W. E. B. Du Bois.* Philadelphia: Running Press, 2002.

Early, Gerald, ed. *Lure and Loathing: Essays on Race, Identity, and the Ambivalence of Assimilation.* New York: Allen Lane, 1993.

Fisher, Rebecka Rutledge. "Cultural Artifacts and the Narrative of History: W. E. B. Du Bois and the Exhibiting of Culture at the 1900 Paris Exposition Universelle." *MFS: Modern Fiction Studies* 51.4 (2005): 741–774.

Fontenot, Chester J., Mary Alice Morgan, and Sarah Gardner, eds. *W. E. B. Du Bois and Race.* Macon, Georgia: Mercer University Press, 2001.

Frederickson, George. "The Double Life of W. E. B. Du Bois." *New York Review of Books* 48.2 (February 8, 2001): 34–36.

342 ◆ COLOR AND DEMOCRACY

Frederickson, George. *The Black Image in the White Mind: The Debate on Afro-American Character and Destiny, 1817–1914*. New York: Harper and Row, 1971.
Gabiddon, Shaun L. "W. E. B. Du Bois: Pioneering American Criminologist." *Journal of Black Studies* 31.5 (2001): 581–599.
Gooding-Williams, Robert. "Du Bois's Counter-Sublime." *The Massachusetts Review: A Quarterly of Literature, the Arts and Public Affairs* 35.2 (Summer 1994): 202–224.
Herring, Scott. "Du Bois and the Minstrels." *MELUS* 22 (Summer 1997): 3–18.
Hubbard, Dolan, ed. *The Souls of Black Folk One Hundred Years Later*. Columbia, Missouri: University of Missouri Press, 2003.
Jones, Gavin. "'Whose Line Is It Anyway?' W. E. B. Du Bois and the Language of the Color-Line." In *Race Consciousness: African-American Studies for the New Century*, ed. Judith Jackson Fossett and Jeffrey A. Tucker. New York: New York University Press, 1997.
Judy, Ronald A. T., ed. "Sociology Hesitant: Thinking with W. E. B. Du Bois." Special Issue: *Boundary 2: An International Journal of Literature and Culture* 27.3 (2000).
Juguo, Zhang. *W. E. B. Du Bois and the Quest for the Abolition of the Color Line*. New York: Routledge, 2001.
Kirschke, Amy. "Du Bois, *The Crisis*, and Images of Africa and the Diaspora." In *African Diasporas in the New and Old Worlds: Consciousness and Imagination*, ed. Geneviève Fabre and Benesch Klaus. Amsterdam: Rodopi, 2004. 239–262.
Lemke, Sieglinde. "Transatlantic Relations: The German Du Bois." In *German? American? Literature? New Directions in German-American Studies*, ed. Winfried Fluck and Werner Sollors. New York: Peter Lang, 2002. 207–215.
McCaskill, Barbara, and Caroline Gebhard, eds. and introd. *Post-Bellum, Pre-Harlem: African American Literature and Culture*. New York: New York University Press, 2006.
McKay, Nellie. "W. E. B. Du Bois: The Black Women in His Writings—Selected Fictional and Autobiographical Portraits." In *Critical Essays on W. E. B. Du Bois*, ed. William L. Andrews. Boston: G. K. Hall, 1985.
Meier, August. "The Paradox of W. E. B. Du Bois." In *Negro Thought in America, 1880–1915; Radical Ideologies in the Age of Booker T. Washington*. Ann Arbor: University of Michigan Press, 1963.
Miller, Monica. "W. E. B. Du Bois and the Dandy as Diasporic Race Man." *Callaloo* 26.3 (2003): 738–765.
Mizrunchi, Susan. "Neighbors, Strangers, Corpses: Death and Sympathy in the Early Writings of W. E. B. Du Bois." In *Centuries' Ends, Narrative Means*, ed. Robert Newman. Stanford, CA: Stanford University Press, 1996.
Moses, Wilson Jeremiah. *Creative Conflict in African American Thought: Frederick Douglass, Alexander Crummell, Booker T. Washington, W. E. B. Du Bois, and Marcus Garvey*. Cambridge, England: Cambridge University Press, 2004.
Pauley, Garth E. "W. E. B. Du Bois on Woman Suffrage: A Critical Analysis of His *Crisis* Writings." *Journal of Black Studies* 30.3 (2000): 383–410.
Peterson, Dale. "Notes from the Underworld: Dostoyevsky, Du Bois, and the Discovery of the Ethnic Soul." *Massachusetts Review* 35 (Summer 1994): 225–247.

Posnock, Ross. "The Distinction of Du Bois: Aesthetics, Pragmatism, Politics." *American Literary History* 7 (Fall 1995): 500–524.

Rampersad, Arnold. *The Art and Imagination of W. E. B. Du Bois.* Cambridge, MA: Harvard University Press, 1976.

Rampersad, Arnold, and Deborah E. McDowell, eds. *Slavery and the Literary Imagination: Du Bois's* The Souls of Black Folk. Baltimore: Johns Hopkins University Press, 1989.

Rothberg, Michael. "W. E. B. Du Bois in Warsaw: Holocaust Memory and the Color Line, 1949–1952." *Yale Journal of Criticism* 14.1 (2001): 169–189.

Schneider, Ryan. "Sex and the Race Man: Imagining Interracial Relationships in W. E. B. Du Bois's *Darkwater.*" *Arizona Quarterly: A Journal of American Literature, Culture, and Theory* 59.2 (2003): 59–80.

Schrager, Cynthia D. "Both Sides of the Veil: Race, Science, and Mysticism in W. E. B. Du Bois." *American Quarterly* 48 (December 1996): 551–587.

Siemerling, Winfried. "W. E. B. Du Bois, Hegel, and the Staging of Alterity." *Callaloo* 24.1 (2001): 325–333.

Smith, Shawn Michelle. *Photography on the Color Line: W. E. B. Du Bois, Race, and Visual Culture.* Durham: Duke University Press, 2004.

Sundquist, Eric J. "Swing Low: *The Souls of Black Folk.*" In *To Wake the Nations.* Cambridge, MA: Harvard University Press, 1993.

Temperley, Howard, Michael B. Katz, and Thomas J. Sugrue. "W. E. B. Du Bois, Race, and the City." *The Times Literary Supplement.* No. 4996 (1999).

"The Study of African American Problems: W. E. B. Du Bois's Agenda, Then and Now." *Annals of the American Academy of Political and Social Science* 568 (March 2000): 1–313.

Warren, Kenneth W. "Troubled Black Humanity in *The Souls of Black Folk* and *The Autobiography of an Ex-Colored Man.*" In *The Cambridge Companion to American Realism and Naturalism: Howells to London,* ed. Donald Pizer. Cambridge: Cambridge University Press, 1995.

West, Cornel. "W. E. B. Du Bois: The Jamesian Organic Intellectual." In *The American Evasion of Philosophy: A Genealogy of Pragmatism.* Madison: University of Wisconsin Press, 1989.

Williamson, Joel. *The Crucible of Race: Black-White Relations in the American South Since Emancipation.* New York: Oxford University Press, 1984.

Wolters, Raymond. *Du Bois and His Rivals.* Columbia, Missouri: University of Missouri Press, 2002.

Zamir, Shamoon. *Dark Voices: W. E. B. Du Bois and American Thought, 1888–1903.* Chicago: University of Chicago Press, 1995.

Zamir, Shamoon. "'The Sorrow Songs'/'Song of Myself': Du Bois, the Crisis of Leadership, and Prophetic Imagination." In *The Black Columbiad: Defining Moments in African American Literature and Culture.* Cambridge, MA: Harvard University Press, 1994.

Zwarg, Christina. "Du Bois on Trauma: Psychoanalysis and the Would-Be Black Savant." *Cultural Critique* 51 (2002): 1–39.